Renate Kirsch | Elke Siehl
Albrecht Stockmayer [eds.]

Transformation, Politics and Implementation

Smart Implementation in Governance Programs

 Nomos

 Deutsche Gesellschaft
für Internationale
Zusammenarbeit (GIZ) GmbH

The views expressed in this publication are those of the authors and do not necessarily represent the views of the Deutsche Gesellschaft für Internationale Zusammenarbeit GmbH.

© Coverpicture: Pauline Heusterberg based on pictures derived from the GIZ data bank

Copy Editor: Robert Furlong

The Deutsche Nationalbibliothek lists this publication in the Deutsche Nationalbibliografie; detailed bibliographic data are available on the Internet at http://dnb.d-nb.de

ISBN   978-3-8487-3738-3 (Print)
           978-3-8452-8051-6 (ePDF)

British Library Cataloguing-in-Publication Data
A catalogue record for this book is available from the British Library.

ISBN   978-3-8487-3738-3 (Print)
           978-3-8452-8051-6 (ePDF)

Library of Congress Cataloging-in-Publication Data
Kirsch, Renate / Siehl, Elke / Stockmayer, Albrecht
Transformation, Politics and Implementation
Smart Implementation in Governance Programs
Renate Kirsch / Elke Siehl / Albrecht Stockmayer (eds.)
371 p.
Includes bibliographic references.

ISBN   978-3-8487-3738-3 (Print)
           978-3-8452-8051-6 (ePDF)

1st Edition 2017
© Nomos Verlagsgesellschaft, Baden-Baden, Germany 2017. Printed and bound in Germany.

Foreword by Sabine Müller

The year 2016 marked a significant change for development cooperation: A new global consensus encapsulated in the 2030 Agenda for Sustainable Development came into effect. With its universal and transformative goals and targets, the 2030 Agenda promotes a conceptual shift from "aid" to "global goods," and from development work to international cooperation. It acknowledges today's global challenges (e.g., climate change, refugees, and migration), and thus confronts development practitioners and partners likewise with the task of finding new ways to implement this joint vision.

Some of the questions include: "How can development programs lead to effective change in complex environments that are characterized as political, non-linear, and only partly predictable in their outcomes?" "What are the rules, principles, or instruments for practitioners to manage implementation in such contexts?" "What can or needs to change about the implementation of development programs in order to enhance development effectiveness and sustainability?"

Recently, initiatives in development organizations, think tanks, and universities have taken up this challenge by exploring in more depth how development programs are implemented and which role implementation has in enhancing the effectiveness of sustainable development cooperation. For example, the World Bank with other development partners started the Science of Delivery and Global Delivery Initiative, Harvard University and the Overseas Development Institute issued a manifesto for Doing Development Differently (DDD), and the Developmental Leadership Program started research programs exploring how leadership, power, and politics influence successful implementation. These are insightful discussions that – as an implementing agency – draw attention and to which we hope to contribute.

Here at the Deutsche Gesellschaft für Internationale Zusammenarbeit (GIZ), we offer locally embedded support for capacity development to public and non-governmental partners. By analyzing our body of knowledge on implementation, we want to contribute to the ongoing international debate and share our experiences and insights, with the intention of advancing the 2030 Agenda and actively promoting the exchange formats provided by the Global Delivery Initiative (GDI).

Based on nine case studies, this book illustrates *how* program implementation unfolded in each case and how program staff maneuvered in complex work environments. The experiences reported by the authors illustrate our mode of work and our ongoing considerations about – what we titled – smart implementation. A central finding is that we rarely have ready-made solutions to local problems. More often, solutions emerge in cooperation with local partners and are then tested and rolled out. Political astuteness, attention to forging cooperation, as well as a focus on addressing local and regional issues are core parameters of our way of implementation. By applying these measures to our cooperation approach, we hope to accompany our partners as technical advisors and facilitators through their transformative processes.

We hope that this volume contributes to a better understanding of the dynamics and frame conditions that shape implementation processes in our partner countries and to the debate on enhancing the effectiveness of development cooperation to achieve the goals and targets of the 2030 Agenda.

Eschborn, March 2017
Sabine Müller (PhD)
Director Sector Departments
Deutsche Gesellschaft für Internationale Zusammenarbeit (GIZ)

Co-Chair of the Advisory Board of GDI

Foreword by Joachim Fritz

Today's requirements for governance programs are more demanding than ever. As the recently published *World Development Report 2017: Governance and the Law* succinctly put it, we moved from "What is the right policy?" to "What makes policies work?" Previously, we referred to generally agreed best models for modernizing the state and its administration. It seemed that solutions and the content of reforms could be easily laid out; they just needed to be implemented. Awareness about what needs to be considered to enhance state legitimacy, resilience, and effectiveness has grown considerably. Consequently, the content of governance reforms has become substantially more complex. The borders between the public and private spheres are blurring, and institutional boundaries are vanishing. At the same time, the complexities of the problems that require governance are increasing, for example in the cases of climate change, international migration, urbanization, and digitalization. As advisors and practitioners supporting governance reforms in partner countries, we are required to continuously develop practices and processes on how policies work in such settings. This requires insights beyond the functionality of the public sector and needs to take the political dimensions of reform into account. Based on the results of two conferences held in 2009, the GIZ Governance and Conflict division reviewed its understanding of change processes and adopted the concept of transformation, which describes development as a non-linear, reflexive, and only partly predictable and manageable process. Subsequently, we improved our political economy analysis instruments and applied them more systematically during program preparation and implementation. Over the last years, we made an effort to craft knowledge on how to better implement governance programs in complex settings. The insightful results of this discussion are presented in the case studies and summarized in the final chapter of this publication.

As GIZ's Governance and Conflict division, we draw two main conclusions from the empirical debates in this book. The first is that the closer integration of governance, peace-building, and security approaches would provide great potential in finding appropriate, innovative, and lasting solutions to the types of governance challenges with which we are asked to assist. The second conclusion is that the way we carry out governance and conflict programs requires institutional space to find the right fit: Space for programs to adapt to local issues is vital for developing solutions that are effective and sustainable.

Knowing how difficult it is to take time out of a busy and hectic work schedule in order to reflect, document, and share experiences, concepts, and lessons, I would like to thank and commend the outstanding efforts of all contributors to this book. We hope that the experiences presented in this publication inspire others to follow and demonstrate how to adapt, analyze, as well as reflect on their work, which are all critical steps when managing an implementation process.

Eschborn, March 2017
Joachim Fritz
Head of GIZ Governance and Conflict Division
Sectoral Department
Deutsche Gesellschaft für Internationale Zusammenarbeit (GIZ)

Acknowledgements

This publication was meant to encourage internal discussions in GIZ's Governance and Conflict division – and it did. Thus, many people contributed to it to whom we owe a word of thanks for their support.

The entire Governance and Conflict division showed great interest and support for this book from the outset. Almost everybody in the division contributed to it at some stage. We would like to thank all planning officers and the respective heads of the four units in the division – Ute Böttcher, Dunja Brede, Elisabeth Leiss, and David Nguyen-Thanh – for their efforts. Ideas for possible case studies were also provided by Nico Lamade and Annette Schmid. Angela Langenkamp went the extra mile to ensure that gender became the focus of one case study. The division's Management Team jointly decided on the concept and selection of cases as well as key messages.

The authors of the case studies and their partners in country form the heart of this publication. They showed stamina in their attempts to convert tacit knowledge into shareable experiences and guts by writing about mishaps, ruptures, failures, and detours with the same level of reflection as when they presented successes. We greatly appreciate that each of them allowed us to challenge and guide them in the development of the case studies. We would like to thank Tim Auracher, Godje Bialluch, Franziska Böhm, Christine Brendel, Thomas Fiegle, Franziska Gutzeit, Lisa Hiemer, Anne Hitzegrad, Astrid Karamira, Ruan Kitshoff, Heiner von Lüpke, Mark Mattner, Yvonne Müller, Jazmín Ponce, Stephanie Schell-Faucon, Markus Steinich, Sabrina Storm, Tobias Tschappe, Christopher Weigand, Agnes Wiedemann, and Melanie Wiskow for the inspiring cooperation. Thomas Meyer is the leader of the program "Legal approximation towards European standards in the South Caucasus." He does not appear as an author, but it was due to his decision and leadership that the South Caucasus case become part of this book.

We asked Verena Fritz and Neil Hatton for external perspectives on implementation challenges in development cooperation, and GIZ in particular. Both have long-lasting working relationships with GIZ and inside knowledge on GIZ's modes of operation. It has been extremely helpful to have them on board to challenge us with their insightful understanding on the subject.

Several ideas and proposals for case studies were submitted that, for various reasons, did not make it into this publication. We thank Chris Backhaus, Peter Dineiger & Annika Wolframm, Christoph Feyen, Daphne Frank, Jörg Holla, Magali Mander & Mathis Hemberger, Hartmut Paulsen, Javier Portocarrero & Luz Gamarra, Jens Pössel, Scherry Siganporia & Sharon Kharshiing, Felix Richter, and Lena Weiler for their interest and contributions.

As editors, we were motivated and felt challenged by the international discussion on implementation and wanted to contribute. Duncan Green and his blog "From Poverty to Power" was an inspirational nudge for us to start this book and share our reflections on implementation. Several blog posts over the last two years have presented examples of how other development organizations have tried to "do development differently." The same holds true for the work of the Politics and Governance Programme at the Overseas Development Institute (ODI). These posts led to wonderfully engaging conversations in front of the coffee machine among staff. David Booth and Alex Duncan sparked the discussion in the sectoral department with their training on political economy analysis. ODI staff invited us to join discussions on Doing Development Differently at ODI and to openly share our implementation experiences, which are based on a different business model than that of many other development organizations. We greatly appreciate their work and their interest in ours. Several of our colleagues in the Governance and Conflict division signed up for the Problem-Driven Iterative Adaptation e-learning course at Harvard. The works of Matt Andrews, Lant Pritchett, and Michael Woolcock and other scholars have inspired our discussions greatly.

Draft versions of articles were circulated to other GIZ divisions and units for comments. Several case studies were also reviewed by partners of GIZ programs and close program allies. The discussions these comments inspired were indispensable for finding our position as an organization on many accounts. We are grateful to Ferdinand M. Amante Jr., Aasmund Andersen, Katharina Brendel, Jens Deppe, Jörg Freiberg, Joachim Fritz, Joachim Göske, Virginia Guanzon, Oliver Haas, Peter Hauschnik, Andrea Kramer, Lothar Jahn, Aziz Jardin, Isabel Lamers, Richard Levin, Ulrich Müller, Zeno Reichenbecher, Petra Riedle, Hanlie Robertson, Anselm Schneider, Budi Sitepu, Paul Smoke, Sonny Syahril, Constanze Westervoss, and Georgia Wimhöfer for their valuable questions, comments, advice as well as their longstanding, trusting cooperation in the implementation of GIZ's governance programs.

Pauline Heusterberg was the intern on the team for six months. She contributed to the introduction and synthesis chapter and polished the manuscript until it shined. Robert Furlong edited the manuscript and Carsten Rehbein was a very patient and supportive publisher. The space and resources required to work on these issues was provided and generously supported by our management. We are grateful to have been given this opportunity, in particular to Sabine Müller and Joachim Fritz.

Contents

Synthesis

Abbreviations

AA	Association Agreement
AusAid	Australian Agency for International Development
BAPPENAS	State Ministry of National Development Planning (Indonesia)
BMZ	German Federal Ministry for Economic Cooperation and Development / Bundesministerium für wirtschaftliche Zusammenarbeit und Entwicklung
CEDAW	Convention on the Elimination of All Forms of Discrimination Against Women
CFAD	Centre for Training and Support for Decentralization / Centre de Formation et d'Appui à la Décentralisation
CLADEM	Comité de América Latina y el Caribe para la Defensa de los Derechos de la Mujer
CMPPO	Co-Management Project and Program Office (Philippines)
CMSC	Co-Management Steering Committee (Philippines)
CoGTA	Cooperative Governance and Traditional Affairs (South Africa)
CoMun	Cooperation with Municipalities
ComVoMujer	Combating Violence Against Women in Latin America
COP	Conference of the Parties
COSERAM	Conflict Sensitive Resource and Asset Management Program
CSC	Civil Service Commission under the President of the Republic of Azerbaijan
CSR	Corporate Social Responsibility
DAR	Department of Agrarian Reform (Philippines)
DCFTA	Deep and Comprehensive Free Trade Area
DCoG	Department of Cooperative Governance (South Africa)
DDD	Doing Development Differently

DeCGG	Decentralisation as a Contribution to Good Governance
DENR	Department of Environment and Natural Resources (Philippines)
DFID	Department for International Development (United Kingdom)
DILG	Department of Interior and Local Government (Philippines)
DJPK	Directorate General of Fiscal Balance (Indonesia)
DoC	Drivers of Change
DPME	Department of Planning, Monitoring and Evaluation (South Africa)
DPO	Development Policy Operation
DPSA	Department of Public Service and Administration (South Africa)
EaP	Eastern Partnership
ECCF	Eastern Cape Communication Forum
EITI	Extractives Industries Transparency Initiative
ENA	Tunisian National School for Administration
EU	European Union
FNVT	Tunisian National Federation of Cities / Fédération Nationale des Villes Tunisiennes
FOCEVAL	Strengthening Evaluation Capacities in Central America
FORCLIME	Forests and Climate Change Programme
GCIS	Government Communication and Information System (South Africa)
GDI	Global Delivery Initiative
GHG	Greenhouse Gas
GIS	Geographic Information System
GIZ	Deutsche Gesellschaft für Internationale Zusammenarbeit
GSP	Governance Support Programme
IRP	Institutional Reform Plan
LRA	Liberia Revenue Agency

M&E	Monitoring and Evaluation
MCAP	Mining Cadastre and Revenue Administration (Liberia)
MCAS	Mining Cadastre Administration System (Liberia)
MENA	Middle East and North Africa
MIDEPLAN	Ministry of National Planning and Economic Policy (Costa Rica)
MIMDES	Ministry for Women and Social Development (Peru)
MIMP	Ministry of Women and Vulnerable Populations (Peru)
MLME	Ministry of Lands, Mines and Energy (Liberia)
MoU	Memorandum of Understanding
NCIP	National Commission on Indigenous Peoples (Philippines)
NEDA	National Economic and Development Authority (Philippines)
NGO	Non-Governmental Organization
NMA	National Minerals Agency (Sierra Leone)
NPA	New People's Army (Philippines)
NT	National Treasury (South Africa)
OECD	Organisation for Economic Co-operation and Development
PAKLIM	Policy Advice for Environment and Climate Change (Indonesia)
PDIA	Problem-Driven Iterative Adaptation
PEA	Political Economy Analysis
PIT	Project Implementation Team
PKPPIM	Center for Climate Change and Multilateral Policy (Indonesia)
PPP	Public–Private Partnership
PSC	Public Service Commission (South Africa)
RDF	Revenue Development Foundation
REDD+	Reduced Emissions from Deforestation and forest Degradation in developing countries
SALGA	South African Local Government Association

SINE	National Monitoring and Evaluation System / Sistema Nacional de Seguimiento y Evaluacion (Costa Rica)
SOE	State-owned Enterprise
TNA	Training Needs Assessment
TWG	Technical Working Group (Philippines)
TWP	Thinking and Working Politically
UK	United Kingdom
UNDP	United Nations Development Programme
UNFCCC	United Nations Framework Convention on Climate Change
USAID	United States Agency for International Development
USMP	University of San Martín de Porres
VAW	Violence Against Women

Introduction

Smart Implementation in Development Cooperation: An Introduction to Issues and Concepts

Renate Kirsch, Elke Siehl, and Albrecht Stockmayer

Designs of international development programs have become increasingly complex over the years. Multi-sectoral and multi-level program[1] designs reflect a growing understanding that change within social systems has to be addressed systemically, that is, programs try to address a social system as a whole and not just one element of it. This is especially apparent in governance programs,[2] which aim at changing the rules of institutions in a social system in order to better serve people. These programs, in particular, are faced with a high degree of complexity, uncertainty, reflexivity, and political deliberation, all of which require specific attention during program implementation. Furthermore, the importance of addressing governance issues across all sectors has been broadly accepted as a means for achieving more sustainable development results. Nowadays, we see governance aspects being integrated into the design of water, health, energy, education, and infrastructure programs at the policy and organizational levels (GIZ, 2012). Therefore, governance programs provide a good example for discussing implementation challenges. In addition, the expectations about the results that can be achieved by development measures have risen, and their fulfillment is being monitored and evaluated with increasing attention by funders and partner organizations. Both aspects influence the design and implementation of development programs (World Bank, 2017).

---

1 The term program is used throughout this article to refer to programs, projects, and investments.
2 GIZ understands "governance as the systems (consisting of actors, rules and structures) that determine how governmental and non-governmental stakeholders reach decisions and use public resources to guarantee public services. Governance includes both the interrelationships between government actors (executive, legislative and judicial) and between government, civil society and private-sector actors that act at all different levels: international, regional, national and local" (GIZ [Deutsche Gesellschaft für Internationale Zusammenarbeit], 2014).

International development organizations and research institutes have renewed their commitment to implementation as a part of the program cycle that is central for achieving the effectiveness of development programs while also being a complex and often unique process in itself.[3] Recent discussions indicate that the understanding of how complex programs are managed and steered – or which rules and principles actually guide implementation – is still limited. This is somewhat surprising, considering the vast and rich experiences of skilled and practiced program staff, who must have this knowledge at their command in their daily work. However, this information seems to be tacit knowledge to a certain degree, difficult to share and discuss widely. This book intends to contribute to the discussion on implementation by making some of this tacit knowledge explicit and practical. Creating strong narratives via case studies is one way to tap into this vast body of underexplored knowledge.[4] It does so by presenting nine case studies of GIZ governance programs[5] that describe the challenges, trigger points, and opportunities program teams encountered during implementation, how they addressed them, and which frame conditions, approaches, and instruments were helpful or hindering. By analyzing these experiences, we hope to identify principles of engagement and management that can guide program staff in implementing more effective and sustainable development operations. Furthermore, we hope to reveal blind spots of what we do not yet understand and outline an agenda for further investigation and knowledge-gathering among development practitioners.

---

3 See Verena Fritz's contribution in this book for a full overview of the discussion.

4 The case study methodology used in this book is based on Yin (2009) as well as the Guidelines of the Global Delivery Initiative (2014, pp. 24–25). Guidelines for writing case studies were developed and shared with all GIZ governance teams (Kirsch, 2015).

5 GIZ implements these programs on behalf of its commissioning parties, that is, the German Ministry for Economic Cooperation and Development (BMZ) and the European Union in Azerbaijan. Australian Aid and the World Bank provided additional finances to the governance program in Liberia. This publication focuses on reviewing implementation experiences in governance programs. Experiences from other sectors are presented in nine case studies, which are included in the GDI library and present experiences in water, health, energy, administration, rule of law, and sustainable supply chain programs; see http://globaldeliveryinitiative.org/global-delivery-library

We start the discussion by reviewing how development organizations engage in implementation. This is followed by revisiting conditions for implementing programs in complex environments and reexamining the tension between two different but mutually valid objectives: space for adaptation and orientation toward process versus orientation toward predefined results. How GIZ handles this tension is then explained by introducing the concept of "smart implementation." The introduction chapter outlines in two sections the conceptual and institutional frame conditions in which GIZ programs operate and what this implies for the way programs are – and can be – implemented. This section includes an introduction to the concept of transformation, which GIZ's governance division adopted in 2013 as a conceptual frame for program design and implementation. These reflections lead to the questions we want to discuss in the nine case studies. Finally, the cases and their implementation challenges are introduced.

Modes of implementation in development cooperation

To start a discussion on implementation, it is worth revisiting in which ways development organizations engage in it. One modality is characterized by an external agency providing funding and technical support to a change process, but the implementation is predominantly the responsibility of the partners in country. This model applies to some bilateral donors and development banks, where loans or grants are offered to finance and facilitate change processes, but the ability to accompany partners in the actual implementation is limited to supervision. Alternatively, additional resources are required to include accompanying technical assistance measures, or technical assistance support is contracted out to a third party. The effectiveness of the development measure is assessed by the degree to which predefined results have been achieved at the end of the program (phase). The process of how the results have been achieved can often only be reviewed from a distance. In a second mode, development organizations accompany organizations in partner countries through change processes by means of predominantly in-kind advisory services. A first distinction to the first model is that these services are offered based on an agreement of joint responsibility between the external organization and the partner for managing the program and achieving results. A second difference is greater attention to process, with the assumption that the way change occurs influences *which* results are achieved and their quality (e.g., degree of public acceptance to, inclusion of, and support by stakeholders for change). A third distinction is a higher degree of flexibility in reshaping predefined results and adapting to changes in the course of implementation. Within the inherent tension between achieving often ambitious and specific results and adapting to partners' interests and course of action, more space exists to accommodate the latter. The mode of engagement here is characterized by the notion that advisory teams accompany the change process of a partner government or institutions, in which the partners determine the overall direction, outcome, and pace. GIZ's mode of delivery falls into this second category. However, both modes of support see implementation as a crucial stage in the program cycle for enhancing development effectiveness, and program teams are eager to better understand what constitutes a successful or smart implementation. This provides the common ground for a joint learning agenda. Being aware of existing differences will facilitate communication across development partners and explain varying levels of attention to specific aspects.

Balancing directive and adaptive approaches in implementation

Implementing organizations operate under two frameworks, that is, a results orientation that focuses on predefined, binding, and measureable results, and a process orientation that focuses on adapting to changes in complex situations. Both frameworks are equally valid but follow a logic that affects the other and might create tension for implementation. On the one hand, the Paris Declaration on Aid Effectiveness stipulates in its fourth principle on "managing for results" that all parties in development cooperation should pay more attention to achieving and measuring results (Organisation for Economic Co-operation and Development, 2005). This initial response resulted in a call for more program quality, transparency, and accountability to partners and taxpayers, and led to the development of new tools and standards, especially in program planning and evaluation. For implementation, this means more direction and clear boundaries in which the program operates, but also less freedom and flexibility to respond to changes that might occur. Furthermore, the political dimension of implementation is neglected, which is often the reason why adaptations become necessary (Eyben, Guijt, Roche, & Shutt, 2015).[6] On the other hand, since 2010 several initiatives in development organizations and think tanks have called for paying more attention to the complexity of the environment in which development programs take place. These scholars and practitioners warn against the application of ready-made solutions that are presented in best practices with the intention of replicating them within different contexts (so-called codified ideas) (Andrews, 2013), as they lead to merely "isomorphic mimicry" – the shell of an institution without the ability to fulfill its intended function, because the rules, structures, and processes do not fit the environment in which it was placed (Andrews, Pritchett, & Woolcock, 2012). These initiatives promote the idea of working in a problem-driven, adaptive, and politically informed way. Here, implementation responds to the dynamics and conditions of local contexts and adapts to them following the direction, form, and pace that the reform program takes. The focus is on solving local problems that occur during implementation. Solutions are identified and legitimized by stakeholders and their broad involvement and endorsements. They are tested incrementally before they are brought to scale. Tight feedback loops support experimental learning and the ability to stay connected to local demands and interests (Andrews, Pritchett, & Woolcock, 2012, p. 1, 2017).

These ideas have been encapsulated in the Doing Development Differently agenda (DDD Manifesto Community, 2014), which is based on Problem-Driven Iterative Adaptation, on Thinking and Working Politically, and the experiences of the UK Overseas Development Institute's work on African Power and Politics and predecessor programs (Andrews, Pritchett, & Woolcock, 2012, 2017; Levy 2014; Wild, Booth, Cummings, Foresti, & Wales, 2015; Wild, Andrews, Pett, & Dempster, 2016; Wild, Booth, & Valters, 2017; Leftwich, 2011; Booth, 2012, 2014). It also relates to the Global Delivery Initiative at the World Bank,[7] which aim to systematically record and document positive and negative implementation experiences from individual programs as objectively as possible using methods of empirical social research, on the basis of which common fea-

---

6 The fact that parliaments have no role and relevance in the agenda illustrates this point.
7 See also http://doingdevelopmentdifferently.com; http://publications.dlprog.org/TWP.pdf; https://www.odi.org/projects/africa-power-and-politics-programme; http://www.globaldeliveryinitiative.org/; http://blogs.worldbank.org/category/tags/science-delivery

tures shall be identified and recommendations derived for comparable cases. All of these initiatives discuss implementation and offer new perspectives and concepts for operation.[8] Verena Fritz's article explains the genesis and core ideas of these initiatives in detail and reviews if – and to which extent – they have informed the way implementation is conducted and what still needs to be addressed.[9] This book is one of GIZ's contributions to this debate, in which we want to present our experiences and discuss how far we have come on some of these issues.

In conclusion, implementation surely needs direction, which is provided by making objectives and results explicit, and by stating how change is assumed to occur in theory. Measuring progress on these dimensions is helpful but not sufficient to ensure effective development. These measures in themselves will not ensure locally accepted, adapted, and sustainable results. For this, the transformative dimension of social change has to be taken into account, which acknowledges that implementation is a non-linear process that occurs with ruptures, reversals, delays, jumps, or simultaneous actions in other processes. Squaring the circle on these mutually valid objectives requires space and time for maneuver. Finding the balance between objectives that serve as landmarks offering guidance along the way in almost never linear change processes is an issue this book investigates.

Defining smart implementation for GIZ programs

The tension that different development objectives can create for program design and implementation was the stimulus for discussions at GIZ in 2009. It was recognized that the implementation process needed to be unpacked, and that a better understanding was required of *how* programs are implemented in order to provide guidance for achieving results that are sustainable and considered valuable by partners. It was acknowledged that portraying an implementation process is not self-evident, as the relationship between programs and their results is neither direct nor causal but non-linear and complex in nature. GIZ proposed to accept complexity, uncertainty, and bounded rationality as given preconditions of its working

---

8 For a comparison of similarities, overlaps and differences of these initiatives, see Algoso and Hudson (2016).
9 See Verena Fritz's contribution in this publication.

environment. As a consequence, joint responsibility for program implementation between partners and advisors, adaptive management based on permanent learning loops, and the incremental development of approaches and instruments was promoted, as this would allow for short feedback loops and easy adjustments during the implementation process. It was restated that, for GIZ's work, a focus on process is critical and determines the kind and quality of results that are achieved. It was also acknowledged that objectives and results might differ from the original program design and need to be adaptable during implementation due to the course the process takes. The essential idea of smart implementation takes the non-linear nature of development processes as a starting point for developing incremental, context-specific implementation strategies. The term smart implementation was coined in two GIZ publications that succeeded these discussions in 2009 and 2010 (Ernsthofer & Stockmayer, 2009; Frenken & Müller, 2010). Core elements of smart implementation entail a flexible and adaptive program management structure, as well as constant monitoring and analysis of the (political) environment.

1 CONCEPTUAL CONSIDERATIONS FOR SMART IMPLEMENTATION: FACILITATING THE COMPLEXITY OF SOCIAL CHANGE

Moving from a linear to a complex understanding of development

Traditionally, development was perceived as being unidirectional. It was assumed that the desired changes would follow once the necessary inputs (technology, knowledge, etc.) were supplied. Changes were believed to happen in a linear fashion and to be foreseeable and steerable. Thus, programs were planned, executed, re-planned, and executed further. Reaching a specific aim was seen as a matter of analyzing the situation, developing the right design, optimizing the available means, and putting them to work. Milestones, benchmarks, and objectives with indicators all appeared to underscore the idea of unidirectional development. It was assumed that programs could be improved and accelerated, and that their results could be scaled-up and transplanted to other cases and countries. Yet, over the years, the shortcomings of such a technocratic, economic-centric, and apolitical approach became obvious. As a response, most aid organizations adopted political goals alongside the common socio-economic ones and established separate governance departments. However, governance programs also used to focus on rather technical issues (Carothers & de Gramont, 2013, pp. 5f., 177).

Over time, the objectives of governance programs in particular shifted from providing technical assistance to rather specific problems geared toward accompanying and facilitating complex reforms and social change processes in partner countries. Consequently, the understanding of how change occurs broadened, and "systems thinking" was increasingly adopted as the conceptual frame for approaching change and designing development measures (Green, 2016b, chapter 1).

Systems thinking[10] accepts that social change takes place within complex and dynamic systems. It can be stimulated by addressing the whole system, not only a single element of it. Change occurs from the inside and requires a critical mass of actors demanding it. Social systems tend to seek stability and a power equilibrium. Thus, the impulse for change can be neutralized and needs to be re-injected over time. Any external engagement leads to change within the system, whether intended or unintended. Measures supporting the change process affect the entire system across all levels (policy, institutional, and individual) and sectors and cannot be confined to the directly intended institution or stakeholder. This interdependence leads to indirect and second-round effects that require attention and response. Social change, as described by systems thinking, is explained as follows:

- It is a non-linear and reflexive process in which each achievement relates back to previous ones. The change process has a direction, but it incorporates loops, ruptures, and side paths. Events might occur immediately, simultaneously, or with tremendous delays. Achievements can be stalled, or even reversed, causing the process to move backward and forward, depending on, for example, political dynamics or changing majorities.
- Progress, acceleration, as well as setbacks and reversals occur when critical junctures or tipping points are reached that determine the future steps in the process.
- Outcomes and impacts can neither be fully known at the outset, nor can they be deduced from existing evidence alone; rather, they emerge as the implementation process moves on.

---

10 For an introduction into system theory, see Simon (1998) and Luhmann (1984).

- Due to the interdependence of factors, stakeholders can steer or manage the process only to a limited extent and become themselves subject to influence and interferences by other parties.

The implication for program implementation is a high degree of uncertainty, uncontrollability, and unpredictability throughout the process. Decision-makers and program managers have to move in an environment where they are faced with insufficient information and often changing parameters. Constant analysis, responsiveness, flexibility, and adaptability are aids for program management that provide space to shape the process instead of only having to react to it (Andrews, Pritchett, & Woolcock, 2012, 2017; Booth & Unsworth, 2014; Root, Jones, & Wild, 2015; Green, 2016b).

Transformation as the conceptual frame for GIZ governance programs

To better incorporate these considerations into program design and implementation, GIZ's governance and conflict division adopted the concept of transformation as a conceptual frame in 2013 (Hübner, Kohl, Siehl, & Stockmayer, 2013).[11] Transformation describes a complex, multidimensional process that encompasses all aspects of political, economic, social, and technological change. Transformation processes are characterized by their heterogeneity and entail diverging actors from politics, administration, the private sector, and civil society, as well as actors from the regional, national, and local levels. Elements of transformation include the changing of structures and institutions, but also changes in human interests, values, and attitudes. Transformation cannot be anticipated with certainty. The concept highlights the simultaneous and comprehensive nature of change processes, which do not always directly respond to defined problems or challenges. There are too many variables at play, and their nature as well as the many interdependences between these variables inhibit predicting the future direction of the process – let alone its effects. Transformation consists of many sub-processes, but they do not follow

---

11 The concept of transformation was influenced by the experiences GIZ made in Eastern Europe and Central Asia in the 1990s and 2000s. The concept paper was developed by Albrecht Stockmayer, Katharina Hübner, Astrid Kohl, and Elke Siehl.

one unified objective (Loorbach, 2010, pp. 161–183). In many cases, transformation responds to past conflicts: It is subject to pressure from delayed reforms, but it is also driven by (often diverging) visions of the future in which actors try to change, for example, the present balance of power or allocation of resources. The relationship between actors is loose and complex, which makes it difficult to fully capture them (in 't Veld et al., 2011, p. 16). Yet, our partners and their institutions are embedded in these processes and will not abstain from trying to manage and interfere in them. Program staff needs to understand the nature of the transformation and remain conscious of the fact that there are only a few stable conditions in it, and that content, alliances, ownership, commitment, and resources change over time. Knowing the history and intention of the transformation is a prerequisite for advisors to offer sound support to partners that are moving within it.

The role of governance in transformation

Every transformation process is (also) a governance process because it addresses interests and power relations as well as rules and resources. However, not every reform is necessarily a transformation, as not all reforms change the society's systemic characteristics or values. Transformation needs governance to give the process direction and drive.[12] Roeland J. in 't Veld et al. explain the double function of governance and call it *transgovernance*:

> Governance relates to social systems. These are reflexive in nature. They learn continuously, with the support of experience, knowledge, revelation and so on. Creating governance means shaping and influencing social system, so governance has therefore to be reflexive in itself. (In 't Veld et al., 2011, p. 9)

The research team asserts that most of the transformative changes take place at a very small-scale level "ranging from technological innovations in niche-markets to adjustments in individual behavioral patterns" (in 't Veld et al., 2011, p. 16). Combined, these small changes lead to profound changes. *Transgovernance* is about finding and fostering such small-scale

---

12 O'Neil and Cammack (2014) illustrate in a case study on Malawi the effects if governance is missing in transformation.

changes, which can – if governed well – lead to greater change and impact (in 't Veld et al., 2011, p. 16).

Governance in transformation supports managing asymmetries and unforeseeable changes. Learning, which results from reflexivity, ensures that actors can reach a certain degree of congruence to move forward. Thus, governance contributes to advancing transformation processes toward sustainable change by maintaining a certain level of stability and reliability in situations of profound uncertainty (in 't Veld et al., 2011, p. 10).[13]

Transformation is political by nature

Politics is the main mechanism by which the deliberation in transformation takes place. It is the political arena where interests and opinions are shaped, voices and proposals are tested, and positions are negotiated. This happens in formal political institutions (parties, parliament) as well as in informal ones (media, social movements, lobbying). Influence and power are exercised to forge constituencies and majorities that support interests and positions. The constellations of interests, majorities, and positions change throughout the process, and it is hard to predict which ideas and political views will gain public support as well as when they will and by whom. Thus, politics is an integral part of any social change process and, therefore, a crucial dimension of program implementation that needs attention and response. Program implementation cannot be confined to its technical dimensions – even if the program works on predominantly technical issues. Any development program causes reactions in the system regarding power relations, the influence levels of actors, and resource allocations, and therefore it is squarely in the political domain of matters. Knowing the political structure, power relations among actors, as well as

---

13 Politics in a strict sense refers to activities and actors within the formal domain of the state. Yet, for understanding the political dimension of development cooperation, a broader view of what constitutes politics is more appropriate. It includes the distribution of power and resources within a society, the assertion of interests, processes of conflict, cooperation and negotiations, as well as the way in which decisions are taken. Thus, the term "political" captures "contestation and cooperation among diverse societal actors with differing interests and power" (Carothers & de Gramont, 2013, p. 13). For a discussion on power in change processes, see Green (2016a, chapter 2).

their motivations and incentives is a precondition for maneuvering as an external advisor within a partner's environment. The concept of transformation accepts that implementation problems might have a technical base, but their political rational always has to be considered as well.

Acknowledging the function of politics in development assistance and in transformation has been proclaimed for a long time (Carothers & de Gramont, 2013; Fritz, Levy, & Ort, 2014; Deutscher Bundestag, 1995, p. 48), but it has proven difficult to translate this idea into operational work. One explanation is that a systematic consideration of the political dimension in program implementation collides with the traditional view of a program: The intention of a program was to insulate the reform from outside interferences in order to address its technical challenges. Politics was perceived as an outside risk that had to be observed, at best, but it was not considered to be something that could be managed or used to advance the agenda (Eyben, 2014, p. 81). The work on Thinking and Working Politically captures this misconception quite well in the following quote but also outlines what kind of mind-shift and skills are required to incorporate a political view into implementation. Working politically in development is easily misinterpreted as insensitive interference, as an invasion of sovereignty and a disregard for principles of ownership and endogenously driven developmental process (Leftwich, 2011).

> [It] means supporting, brokering, facilitating and aiding the emergence and practices of developmental or reform leaderships, organizations, networks and coalitions, in the public and private fields, at all levels, and across all sectors, in response to, and in concert with, initiatives and requests from local individuals and groups. It means *investing in processes* designed to support the formation and effectiveness of developmental coalitions, sometimes over long periods, committed to institutional reform and innovation by enhancing not just technical skills (the conventional domain of capacity building) but also the political capacity of organizations in areas such as negotiation, advocacy, communication and the generation of constructive policy options. It may involve supporting processes which lead to "political settlements" whether these be at the macro-levels or in specific policy sectors. (Leftwich, 2011, p. 8)

Conducting political (economy) analysis (PEA) and using this information for program appraisal, design, and implementation was a first attempt to accommodate this new thinking. Several development organizations piloted approaches to incorporate political economy analysis more systematically in their work (Fritz, Levy, & Ort, 2014; Booth, Harris, & Wild, 2016). However, the effects of this effort have been marginal on how development programs are implemented. One explanation is that the operational approaches have not changed as well, so that the program staff is obliged to follow the rules of headquarters rather than partner demands. In this case the information provided by political economy analysis can hardly be translated into operational work, as no space exists for doing things differently (Development Leadership Prôgram, s.a.). Verena Fritz explains in her article why it took several loops to learn how to integrate the results of such analysis into daily work.[14]

Yet, there is another political dimension that influences the implementation of programs. Donors and development organizations formulate their values and interests in the form of sector policy or guidance papers, which at least serve as references (if not binding guidelines) for operational staff in country settings. They also influence the frame in which operations take place and how they are conducted. Shifts in donor priorities may require adaptations in the implementation of programs that are not locally-led and problem-focused.

In summary, the focus of implementation has slowly shifted from the technical to the political domain. The concept of transformation accepts that implementation problems might have a technical base, but their political rational always has to be considered as well.

Implications of adopting the concept of transformation for smart implementation

Adopting the concept of transformation as the conceptual frame of GIZ governance operations has implications for how implementation is approached. Four points can be stated.

First, knowing that we act in conditions of transformation changes how we relate to a program. It is merely one element of support in a wider array of internal and external activities. It is hardly the main driver of – or an indispensable contribution for – change. Only multiple actions over a longer period of time will lead to transformation.

Second, implementation in conditions of transformation requires a sound understanding of the environment, details about the drivers of

---

14 See Verena Fritz's contribution in this publication; see also Fischer and Marquette (2014).

change, the formal and informal institutions, and the political, social, and economic dynamics, including power relations. All of this requires analysis, instruments, and approaches that go beyond the sector perspective and take political and cross-sectoral aspects into account.

Third, to be able to address the political dimension in transformation, advisors not only have to understand the political context in which they work but need to be able to move within it in order to create scope of action for partner institutions. Hence, the importance of conducting political (economy) analysis is apparent, but it has to be current to be relevant for teams.

Finally, the concept multiplies the roles that program staff have to take on while straddling between technical, political, and managerial challenges in the attempt to support partners in their function while steering the next steps of a transformation. The case studies illustrate how program staff take up the role of technical experts; political and social analysts; organizational development advisors; conveners of new ideas; and brokers of new cooperation efforts and partnerships at different stages of the implementation.

The following section explores whether the institutional arrangement of German development cooperation can provide the conditions for GIZ governance programs to implement them in this spirit.

2 INSTITUTIONAL CONSIDERATIONS FOR SMART IMPLEMENTATION

GIZ – an implementing agency for sustainable development

The Deutsche Gesellschaft für Internationale Zusammenarbeit GmbH (GIZ) – the German agency for international cooperation – is a limited liability company under German private law with a public-benefit corporate purpose. GIZ is owned by the Federal Republic of Germany, represented through the Federal Ministry for Economic Cooperation and Development (BMZ) and the Federal Ministry of Finance. GIZ's purpose is to promote international sustainable development and to support the German federal government in achieving its objectives in this field. BMZ and increasingly other German ministries and international donors commission GIZ to prepare, implement, and assess development cooperation measures in the field of capacity development. The division of labor between the German government and GIZ is specified in concrete terms in regulations and guidelines, such as the Federal Guidelines for Bilateral Financial and Technical Cooperation, the General Agreement, and the joint Code of Conduct for BMZ, GIZ, and KfW Development Bank. A code of conduct regulates the working relations.[15] Whereas BMZ is responsible for setting policies, for commissioning, and for controlling implementers, GIZ implements these measures independently, together with the partners. The principle of joint responsibility for achieving objectives gives partners a decisive role in the planning and implementation of programs.

Since the mid-1970s, when GIZ's precursor organization was founded, several arrangements defining the commissioning procedure and delivery between BMZ and GIZ have been in operation: Originally, the logical framework was at the heart of the commissioning framework as the yardstick by which to measure the success of a program. The logical framework outlined a program's objective, purpose, required inputs and resources, expected outputs, main activities, and anticipated results and assumptions with a strong focus on fixed input and output indicators.[16] GIZ adapted the logical framework approach to its needs, added the problem analysis phase, and introduced ZOPP (goal-oriented project planning) as a standard tool in 1983 (GTZ [Deutsche Gesellschaft für Technische Zusammenarbeit], 1988), which was accompanied in 1998 by Project Cycle Management (GTZ, 1995, 1997). However, criticism to the logical framework approach cited that it was too rigid, linear, and mono-causal; it did not allow for necessary adjustments during program implementation; and that it focused too much on the output level rather than on outcomes. This led to the adoption of a new commissioning framework between BMZ and GIZ in 2002. The need for change was described as follows at the time: "A higher degree of flexibility for implementing projects is urgently called for because, at the core of technical cooperation, we increasingly find the support of complex social transformation processes taking place in a dynamic environment" (BMZ/GTZ [German Federal

---

15 KfW stands for Kreditanstalt für Wiederaufbau (Bank for Reconstruction) and is another German implementing organization in the field of development cooperation. The KfW Banking Group includes the KfW Development Bank that implements development finance on behalf of the German government and other international donors, often in close cooperation with and complementary to GIZ's technical cooperation programs.

16 For a brief introduction into Logical Framework Analysis, see World Bank (2005) and European Commission (2004).

Ministry for Economic Cooperation and Development / Deutsche Gesellschaft für Technische Zusammenarbeit], 2006, p. 3).[17]

The new commissioning framework between BMZ and GIZ introduced the inclusion of a results model that outlines in detail the theory of change for achieving the stated objectives. Furthermore, a GIZ program proposal now includes a statement about which outcomes will be achieved by GIZ and the partner organization within a proposed time frame. This led to a scaling-down and more realistic formulation of program objectives and indicators. Thus, against the promise of achieving results and a joint agreement on objectives, more flexibility and discretion on how to steer and manage implementation has been granted to GIZ. This commissioning framework ensures that GIZ's implementation mandate is sufficiently broad so that it can – and must – use its discretion to reach objectives in a way best suited to the local context. Most implementation decisions are therefore taken within the local context, or at least very close to it. This allows for a high degree of adaptability to the local situation. Changing the program outcomes and core activities is possible with reasonable administrative effort and in agreement with BMZ throughout the implementation phase of a program (usually a three-year time period), if the unpredictable change dynamics in the country suggest it.

Based on the theory of change, which is developed during program appraisal, many GIZ programs are designed in a multi-level approach and target the policy (macro), the institutional (meso), and the individual (micro) levels with core measures at each level. The advantage for implementation is that, if progress is slow on one level, activities can be rerouted to a second or third level. This provides flexibility, for example by providing time to await political decisions to be taken, public opinions or majorities to be forged, and administrative obstacles or capture to be overcome – all while staying engaged and without jeopardizing the support to the overall transformation.

GIZ's management model Capacity WORKS

In response to the shifting conceptual and institutional priorities of the organization, a new management model for shaping and steering coopera-

---

17 Author translation; BMZ/GTZ (2003, pp. 3, 5, quoted in BMZ/GTZ, 2006, p. 3).

tion was developed and found its expression in Capacity WORKS (GIZ, 2015; Beier, 2015; Maurer, 2013). It, as well as the concept of transformation, translates conditions of social change into guidance for implementers. Its rationale is briefly explained in this section.

Cooperation is the cornerstone of social development, as no single actor can initiate or manage change processes. Furthermore, in order to be sustainable, change has to evolve from within a society rather than being triggered from the outside. Thus, working with partner countries in cooperation systems lies at the heart of development assistance. However, acknowledging the crucial importance of cooperation does not necessarily make the task of managing it any easier.

Difficulties stem from the different management requirements of cooperation systems compared to hierarchical organizations. Generally, organizations are centered around the provision of a good or service and are composed of a particular set of goals or interests, structures, and processes. Internal hierarchies traditionally form the basis of managing such organizations. These closed structures not only enable management in its strictest sense but require it in order to organize, design, and implement production processes. Cooperation systems, in turn, need a different form of management. They are usually based on a convergence of interests and depend on negotiations between partners on eye level to reach a majority vote or a consensus. Directive, hierarchal instructions would be most likely rejected, as they undermine the principle of engagement, which is voluntariness and common purpose.

Actors enter cooperation systems as partners, but nevertheless will follow their own goals. Thus, to jointly develop a strategy or theory of change that is supported by all partners, it is often a time-intensive but crucial exercise at the outset to ensure fruitful cooperation. Steering structures are adopted by most cooperation systems, even if they differ to those in hierarchal organizations. However, cooperation partners remain autonomous in deciding whether – and to what degree – they wish to cooperate.

Drawn from the practical experiences gained from different programs and countries over the course of six years, patterns were identified that shape fruitful cooperation. These patterns – summarized in the five "success factors" strategy, cooperation, steering structure, processes, and learning and innovation – form the basis of GIZ's cooperation management model and can be summarized as follows:

Strategy: A joint strategy to achieve the negotiated objectives is the initial point for successful cooperation

Cooperation: Negotiation, clearly defined roles, and trust form the basis for fruitful cooperation

Steering structure: Agreements on how the actors involved will jointly prepare and take decisions guide the cooperation system

Processes: A clear understanding of which new processes need to be established or which existing processes need to be modified in order to reach joint objectives is part of successful cooperation systems

Learning and innovation: Cooperation partners create an enabling environment for innovation by enhancing the learning capacities of all actors involved

These five success factors together form a management model for analyzing and understanding cooperation systems and their mechanisms in a structured way. The analysis and the subsequent developed implementation strategy provide orientation in complex environments and offer a way to develop a common language shared among all partners. Capacity WORKS as a management model supports cooperation partners in articulating what they wish to achieve and how they intend to do so. Thus, by jointly interpreting the reality and developing a vision for a desirable future, a common ground for joint action is created (GIZ, 2015, p. 2).

For each of the five success factors, Capacity WORKS offers tailored tool boxes, which can serve as an inspiration in actual cooperation systems. Yet, as implementation processes are unique and context-specific, it does not attempt to provide ready-made answers to particular challenges.

Neil Hatton's article in this book[18] discusses the implications of a systems perspective in organizations and for their management. He also explains the rationale and the design of Capacity WORKS in more detail and highlights implementation challenges from an organizational development perspective.

3 QUESTIONS CONCERNING IMPLEMENTATION IN THE NINE CASE STUDIES

The outlined conceptual and institutional frame in which GIZ governance programs operate define the space and scope in which – and how – implementation takes place. In this publication, we want to review how these conditions play out in practice, and how program teams maneuver within

---

18 See Neil Hatton's contribution in this book.

them. For this, the implementation challenges and processes of nine GIZ governance programs are retraced. The findings are presented in the form of case studies. Each program team was asked to reflect on their implementation process with the following five questions in mind (GIZ, 2015):

- What kinds of challenges occurred during program implementation? What did working in uncertain, unpredictable, complex, and political environments mean in your case?
- How did program teams and partners orient themselves in complex and unpredictable environments?
  - Which principles, instruments, or approaches were referred to or adopted?
  - What kind of analysis was used? How was insufficient information handled?
  - How did teams and partners learn?
- Were there tensions between achieving predefined results and adapting to changing circumstances? How were they handled?
- Which frame conditions (at the level of the development organization and in country) were conducive or hindered implementation in complex environments?
- What aspects of implementation were transferrable between contexts and countries, and what was context-specific and needed to be newly created?

The case studies of GIZ cover a wide array of countries and governance issues. All programs were shaped by context-specific dynamics and faced different challenges. The authors describe the process of moving from a plan to a program design and via implementation toward results. They reveal the implementation challenges they faced and retrace how changes occurred in specific cases, revealing contradictions, setbacks, mishaps, and power struggles as much as the opportunities, luck, encounters, and coincidences that occurred while bringing a program design into reality. Critical junctures as well as course corrections are normal in a complex change process and are explained. Furthermore, it is discussed how alliances were forged, what manipulations occurred, how informal arrangements were formed and negotiated to make them formal, and what it took to convince stakeholders of an idea or approach that was not a priority at the outset.

As an introduction, the governance themes and implementation challenges of each case study are briefly outlined.

Liberia, which, despite being well-endowed with natural resources, remains one of the poorest countries in the world and faces the challenge of how to turn resource wealth into sustainable and inclusive development. The case study describes how the GIZ governance program assisted the government of Liberia in improving the way it **administers mining licenses** in order to create regulating mechanisms and to cut down on corruption. It is revealed how capacity constraints and donor pressure influence implementation in a rather fragile environment. Furthermore, as the system introduced had previously been applied in Sierra Leone, the case study depicts which elements of a certain approach can be reproduced – and to what extent implementation depends on the local context.

Among many other reasons, the public administration's bureaucratic despotism was one element that triggered **Tunisia's** revolution in 2011. In accordance with Tunisia's new constitution, GIZ is supporting the implementation of the guiding principles of **democracy, decentralization, and a public administration** that is at the service of the citizens and the common good. The program described in the case study include activities such as the trainings of Tunisian officials, supporting a sector ministry in decentralization, transforming Tunisia's training center for decentralization, and fostering the involvement of young people in local politics. The case study reveals how programs have to cope with challenges that arise from political uncertainty and high public expectations. In addition, the practical relevance of joint learning and an incremental course of action are exemplified.

Supporting the reform of the **public service administration** was the aim of the GIZ program in **South Africa**. Yet, a lack of coordination and collaboration between different spheres of government and a certain attitude of "silo thinking" rendered the development of a common approach for a government-wide monitoring and evaluation system and the introduction of community media support quite challenging. The case study reveals how establishing new forms of cooperation and providing spaces for exchange can lead to a joint vision of change that shapes implementation.

The case study of **Costa Rica** traces the implementation of a GIZ program that supported the government in improving and **strengthening its monitoring and evaluation capacities**. Mistrust as well as a lack of dialogue and communication between different units and departments were some of the challenges the program faced. However, it is shown how creating space for communication and learning and (maybe more important) how constant monitoring and feedback raised acceptance for a new and controversial policy. The case study is structured around Capacity WORKS and, thus, exemplifies to what extent the management model of GIZ provides support and orientation for implementers.

The GIZ team in **Peru** enjoyed more leeway than what is usually given to program teams. Set up as an advocacy program with the broad objective of contributing to the fight against **violence against women**, they were able to independently select their partner and choose their focus area. The team decided to explore new ways by trying to engage the private sector. Although the program was not restrained by a rigid program structure, the case shows that even moving between the intermediary objectives, alliances, and main protagonists, there were constantly new challenges, some that even threatened to make the program unviable. These challenges were overcome by equally unexpected resources – some new and unknown, some known but underestimated.

The example of the **South Caucasus** traces the process of **introducing a new administrative law** to make public authorities accountable to their citizens in Armenia, Azerbaijan, and Georgia. The approach of the three programs was similar, but implementation processes varied considerably according to the different reform dynamics within the countries. Thus, each country produced its specific critical juncture, and the case study reveals how the different programs responded to these context-specific challenges.

In **Azerbaijan**, GIZ supported the capacity-building of the national Civil Service Commission. The management and coordination of civil servant training and professional development across state bodies was provided through the development of a training strategy and the implementation of training policies and curricula. This program is especially interesting because it was carried out with additional funding from the EU with different institutional arrangements compared to those between GIZ and BMZ. The EU conditions provided a different scope to adapt elements of the program during implementation in view of local changes and increased complexities. How this affected implementation and the program as such is traced in the case study.

The case study on the **Conflict Sensitive Resource and Asset Management Program** in the **Philippines** depicts some of the challenges that program implementation faces in environments affected by violent conflicts between the government and armed non-state actors. Taking as an example the support provided to a city on the island of Mindanao from

2011 to 2014, the case study analyzes how to assist government agencies to foster inclusive and sustainable socio-economic development in a volatile conflict situation. It also illustrates what guided partners in addressing implementation challenges, such as the lack of access to a classified forest area by both GIZ and the local government due to the security situation. It shows how – despite several setbacks – mistrust among the actors was overcome.

The case study of **Indonesia** describes the challenges of establishing **financing mechanisms for climate change mitigation** that are guided by principles of **good financial governance**. It illustrates efforts by GIZ teams from different backgrounds to develop a coherent advisory approach. It focused on engaging various partner institutions with different interests regarding climate change mitigation policies and fiscal decentralization. Besides discussing opportunities and challenges within a bilateral development cooperation agency to offer ad hoc, multi-sectoral advisory services to partners, the case study also stresses its limitations within a real-time reform process in Indonesia.

Prior to the presentations of the case studies, the book presents two other articles that discuss conditions for successful or smart implementation. One is from the perspective of the World Bank capturing the PDIA and DDD discussion, and a second one is from the perspective of organizational development and discusses GIZ's management model Capacity WORKS. The findings and results of the nine case studies will be reviewed in the final chapter of this book, in which an outlook to the next steps in the debate on implementation is given.

References

Algoso, D., & Hudson, A. (2016, June 9). Where have we got to on adaptive learning, thinking and working politically, doing development differently etc? Getting beyond the people's front of Judea. *From Poverty to Power.* Retrieved from http://o xfamblogs.org/fp2p/where-have-we-got-to-on-adaptive-learning-thinking-and-work ing-politically-doing-development-differently-etc-getting-beyond-the-peoples-front -of-judea/

Andrews, M. (2013). *The limits of institutional reform in development: Changing rules for realistic solutions.* Cambridge: Cambridge University Press.

Andrews, M., Pritchett, L., & Woolcock, M. (2012). *Escaping capability traps through Problem-Driven Iterative Adaptation (PDIA)* (CGD Working Paper 299). Washington, DC: Center for Global Development. Retrieved from http://www.cgdev.org/con tent/publications/detail/1426292

Andrews, M., Pritchett, L., & Woolcock, M. (2017). *Building state capability. Evidence, analysis, action.* Oxford: Oxford University Press.

Beier, C. (2015). Vermittler zwischen den Welten. *OrganisationsEntwicklung, 2,* 46–51.

BMZ/GTZ (German Federal Ministry for Economic Cooperation and Development / Deutsche Gesellschaft für Technische Zusammenarbeit). (2003). *Handreichung zur Bearbeitung von AURA Angeboten.* Eschborn: GTZ.

BMZ/GTZ. (2006). *Handreichung zur Bearbeitung von AURA Angeboten.* Eschborn: GTZ.

Booth, D. (2012). *Development as a collective action problem. Addressing the real challenges of African governance* (Synthesis Report of the Africa Power and Politics Programme). London: Overseas Development Institute.

Booth, D. (2014). *Aiding institutional reform in developing countries: Lessons from the Philippines on what works, what doesn't and why* (ODI Working politically in practice series, Case Study no. 1). Retrieved from https://www.odi.org/sites/odi.org.uk/files/odi-assets/publications-opinion-files/8978.pdf

Booth, D., Harris, D., & Wild, L. (2016). *From political economy analysis to doing development differently: a learning experience* (ODI report) London: Overseas Development Institute. Retrieved from https://www.odi.org/sites/odi.org.uk/files/odi-assets/publications-opinion-files/10205.pdf

Booth, D., & Unsworth, S. (2014). *Politically smart, locally led development* (ODI Discussion Paper). London: Overseas Development Institute.

Carothers, T., & de Gramont, D. (2013). *Development aid confronts politics: The almost revolution.* Washington, DC: Carnegie Institution.

DDD Manifesto Community. (2014). *Doing Development Differently manifesto.* Retrieved from http://doingdevelopmentdifferently.com/the-ddd-manifesto/

Deutscher Bundestag. (1995). *Zehnter Bericht zur Entwicklungspolitik der Bundesregierung.* Retrieved from http://dip21.bundestag.de/dip21/btd/13/033/1303342.pdf

Development Leadership Program. (s.a.). *Thinking and working politically.* Retrieved from http://publications.dlprog.org/TWP.pdf

Ernsthofer, A., & Stockmayer, A. (Eds.). (2009). *Capacity development for good governance.* Baden-Baden: Nomos.

European Commission. (2004). *Aid delivery methods – project cycle management guidelines, vol. 1.* Retrieved from http://ec.europa.eu/europeaid/sites/devco/files/methodology-aid-delivery-methods-project-cycle-management-200403_en_2.pdf

Eyben, R. (2014). *International aid and the making of a better world.* London: Routledge.

Eyben, R., Guijt, I., Roche, C., & Shutt, C. (2015). *The politics of evidence and results in international development. Playing the game to change the rules?* Warwickshire, UK: Practical Action Publishing Ltd.

Fisher, J., & Marquette, H. (2014). *Donors doing political economy analysis. from process to product (and back again?)* (Research Paper 28). The Development Leadership Program. University of Birmingham, UK.

Frenken, S., & Müller, U. (Eds.). (2010). *Ownership and political steering in developing countries.* Baden-Baden: Nomos.

Fritz, V., Levy, B., & Ort, R. (Eds.). (2014). *Problem-driven political economy analysis: The World Bank's Experience.* Retrieved from https://openknowledge.worldbank.org/handle/10986/16389

GIZ (Deutsche Gesellschaft für Internationale Zusammenarbeit). (2012). *Das Zusammenspiel zwischen Sektoren und Governance aus Sicht der Abteilung 42.* GIZ Abteilung 42 Good Governance und Menschenrechte. Taskforce Governance in Sektoren. Eschborn: Author.

GIZ. (2014). *Our understanding of good governance. How we support reform and transformation processes.* Eschborn: Author.

GIZ. (2015). *Cooperation management for practitioners: Managing social change with Capacity WORKS.* Wiesbaden: Springer Gabler.

Global Delivery Initiative. (2014). *Delivery case study guidelines.* Retrieved from http://www.globaldeliveryinitiative.org/sites/default/files/pages/delivery_case_study_guidelines_-_english.pdf

GTZ. (Deutsche Gesellschaft für Technische Zusammenarbeit). (1988). *ZOPP (an introduction to the method).* Eschborn: Author.

GTZ. (1995). *Project Cycle Management (PCM) und Zielorientierte Projektplanung (ZOPP), Ein Leitfaden.* Eschborn: Author.

GTZ. (1997). *ZOPP. Objectives-oriented project planning.* Eschborn: Author.

Green, D. (2016a). *How change happens.* Oxford: Oxford University Press.

Green, D. (2016b, December 8). Adaptive management looks like it's here to stay. Here's why that matters. *Oxfam International.* Retrieved from https://blogs.oxfam.org/en/content/adaptive-management-looks-it%E2%80%99s-here-stay-here%E2%80%99s-why-matters

Hübner, K., Kohl, A., Siehl, E., & Stockmayer, A. (2013). *Aus der Praxis für die Praxis. Transform*ation – *Zum Verständnis.* Ein Rahmenkonzept der Abteilung Good Governance und Menschenrechte. Eschborn: Deutsche Gesellschaft für Internationale Zusammenarbeit.

In 't Veld, R. J., Töpfer, K., Meuleman, L., Bachmann, G., Jungcurt, S., Napolitano, J., Perez-Carmona, A., & Schmidt, F. (2011). *Transgovernance. The quest for governance of sustainable development.* Potsdam: Institute for Advanced Sustainability.

Kirsch, R. (2015). *Book project: Smart implementation in governance. Guidelines for writing a case study on implementation.* Retrieved from http://www.good-governance-debates.de/wp-content/uploads/2015/03/Guidelines_SM_case-studies_final.pdf

Leftwich, A., (2011). *Thinking and working politically: What does it mean, why is it important and how do you do it?* Retrieved from http://www.gsdrc.org/document-library/thinking-and-working-politically-what-does-it-mean-why-is-it-important-and-how-do-you-do-it/

Levy, B. (2014). *Working with the grain. Integrating governance and growth in development strategies.* Oxford: Oxford University Press.

Loorbach, D. (2010). Transition management for sustainable development: A prescriptive, complexity-based governance framework. *Governance: An International Journal of Policy, Administration and Institutions, 23*(1), 161–183.

Luhmann, N. (1984). *Soziale Systeme. Grundriß einer allgemeinen Theorie.* Frankfurt am Main: Suhrkamp Verlag.

Maurer, M., Glotzbach, S., & Görgen, M. (2013). Balance-Stück in vier Akten. Die Einführung eines systemischen Managementmodells in der GIZ. *OrganisationsEntwicklung, 2,* 76–83.

O'Neil, T., & Cammack, D. (2014, May). *Fragmented governance and local service delivery in Malawi* (ODI report). London: Overseas Development Institute. Retrieved from https://www.odi.org/sites/odi.org.uk/files/odi-assets/publications-opinion-files/8943.pdf

Organisation for Economic Co-operation and Development. (2005). *The Paris Declaration on Aid Effectiveness.* Retrieved from https://www.oecd.org/dac/effectiveness/34428351.pdf

Root, H., Jones, H., & Wild, L., (2015). *Managing complexity and uncertainty in development policy and practice* (ODI report). London: Overseas Development Institute.

Simon, F. (Ed.). (1998). *Lebende Systeme.* Berlin: Suhrkamp Taschenbuch Wissenschaft 1290.

Wild, L., Andrews, M., Pett, J., & Dempster, H. (2016). *Doing development differently: Who we are, what we're doing and what we're learning.* ODI Politics and Governance Programme. Retrieved from https://www.odi.org/publications/10662-doing-development-differently-who-we-are-what-were-doing-and-what-were-learning

Wild, L., Booth, D., Cummings, C., Foresti, M., & Wales, J. (2015, February). *Adapting development. improving services to the poor* (ODI report). London: Overseas Development Institute. Retrieved from https://www.odi.org/sites/odi.org.uk/files/odi-assets/publications-opinion-files/9437.pdf

Wild, L., Booth, D., & Valters, C. (2017, February). *Putting theory into practice. How DFID is doing development differently* (ODI report). London: Overseas Development Institute.

World Bank. (2005). *The logframe handbook: A logical framework approach to project cycle management.* Retrieved from http://documents.worldbank.org/curated/en/783001468134383368/pdf/31240b0LFhandbook.pdf

World Bank. (2017). *World Development Report 2017: Governance and the law.* Washington, DC: Author. Retrieved from http://www.worldbank.org/en/publication/wdr2017

Yin, R. (2009). *Case study research: Design and methods.* Applies Social Research Methods Series. 4th edition. Thousand Oaks, CA: SAGE.

Tackling Implementation Challenges
in Development Organizations

Polka or Parker? What Management Could Learn About Smart Implementation from Music

Neil Hatton

> "Philosophers have only interpreted the world. The point is, however, to change it."
> — Karl Marx, Eleven Theses on Feuerbach (also inscribed on his grave)

"You can't change the way Manila looks, you can change the way you look at Manila."

This sentence – from a Filipino acquaintance of mine, Carlos – taught me a very important lesson in life. At the time that he said this, I had been living in Manila for more than three years and was feeling negative about the city. It was dirty, crime-ridden, clogged with traffic, architecturally uninspiring, and a difficult place to live in all around. No matter how often I tried to convince myself that the biggest shopping mall in Asia really was a fascinating thing, I still could not convince myself. I complained about this to practically everybody who was willing to listen (and even some who were not). Carlos took me by the hand one evening and walked me around the city to look at the sights and sounds that I had been looking at daily for three years. He told me many things that I did not know, casting old facts in a new light, and he wove a story that got me to like – if not fall in love with – Manila. He literally changed the way I looked at the city.

This personal lesson is similar to one I feel we need to implement when discussing "smart implementation" in development projects. We have been looking at many of the same things for many years and trying to make it smarter in many ways. The problem here is not the skills level or amount of effort, but rather the way we are looking at it. Management theory has a particular way of looking at things and a logic that leads us – in development contexts – down a blind alley. But if we are prepared to look at the "problem of implementation" in a different way, many of these difficulties turn out not to be so hard after all. Herein lies the route to "smart" implementation – not working harder but, rather, smarter.

In this brief chapter, I try to describe and assess other sources of inspiration that are available to us to help us with this challenge. Which other alternatives are available? How can we integrate these alternatives into our personal and, above all, organizational repertoires? These questions are fruitful, as they reveal a lot along the way about our individual and collective attitudes to management, change and social systems.

This chapter is loosely structured as follows. In the first part, I look at why social systems behave in a fundamentally different fashion than mechanical systems, on which most of our management theory is based. I also explore why this simple insight has found no place in management theory. In the second section, I expand on this to look at the fundamental differences between organizations and cooperation systems or multi-stakeholder partnerships and the requirements that this implies for the development goals that must be achieved through such partnerships. I then take a small detour and look more closely at the process of developing a jazz tune, which has many parallels to our work in development. On the basis of these insights, I try to sketch out a smart implementation, but one that lies distinctly in the real world of craft and not science. Lastly, I describe some of the experiences that the Deutsche Gesellschaft für Internationale Zusammenarbeit (GIZ) has had in this area, both in terms of developing a model for such interventions as well as the challenge of changing its organization to make it an explicit core competence of the company as a whole. Along the way, I try to illustrate the argument with examples from the work of GIZ to make it less technical and more accessible to a wider audience, while still attempting to retain a vestige of academic rigor.

Lost in triviality

The management world is still basically wedded to the belief that organizations and social systems are essentially trivial (in the sense of them being mechanical, not in the sense of them being unimportant[1]) and can be 1) understood and 2) changed in an input-output and goal-oriented fashion. This comes from the origins and birth of modern management and

---

1 This does not mean that they are not important; however, they are not simple. Even trivial systems can be very, complicated, for example the logistics system of DHL. They are not, however, complex.

Frederick Taylor.[2] This paradigm of management came from engineering and the application of such principles to the analysis and organization of the tasks of manufacturing. This ushered in a revolution in organization second only to that of the industrial revolution. It found a permanent home in the specialization of conveyor-belt production, which enabled the production of the Model-T Ford and gave birth to the hierarchical and functionally-specialized organizations that produced it. This Taylorist paradigm is still dominant in virtually all modern thinking and writing about management. It goes so deep that it has gained the status of an implicit and rarely questioned truism, regardless of its validity. It is our experience that there is a huge difference between the mechanistic and predictable view of "scientific management," as Taylor himself called it, and the behavior of social systems. When the change process (e.g., the production of a car) takes place in a situation where both the process of assembly of the machine as well as the behavior of the workers can be by and large controlled, this paradigm works.[3] As soon as the social interaction of the actors in the change process becomes important (e.g., the design and implementation of a better health system), this paradigm breaks down irrevocably. It seems odd to even have to state this, as development practitioners have experienced this daily for many years, but the consequences are worth dwelling on.

The reason for this difference is worth exploring in more detail. A mechanical (or to give it its technical name, a "trivial"[4]) machine is one that reliably converts input A into output B. Its inner workings can be pre-

---

2 This initial insight was systematized and perfected a few years later across the city in Detroit by his General Motors colleague Alfred Sloan, who gave his name to the eponymous management school. For the sake of legibility, I shall refer to this approach as "Taylorism," even though the correct epithet would really be "Taylorist/Sloanist," but then I would sound like Marxist revolutionaries and you would never finish reading.

3 This model assumes, of course, that the workers do not form unions or go on strike for better pay or fall in love with each other or fight each other or any of the other myriad things that assembly line workers (and human beings in general) actually do.

4 For those interested, this is a very short summary of the work of the Austrian cyberneticist and systems thinker Heinz von Förster, who illustrates this point brilliantly in his paper "Abbau und Aufbau." The paper is out of print, but it is reproduced in Simon (1998) in German. It is instructive that, to the best of my knowledge and research, this paradigm-defining paper (along with many other texts in the systemic/cybernetic tradition) have never been translated into English.

cisely described, and if it does not work as planned, a suitably qualified person can intervene and repair the machine so that it works as it should. This is exactly how machines should and do work, from simple (a pencil sharpener) to complicated (cars and computers). A non-trivial system, on the other hand, converts A into B, but also (and depending on the situation) into C, D, and even X, and under certain circumstances Z. Inputs are only loosely converted into outputs (as anyone who has tried to teach a child French vocabulary will know). Its inner workings cannot be described, and if it does not work as planned, it is not easy to "repair" it – as anyone who has tried to "repair" a student, employee, colleague, or partner will testify (the suitably qualified people here being teachers, psychologists, managers, parents, husbands, and wives). And we should not forget that the job of capacity development and developmental transformation at an international level that we address here is a much higher and more complex challenge than individuals, families, or single organizations. As the examples suggest, this starts with psychological (i.e., people) systems – people cannot be changed in the input-output fashion described above, although it has not stopped organizations, schools, and governments over the millennia from trying. Social scientists refer here to "complex" as opposed to "complicated" systems – systems that are so complex that they cannot be modeled, explained, or designed/operated/repaired like their trivial counterparts.

But that is precisely what we attempt to do every day in organizations, is it not? And the tools that we have available (the word "tool" is in itself a giveaway) are all based on the Taylor paradigm of the mechanical system – the wrenches and hammers of social engineering.[5]

Gregory Bateson: What is the difference between kicking a tin can and a dog? Gregory Bateson (1972), the social anthropologist, is famous for asking what the difference between the two (hypothetical, we hope) questions was. His answer illustrates the difference that indeed makes a difference.	Kicking a can involves the precise calculation of the angle and point of contact, the force required to propel the can, and the required distance to get it out of our way based on its size, shape, and weight. The average child can do this quite well before their 10th birthday.

---

5 Mark Twain summed this up neatly when he said, "If your only tool is a hammer then every problem starts to look like a nail."

Kicking a dog is similar, but also very different. Before I make contact with the dog (or more precisely, his rear end), both the dog and I start to think. The force with which my foot connects with the dog to get him out of my way remains a constant variable to be calculated – but the reaction of the dog (runs away with his tail between his legs; barks and runs away to get reinforcements; stands up, growls, and bites me) depends on the complex inner workings of the dog (what kind of experience has he had with people and kicking?). Moreover, my experience of kicking dogs (assuming I really do such a thing) is also relevant. Did all the dogs that I kicked run away, or did one of them bite me? Will this affect the force or conviction with which I connect with the dog? I can hope and project what will happen (according to my experience with dogs), but until the dog reacts, I cannot know it in the sense that I can know where the tin can will land.

And kicking cats is a different discipline altogether (you have to catch them first).

Clearly, social systems are non-linear in their behavior and are based on so many variables that have to do with the past experiences of the participants that they are at best unpredictable and at worst completely baffling. This places the social engineer in a dilemma. Teachers, parents, psychologists, and especially managers (not to mention development professionals) want and need to be able to influence these complex systems, and indeed they do, every day – but not with the mechanistic repertoire of hammers and screwdrivers. Fritz Simon (building on an earlier observation of Sigmund Freud) summed up the dilemma of the social engineer when he described teaching, education, and psychotherapy as "impossible professions" (Simon, 2002, but originally from Sigmund Freud) – based on a paradox of having to intervene to achieve a specific goal in a system that cannot be made to function in a predictable manner. Such professions – to which the development worker also belongs – have to live with the paradox of being responsible for producing results in systems: a) which they do not and cannot fully understand; b) which do not let themselves be influenced by them if they do not want to be; and c) for which the development worker only has the hammer provided to him by Mr. Taylor.

Lip service is paid to this insight in more modern management theory, but not in practice. The understanding of social systems (organizations or development contexts) leads to a kind of window-dressing of the change management projects. The literature praises "participation" and the involvement of the staff and stakeholders in the process (rather than seeing them – as Taylor did – as pawns in a chess game to be moved and sacrificed at will). This remains superficial – organizations and management theory are still dominated by the "machine-trivial" paradigm and not by the "social-complex" model. Moreover, the task of the development professional and their organizations is at a higher level of complexity than even this, as we see in the next section.

Cooperation systems and development partnerships are not organizations

Having seen that our concepts of management and organizations are somehow stuck in the early part of the last century, we must now confront a second uncomfortable truth. Even if the management concepts had kept up with the recognition of the uncontrollability and unpredictability of social systems, we in development cooperation contexts are not just dealing with individual organizations but rather partnerships and coalitions spanning many stakeholders, from the government to the private sector as well as civil society.

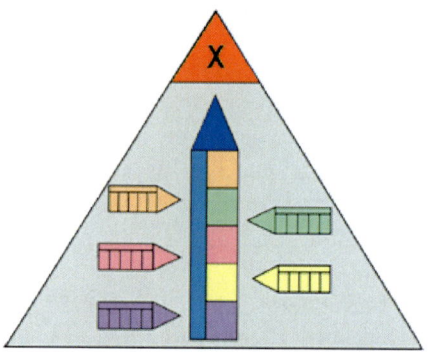

These partnerships and multi-actor projects are not just fashionable, they are born out of the recognition that the problems that the international community is faced with (climate change, social inequality, peace and conflict) are not solvable by the efforts of a single organization. We could not build the super organization that would be able to do all this. Rather, we are reliant by necessity on the contributions, resources, and participation of a diverse range of organizations – from the government to the private sector and civil society. The international consensus is clear about this,[6] but it is less clear about some of the consequences that this brings with it. One of these is the fundamentally opposed logical systems of organizations and cooperation projects, partnerships, and alliances.[7] In order to understand this, it is necessary to look a little more closely at the classical organization as well as the development project or partnership.

A classical **organization** organizes its internal processes so as to "produce" a good or service that is useful to its clients. Internal component processes here include, for example, strategy, marketing, controlling, as well as personnel management. These component processes combine to produce the "product" – be it goods or services – of the organization.

Several characteristics of this organizational form are relevant for consideration here. Organizations of this type are characterized by *formal goals* and *hierarchies* of managers and employees. Employees must pass through rituals of hiring (and sometimes firing), are subject to disciplinary rules while members of the organization, and are required to comply with decisions made by managers, often reflected in their individual goals and salaries and backed up by considerable internal sanctions (and occasionally rewards!) as well as external support from civil law.

Organizations develop in this way a particular and individual character over the course of time with rules, structures, and processes that reflect this. During the course of our work in an organization, we are obliged to work with colleagues who we would not choose as friends, we do things that we would probably not do voluntarily in our free time, and abide by decisions that we do not agree with, would certainly question, and maybe refuse to comply with if they were taken by friends or family members. Being a member of an organization imposes restrictions and claims on our behavior. This closed structure not only *enables* management in its strictest sense, but also *requires* it – to organize and implement the processes through internal hierarchy that is required to produce the product or service of the organization and specify and differentiate the component activities and processes that go into producing it.

---

6 The 2030 Agenda that places great emphasis on partnerships as a key implementing method is a singular example among many.

7 There are many definitions and names for such undertakings, which are often specific to individual donors and their systems. Multi-stakeholder partnerships, projects, alliances, networks, and cooperation systems are all, however, elementally similar in the characteristics that are relevant here.

"Classical management" in all its forms – and certainly in the variation represented by Taylor and discussed in the previous section – is predicated upon this basis: an active management function that can design, implement, and improve component processes that combine to produce the organization's product. Good organizations are well-managed, poor organizations are badly managed. Good management is a major source of competitive advantage in modern organizations, and poor management is often at the root of the demise of once-great industry champions.[8]

In contrast to this is the situation of a *development project*,[9] characterized by a high degree of cooperation, negotiation, and fluid structures.

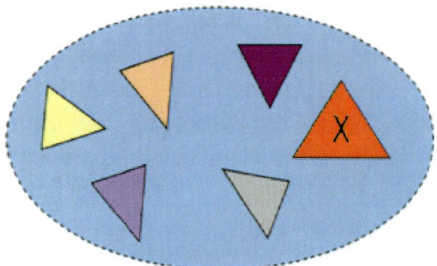

Here, the products of the individual organizations are combined together into a network of contributions that seek to address particular problems at a country, regional, or global level. This is a *multi-organizational* context based on a convergence of interest rather than any formal, hierarchical basis. Rules and decisions are made and taken through negotiation and cooperation rather than formal management processes. "Management" – in the hierarchical sense described above – cannot take place here.

---

8 According to *The Economist* ("Measuring management," 2014), 30 percent of the productivity gap between the United States and Europe can be explained by this factor alone.

9 By "development project" we mean here a project that is a voluntary agreement between independent actors in pursuit of some kind of societal goal. This is in contrast to a firm's or organization's internal project in which employees of the same organization come together from different departments to achieve an individual organization's or firm's goal. They are outside of the usual departmental structures in an interdisciplinary project team but remain employees of the organization in the sense described above. They are subject to the logic and management discipline of the classical organization outlined above.

Similarly, classical management techniques predicated on the logic of the organizational/management system cannot work either. Management here is predicated on – and requires – hierarchy and a classical approach to decision-making. This is precisely what is missing in collaborative and participatory development projects. But management is also required in such partnerships. Decisions about strategy, participation, funding, planning, organizing, and implementing activities as well as monitoring and evaluating such projects still have to take place here if the partnerships are to achieve their goals; it is just that the motor that makes it possible (hierarchical management in the Taylor sense) simply does not exist.

The challenge facing all development practitioners is to develop adequate management systems and tools that are feasible, acceptable, and suitable for such multi-organizational contexts. Being "smart" here first involves recognizing the real dilemma that we find ourselves in and not just rushing in with quick fixes that do not (and cannot) work. Development cooperation projects need "smart" here to equate to the acknowledgement of the context in which it operates – not hierarchy but negotiation. This simple but fundamental insight of the difference between organizations and cooperation systems really does make a difference. It explains the need for a fundamentally different way of doing things in projects and partnerships in a cooperative context, as well as why "more of the same" from the classical management context simply will not work.

Polka or Parker?

Having already said that most organizations march to the beat of a rather old-fashioned drum, it is time to adopt a metaphor to make the point more strongly. It is as if the organizations in which we work and are socialized are analogous to classical music – a body of theory and practice developed between the Renaissance and the 19th century. Classical music had (and still to a large extent has) fixed ideas about orchestras, instruments, composition, musical theory, and the like. Our organizations are the guardians of this classical tradition. Our introduction and socialization into them is governed by the Taylor paradigm, the theory of organization (and reorganization) is governed by hierarchy and the organizational chart; when we think about the organization, we articulate our thoughts (just like classical composers) in the scales and chords of the Taylorist paradigm. But where organizations have stayed by and large still, music has moved on to encompass a myriad of new instruments, musical theories, compositions, and performances in a way that organizations and their underlying theory have not. One of the most relevant for this analysis is jazz – a combination of composition and improvisation that was a major innovation in its time (see box below).

Development professionals and organizations that have understood and embraced the fundamental cooperative nature of the partnership systems in which they work, however, are playing in a jazz combo with their partners. They do this very well (and successfully), but when they return to their organizations and report on what they did in the form of best practices or contributions to knowledge-management networks, they tend to fall back into the language of classical socialization.[10] Try writing down a brilliant jazz solo in musical notation and it loses its force; try repeating a jazz improvisation and it falls flat. Each performance lives for the moment – the band, the audience, the atmosphere, the city.

This metaphor cannot, of course, be taken too far. But the basic picture – we are talking, practicing and playing Beethoven (a "polka" from Johann Strauss) in our organizations. But playing in a jazz combo with our partners ("The Bird," Charlie Parker) in partnerships and projects in developing countries sums up the slight feeling of schizophrenia that many successful development practitioners have: Polka or Parker?

"Dohhh – those jazz guys are just makin' that stuff up!" – Homer Simpson Jazz improvisation is the process of spontaneously creating fresh melodies over the continuously repeating cycle of chord changes in a tune. The improviser may rely on the contours of the original tune, or solely on the possibilities of the chords' harmonies. The trick to jazz improvisation is	playing music with both spontaneous creativity and conviction. Members of a jazz band will have a basic structure given by the tune and the series of the (normally) 12 bar repetitions that structure it. Band members will alternately play backing and improvise solos, sometimes tossing musical ideas and phrases back and forth to develop and expand. There is no standard tune, rather the

---

10 To develop the image a little further, one consequence of the above is that the "language" spoken in an organization such as the GIZ (or any other large development organization) is that of 1) triviality and 2) hierarchy implied in the "classical" Taylor paradigm. That means that tools and instruments or even lessons learned (best practice and the like) are articulated in the language of the organization (trivial and hierarchical) and need its hierarchy to be repeated in other organizations.

jazz players listen to each other's playing to pick up hints and signals from the others. Some ideas are good for piano, some are better played on the bass, and others need brass to develop their full potential. Some ideas can only be developed together; others are really solo. The end result is a complex interlay of rhythm and harmony, mixed into a basic tune that is composed in advance and forms the backbone of the piece.

But not everything is free (unless it is free jazz). The players have rigorous technical and musical training that enables them to master their instruments and the compositions they play. They spend many hours learning the chords and scales that are the grammar and vocabulary of the tunes that they play and the melodies that they create when onstage with their band. The result is mostly neither 100 percent improvisation nor 100 percent composition but a skillful mixture of both, balancing the elements as well as the musicians in the band.

Jazz musicians are not the only ones to improvise; classical musicians such as Bach, Handel, Mozart, and Beethoven were all masterful improvisers.

Smart implementation is art and craft – and not the science (of delivery)

The implementation of development projects in international cooperation contexts needs to place much more emphasis on organizing and less on implementing. This requires an understanding of development management as performance art akin to jazz music, by which we mean improvised, flexible, intuitive, and always sensitive to the context, and that these attributes are positively connoted and part of the dialogue and learning inside of our organizations. At the moment, we really are letting our development practitioners out in the field develop fine music together with their partners, but when they come back to their organizational bases, they often struggle to capture what they have done in classical notation. This is a challenge not only for balancing the respective needs of the two sides (hierarchical management in organizations, and cooperation management in development projects and partnerships) but also for establishing cooperation management (jazz) as a legitimate and concrete body of knowledge and practice with an institutional memory for learning and establishing the tools, instruments, theory, knowledge, skills, and attitudes associated with it.

Finding this performance art, taking it out of the realm of personal and individual intuition and gut feeling, and giving it a voice inside the decision-making processes of our international development organizations and networks is a great challenge. Building our organizations in a way that they can allow for such a hybrid transmission (classical music inside the organization and jazz in cooperation projects) requires a high degree of skill on the part of the organizations. To make an explicit organizational core competence out of an implicit individual intuitive skill is a challenge indeed. But this very skill of balancing the two worlds is what is required of the individual practitioners in their everyday work as well as the organizations that they work for. Indeed, the very nature of the multi-stakeholder partnerships that we need to forge to find answers to the challenges of the 2030 Agenda for Sustainable Development and the problems of global governance demand this from us all.

It may be a source of disappointment to those brought up in the classical paradigm that there really is no such thing as a "science" of implementation, but rather a craft set composed of skills, knowledge, tools, models, and techniques that have evolved over the course of many decades, and that have now found a legitimate voice in the shape of cooperation management. Much as the jazz musician has learned their trade of technique, scales, theory, phrasing, and composition that can rival that of the classical musician, so too has the development practitioner acquired a considerable body of experience and knowledge that deserves recognition and attention alongside that of their classical counterpart of management. But as with management in organizations, its exercise is context-sensitive (culture and content) as well as intuitive (there are no blueprints for social change), and the experienced practitioner builds all this into their behavior when active in such contexts.

Capacity WORKS as an attempt to codify jazz improvisation

To take the epitaph of Marx seriously, we have to start thinking about changing the world rather than just analyzing it. Here there is a crucial difference between the academic discipline of understanding and analyzing, and the more pragmatic job of the change manager. Coming out of the industrial and commercial world of consulting, where good money is to be had guiding organizations through the process of change and development, there is a large body of practice (if not of theory) that underpins this. Although academics have consistently and rightly noted the lack of scientific rigor of the management world,[11] this has not stopped the change managers from earning credibility in business. The change manager is a pragmatist who collects and uses tools and instruments pragmatically and does not let him or herself be bothered by such a theoretical understanding of the world that makes their work impossible.[12]

This was more or less the situation 15 years ago in GIZ, as the organization (or at least parts of it) struggled with the questions of what it actually did "in the field" when it was implementing its projects, and when and why it was successful (or unsuccessful).[13] The first and intuitive answer of the organization was simply that there were a small amount of very good project managers around who were good at what they did. The implication of this was that such people had to be "cloned" in order to increase their numbers in the organization. When the organization had cloned enough of these star project managers, it would be more successful. This logic was seductive and fit the most widely held paradigm of change, namely that the activities of heroic individuals (leaders, managers, and other charismatic persons) are the key elements of change processes. Although change processes need people, they are a necessary but not sufficient condition of the systemic change process in which organizations, networks, and whole sections of society are required to work in harmony over an extended period to bring about sustainable societal change. Indeed, many change processes in development contexts fail, despite such good and qualified people, and the oversimplification of such processes – reducing them to the consequences of the actions of a few individuals – is as lazy as it is wrong. This is where the overwhelming donor emphasis on

---

11 They see "management" more as an eclectic mixture of psychology, sociology, as well as a smattering of engineering and natural sciences rather than a body of theory in its own right.

12 It is no accident that the profession of change manager originated not in Europe but in the United States, where the roles of theory and practice are often reversed and where pragmatism and experimentation enjoy a better reputation.

13 The mode of delivery of the German Federal Ministry for Economic Cooperation and Development (BMZ) and the GIZ is and was unusual here in the context of international development. German policy is and was always more favorable to the implementation of projects together with partner countries. This involved financial support and personnel in the recipient countries in temporary project structures, as opposed to budget support or basket funding of sectors more popular with other donors. Budget support and the like is not affected by the characteristics of cooperation systems identified here.

human capacity-development not only fails to improve the systemic capacity of a society but can actually harm it, as people are trained out of their jobs in organizations that do not change with them. Most donor-induced capacity-development strategies concentrate almost exclusively on the human factor and neglect the other crucial aspects.

GIZ[14] gathered these individuals and examined in a lengthy and sys-tematic process what it was that they did. This was at first tantamount to heresy; it was simply not possible to compare the efforts of such people as diverse as this. Banking projects could not be compared to agricultural ones, nor agricultural states with emerging economies, and Africa had nothing to do with Latin America, surely! After this initial hilarity on the part of the participants had subsided, they shared in a first step their "tips and tricks" – their personal toolbox of instruments and tools that they used to do their jobs. Of course, many were technical and had to do with spe-cific bodies of professional knowledge that were relevant for their sectors or fields of intervention. After a while, however, other kinds of tools emerged. These were on a more unconscious and less articulated level from those that were technical and mixed in a creative way with them. Interestingly, these tools seemed to come from a common toolbox in which bankers and educationalists, farmers and governance specialists, as well as colleagues from diverse regions, cultures, and countries all seemed to have something in common. This was basically the level of social change outlined in the previous sections – not directing a trivial system to produce particular products, but rather "massaging" the social system toward common goals by building coalitions, discussing topics, and facili-tating new ways of working that were in any one context technical, but also generic – a 12 bar blues improvisation on a basic melody.

There was even a layer below this. After the practitioners had emptied their pockets and all the Swiss army penknives, rabbits' feet, and balls of string were lying on the table, there was something else still left, intangi-ble but real. Alongside the generic instruments and tools that they used to do this that were common across all sectors and cultures, there was an implicit and underlying body of knowledge about how and when these tools were best used. This third level of practice was so faint that it was almost at the level of the subconscious. Just as Parker did not play any old

---

14 Of course, at the time of doing so, the GIZ was still the Deutsche Gesellschaft für Technische Zusammenarbeit GmbH (GTZ) and only took on its current form in 2011.

stream of notes (despite what Homer Simpson might think) when he recorded *Ornithology* but rather an intuitive and complex melody based on a lifetime of study and technical mastery, so too with the development practitioners, who did not just throw in tools, instruments, or interventions but rather had a common theory about *what* was needed *when*, also based on a lifetime of reflective practice and technical mastery. At a time when virtually every development organization on the planet already had tool-boxes for capacity development and tools coming out of their ears, these colleagues also had a **model** of **what** was needed and **when**.[15] This was the genesis of the **model** of change in cooperation (i.e., social) systems. This was the birth of Capacity WORKS as an insight into how these change processes really take place, and the initialization of a debate about a body of knowledge that, up to then, was (and still is) being conducted with the language and vocabulary of Taylorist management. It is not an exaggeration to say that this insight was the start of the codification of a body of knowledge about change management in social systems that continues to this day, and is by no means over. Project managers with experience, upon seeing Capacity WORKS in its finished form, were able to say, "I recognize that," as it reflected their good and intuitive craft, built up over many years and passed on, in some cases, from generation to generation. New project managers entering the organization were presented with a codified body of knowledge, practice, and theory that enabled them to go out into the world and (together with many others) change it. GIZ was thereby able to say that they had an institutional body of knowledge that was independent of the people in the organization – a real organizational capacity.

Capacity WORKS

Emerging out of the basic recognition described in the earlier sections – namely that a) social systems are not trivial systems but highly complex, b) cooperation systems cannot fall back on the basic logic of hierarchical organizations for decision-making, as well as c) the empirical observation

---

15 It would be wrong to suggest here that these three discoveries took place sequentially in the course of such a mythical debriefing of GIZ colleagues. This was a process that took many months, with different groups and with many blind alleys, one-way systems, and deviations that all led to the goal.

that clever development practitioners had been doing all of this regularly and for a long time – the model of Capacity WORKS as well as the choice of instruments began to emerge as an answer and evolved over about four years to completion in its first form. GIZ needed some kind of professional support for its staff in designing and implementing ever more complex projects that were increasingly oriented toward a comprehensive capacity-development approach. This involved working on the three levels of people, organizations, and society, as well as making sure that these were linked with each other in a capacity-development strategy. The astonishing thing here is that, since then, there have been numerous updates[16] to the model and its tools, but the basic structure has remained unchanged: 5 success factors and about 40 tools to support them. The basic insights described here remain valid and have stood the test of implementation in the field.

Capacity WORKS is not the Holy Grail and has no claims to be the one and only solution to the challenges of working with cooperation systems. It has, however, been able to capture these good practices, enrich them with an overarching and explanatory model as well as a theory of change in societal systems, and (at least try to) anchor them in a large bilateral development agency as a core organizational skill. In this aspect, it is rather unique in the development context.

Introducing Capacity WORKS into GIZ

The development process involved the debriefing described above, which took place over a two-year period, followed by a two-year pilot worldwide in GIZ. After having assessed the suitability and practicability of the model and its tools for the GIZ context, it was rolled out into the organization in a two-year mainstreaming process that involved a massive investment in training at all levels in the organization (as well as outside) and the adaptation of rules, structures, and processes to accommodate Capacity WORKS in all aspects of the organization. As with the painting of long bridges, when the organization got to the end, it had to start at the begin-

---

16 Four to date (2016).

ning again, and so the seamless integration of Capacity WORKS into the organization is an ongoing and never-ending task.[17]

The model

The deepest level of insight working with the development practitioners was that (as described above) they had an intuitive model of how social systems develop and change, and as a consequence, a model of practice of how and where and when to intervene in them to "massage" change in the desired direction.

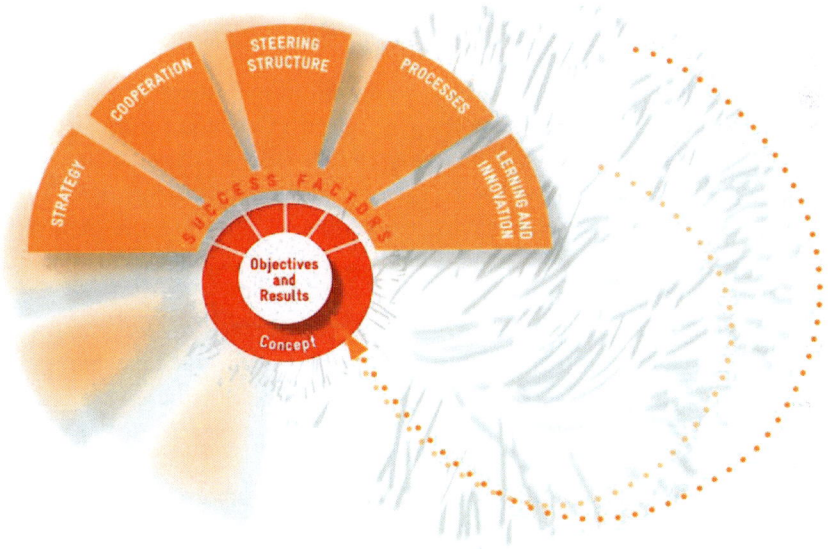

There are many relevant elements represented visually here. The first and most striking is that, as described above, all successful managers of development projects were doing similar things (or rather, they were encouraging their cooperation partners, with their help and support, to do particular

---

17 This change will not be described in detail here. Readers interested in this should read the article from Glotzbach, Maurer, and Görgen (2013) that describes precisely this (only in German).

things). Virtually all of the practitioners involved, irrespective of geography, sector, or situation, were doing things that fell into five broad categories – the success factors. I expand on this below. None of these success factors are in themselves radical or complex – they refer to elements that are more or less common sense. These success factors deliberately only occupy the top half of the model visually representing the idea that we are dealing with an open system that is susceptible to many influences other than those related to the project. Also, these success factors are not numbered or sequenced in any way. No one success factor is more important than the other, and there is no "step one" or starting point. The model can be accessed at any time and from any angle – there really is no need to start from the beginning and work your way through. To colleagues being introduced to the model, this came either as a complete relief or as the greatest provocation imaginable.

Secondly, these "success factors" were not ends in themselves ("cooperation is good and more cooperation is better") but rather a means to an end. The end, represented by the small white disc in the middle, is the objectives and results for which GIZ received its commission from BMZ in the first place. Thus, the discussion was not "Who are the best partners?" but rather "Which partners do I need to achieve the results that need to be achieved?" Underlying all of this is the red disc, here rather cryptically entitled "sustainability." This is a reference to the framework of sustainable development, within which all our efforts take place and which forms a kind of moral and ethical platform upon which we build.

Thirdly, building on the idea that there is no chronological order in which these success factors have to be taken, there is also no fixed timescale for their implementation. The success factors can be worked through in a team meeting in 45 minutes to get a quick snapshot of the project, they can be used to guide a project appraisal or evaluation of its management structure, and they can be used to guide and structure an implementation phase of a complex project cycle over several years.

Lastly, there is no right or wrong way to use Capacity WORKS. Some projects adopt a light approach whereby adapted elements are used from time to time, others use it explicitly as a structure for planning and implementing together with their partners, while others use the tools and instruments as stepping stones in their own creative processes and interactions with their partners, developing new and adapted offshoots of basic instruments.

The most obvious elements remain, however, the success factors. These are the groups or categories of activities that the successful project managers used to effectively "manage" the cooperation system. There are five.[18]

Strategy

All practitioners were very good at – and careful to build – a common strategy among the relevant actors about "why" this change project was required. A common (and positive) vision of the future (not a deficit and problem-oriented view of the past) unites diverse actors and focuses and synergizes the energy and resources of the participants. Successful practitioners invested time and resources in a communicative and social process of strategy formulation with partners – not dictating from above as in organizations, but building and cajoling from the side. All good development practitioners recognized the need for a common, agreed, and well-understood strategy that all parties could sign up to. At the same time, they were aware that it was not enough to simply impose this from the outside or let a well-paid international consultant write it. Rather, they designed a process that enabled the participants to grapple with the meaning and the significance of this project and its goals for themselves. The selection of tools reflects this and provides the development practitioner and their partners with a suite of tools for collectively analyzing and elaborating strategic options and deciding collectively which are the most promising.

Cooperation

Only when the participants in a cooperation system acknowledge that they are all dependent on each other can the system be successful. Although asymmetries of power, knowledge, and resources remain, each actor has a part to play, and without it nobody gets to the final goal. Only when this mutual dependency is explicitly acknowledged can the cooperation system move forward. Similarly, as remarked above, cooperation is a means to an end here (the achievement of the goals) and not an end in itself. Coopera-

---

18 This is of course a very short summary. Please see Deutsche Gesellschaft für Internationale Zusammenarbeit (2016) for more details.

tion is expensive and time-consuming and must be used sparingly – as much as is necessary, and as little as possible to achieve the goals. More cooperation is not always better, and the economy of cooperation must be considered as paramount. The differentiation concerning roles and responsibilities within the project structure as well as the relevant contributions the partners make need to be discussed, negotiated, and agreed upon. The toolbox provides a wide range of tools for the mapping, analysis, discussion, and negotiation of cooperation roles as well as for their maintenance and development.

Steering structure

Good development practitioners built a solid decision-making structure for the lifetime of the project that enabled decisions among the actors about resources, financing, planning, implementation, monitoring, evaluation, and conflict to take place without recourse to organizational structures. A development project has to take decisions daily about management, and it needs an adequate structure to do this. Analog to the discussion on cooperation, this too is dependent on the goals of the project. A regional project will have a more complex steering structure than a national one. The toolbox provides a structured set of tools that enable the development practitioner – together with their partners – to design, build, and maintain a steering structure adequate for the complexity and the goal structure of the project. Given the recent research and evidence concerning the lack of impact of global partnerships as crucial elements for achieving the 2030 Agenda targets,[19] and the fact that the reason for this failure was largely to be found in the lack of effective governance (Pattberg, 2012) (i.e., steering) structures, this insight appears now to have been confirmed by independent research.

---

19 A recent study of 348 global partnerships registered in the UN Commission for Sustainable Development database found that 80 percent either achieved nothing (37%) or only achieved things that were not related to their objectives (43%) (Pattberg, 2012).

Processes

Our successful development practitioners had a keen managerial eye for the processes by which the change takes place. Sometimes these are existing processes in organizations or cooperation systems and networks that need to be improved. Sometimes radical new and innovative processes need to be first invented, designed, piloted, and then scaled-up. The management (change processes) of the project as well as the permanent processes in the sectors and countries where the sustainable change is to take place need to be analyzed, designed, managed, and improved. The design and introduction of processes that take place between independent organizations (e.g., local area development processes) is a huge challenge for all development participants and requires care and attention to detail.

Learning and innovation

Successful development practitioners paid more than lip service to the concept of learning. Not just concentrating on what individuals had to learn, but considering the system as a whole in its learning needs and interdependencies, such practitioners instituted a process of reflection and learning (together with partners) on an individual, organizational cooperation system as well as on policy level. Only in this way can change be sustainable.

All of these factors are complemented by tools (42 in total) in a **toolbox**[20] that are clustered in the success factors and that enable change managers and development practitioners to intervene in such systems and design processes and activities that reflect on them. There are between 6 and 10 tools per success factor that can be used in differing situations according to need. They vary in complexity: from simple back-of-the-envelope discussions that can take place at almost any time to larger processes that can take many weeks or even months to complete.

---

20 Similarly, the discussion or even description of the tools would overstretch the scope of this article. Please see the Capacity WORKS handbook for more details on this (or go to the GIZ website: http://www.giz.de).

Conclusion

We said at the beginning that the purpose of this theoretical mystery tour was to try to "work smarter not harder," in the sense of smart implementation in development projects. We also said that this could not involve doing more of the same, just better – but rather to change the way we look at the problem. This we have illustrated with a theoretical look at the way in which social systems really change and not how we would like to see them. It is not easy to change one's perspective – anybody who has ever had to really change knows how difficult it is to separate oneself from cherished notions and beliefs.

Our entire management theory of the last 100 years has been built on rather shaky foundations. The insights from engineering and the natural sciences concerning the technical organization of production processes simply cannot be transferred wholesale into the area of social interaction. The attempt to make our implementation processes in development projects by being smarter in the way in which we apply the wrong knowledge cannot be the answer to the question posed by this book. This can be done better by looking at and learning the secrets of success of those (impossible) professions that deal successfully with change at a social level every day. This argument applies completely to organizations, but an additional element that complicates our work in development cooperation is the recognition that such projects are not organizations but rather cooperation systems that lack the hierarchy found in organizations to manage themselves and direct their change processes. This lack of hierarchy is only a problem if you are looking at the problem of social change in the wrong way. To borrow the maxim of Carlos with which I started the chapter: you cannot change the way social systems work, their basic laws and paradigms; you can, however, change the way you look at social systems. Borrowing even a few of the tools built up by the systemic schools of thinking – from biology to physics and psychology – can give us a whole new way of looking at the problem, and successfully changing these systems in a way that fits our moral and social values.

This can be seen very well in the other case studies in this book. The colleagues working in all these situations were apparently in completely different situations. No one in their right mind would dare to compare the contexts of mining in Liberia, climate mitigation financing in Indonesia, and creating safe work environments for women in Latin America with each other. Quite apart from their linguistic and cultural differences, the context, and the professional expertise required, the actors and political contexts were all diametrically opposed to a common understanding or comparison. But they all did similar things; much like in the development process of Capacity WORKS, it is apparent from reading about what they did that they acknowledged the context and consequences of the cooperation system and the realities of the actors and their relationships within it.

The ideas and thoughts in this book and this chapter were always relevant to the management of cooperation systems in the past. Given the newfound enthusiasm for such cooperation systems – called partnerships and multi-actor partnerships – and their pivotal role in the achievement of the 2030 Agenda, this discussion has gained a new relevance. Especially when one looks at the rather sobering evidence concerning the lack of success of such partnerships, this debate has a lot to offer – both theoretically as well as practically. The lack of success (noted earlier) of such partnerships is universally attributed to the poor "governance" of the partnerships.[21] By governance, the commentators quote such issues as partners, equipment, rules, regulations, and processes, whereby the actors in the partnership can transform will and commitment into concrete outputs such as services or standards. This fits neatly with the ideas and philosophy with which GIZ, through Capacity WORKS, has been working the last 10 years.

To all the smart implementers in the world, even if they did not know they were, please keep making it up! Homer Simpson and I will both be very grateful.

References

Bateson, G. (1972). *Steps to an ecology of mind*. Chicago University Press.

Deutsche Gesellschaft für Internationale Zusammenarbeit. (2016). *Cooperation management for Practitioners: Managing social change with Capacity WORKS*. Wiesbaden: Springer Gabler.

Glotzbach, S., Maurer, M., & Görgen, M. (2013, April). Balance-Stück in vier Akten. Die Einführung eines systemischen Managementmodells in der GIZ. *Zeitschrift für Organisationsentwicklung*, 76–83.

---

21 "There is a clear correlation between the effectiveness of a partnership and its process management" is one of many comments in this vein; quoted from Liese and Beisheim (2011).

Liese, A., & Beisheim, M. (2011). Transnational public-private partnerships and the provision of collective goods in developing countries. In T. Risse (Ed.), *Governance without a state? Policies and politics in areas of limited statehood* (pp. 115–143). New York, NY: Columbia University Press.

Measuring management. (2014, January 18). *The Economist*. Retrieved from http://www.economist.com/news/business/21594223-it-no-longer-just-plausible-theory-good-management-boosts-productivity-measuring

Pattberg, P. (2012). *Public private partnerships for sustainable development*. Cheltenham: Edward Elgar.

Simon, F. (Ed.). (1998). *Lebende Systeme*. Berlin: Suhrkamp Taschenbuch Wissenschaft 1290.

Simon, F. (2002). *Die Kunst, nicht zu lernen*. Heidelberg: Carl-Auer-System Verlag.

Doing Development Differently: Understanding the Landscape and Implications of New Approaches to Governance and Public-sector Reforms

Verena Fritz

Seeking to accelerate development, the agencies and individuals involved have regularly advanced new ideas of how external support can function better, deliver more, and achieve greater impact. There has been a particular flourishing of new ideas within the broad field of governance and public-sector reforms in the 2000s.

This chapter starts off with a review of the "landscape of new ideas," focusing on five proposed approaches in particular: political economy analysis (PEA), Problem-Driven Iterative Adaptation (PDIA), Doing Development Differently (DDD), Thinking and Working Politically (TWP), and the "science of delivery." It sets out the "problem-diagnostic" that underpins each of these approaches, how they overlap and differ, and what they suggest to do differently. It then turns to what the World Bank, as one particular development agency, has done over the past decade, including how teams have sought to use such new approaches in various countries. It also provides a brief reflection on the *World Development Report 2017: Governance and the Law*, which is the first *World Development Report* since 1997 to squarely focus on governance. The final section sets out some of the implications that can be drawn from the past 10 years and what the important next steps going forward are so as to make projects that support a strengthening of governance more effective.

What does the landscape of new ideas look like?

The initial movement toward new ideas for development emerged in the early 2000s in the United Kingdom (UK). It grew out of a recognition that (i) fixing the macro-economic and trade policy environment was important, but not sufficient to stimulate growth and poverty reduction, and (ii) that even though good policy and institutional prescriptions were available for a range of sectors, these were often not taken up, or were implemented in a way that did not truly lead to the expected governance improvements. The UK may have offered particularly fertile ground for engaging these ideas, given that a number of universities have substantial development policy programs, and these have, in turn, a relatively close relationship with the country's official development agency, the Department for International Development (DFID). In addition, the UK has a range of development think tanks as well as substantial policy departments in its large development charities.

As captured by Warrener (2004), tracing the emergence of the "drivers of change" (DoC) approach, an authorizing environment was provided in the late 1990s and early 2000s by the then Secretary of State for International Development, Clare Short, who felt that understanding the politics underpinning opportunities for poverty reduction was essential.[1] The agency began to hire more governance advisors as well as to develop an initial framework for looking at DoC between 2000 and 2003. The idea of this approach was to identify the underlying stakeholder incentives and other factors that lead to policies and policy implementation which go against accelerating development and poverty reduction. The general assumption was that understanding such drivers and making them more explicitly part of the process of selecting and designing development interventions would enable greater effectiveness. How exactly this would happen was not precisely articulated at this stage.

Between 2003 and 2004, about 20 DoC-type studies were carried out by different DFID country offices, including in Bangladesh, Nigeria, Colombia, Pakistan, and others across the regions (Warrener, 2004). The main focus of the studies was on the political system, the policy process, and the budgeting process, and how these facilitated or hindered efforts at poverty reduction and expanding service delivery. Corruption was a major theme in several of the studies, mainly as a driver preventing change, or undermining efforts at improvements. Most studies were carried out at least to a significant extent by external consultants, whereas some, such as the Malawi DoC analysis, were carried out by regular staff based in country offices.

Key benefits were felt to be: a greater insight into the complexity of operating environments, greater attention to elite incentives, a better understanding of why certain programs had worked or failed, and also a

---

1 Short held this role from 1997 to 2003.

more comprehensive way of thinking about potential future scenarios of countries over the short, medium, and long terms. A main challenge was operationalization, that is, what to do differently, how to interpret the findings in terms of implications, and how to balance insights from the analytic work with pressures to disburse funds that were being increased for many country offices (Department for International Development, 2005). A further thorny issue remained as to whether the analysis could be developed jointly with partner governments and/or with other development partners, and whether the resulting reports should be made publicly available. Around the same time, a few other development partners began experimenting with versions of PEA, including Sweden and the Netherlands (Organisation for Economic Co-operation and Development, 2005), primarily targeting country-level analysis.

A new wave of political economy work emerged in the World Bank in the late 2000s – in part stimulated by a large-scale trust fund that was provided by the UK jointly with Australia, the Netherlands, and Norway (Van Heesewijk, 2014). In earlier years, individual World Bank country teams had started undertaking or commissioning political analysis, but these efforts were very individualized and remained little-known outside the particular teams. One of the key limitations of such an approach was to have little learning across teams.

The World Bank teams that started engaging on a wider use of political economy perspectives sought to learn some of the lessons from the DoC work at DFID as well as similar frameworks used by other development partners. In doing so, they proposed the idea of "problem-driven analysis," that is, focusing the analytic effort on a particular set of questions and operational challenges from the outset, with the intention to make the resulting recommendations more directly operationally relevant and usable. Furthermore, to facilitate the exchange of ideas and experiences across teams undertaking PEA – in different sectors and regions across the Bank – a Community of Practice was established in late 2009. However, different from DFID, high-level endorsements of such a perspective and of deliberate analysis remained ambivalent.

Over the following years, more than 300 pieces of PEA were undertaken across the World Bank. Sectors included agriculture, energy, water, extractives, forestry, financial sectors, health, and education, as well as macro-fiscal management, and others. In many sectors, there are some very challenging incentive issues concerning the protection of national and public interests, such as: ensuring that power tariffs are fair but also enable investments; protecting and renewing forests in the face of the potential profits from illegal logging; recording and protecting the land rights of poorer individuals or groups; or ensuring that commercial banks are well regulated rather than allowed to extend insider loans for which repayment is not expected to be enforced. Members of political and commercial elites as well as individuals up and down the income ladder often face incentives to seek out individual income opportunities – engaging in illegal logging, seeking a favorable loan, or grabbing land – that harm collective interests. Making development interventions in these sectors even somewhat more effective is important to achieve progress on sustainable and shared prosperity.

The World Bank's 2009 Good Practice Framework recognized explicitly that PEA can target country-level dynamics as well as specific sectors and individual development interventions/projects. Especially the latter two are directly targeted at identifying what interventions are likely to be most feasible in a given context and period of time. They also seek to capture potential opportunities for "stretching" the available space for reforms, for example through understanding in greater detail the specific vision of country stakeholders for reforms (which may differ from what development agencies consider as best or standard practice), their ability to convince others about the merits of a development effort or reform, and how they can best be supported. A general guiding idea is that "first best solutions" inspired by economic or other technical theories may not work in practice in a development context, and that identifying flexible solutions is what matters most, even if they deviate from what is considered to be technically optimal.

Over time, other agencies have also developed frameworks for PEA, and/or have sought to make staff more aware of political economy risks and how these can potentially be addressed, or at least more actively taken into account. This has included the Danish International Development Agency in 2009, the German Federal Ministry for Economic Cooperation and Development (BMZ) in 2010, the European Union in 2011, the Asian Development Bank in 2011 (see Serrat, 2011), the United States Agency for International Development (USAID) in 2016, the International Monetary Fund, and others. Although this has some commentators wondering whether there are competing frameworks, there is actually a lot of commonality, and it involves tailoring a core set of ideas to the specific needs and operating models of different agencies. For example, similar to the World Bank's approach, USAID's *2016 Field Guide* to PEA emphasizes the need to pursue "problem-focused" approaches. What has varied more across agencies than the contents of these frameworks has been the specific motivations and the degree of management-level endorsements and, accordingly, subsequent efforts to actually use such approaches in seeking to adapt operational practices.

Furthermore, one key challenge for any general methodology is that it cannot be tailored to the specific set of issues and incentive problems in various sectors; this matters for making political economy perspectives readily usable by sector teams. Thus, in addition to general frameworks, there are also some sector-specific notes, albeit still only for a few sectors, such as urban water. Such tailoring to specific sectors and types of reform challenges is very important in order to further increase potential operational usefulness and ease of use. It can also involve some innovation within sectors in terms of what are assumed to be standard good practices – as these can be "too optimal" and make unrealistic assumptions about stakeholder incentives and institutional capabilities that do not hold in most low- or even in middle- (and high-) income countries.

In parallel to these efforts at making political economy operationally relevant and useful, another new approach that has emerged since the late 2000s has been Problem-Driven Iterative Adaptation. The idea was advanced by Michael Woolcock, Lant Pritchett, and Matt Andrews. The problem-diagnostic of political economy perspectives and of PDIA overlaps in some respects, but also differs in important ways. Whereas political economy perspectives emphasize that there can be powerful incentives that vitiate against making and implementing policies that promote development, PDIA emphasizes that development partners tend to impose solutions externally, and that development solutions agreed upon among local stakeholders are more likely to work. Furthermore, PDIA was developed with a more specific focus on public-sector reforms and institutional strengthening, whereas PEA has been utilized for a wide range of sectors.[2] PDIA also emphasizes the notion of "capability traps" and the idea that development partners tend to overstretch existing capabilities and, as a result, hinder rather than promote effective institutional strengthening.

As a combination of the PEA and the PDIA perspectives and insights, the proposal of Doing Development Differently emerged in 2014, being a

---

2   In part, PDIA also draws on the development policy thinking of the Paris Declaration of 2005, which emphasized the need for developing countries to be in the driving seat of development efforts.

synthesis of the two ideas of pursuing implementation that is politically smart as well as using iteration in identifying and pursuing solutions.[3] It also brings on board ideas of seeking rapid results – that is, small but concrete steps toward progress implemented rapidly instead of investing in big upfront plans. This approach had initially become popular in the mid-2000s as a management tool applied to development challenges (see, e.g., World Bank, 2008). As noted also by Booth, Harris, and Wild (2016), given the DDD term's attractiveness (and broadness), it is also being stretched in various directions.

The core proposals on DDD are set out by Andrews, Pritchett, Woolcock, and their collaborators across various publications (see, e.g., Andrews et al. 2012, 2016). One of their main starting points was complexity – and the need to adapt to changes that could not be foreseen at the outset of a development project. Some of these changes may be due to political developments, others because of fragile situations or because of the way any situation can evolve in unexpected ways. The PDIA approach recapitulates earlier ideas raised by the famous "political economist" Albert Hirschman from his experience of implementing projects on behalf of the World Bank in the 1950s in Latin America. Hirschman noted at the time the need for greater flexibility and for revisiting how best to approach improvements in an iterative way, rather than presuming that "what to do" could be fully specified at the outset. In recent years, the DDD approach has gradually moved toward a greater level of specification of what this could mean and how DDD proposals could be operationalized by development agencies – for example, see a recent paper proposing a move from a "Logframe" to a "Searchframe" (Andrews et al., 2016).

A year earlier, in 2013, a somewhat less well-known effort was launched as Thinking and Working Politically.[4] The main emphasis is to work in "politically smart ways" and to focus on the translation of political economy insights and to actually take different approaches. The intention is to establish TWP as an international Community of Practice across different development agencies and other stakeholders such as think tanks, academic departments, and others.

Apart from these specific efforts made within – or closely linked to – development agencies, there is a wider intellectual debate on international

---

3 See homepage at http://doingdevelopmentdifferently.com/
4 See homepage at https://twpcommunity.org/

development that has increasingly emphasized the need to consider political economy factors. This has included several widely read publications such as Acemoglu and Robinson's 2012 *Why Nations Fail*, various essays by Dani Rodrik, as well as Carothers and de Gramont on the "almost revolution." Courses on "Political Economy of Development" and variations thereof have been widely offered at a number of universities; research on issues such as vote-buying practices, electoral systems and their implications for policy choices, the role of information, and other issues has expanded considerably over the past decade. One major effort to review and synthesize what this literature implies for the work of development agencies is the *World Development Report 2017: Governance and the Law*, discussed further below.

A further idea – linked to the arrival of Jim Kim as the 12th President of the World Bank in 2012 – has been the "science of delivery" (Wagstaff, 2013). The problem-diagnostic of this approach – based on the healthcare sector – is that, despite a great deal of *scientific* innovation that is focused on a better understanding of the causes of diseases and better medicines, innovation with regard to supplying healthcare effectively and affordably to populations has been much more limited and uneven. Based on this problem-diagnostic, a Global Delivery Initiative (GDI) was established in 2015 as an initiative with a total of 36 partners, including bi-and multilateral development agencies as well as think tanks, NGOs, and academic institutions.[5] In terms of how to improve delivery and development effectiveness, the GDI is more of a "big-tent" initiative that has assembled a range of proposals of what to actually do differently, ranging from specific financing arrangements to community empowerment, to the use of PEA and PDIA-inspired approaches. The latter includes several of the case studies on efforts in Nigeria at innovative project design and implementation, which involved strong up-front analysis of political economy incentives and constraints as well as embedding staff with a political economy perspective and focus in the subsequent operational engagement (Hima, Santibanez, Roshan, & Lomme, 2016).

The key challenges that these interrelated approaches confront is "how to make development practice different" and to prove that doing so actually increases the development effectiveness of interventions – their ability to be well-implemented, to have a significant and sustained impact, and to

---

5 See homepage at http://www.globaldeliveryinitiative.org/about-us

avoid unintended consequences such as (reinforcing) elite capture. A related challenge is the fact that, in an increasingly fast-paced world of ideas and policy proposals, it can be hard to sustain the focus on any particular approach or issue long enough to actually pursue a full sequence: from conception to doing something differently, to lesson-learning about whether this worked and made a difference, and finally to potential for wider application. A set of these challenges have been aptly summarized in the book by Carothers and de Gramont (2013), *Development Aid Confronts Politics: The Almost Revolution.*

As highlighted in Carothers and de Gramont's book as well as by Booth et al. (2016), although attention to political economy factors has significantly increased in recent years, there is still a gap to more fully "doing things differently" in terms of operational approaches, both with regard to core governance and public-sector projects, and to governance aspects across a wide range of sectoral issues – from seeking to improve the design of energy subsidies to better land management and reducing absenteeism of teachers and nurses in the education and health sectors.

Doing things differently is challenging. It requires some consensus among those involved – including country stakeholders – in developing an intervention and implementing it as well as consensus about what is to be done differently; it also encapsulate the notion of continuous learning. Such consensus can be difficult to develop and sustain. This especially remains the case as long as doing so, on the one hand, runs counter to standard incentives and business processes among development agencies, and, on the other hand, as long as such concepts and ideas are not shared and discussed more widely with country stakeholders.

What has the World Bank done differently in its engagement?

As outlined in the section above, an initial key contribution of the World Bank's approach to PEA has been to emphasize a *problem-driven* perspective, that is, to focus the analytic attention on specific issues that are expected to be challenging for project design, implementation, or impact. This brings the analysis closer to potential actions that a development agency can take. This may lead to questions such as whether or not to engage in a sector at a particular point in time, for example banking-sector regulation, or whether to seek improvements in the power sector, and also how best to calibrate the engagement. Often, this involves identifying the

available space for reforms and areas in which a government is truly interested in achieving progress.

Taking a problem-driven approach does not mean letting go of trying to
understand country-level drivers. Often, country-level political economy
dynamics influence the situation in various sectors – whether agricultural
subsidies are provided to keep rural voters loyal, or whether advantageous
loans to political insiders become a problem, or even which company gets
contracts for improving government processes, from public financial management to land registries. The importance is to hone in on how this plays
out with regard to a particular set of public goods or services, the business
environment, etc. A problem- or issue-specific perspective also helps to
bring economic drivers more closely into view, since it drills into the particular gains and rents available; the reasons why some stakeholders may
not want to change the status quo.

Problem-focused analysis can also involve focus-group discussions or
surveys to understand more closely what the expectations and concerns of
citizens are. Citizens may oppose certain solutions, even though they are
intended to reduce poverty and improve livelihoods. For example, citizens
may not trust that governments will compensate for the removal of subsidies through greater spending on social benefits, or they may not believe
that registering as a taxpayer and paying taxes will indeed contribute to
better roads and better schools.

Across the World Bank, problem-driven PEA has been used in a number of sectors – the provision of urban water (Manghee & Poole, 2012),
nutrition policy reforms (Natalicchio, Garrett, Mulder-Sibanda, Ndegwa,
& Voorbraak, 2009), improving approaches in the forestry sector (Kishor,
Castillo, & Nguyen, 2015), considering how to induce better cross-border
collaboration for watersheds (ongoing), civil service reforms (Nunberg,
Barma, Abdollahian, Green, & Perlman, 2010), natural resource management (Barma, Kaiser, Le, & Vinuela, 2012), and more effectively reforming energy sectors (Kojima, Bacon, & Trimble, 2014). Many staff members and managers in various sectors – frustrated by the inability to gain
traction or concerned about risks that are apparent, but the details of which
are not well understood in many instances – have sought to undertake or
commission political economy analytic work. In some sectors, there has
been a systematic effort comprising coordinated analyses of multiple
countries; in others there have been thus far only a handful of applications
for particular countries and sector challenges. In the latter, analysis has
often been focused on specific aspects and questions related to a planned

project, or a project that is under implementation but experiencing challenges.

Despite a substantial uptake, it has not been easy or straightforward to bring the resulting insights into project design and implementation in a consistent manner – that is, to fully implement such an approach. This is also highlighted by the *World Development Report 2017: Governance and the Law* (World Bank, 2017, p. 35). Some challenges in this regard are related to the business model of lending to governments. The strength of the lending model is that it assumes that governments which borrow funds have a real interest in realizing what they borrow for (e.g., improvements in the health sector, the agricultural sector, etc.), and they also have the best possible insights into their own capacities to handle a given development effort. Governments are in the driving seat with regard to what happens once funds are allocated, with supervision exercised by the Bank. At the same time, this model does not really foresee deep, continued engagement with stakeholders during implementation – and hence it also does not allocate resources for it. To some extent, therefore, up-front PEA that influences project design and other key decisions is somewhat easier to combine with existing operating models than a PDIA approach, for which continuous engagement is central.[6] In this regard, grant-financed technical assistance – or a combination of grant and lending funds – offers greater opportunity.

As noted on the application of PEA for Development Policy Operations (DPOs) (i.e., budget support rewarding reforms undertaken) in 2016, some DPO teams – notably in Afghanistan, Burkina Faso, and Mozambique – have used PEA effectively to better understand government ownership of reforms up front and target the operation accordingly. Additionally, more informal PEA considerations have influenced operations in the West Bank and Gaza and in Malawi. No comparable evaluation paper is currently available for the other main operational modality: investment project

---

6 Moreover, experience demonstrates that for various reasons, governments frequently overestimate or overstate their own capacity and sustained commitment to implementing development efforts – at least some of which could be addressed through a combination of good up-front analysis *and* continuous engagement during implementation.

financing. The overall finding is that for DPOs, PEA is still done rela-tively infrequently.[7]

Still, there are some important opportunities that teams have used to various degrees. Firstly, PEA has helped teams to gain insights into coun-terpart interests and incentives that otherwise might have taken a much longer time to acquire. It has helped to shift the policy dialogue away from reforms that had repeatedly been tried but failed, and moved them to areas that offered greater opportunity for traction. For DPOs, using a political economy perspective and analysis has allowed for identifying reforms that governments are not only committed to approving formally, but also to actually implement. It has also supported innovations in how country teams engage on challenging issues, including engaging on natural resource extraction in several countries (e.g., Burkina Faso, Mongolia), which entails the challenge to contain rent-seeking as well as opportunities to significantly improve fiscal revenues.

Furthermore, while continuous and more intensive engagement with stakeholders is not part of the standard operating and funding model, teams have often sought out additional resources to be able to do so. A number of teams – in Nigeria, the Philippines, the Dominican Republic, Mozambique, Mongolia, and elsewhere – have been able to raise Trust Fund resources to be able to engage in a more continuous and iterative way. Having innovative analysis in hand has often greatly facilitated such efforts. The following section turns to some of these specific applications.

Applications in country

As emphasized above, more intensive uptake and use of political economy drivers has happened in a subset of countries for which initial analysis was produced. In particular, uptake has rested on three main factors: significant interest by the Country Director, the presence of one or several team mem-bers able to deliver innovative engagement, and the ability to mobilize additional funding. As noted above, because a political economy perspec-tive emerged in the World Bank Group more as a "bottom up" effort than

---

7 In fiscal year 2015, the World Bank Group, that is the International Bank for Reconstruction and Development and International Development Association com-bined, approved 300 new operations, see http://www.worldbank.org/en/about/annua l-report/fiscalyeardata

a "top down" one with (high-level) management endorsement, opportunities for deeper operational experimentation have been somewhat constrained.

One recent example is Nigeria – a country with the Bank's largest program in Africa, but also many unresolved governance and development challenges. In the early 2010s, the team began developing a set of political economy analytic studies that focused on several strategic as well as service-delivery sectors and policy areas. This included a country-level analysis as well as sectoral studies focused on natural resource management/the oil sector, fiscal transfers, water and irrigation management, agriculture, health, and the power sector.

The initial analytic effort was followed in 2014 by the introduction of a "Governance, Conflict, and Gender Filter," that is, a mandatory review of all other analytic and operational work from these perspectives.[8] For operational interventions, the main thrust of the filter has been to review whether operations take the governance context and dynamics into account in a way that is likely to work and be constructive; the likelihood and consequences of conflict (e.g., in the area of project implementation); and the likely impact of an intervention on men and women. For analytic work, similar questions have been applied, in particular at the concept note stages, that is, when defining the scope of work and assessing whether a greater emphasis on governance, conflict, or gender dimensions should be included. If needed, the governance team was also able to provide more in-depth involvement, analysis, and recommendations to sector teams.

For a large country with a sizeable number of operations and analytic tasks being undertaken, implementing such a filter has required considerable staff and consultants' time. The purpose of the filter has been to identify what engagements are politically and institutionally feasible and likely to have an impact in a complex and challenging environment. The reviews were also based on ideas about "islands of effectiveness" (Therkildsen, 2008; Bain, 2016; Barma et al., 2014), which are one way of seeking out progress in contexts where overall governance improvements have proven to be difficult.

---

8 This section draws on Bain (2016, 26ff.), Thomas (2015), Van Heesewijk (2014). The filter still continues to be used as of 2017. A similar filter had been in use for some years in the Philippines (which later evolved into other innovative governance engagements).

As the team leading this effort found out in an initial review undertaken in 2015, the filter was particularly effective when proposing concrete and specific adjustments to projects being prepared. It was also particularly effective when initial comments were provided early and subsequently followed up through further review and exchanges as the plans for projects were concretized. Engagement was particularly intense with three projects: one in agriculture (staple crop processing zones), one in social protection, and a health sector "Program for Results" operation (i.e., an operation where funds are disbursed according to the progress measured by disbursement-linked indicators).

In each of these projects, adjustments were made to make the projects both more "politically savvy" in terms of developing greater buy-in from stakeholders – including elites, intended beneficiaries, and potential disrupters – and more "iterative" and learning-oriented through a process of piloting approaches and seeking feedback on what works, before broadening the scope. In particular for the health sector, the design that was developed sought to learn lessons from better-performing states and to integrate these into the approach in other states. Trust Fund resources enabled the contracting of a local network of delivery facilitators, whose contracts in turn are linked to the level of progress being achieved.

In addition to these up-front efforts and ongoing engagements with projects under implementations, the team also sought to learn lessons from completed projects through a series of "Delivery Case Studies." However, contrary to many ex post assessments that focus on identifying why political economy factors prevented progress, the studies were focused on identifying and explaining relatively successful operations.

One crucial factor for the Nigeria program was the deep engagement of the governance team for selected operations on specific operational processes and decisions – for example, on how to plan the disbursement schedule in a way to be consistent with initial piloting and lesson-learning focused on stakeholder reactions and choices, and subsequent scaling-up; on project implementation manuals to ensure that such manuals also reflect the different approach being pursued; on the specific design of "disbursement-linked indicators" and so on. Such continuous attention has been crucial to avoid having good up-front considerations falling by the wayside or making them much diminished when actually putting the operations into practice. Doing so also involved significant efforts at bringing on board a wide range of staff and consultants involved in these operations.

The Nigeria Governance Filter and Program for Adaptive Learning built on, and further developed, efforts at innovative governance engagements in the Philippines, Mongolia, Kenya, Burkina Faso, and elsewhere. A governance filter was used in the Philippines starting about 2009 to better identify what projects and specific project approaches might be feasible. There has also been recent innovative work on the roads sector, seeking to link technology, transparency, and changing incentives for politicians to be able to focus on actually delivering improvements in rural road construction and maintenance (Kaiser, 2016). In Mongolia, the team invested in better understanding government policy decisions, going against international advice in a number of areas – from better natural resource management to fiscal management, to the design of social protection programs.

The World Development Report 2017 and its potential influence

The *World Development Report 2017* focuses on governance and the law. It is the first such report in 20 years to be dedicated squarely to the role of institutions and of governance in development. Moreover, the report puts political economy drivers of development front and center. It outlines the need to rethink the approach to governance and emphasizes the importance of seeking functional improvements, rather than institutional forms, to emphasize the role of power asymmetries (and interests) relative to focusing on capacity constraints – and the *role* of law – rather than the rule of law. In its key chapters, the report focuses on the effects of governance and governance dynamics on three key development outcomes: security, growth, and equity.

In some ways, the report reflects the current state of thinking on governance: It is a sprawling agglomeration of ideas and evidence from a wide range of countries and sectors. The report is very clear in setting out why "first generation" governance interventions have often not worked, or not worked as intended. In a nutshell, the logical sequence that governance is critical to sustainable and equitable development – and that once this is recognized, governance can be improved rapidly – has been contradicted by events.

The report then explores the roles of citizens, shifting elite bargains, the media, and international actors and networks as potential drivers of change. One of the major contributions of the report is exploring how change has eventually been galvanized in many countries that made the transitions from low- to middle-income and from middle- to high-income levels.

A central challenge for the World Bank and for the international community and those parts of it focused on strengthening governance is how to operationalize the findings from the report. Operationalization of ideas has typically been the easiest when the guidance is simple and clear-cut, whereas developing the next generation of governance interventions based on the evidence accumulated thus far needs to be flexible and adaptive, as different country contexts and dynamics offer varying opportunities.

As with regard to the initial emergence of attention to governance and to the importance of political economy drivers, DFID has been a frontrunner in terms of efforts at operationalizing some of these insights. It has sought to do so in a way that seeks to avoid condensing insights into complex dynamics of how governance evolves, and efforts at improvements can be made into simplified standard guidance. Interestingly, the Smart Rules – introduced in 2014[9] – flip the traditional perception of a good technical program design on its head. As the first test of technical quality of a proposed intervention, the rules guide teams to ask whether it is likely to be feasible and to work as intended, given the political economy context. This is followed by establishing the impact on poverty, the likelihood of sustainability, and avoiding to do harm in terms of reinforcing predatory institutions or exacerbating conflict. The rules also emphasize the need for programs to be evidence-based, that is, to develop interventions based on pertinent evidence prior to the operation as well as to make adjustments over time in response to evidence about what is working. These guiding principles for technical design are then embedded in a framework of operating procedures around how to develop a "business case" for a particular intervention, following procurement and other relevant guidance, and so on.

In general, development agencies could have a great deal to gain from greater deliberate experimentation with some of the core new ideas and approaches being proposed. For example, greater attention to political economy dynamics and adapted designs targeting feasible functional improvements could be deliberately built into selected projects while let-

---

9 See homepage at https://www.gov.uk/government/publications/dfid-smart-rules-better-programme-delivery

ting other but similar projects pursue a more traditional design – in countries with a roughly similar potential for improvements. This would allow for revisiting after two to three years whether there has been a noticeable difference in progress made. A key challenge for such an "evidence-based" operationalization is that it takes a considerable period of time – relative to an international development community that tends to be driven by much faster-changing fashions and areas of attention.

Still, as indicated by the follow-up process to the *World Development Report 2011* on fragility and conflict, and the new efforts being made with regard to fragile states for the forthcoming International Development Association 18 (covering the period of mid-2017 to mid-2020), when a *World Development Report* addresses issues that are widely felt to be pressing, the effects can be significant and long-lasting. At least somewhat similarly, the *World Development Report 2017: Governance and the Law* touches on aspects of development that have gained much greater attention from many quarters in recent years. This increases the likelihood that various institutions will seek to follow some of the ideas that the report proposes. One aspect that is already noticeable is a growing emphasis on political economy skills and experience in its utilization for project design and implementation in various job descriptions. Another important aspect is that, as a flagship document, the *World Development Report 2017: Governance and the Law* elevates the concern about second-generation approaches to strengthening governance – and the need to do things differently to the corporate level of a major international financial institution – and gives it substantial international visibility. As discussed above, such a higher-level endorsement has been a missing ingredient to date.

What are the emerging lessons from implementation and the outlook for cooperation?

When proposing to engage in full-fledged testing of proposed new approaches to strengthening governance, it is important to draw emerging lessons from implementation that have been made available thus far. Some of these lessons are set out in Fritz et al. (2014) and developed further here based on the most recent experiences.

A first, central lesson is that one-off, up-front analysis is rarely sufficient. The contexts in which we are seeking governance improvements are typically volatile, and conditions, stakeholders, and challenges evolve.

This does not imply that voluminous reports have to be produced on an annual or biannual basis. However, it means that initial information needs to be revisited and reanalyzed (possibly resulting in a PowerPoint or similar type of short summary), and that the implications for development interventions need to be discussed – within teams as well as between teams and authorizing managers, and with the country stakeholders involved – at least on a yearly basis.

The Nigeria team has followed such a model that very deliberately seeks to engage in repeated understanding of the evolving situation and in a continuous engagement of staff on addressing the calibration of specific operational steps.

A further important lesson is that there can be different interpretations in terms of "what to make of" specific political economy drivers. For example, when a key government official is replaced or if government proceeds with politicizing a certain policy area – whether it is public financial management, agricultural extension services, or land administration – what is the best way to react?

Dynamics perceived to be worsening can be particularly challenging to address. For example, if a major corruption scandal emerges, highlighting the power of elite interests opposed to using public funds in the interest of citizens and overall development, should ongoing efforts at strengthening governance be reinforced, continue as before, or rather be scaled back? Should a project seek increased dialogue with elites in response, or rather focus more strongly on working with "untainted" stakeholders? But who might have less leverage to actually influence the situation?

In many such situations, PEA suggests that an approach that is neither too normative nor too naïve – nor too cynical – is best. Elite capture and weaknesses in accountability need to be expected rather than come as a surprise, and a good response can be to "speak truth to power" in various forms as well as to continue to work on strengthening accountability and state capabilities to make the abuse of funds more difficult, and more likely to be detected. At the same time, agreeing and pursuing a balanced response among teams – and more broadly among development partners – can be challenging, as some are likely to want to "punish more" and others to just continue as before.

Potential windows of opportunities can also pose a puzzle in terms of how best to capitalize on them and how far to seek to accelerate progress without overstretching. Teams have to confront such questions when working with new governments that are genuinely seeking to move their country's development onto a better and more equitable path, but which also often face entrenched interests – whether in Ukraine in 2004, in the Philippines in 2010, or in Nigeria in 2015 – as well as the problem of trying to generate change, starting with deep institutional dysfunctions.

Given the challenges with interpretation and drawing implications that are actionable for a particular project or program, it seems crucial to establish processes for discussion among team members with different backgrounds as well as with country stakeholders and authorizing managers. Such discussions are most likely to bring out different options as well as risks and can help teams to identify what adjustments are most likely to have the intended effects. The choices can then also be documented for subsequent continuous learning of what works. Where there are other development partners present in a country who are similarly seeking to take more flexible and political economy-informed approaches, this can also be an important asset in terms of exchanging insights as well as options.

A further important point is that there can be challenging normative judgments. Poverty and poor governance go together – because governance is crucial to development, countries that are poor today tend to have a history of poor governance and frequently have entrenched governance problems. As a consequence, there is a strong likelihood of the presence of "dirty politics," a privileging of loyalty over merit in managing the civil service, fluctuating political commitment to reforms and service-delivery improvements, and so on. Implementing a project seeking to strengthen governance in such contexts can be daunting and can pose challenging normative questions. In particular, it is for these types of challenging contexts with limited opportunities that it is important to consider what it means to seek Doing Development Differently.

To date, efforts at PEA and DDD have mainly been applied to two types of country contexts: (i) those that are somewhat or largely open politically (i.e., in democratic or semi-democratic environments), and (ii) those that appear as particularly difficult and intractable, and for which management feels that standard technical approaches have failed, such as those evidenced by cancelled operations as well as limited uptake and disbursements. In politically more open countries, governments are typically less sensitive to external analysis. At the same time, there can be more opportunities for engagement, in particular in terms of building broader support for a particular reform effort, working with civil society on monitoring actual policy implementation, and hence closing the gap between "laws on the books" and their actual application, and so on. Integrating "political economy smart approaches" and efforts at iterative engagement can be more challenging in contexts where many previous efforts at strengthening institutions and improving governance – whether at the core or in particular sectors – have previously failed. Doing so can still result in some useful adjustments to how an intervention is designed and implemented – with regard to the likely acceptance by stakeholders, feasibility, and possibly targeting islands of excellence – but it is inherently difficult to have a transformative impact in the short to medium term.

A key challenge for evidencing whether political economy-informed and iterative approaches can actually move the needle on development effectiveness relative to a context's degree of difficulty is that it requires comprehensive coverage: from initial project design to the design of specific implementation processes and decisions about adjustments, and so on. Achieving such a coherent approach has proven very hard, in practice. Firstly, doing so is not part of standard guidance, staff incentives, and budget allocations. Secondly, among the three to four key stakeholders committed to such an approach, at least one will move on within one or two years, given typical rotation patterns. "Doing things differently" and not being well-aligned with standard staff incentives – which may center more on disbursements, timeliness of reporting, and so on – increase the likelihood that the staff and managers replacing an original team are less likely to follow through with such an effort. It is in this regard that the *World Development Report 2017: Governance and the Law* and its operationalization are crucial: By giving considerations about political economy drivers, incentives, and interests greater prominence, it may lead to stronger and more widespread emphasis as well as the greater demand by managers that project teams seek to operate accordingly. Such nascent mainstreaming will be essential to allow more "experiments" to mature over a full project cycle rather than being concentrated primarily in the design stages but not followed through on subsequently.

Within development agencies, a key challenge in particular of adopting flexibility in implementation is how to allocate decision-making powers and accountability. Although some problem-driven adaptation happens continuously in any development project, there is also a strong emphasis on compliance with rules and processes as well as on pursuing pre-defined goals and targets based on which successes will be assessed. Although it is possible to change goals and targets during implementation, this often involves significant bureaucratic transaction costs and extensive justifications from project teams to authorizing managers, and hence it is typically done, at most, once or twice over the lifetime of an intervention of five years, for example.

At its core, PDIA and DDD would devolve decision-making authority over adjustments from high-level decision-makers in aid agencies to country and project teams working on continuous problem-solving with the stakeholders concerned. The open-endedness in terms of what the reform efforts would achieve is a difficult fit for systems in which several layers of donor-agency managers seek to authorize clearly ex ante specified sets of changes that are formally agreed with country governments, which teams and contracted consultants are then expected to pursue and deliver on.

With more flexible processes, many stakeholders will be able to find more adapted and effective approaches, and potentially significant time and costs can be saved. A risk is that flexibility can also be poorly used or abused – for example, if flexibility results in too many initiatives going in different directions, if those meant to work on implementing an intervention use flexibility to reduce their level of effort, or if certain stakeholders seek to pull away from initial reform commitments, as they de facto prefer the status quo. Guarding against such risks is likely to require new efforts at documentation and at measuring progress. Such efforts could be quite substantial and complex, but they could potentially also be more meaningful in terms of focusing on impacts rather than ex ante statements and justifications, and of being able to contribute to ongoing adjustments.

Going forward, a crucial opportunity is to build on what has been done so far and to engage in systematic, deliberate, and well-monitored piloting, implementation, and selective mainstreaming. As all the different approaches and strands of thought discussed in this chapter indicate, there is a widely shared sense that existing approaches to development have not delivered as much, or as consistently, as has been hoped for. This fundamental problem-diagnostic is shared by political economy perspectives as well as by PDIA, DDD, and the GDI. Further exchanges between these perspectives would also be helpful.

The new approaches outlined here have a potential to reduce the number of failed interventions and to increase the development effectiveness of interventions in a range of contexts and sectors. Development interventions that are designed with incentives and interests in mind are more likely to successfully address the problem of post-intervention sustainability than projects that run counter to incentives.

In addition, there is greater scope for dialogue with stakeholders in developing countries. The default mode often is to engage in a polite dialogue around what development efforts are to be financed rather than to go more deeply into questions of why past interventions may not have been fully successful and how to approach similar efforts differently going forward. Bringing innovation into this dialogue is possible but requires some calibration. Being confronted with a wide range of new ideas – from leadership development to the science of delivery to PDIA – can be confusing for country partners, so putting these ideas into tangible, everyday terms that relate to specific development problems matters. At the same time, counterparts often appreciate efforts at taking country contexts more seriously and trying to understand in greater detail what the problems are and how they can be resolved. Such in-depth discussions can also help to identify what solutions – regarding land tenure or strengthening a civil service, and others – might actually work in contexts in which fiscal resources remain scarce, and institutional constraints such as a slow or corrupt judiciary are unlikely to improve significantly in the short to medium term.

There continues to be an urgent need to further increase development effectiveness of reform efforts and the external interventions to support these. The great opportunity is to begin a period of innovation in implementation and of much more systematic exchange and learning on "what works," both within individual agencies and institutions and across them. This could also result in better insights into what efforts can be transferred from one situation to another, and which ones are less transferrable, and why. There are also risks: One is that innovation runs on too many separate tracks; a second is that ideas keep running ahead of implementation and are not systematically translated into finding – and more broadly applying – better practices.

References

Andrews, M., Pritchett, L., & Woolcock, M. (2012). *Escaping capability traps through Problem-Driven Iterative Adaptation (PDIA)*. Faculty Research Working Paper Series no. RWP12-036. Washington, DC: Center for Global Development.

Andrews, M., Pritchett, L., & Woolcock, M. (2016). *Doing iterative and adaptive work* (CID Working Paper No. 313). Center for International Development,. Cambridge, MA: Harvard University. Retrieved from http://bsc.cid.harvard.edu/files/bsc/files/

Bain, K. (2016). *Doing Development Differently at the World Bank. Updating the plumbing to fit the architecture*. London: Overseas Development Institute.

Barma, N. H., Kaiser, K., Le, T. M., & Vinuela, L. (2012). *Rents to riches? The political economy of natural resource-led development.* Washington, DC: World Bank. Retrieved from https://openknowledge.worldbank.org/handle/10986/2381

Booth, D., Harris, D., & Wild, L. (2016). *From political economy analysis to Doing Development Differently: A learning experience.* London: Overseas Development Institute. Retrieved from https://www.odi.org/sites/odi.org.uk/files/odi-assets/public ations-opinion-files/10205.pdf

Carothers, T., & de Gramont, D. (2013). *Development aid confronts politics: The almost revolution.* Washington, DC: Carnegie Endowment for International Peace.

Department for International Development. (2005). *Using drivers of change for improving aid effectiveness.* Retrieved from http://www.gsdrc.org/docs/open/doc83. pdf

Hima, H., Santibanez, C., Roshan, S., & Lomme, R. (2016). *Nigeria's national Fadama Development Project series: How to build a pilot into a national program through learning and adaptation.* Washington, DC: World Bank. Retrieved from http://www.globaldeliveryinitiative.org/sites/default/files/case-studies/k8773_fadam a_nigeria_cs_p4.pdf

Kaiser, K. (2016). *Drones for better roads: Pointers from the Philippines.* Washington, DC: World Bank. Retrieved from http://blogs.worldbank.org/governance/drones-bet ter-roads-pointers-philippines

Kishor, N., Castillo, S., & Nguyen, N. P. (2015). *The political economy of decision-making in forestry: Using evidence and analysis for reform, program on forests.* Washington, DC: World Bank. Retrieved from http://documents.worldbank.org/cura ted/en/635501468180853227/pdf/101750-WP-PROFOR-WrkingPaper-PoliticalEco nomy-Box393265B-PUBLIC.pdf

Kojima, M., Bacon, C., & Trimble, C. (2014). *Political economy of power sector subsidies: A review with reference to sub-Saharan Africa.* Washington, DC: World Bank. Retrieved from https://openknowledge.worldbank.org/bitstream/handle/1098 6/19986/895470REPLACEM0ies0for0Web0posting.pdf;sequence=1

Manghee, S., & Poole, A. (2012). *Approaches to conducting political economy analysis in the urban water sector.* Water Papers. Washington, DC: World Bank. Retrieved from http://water.worldbank.org/sites/water.worldbank.org/files/publicati on/water-Approaches-Conducting-Political-Economy-Analysis-Urban-Water-Secto r_0.pdf

Natalicchio, M., Garrett, J., Mulder-Sibanda, M., Ndegwa, S., & Voorbraak, D. (2009). *Carrots and sticks: The political economy of nutrition policy reforms.* Washington, DC: World Bank. Retrieved from https://openknowledge.worldbank.org/bitstream/h andle/10986/13746/482870WP0Carro10Box338893B01PUBLIC1.pdf?sequence=1 &isAllowed=y

Nunberg, B., Barma, N., Abdollahian, M., Green, A., & Perlman, D. (2010). *At the frontier of practical political economy operationalizing an agent-based stakeholder model in the World Bank's East Asia and Pacific region* (Policy Research Working Paper, 5176). Washington, DC: World Bank. Retrieved from http://documents.world bank.org/curated/en/707011468026130816/pdf/WPS5176.pdf

Organisation for Economic Co-operation and Development. (2005). *Lessons learned on the use of power and drivers of change analyses in development co-operation: Final report*. Paris: Author. Retrieved from http://www.gsdrc.org/docs/open/doc82. pdf

Serrat, O. (2011). *Political economy analysis for development effectiveness*. Asian Development Bank. Retrieved from https://www.adb.org/sites/default/files/publicati on/29206/political-economy-analysis.pdf

Therkildsen, O. (2008). Public sector reforms and the development of productive capacities in the LDCs. In *The least developed countries report 2009: The state and development governance*. Background Paper No. 1. Geneva: UNCTAD.

Thomas, M. (2015). *Making governance work for sectors – A summary of sector and project level political economy work in Nigeria during FY15*. Washington, DC: World Bank. Retrieved from http://documents.worldbank.org/curated/pt/423981468 185963704/pdf/102161-WP-P151718-Box394822B-PUBLIC-Nigeria-PEIA-Summ ary.pdf

Van Heesewijk, P. H. (2014). *Holding a mirror to the Governance Partnership Facility (GPF): $89 million multi-donor trust fund releases annual report*. Washington, DC: World Bank. Retrieved from http://blogs.worldbank.org/governance/holding-mirror -governance-partnership-facility-gpf-89-million-multi-donor-trust-fund-releases-an nual

Wagstaff, A. (2013). *So what exactly is the "science of delivery"?* Washington, DC: World Bank. Retrieved from http://blogs.worldbank.org/developmenttalk/so-what-e xactly-is-the-science-of-delivery

Warrener, D. (2004). *The drivers of change approach*. London: Overseas Development Institute. Retrieved from https://www.odi.org/sites/odi.org.uk/files/odi-assets/public ations-opinion-files/3721.pdf

World Bank. (2008). *The rapid results approach: A tool for leadership development and institutional change*. Washington, DC: Author. Retrieved from https://openkno wledge.worldbank.org/handle/10986/9518

World Bank. (2017). *World Development Report 2017: Governance and the law*. Washington, DC: Author. Retrieved from http://www.worldbank.org/en/publication/ wdr2017

Case Studies

Reforming Liberia's Mining License Administration System: Circumventing Implementation Challenges by Adapting Lessons from Sierra Leone

Astrid Karamira and Mark Mattner

Executive Summary

Despite being well-endowed with natural resources, Liberia is one of the poorest countries in the world. Its overall challenge is to turn resource wealth into development, but it is instead afflicted by the adverse effects of resource exploitation. Although government revenues from mining do not automatically result in equitable development, the country has few other options to raise development funds. In order for potential to turn into reality, and for mining revenues to turn into development, it needs strong regulatory systems, a good investment climate, and institutions that can ensure that mining operators abide by legal requirements and provide decent employment opportunities.

In this broader context, a specific challenge is that Liberia has a very weak mining license administration system. Putting in place a solid system in this regard is crucially important for two reasons. First, the system manages both the fiscal and social terms of a license agreement. The absence of a functioning mining license administration system creates space for corruption, as company and government individuals do not have to follow a certain set of rules, but instead have the opportunity to agree on individual terms with regard to taxes and license fees. Second, the license management system is the mechanism through which the state monitors fiscal and social license compliance. Until recently, the government of Liberia has been unable to monitor whether license holders were making the many different payments that were due during the lifecycle of the mining license. Large parts of the mining economy were essentially unregulated.

Against this background, the paper discusses how the Deutsche Gesellschaft für Internationale Zusammenarbeit (GIZ) Regional Resource Governance in West Africa program is assisting Liberia in improving the way it administers mining licenses.[1] How best to support complex change processes that involve multiple levels of capacity development in a fragile environment? What principles of engagement and management should be applied? Which are the main success factors for effecting sustainable change? The specific activity analyzed in this regard is the implementation of the Mining Cadastre Administration Support Project (MCAP) approach, developed and supported by the Norwegian non-profit organization Revenue Development Foundation (RDF) and applied successfully in Sierra Leone since 2009. MCAP is designed around the provision of a modern IT-system that is flanked by long-term capacity development and advisory services. In the two years since its introduction, the system has already yielded a number of tangible benefits in Liberia. The Ministry was able to lift the moratorium on exploration licenses in March 2014. All industrial licenses for large mining companies and most semi-industrial licenses for medium-sized mining operations are processed through the system. This means that there is a single place with all license-holder information and a central tool for administering the license.

In supporting these change processes, GIZ had to engage with two main implementation challenges. First and foremost, any reform effort in a "fragile" governance context would inevitably have to identify capacity constraints as being the central implementation challenge. This is certainly true in Liberia. Although international donors frequently contribute to addressing some of those gaps in the medium term, achieving sustainable results is considerably more difficult. In addition to capacity constraints, the second major implementation challenge is adapting the approaches and lessons learned in Sierra Leone to the local conditions of the Liberia context. Observing the gains made in Sierra Leone raised expectations in this new mining license management system and built pressure for swift implementation in Liberia. However, what looked like a possible template for transfer was in reality a context-specific response to local challenges.

In order to overcome these challenges and to institutionalize outcomes and results, the GIZ Regional Resource Governance program pursues a comprehensive capacity-development strategy that combines individual training, institutional development, and policy advice at the macro level. In the course of implementation, it also capitalizes on the linkages and synergies created by embedding MCAP implementation into its broader

---

1 GIZ implements the program on behalf of BMZ.

partnership portfolio in the sector, which includes revising the Mining Act and associated regulations, supporting a comprehensive capacity-development strategy for the Ministry of Lands, Mines and Energy (MLME), and developing a strategy to regulate small-scale mining. In addition, close collaboration with the World Bank in the early stages of the process ensured that seed funding was available at critical early junctures and that both the World Bank and GIZ provided coherent advice to the MLME. A delegated cooperation agreement with Australia similarly enhanced coordination.

The paper concludes by outlining a set of lessons learned, based on the "smart implementation" principles that form the basis of the present volume. The experience described points to the vital importance of partner *ownership*. Although this is a trite observation on the surface, it is a real challenge to support partners in making genuine choices (in this case, for the MCAP) when they are often under donor pressure and have only insufficient capacity or information. The discussion also illustrates the importance of working within partnership contexts for a *sustained period of time*. It is unrealistic to expect substantial and sustainable change in fragile environments within three-year planning horizons. It takes time to build trust, adapt approaches to local conditions (no "big bang"), and to proceed in an *iterative manner* that allows for learning and continuous improvement. It is also clear that capacity-development activities – such as the ones discussed in this paper – require *integrating technical, political, process, and organizational development advice*. This means that GIZ advisors have to show flexibility in taking on different roles at different times in the process. The GIZ model of capacity development at different levels is well-suited in this regard.

Introduction

The well-known governance challenges in Liberia's mining sector came to the fore in early 2012, when the MLME declared a moratorium on issuing new exploration licenses. It was forced to take this decision after a rapid diagnostic funded by the World Bank uncovered that many mining plots had been awarded as license areas to multiple investors. These geographic overlaps seemed to justify worries that the ministry was unable to adequately manage the mining sector. Such a moratorium would reflect a serious crisis in any mining economy, because it meant that investors could no longer legally be granted the right to search for new mineral deposits. For Liberia, the timing was especially critical because it coincided with one of the longest and most pronounced mining booms in modern history. For a country that had recently escaped civil war and was planning to turn to mining as a source of development finance, it was clear that something had to be done – especially since those investors that were willing to abide by recognized legal and ethical standards were now discouraged from making their investments.

This paper focuses on the reform steps taken by the MLME in improving the way it administers mining licenses. With initial assistance from the World Bank and more in-depth advice from the GIZ Regional Resource Governance program, the ministry identified the MCAP approach, developed and supported by the Norwegian non-profit organization RDF and implemented successfully in Sierra Leone since 2009, as being a suitable model for its own efforts. The paper discusses how the GIZ program helped the MLME adopt this approach. As the main supporter of MCAP in Sierra Leone and as the main partner of the MLME in Liberia, the Regional Resource Governance program played a central role in transferring the requisite knowledge and lessons learned from Sierra Leone, and in tailoring the overall approach to the specific situation in Liberia. It did so by embedding this activity in its overall partnership portfolio with the MLME, which also included revising the Mining Act and associated regulations, supporting a comprehensive capacity-development strategy for the ministry, and developing a strategy to regulate small-scale mining, which had been continuing largely unregulated in rural areas due to the lack of administrative reach of the ministry. In addition, close collaboration with the World Bank in the early stages of the process ensured that seed funding was available at critical early junctures and that both the World Bank and GIZ provided coherent advice to the MLME. Full roll-out and implementation of MCAP began in July 2013 after the government of Australia made a financial contribution to the GIZ Regional Resource Governance program just as the MLME had decided to adopt MCAP.[2]

---

2   Australia contributed to the GIZ Regional Resource Governance program through a three-year delegated cooperation agreement, which funded MCAP implementation and a host of other activities. The agreement ended in July 2016. The work now continues with funds from the German Federal Ministry for Economic Cooperation and Development (BMZ).

Development challenge

Despite being well-endowed with natural resources as an established exporter of iron ore, gold, diamonds, timber, and rubber, Liberia is one of the poorest countries in the world. It ranks near the very bottom of the key development indicators (e.g., Liberia was ranked 175 out of 187 in the 2014 Human Development Index). Its overall challenge is to turn resource wealth into development, but it is instead afflicted by the adverse effects of resource exploitation. In this broader context, a specific challenge is that the country has a very weak mining license administration system. Putting in place a solid system in this regard is crucially important for two reasons. First, the system manages both the fiscal and social terms of a license agreement. The absence of a functioning mining license administration system creates space for corruption, as company and government individuals do not have to follow a certain set of rules, but instead have the opportunity to agree on individual terms with regard to taxes and license fees. Second, the license management system is the mechanism through which the state monitors fiscal and social license compliance. Prior to the introduction of MCAP, the ministry was unable to monitor whether license holders were making the many different payments that were due to the government during the lifecycle of the mining license. Large parts of the mining economy were essentially unregulated.

Implementation challenges

Any reform effort in a "fragile" governance context would inevitably have to identify capacity constraints as being the central implementation challenge. This is certainly true in Liberia. Although international donors frequently contribute to addressing some of those gaps in the medium term, achieving sustainable results is considerably more difficult. In order to overcome this challenge and to institutionalize outcomes and results, the Regional Resource Governance program pursues a comprehensive capacity-development strategy that combines individual training, institutional development, and policy advice at the macro level. This approach is in line with the standard approach of GIZ to capacity development and can also be used to disaggregate specific capacity gaps encountered in the course of introducing MCAP in Liberia.

- At the *individual level*, many MLME staff members do not possess the necessary training, qualification, or formal education required for their positions. Although they generally have extensive practical knowledge of mining issues, they are often unable to apply this knowledge systematically toward implementing a coherent approach to mining-sector regulation. They are also faced with highly qualified and better paid mining-company staff. A number of the mining inspectors at the MLME have no formal training related to the mining sector, even though this is a prerequisite to conduct meaningful inspections of mining sites, which is a highly technical activity.

- At the *institutional level*, responsibilities within the MLME are often unclear, leading to administrative inefficiency and lack of collaboration between different units. For example, mining licenses have long been awarded even though there is no explicit legal guidance governing the process. As is discussed below, a new Mining Act and a set of regulations for implementation have been drafted with the assistance of the GIZ program, but they have not yet been formally adopted. In this environment, it is difficult for even the most motivated staff members to effect change or even to conduct their functions. In addition, shortages of equipment and frequent power cuts meant that until 2012, mining license information (including geographical information on mining plots and fee-payment data) were held largely in paper form at the MLME central office, impeding easy access to – and exchange of – information.

- At the *policy level*, the government has so far been unable to devise a fully coherent system of mineral governance, which means that there are other agencies in addition to the MLME with often competing mandates and authority. Despite the importance of the mining sector for the economic and social development of the country, inter-agency coordination and cooperation in the sector is difficult to achieve. In the case of payments made by mining companies, including license fees and production royalties, all payments are made to the Liberia Revenue Agency (LRA) and its predecessor agencies. Although data exchange is improving because of MCAP, revenue authorities often did not inform mining authorities of non-payments in the past, severely hampering the government's ability to collect revenues. The fact that industrial mining contracts typically involve large sums over long periods (particularly for iron ore), the various institutions and specific actors within them have a sustained interest in maximizing their roles in contract negotiations and license management. Finally, the government has been unable to provide effective donor coordination in the sector and, as is seen below, donors do not always agree on the best approach to strengthening the license management system.

In addition to capacity constraints, the second major implementation challenge to introducing MCAP at the MLME is adapting the approaches and lessons learned in Sierra Leone to the local conditions of the Liberia context. The key impetus for Liberia to choose MCAP came from an in-depth study-tour in 2012, supported by GIZ, during which senior MLME officials had the chance to familiarize themselves with the system in Sierra Leone. Observing the gains made in Sierra Leone raised expectations in this new mining license management system and built pressure for swift implementation in Liberia. However, what looked like a possible template for transfer was in reality a context-specific response to local challenges. Hence a one-to-one transfer of the system to Liberia was not a viable option.

Sierra Leone is a fragile state that is in many ways structurally similar to Liberia. Both have exited from civil war in recent times and both are facing severe capacity constraints. However, in the mining sector, institutional and policy capacity in Sierra Leone is significantly stronger than in Liberia. The reasons for this go beyond MCAP. With the support of the World Bank, Sierra Leone created a stand-alone National Minerals Agency (NMA). This agency was staffed by the best civil servants available and has strong leadership and a clear legal mandate. This meant that an introduction of the system had support across the board and that there was only little institutional resistance. Although the NMA and its overseeing Ministry of Mines and Mineral Resources were at odds initially about their respective roles, a consensus was eventually reached that located responsibility for mining license management with the NMA. In addition, eight Sierra Leonean engineers had been trained in Ghana and returned home with master's degrees even before the NMA was created. These engineers took a pivotal role in the success of the NMA, as they were all given key positions in the newly created agency. Nevertheless, owing to the challenging context, the system also continues to experience a number of significant challenges, such as the reluctance of a politically appointed body at the ministry to grant the necessary approval for cancelling licenses on technical grounds.

Structure of the paper

Against this background, the overall analytical question that this paper addresses is how best to support complex change processes that involve all three levels of capacity development in a fragile environment. What principles of engagement and management should be applied? Which are the main success factors for effecting sustainable change? In answering these questions, the paper uses the case of transferring the RDF's Mining Cadastre Administration Support Project approach, MCAP, from Sierra Leone to Liberia. In doing so, it considers a set of operating principles proffered in *The Role of Ownership and Political Steering for Development Results.*[3] The specific focus is on the following five principles: (i) adoption of a multi-stakeholder approach, (ii) focusing on developing genuine partnership systems, (iii) operating in a mode that integrates technical, political, process, and organizational development advice, (iv) context-specific and incremental implementation of interventions, and (v) long-term engagement in the transformation and reform process to ensure direction and results. Since the implementation of the MCAP approach is currently ongoing and the Regional Resource Governance program has made a long-term commitment (subject to commission by the German Federal Ministry for Economic Cooperation and Development) to its support, any analytical insight at this stage can only be illustrative. But given the precarious nature of program implementation in fragile states, it is expected that the insights yielded will nevertheless be relevant and interesting to a wider audience.

The remainder of this paper is structured in three sections. The first sketches the operational context in which MCAP implementation is taking place. The second traces the steps taken throughout implementation along the three dimensions of capacity development: individual, institutional, and policy. The final section then draws out the lessons learned in the context of the present volume's "smart implementation" framework.

---

3 Please see S. Frenken, M. Jacob, U. Müller, and A. Stockmayer (2010). The role of ownership and political steering for development results. In S. Frenken and U. Müller (Eds.), *Ownership and political steering in development countries*. Baden-Baden and Bonn: Nomos and GIZ.

Context

The potential of the mining sector to provide domestic development resources for Liberia's future is huge. In 2013, the country reported gross domestic product growth of 8.1 percent. This growth was primarily due to rapidly growing iron ore exports and a related construction and services sector. The mining sector's share in the overall economy stood at approximately 10 percent, with very positive growth forecasts. In fiscal year 2012/2013, revenues from the extractive sector amounted to about $38 million, which was about 6.9 percent of government revenue. At the time, two industrial iron ore mines had already begun operation, with two more fully explored and ready for construction. One industrial gold mine was also producing, with a second under construction. There was also a growing number of medium-sized gold and diamond mines and a large micro-mining sector. Yet, to date, the mining sector has contributed very little to inclusive economic growth and employment. Specific commodities (particularly diamonds) played an important role in the financing of long and brutal cross-border civil wars in both Liberia and Sierra Leone. Today, as before, small-scale mining supports the livelihoods of a large number of people in rural areas (estimates of the number of people are generally unreliable), with miners toiling often under very precarious conditions in remote areas.

Although government revenues from mining do not automatically result in equitable development, mining economies such as Liberia are left with few options to raise development funds. In order for potential to turn into reality and for mining revenues to turn into development, they need strong regulatory systems, a good investment climate, and institutions that can ensure that mining operators abide by legal requirements and provide decent employment opportunities. Liberia has recognized this imperative, which has become all the more pressing of late because of rapidly falling iron ore prices and increasing competition for reputable investment. As such, the government has committed to pursuing a reform agenda guided by the regional framework prescribed by the African Union's Africa Mining Vision and other international standards.

Turning this overall commitment into specific steps continues to pose challenges due to capacity gaps on the part of the government but also on the part of civil society, which often lacks the ability to hold government institutions to account. This does not mean, however, that there have not been some notable successes. In the areas of combating corruption and mismanagement through transparency, for example, Liberia passed a law in 2009 to provide clear rules for the implementation of the Extractives Industries Transparency Initiative (EITI). This global standard demands that natural resource companies disclose all payments made to government agencies, while those agencies in turn disclose all payments received by the companies. Also in 2009, Liberia became the first African country to be fully compliant with the requirement of the initiative. Since then, the local EITI chapter, partially in partnership with the Regional Resource Governance program, has repeatedly been praised for devising innovative activities to enhance the use of EITI data to hold public officials to account. For example, since 2012, high school students have formed debate clubs to discuss the policy challenges related to natural resource management, culminating in a high-profile annual debate competition.

At the very technical level of mining-sector regulation, the MLME holds the key to implementing reforms. The GIZ Regional Resource Governance program has become the ministry's main external supporter over the years and is now supporting a holistic set of interrelated activities. The first activity is the ongoing update of the formal legal framework of mining-sector regulation. The current Mining Act of 2001, adopted under dictator Charles Taylor during the civil war, does not reflect the principles of a modern mining regime (or of good governance) because it concentrated the decision to award mining licenses almost purely in the hands of the executive branch and provides next to no avenues for redress. In addition, because of a lack of coordination among government ministries and international donors, a myriad of related laws have been adopted that affect mining-sector regulation but either contradict each other or the Mining Act (which is, despite its flaws, the mining law in force). Finally, there are only two implementing regulations available that guide officials at the MLME in applying the Mining Act. In reality, the application of legal provisions is often a result of practice and negotiation – a situation that neither reassures investors nor facilitates governance oversight. A more modern Mining Act has been drafted and a set of detailed regulations have been developed through a consultative process with the assistance of GIZ and are now available to the MLME for introduction to the legislature.

The second component of GIZ assistance to the MLME is the creation of a capacity-development plan that maps its existing capacities against those needed to fulfill its minimum statutory obligations under the updated Mining Act. Taking into account the capacity needs at all three levels, the plan makes detailed proposals for training measures and administrative restructuring. In this vein, the plan will allow the MLME to solicit and coordinate contributions from donor partners. Crucially, it also contains a strategy to decentralize the MLME's function to key mining districts in rural areas in order to improve the services that are available to small-scale miners there, who currently have to travel to the capital, Monrovia, to obtain a license. This is a barrier to compliance, as traveling to the capital city is costly and time-consuming for the miners. The third activity supported by GIZ is the drafting of a regulatory roadmap for the small-scale mining sector. Small-scale mining remains an important livelihood activity in rural areas but is essentially unregulated, due primarily to capacity constraints on the part of the MLME.

The fourth area of GIZ support to the MLME, and the focus of this section, is the implementation of MCAP in order to improve the efficiency of mining license management. MCAP essentially consists of three components, which combine the provision of a technical IT-solution with long-term advisory services. The first is an IT-platform (Mining Cadastre Administration System, MCAS), which provides a cost-effective solution for managing the multiple administrative steps that are necessary to ensure that mining licenses are managed effectively. These range from recording license applications when they are made to ensuring that all legally required steps are taken in the course of approval, including checking for fee-payment and geographic overlaps. The RDF does not charge users license fees for the software system. Additionally, improvements made to the system in one country are transferred for free to other implementing countries. The second component is ongoing advice from a team of long-term resident advisors. These advisors not only support the administrative staff responsible for processing licenses in rolling out the IT-system. In addition, they support the relevant government institution in improving their administrative procedures on an ongoing basis to identify the training needs required to enhance operations and to support collaboration with the multiple agencies involved in collecting revenues. In Sierra Leone, the latter culminated in the establishment of the intra-governmental Extractive Industry Revenue Task Force, which today exerts strong ownership over collecting data that is useful for enhancing government receipts from the mining sector. The third component of MCAP is an Online Repository, which, subject to some legal constraints related to tax law, publishes license ownership and fee-payment data on the internet for investors and civil society to access anytime for free. This is intended to not only attract investors by making it easier to identify available plots, but also to facilitate civil society oversight by facilitating access to information.

In the two years since its introduction, the system has already yielded a number of tangible benefits in Liberia. The moratorium on exploration licenses was lifted in March 2014. All industrial licenses for large mining companies and most semi-industrial licenses for medium-sized mining operations are processed through the system. This means that there is a single place with all license-holder information and a central tool for administering the license. In addition, a data-sharing agreement with the LRA (where license payments are made) has been defined and payment data is being shared systematically. On this basis, the Online Repository makes payment and license data available to the public. The number of mining operators with valid tax ID numbers – a precondition for payment – has also rapidly improved. This led to an increase in the LRA tax rolls: from 43 to 128 companies, with another 86 companies having already been identified. However, only 17 of these companies submitted tax returns in 2014. Thus, there is still a lot to be done with regard to tax compliance. There are two remaining challenges. The first is that not all licenses are processed through the system. Instead, personal relationships are sometimes used to move files forward and specific officials insist on making specific decisions. The second and related challenge is that the system acts primarily as a cadastral system in which data is kept and it has not been fully applied to redesign processes. In essence, the MLME continues to lack the institutional and policy capacity to fully embed the system in its administrative procedures and processes.

The remainder of this paper illustrates how the GIZ Regional Resource Governance program supported the achievement of these successes and has been addressing the remaining challenges in MCAP implementation. One key element in this regard is that supporting MCAP is an integral part of a holistic approach that combines the interrelated change processes undertaken by the MLME and supported by GIZ. The ongoing update of legal frameworks – and the development of a capacity plan for the MLME in particular – complement MCAP implementation.

Tracing the implementation process

The implementation process of MCAP in Liberia began roughly in 2011, when the MLME began to consider changing the cadastral system it was using at the time. The process can be divided in three stages for analytical purposes. The first is the period of *orientation*, in which the MLME considered its options and decided on the system (2011–2013). The second is the period of *adoption* of the system (2013–2015), when the software was rolled out and advisors from the RDF were deployed to the ministry. The third is the period of *mainstreaming* (starting in 2015 and continuing to date), during which time the IT-system has been fully functional, but license management procedures need to be updated to reflect optimal practice. The remainder of this section traces the process of implementing MCAS in Liberia along these three stages, and the steps taken by the program and its partners in dealing with the implementation challenges they were facing at each stage. Analytically, reference is made to the GIZ capacity-development framework outlined above, which disaggregates capacity at the individual, institutional, and policy levels.

Orientation stage

The orientation stage began with the observation by senior staff members that the system in use in the Cadastral Unit was no longer fit for purpose. Through a grant from the United States Agency for International Development (USAID) administered by a contractor, the Unit had been provided with computer hardware and the IT-cadastral software Flexicadastre, offered on commercial terms by the software company Spatial Dimensions. Although the software is used successfully around the world by mining agencies and companies, it had not been fit for purpose at the MLME, since the contractor appears not to have adequately taken into account the specific needs of the ministry. It also had not complemented software provision with a long-term capacity-development program for the Cadastral Unit and other relevant parts of the MLME dealing with mining licenses. With only a small number of short training programs by visiting experts furnished by Spatial Dimensions, Cadastral Unit staff therefore were unable to operate the system effectively. Many licenses that had already been issued continued to be recorded on paper, making monitoring of payments and other aspects of compliance exceedingly difficult.

In addition to the lack of individual capacity to use the software, the MLME also lacked the institutional capacity to integrate the Flexicadastre software in its license-awarding processes and in the way in which different units in the ministry collaborated and communicated. Because the

Geographic Information System (GIS) team did not see any added value in the system – as they were unable to use its features properly – they maintained the license registry in a separate database using specialized ArcGIS software instead. Since the system was not used systematically, the de facto license registry was the tenement map maintained by the GIS officer, and not the system database. In other words, licenses continued to overlap as they had during the old paper-based system. As mentioned at the outset, this is one of the worst conceivable failings of a license management system. Finally, since Flexicadastre is commercial software, license fees were to be due on the existing cadastre system every year, even though there was no budgetary allocation to meet this expense. In sum, the provision of Flexicadastre ultimately failed because of the lack of a genuine partnership that could develop a joint vision for addressing multiple levels of capacity development.

The GIZ Regional Resource Governance program had only commenced operations in Liberia in late 2010 and had therefore not been involved in the process leading up to this point. Because of the apparent gaps in the system, however, the MLME now turned to the World Bank and GIZ for assistance. After consultations, the three partners jointly engaged the RDF to conduct a detailed assessment of overlaps. The results of this assessment then prompted Minister Sendolo to impose a memorandum on exploration licenses on the grounds that the Cadastral Unit could no longer guarantee the integrity of the licensing system. This presented the entry point for introducing MCAP based on lessons from Sierra Leone and for applying the more holistic advisory approach taken by GIZ. Although the USAID contractor had simply provided computer hardware and the Flexicadastre software, they had not taken into account that the staff members at the Cadastral Unit in the MLME needed a long-term capacity-development program in order to be able to effectively use the system. Furthermore, they had not planned for accompanying institutional support for the MLME. This, however, was urgently needed, as the license-awarding process has to be connected to other institutional processes, such as the proper implementation of mining regulations related to awarding licenses. The GIZ program at that moment benefited from being perceived as a new actor with less-entrenched local interests but more operational experience in Sierra Leone, due to its longer presence there. To use this momentum, the program organized an instruction tour for senior MLME officials and representatives of the Cadastral Unit to observe the functioning of MCAP in Sierra Leone firsthand. During this trip, the Liberian delegation felt that the MCAP approach could be a better way of dealing with the challenges they were facing.

Upon return to Monrovia, MLME staff discussed the detailed implications of their technical choices with GIZ, the World Bank, and the RDF as well as internally. After concluding these discussions, the MLME decided to request support from the GIZ Regional Resource Governance program and roll out MCAP on account of the way in which it had helped increase the efficiency of mining license management in Sierra Leone. Unlike Flexicadastre, the software license is not subject to any type of license fees from the government, as the provider, RDF, is a non-profit organization. At the time the decision was reached, however, the GIZ program had already made a commitment to support the updating of the Mining Act (a costly endeavor on account of the legal expertise required) and had no immediate funding for MCAP implementation available. Instead, as a stop-gap measure, the World Bank was able to fund a rapid technical mission by the RDF that removed the most glaring and damaging geographical overlaps in licenses already awarded. Despite these funding constraints, the MLME made its own decision to change the license management system based on the technical advice provided by GIZ and the World Bank, even though neither agency was able to induce this decision with the promise of immediate funding. Joint efforts were made to solicit funding, further enhancing the nascent partnership and keeping momentum going without yet being able to adopt the system.

Adoption stage

The opportunity for moving on to the adoption stage came when Australia announced its intention to become a new development partner supporting mineral resource governance in Liberia in 2012. Because Australia is a mining economy with a large number of exploration companies working in Africa, Australian Aid (AusAid) had determined that assisting the license management system should be a central priority for their proposed assistance program. This message was buttressed by the MLME itself, as senior officials wrote to AusAid requesting support in implementing the MCAP system. Since AusAid did not intend to set up their own program structures in Liberia, they approached the GIZ Regional Resource Governance program to propose partnership through delegated cooperation. In essence, this arrangement allowed Australia to channel its funding through the existing GIZ program under a global German-Australian agreement. In addition to facilitating coordination among development partners, funding under this arrangement had the added benefit of allowing the GIZ program to propose additional activities that would strengthen the MLME overall and enhance the structures in which MCAS could successfully be implemented. To complement MCAP, the additional activities that AusAid would fund were the development of implementation regulations for the updated Mining Act, a capacity-development strategy for the MLME, as well as a roadmap for regulating small-scale mining.

The agreement with AusAid was signed in mid-2013, after which time MCAP implementation could begin in earnest. The initial focus on rolling out MCAP was to move license data from the old Flexicadastre system and the remaining paper-based records to the new MCAS IT-system at the Cadastral Unit. However, it was discovered that the data in the Flexicadastre system was of rather poor quality. Therefore, digitization of data was done exclusively from the paper archive. Moving forward, staff also had to be trained in using the system to process new applications and, in particular, to ensure that license fees paid at the LRA were captured by the system so that the MLME could track payment obligations by license holders. As in Sierra Leone, the bulk of training was delivered by an RDF Revenue Specialist, who was resident at the Cadastral Unit full-time, with occasional support from software specialists and other RDF staff knowledgeable in specific aspects of license management. This model of embedded capacity development allowed individuals in the MLME to develop a trusting relationship, with the trainers addressing their individual capacity gaps.

An unexpected opportunity for testing the utility and results of the embedded capacity-development approach came in August 2014, when the RDF advisor had to suddenly leave Liberia due to the Ebola epidemic. Although he continued mentoring the Cadastral Unit team from afar until his return in March 2015, staff members found themselves on their own. What is more, there was no more external presence in the Cadastral Unit to ensure that individuals acted in the interest of the system and not only in their self-interest. Excitingly, however, the system held up and mining licenses continued to be processed by the MCAS software during the Ebola period. License fees continued to be collected despite the fact that the economy had largely ground to a halt. This showed that adopting a long-term approach to building capacity could work even under very challenging conditions.

In addition to the work on the MCAS IT-system and training in the Cadastral Unit, progress was also made on the issue of inter-ministerial cooperation. Here the inauguration of an inter-agency task force on mining revenue responsible for institutionalizing data-sharing among relevant agencies was instrumental. To date, the group has developed data-sharing agreements between the MLME, which is responsible for mining license management; the LRA, where all payments are made; and the Ministry of Finance, which is responsible for revenue policy. The sharing of data between these three institutions is important, as only then can the Liberian state be sure that the amounts of taxes companies pay to the LRA correspond to what they are supposed to be paying according to the license they hold. An RDF advisor has also been placed in the LRA to facilitate building an IT-link to automatically connect the LRA system with MCAS so that payment data can be reflected in real time.

At the same time as MCAP implementation progressed, the MLME continued to work on the other activities supported by the GIZ Regional Resource Governance program. Despite the fact that these parallel processes (particularly the Mining Act update and the MLME capacity-development plan) provided an ideal opportunity for enhancing workflows and procedural elements of license management, less progress has been made in formalizing administrative procedures within the MLME. This is mainly due to the huge challenge presented by institutionalizing new rules and procedures in government institutions in fragile states. In practice, applicants for small- and medium-scale licenses still do not always file their application at the Cadastral Unit for it to be inputted into MCAS. This is different to the situation in Sierra Leone, where the introduction of the NMA provided an opportunity for creating new procedures from scratch, and for putting the Cadastral Unit at the center of the license administration process. In Liberia, by contrast, many applicants continue to meet with specific MLME staff first, particularly in the Bureau of Mines, and ask them to forward their applications on an individual basis. Although these applications will eventually be reflected and deposited in MCAS, this practice allows for continuous nontransparent activities and bypassing of the official license approval process. In other words, although some improvements have been made in terms of building institutional capacity by awarding licenses through MCAS, the license management system has still not been adopted evenly across the MLME. To this date, individual staff members can still influence and divert the process if they choose to do so. This situation reflects the fact that administrative provisions have not been updated at a similar speed as the IT-system. Whereas the IT-system that is being used to administer licenses in the mining sector is fully functioning – and thus has the potential to bring full transparency into the license-awarding and license-administering process – formal provisions for the license system are still missing. This demonstrates that capacity development at the individual level is more easily achieved than at the institutional level.

Mainstreaming stage

Further anchoring and mainstreaming MCAS in institutional structures of the MLME has been the focus of the third implementation period (since late 2015). The system is now fully operational but is not being used to its full potential in day-to-day license management. As in the Sierra Leone example, an Online Repository has gone live and allows the public to access license data online for free. The database contains license-holder and payment information on many licenses, but it is not yet complete and updated enough to attract investors or support civil society in overseeing the licensing process. In addition, the data link between the LRA and the MLME is to be tightened, and exchange protocols with the systems of other agencies, such as the Environmental Protection Agency, have yet to be developed.

In view of these remaining challenges, the focus has shifted to institutional capacity development to consolidate and expand on the gains made to date. The MLME is at times not able – or reluctant – to decisively take decisions on specific aspects of MCAP implementation, such as promulgating clear administrative rules within the institution so that all licenses are processed by the system. It is hoped that implementation of the MLME capacity-development plan, which contains recommendations to that effect, will help in this regard. This process will be supported by GIZ and will underline the utility of the holistic approach to supporting change processes taken by the Regional Resource Governance program.

At the third level of the capacity-development strategy (policy), decisions on important policy areas that could strengthen MCAS, such as license provisions in the new Mining Act and its regulations, have been delayed and postponed repeatedly. The draft Mining Act and its regulations have been completed with the support of GIZ and are now available to the MLME, reflecting good international practice and a nationwide consultation exercise. This draft Mining Act and the regulations have been developed in a multi-stakeholder process led by the MLME and the GIZ program. After final validation by the MLME, they could be introduced to the legislature, but no such steps appear to be imminent. Although this reluctance is, to some extent, political in nature in the run-up to national elections in 2017, it also reflects reluctance on the part of policy-makers to fully commit to one specific course of action. There is therefore still a possibility that the Mining Act – as it has been developed in a multi-stakeholder approach – might never be passed. If this scenario became reality, it would considerably complicate further reforms because one key element would have stalled. At the same time, some regulations could still be adopted by the executive without the new Mining Act coming into force and would already much improve governance processes. In addition, MCAP implementation could still proceed at the MLME and in partnership with other agencies, albeit without the additional tailwind from a new legal framework. Finally, the GIZ program is now facing the additional challenge of being the MLME's only development partner, since the AusAid delegated cooperation has ended and the World Bank and USAID have ceased their assistance to the MLME. This is relevant because a well-coordinated group of partners can play a constructive role in supporting and speeding-up specific change processes.

While continuing its long-term approach to capacity development, training, and mentoring, the Regional Resource Governance program will seek to address this situation in two main ways. The first is to build alliances with other development partners and advocate for their return to supporting the MLME. If well-coordinated, multiple donors can raise the overall number of incentives for genuine reforms, or at least ensure that a push for reform remains on the agenda and gained achievements are consolidated. This might seem contradictory to putting the country in the driver's seat. Furthermore, it might give the impression of GIZ undermining the MLME's ownership in the validation process of the draft Mining Act. However, the Regional Resource Governance program does not act arbitrarily and without consulting its partner but offers targeted advice through its existing partnership structures. Additionally, more donor support to the MLME is primarily in the interest of the Liberian government. It also needs to be taken into consideration that German support to Liberia with regard to resource governance is not unlimited. As mentioned in the beginning of this paper, achieving sustainable results often remains elusive. If there were other donors to support the MLME's reform processes, the chances for achieving sustainable results would increase, since change processes could be accompanied through external advisors for a longer period of time. At the same time, the program will seek to connect its multiple workstreams more tightly in order to provide a more cohesive package of support to address identified capacity-development gaps. In particular, it will try even harder to advise that the package of activities will only yield sustainable results if all are implemented in lockstep, and that they have been designed based on the MLME's explicit request and choice. Although significant achievements have been made, the objective will now be to consolidate them. Against the current slump in commodity prices, this is imperative to ensure that mining will contribute to growth and prosperity in Liberia one day.

Lessons learned

How do the central hypotheses identified concerning different principles of implementation at the outset hold up in the context of the implementation experience described above? In terms of the adoption of a *multi-stakeholder approach*, it is clear that an important success factor in any complex advisory and change program is the coordination of multiple donor agencies. This is particularly true when national partners are not able to play this coordination role. In this particular case, the interagency approach – including Germany and Australia as bilateral donors, the World Bank as multilateral donor, and the RDF as international non-governmental organization – played a positive role. Early support from the World Bank and partnership with AusAid were important factors in facilitating the rollout of MCAP and in supporting the MLME in making a technical decision tailored to its own needs that it could fully own.

On the side of national partners, a *multi-stakeholder approach* to enhance cooperation is equally important, given the complex institutional environment in which agencies often work side-by-side or have structural incentives for competition. In the present case, this is being accomplished through data exchange between revenue and mining agencies, channeled by a formally constituted Task Force. This benefits all agencies involved by clarifying priorities and improving available data. External actors such as the RDF and GIZ can play a useful role in facilitating interactions and exchanges between different government institutions to promote cooperation. The key reason for this is that they are perceived by actors to not have vested interests and can thus act as independent facilitators. In the field of mineral resource governance, German cooperation has a special advantage, as they are perceived as an honest broker and are well-trusted by the partner, given the fact that Germany does not have a strong mining industry. In addition, GIZ implementation principles embodied in the management tool of GIZ *Capacity WORKS* imply very close relations to the partner ministry MLME on a daily basis, which represents a considerable strength in terms of program implementation.

Within national institutions, there are often competing interests that can hamper the implementation of change processes. This has also been the experience of MCAS implementation in Liberia, as not all staff have been willing so far to formalize their informal processing of mining licenses by adopting the new system. Broad internal steering mechanisms for change processes can be a way to bring more staff members on board and give them a positive stake in the transformation of their role. At the end of the day, however, administrative agencies are hierarchical systems, albeit with accountability and checks-and-balances. Care needs to be taken to avoid undermining administrative capacity (and effective line-management) by imposing generic steering structures that are too broad and not sufficiently tailored to the specific task. A carefully calibrated program of capacity development at all three levels (policy, organization, and individual) can help make the right decisions in this regard and needs to be designed on a case-by-case basis.

In terms of focusing on developing genuine *partnership systems*, the experience described above points to the vital importance of partner *ownership*. Although this is a trite observation on the surface, it is a real challenge to support partners in making genuine choices (in this case, for MCAP) when they are often exposed to different donor preferences and have only insufficient capacity or information. In the discussion above, it was not easy for the MLME to choose and implement its own preferred solution, considering that USAID had been supporting and implementing another license management system with the MLME. Smart implementation here means finding the right balance between providing technical advice and leaving enough space for independent decision-making by partners. However, partnership also implies the need for making specific policy decisions in the absence of donor-imposed solutions. At present, the MLME has reached a stage where such decisions are very much needed to ensure further progress. Pace and timing are very important in any reform process. Smart implementation is adjusting to the pace of the reform dynamics in the partner country and accepting when decision-making processes take more time than the project proposal foresees. A multi-layer approach is thus very helpful, as it allows for diverting resources to a different layer, if the process takes more time at one level.

The discussion above also illustrates the importance of working within partnership contexts for a *sustained period of time*. It is unrealistic to expect substantial and sustainable change in fragile environments within three-year planning horizons. It takes time to build trust and adapt approaches to local conditions. The option of a "big bang" solution is highly unlikely in such a context. Proceeding in an *iterative manner* that allows for learning and continuous improvement over time seems to be the principle of smart implementation instead. The example of providing only the IT-systems and to hope for the best, or worst, of the application is a point in case. Although the activities described above are ongoing, the available evidence suggests that continuous mentoring by locally based advisors (embeddedness) is the only viable approach in fragile environments. The fact that mining licenses continued to be processed in MCAS during the Ebola crisis is one such point of illustrative evidence.

It is also clear that capacity-development activities – such as the ones discussed in this paper – require *integrating technical, political, process, and organizational development advice*. This means that GIZ advisors have to show flexibility in taking on different roles at different times in the process. The GIZ model of capacity development at different levels is well-suited in this regard. In other words, the success of a technical activity such as mining license management hinges on other activities such as legal/procedural reform and individual/institutional capacity development. Ideally, the overall sequence will be designed in a way that puts relatively easy quick-wins first (IT-solution in this case) and then use the momentum to address the harder procedural issues. However, care needs to be taken not to wait too long with the latter, because ultimately it is determinant of final success. Furthermore, program managers need to be given leeway to shift programmatic focus in consultation with their partners, if they feel that insufficient progress is being made or if new opportunities emerge during implementation. Such learning – and the ability to adapt to ever-shifting circumstances – is another important element of smart implementation. Overall, this kind of *incremental engagement* has essentially been the implementation approach used by the GIZ Regional Resource Governance program to date, and efforts will be made to further capitalize on the various concurrent support processes ongoing in partnership with the MLME.

Reforming the Legacy of an Authoritarian State: The Case of Tunisia

*Markus Steinich, Thomas Fiegle, Anne Hitzegrad, and Agnes Wiedemann**

Tunisia's revolution in 2011 was triggered by, among other reasons, the public administration's bureaucratic despotism. To address this, Tunisia's new constitution, which was approved in January 2014, contains the guiding principles of democracy and decentralization as well as a public administration at the service of the citizens and the common good. It thus entails a major public-sector reform program that aims at a complete overhaul of the country's public administration and its relationship with the citizens. This leaves the country with an overwhelming implementation challenge.

Financed by the German government,[1] the Deutsche Gesellschaft für Internationale Zusammenarbeit (GIZ) has been supporting governance reforms at the municipal, regional, and national levels in accordance with the new constitution. This article deals with the following four implementation processes:

1. *Governance training for change: How to train Tunisian officials to enable change*
2. *Making a sector ministry fit for decentralization: How to support a disoriented line ministry with a centralistic culture to become an active proponent of local and regional autonomy*
3. *Transforming Tunisia's training center for decentralization: How to improve the response to existing and new training requirements at the municipal, regional, and national levels*
4. *Municipalities acting for tomorrow – Bringing youth to the table: What a "youth-friendly city" can look like, and how stakeholders can contribute to a local youth policy*

---

* All authors are GIZ staff who are currently working – or have worked until recently – in Tunisia: Agnes Wiedemann and Thomas Fiegle work as project directors; Anne Hitzegrad is a governance expert; Markus Steinich is the acting cluster coordinator.
1 GIZ implements the program on behalf of BMZ.

Based on these cases, the following guiding principles for implementation were identified: Trust is necessary to enable the identification of partners' needs; long-term partnerships are useful for trust-building and scaling-up; action-training or training for change increases the possibility of real change; change has to take place on the individual, organizational, and system levels; participation is essential for ownership, integration, and knowledge management; and, finally, cooperation with national and international expertise broadens support quality and coverage.

Context of the case study

Mohamed Bouazizi was one of many young men frustrated by oppression and a lack of prospects. He had complained about harassment by officials on several occasions, but the confiscation of his wares in December 2010 and yet another beating by officials pushed him over the edge. In protest, he set himself on fire in front of the governor's office. In an attempt to calm public outrage, Tunisia's long-time president, Ben Ali, visited the unconscious Bouazizi in the hospital. However, public sympathy and anger inspired by Bouazizi's death finally led to the ousting of Ben Ali and his regime. Uprisings also erupted in other North African and Arab countries, such as Egypt, Libya, and Syria, and collectively became known as the "Arab Spring."

One of the main triggers of Tunisia's Freedom and Dignity Revolution was this despotism of the public administration. Three years after the death of Bouazizi, the revolution's quest for freedom and democracy finally found its expression in Tunisia's new constitution, approved in January 2014. It contains in its guiding principles (Arts. 1–20) the following prescriptions:

- Having taken a leading role during the Arab Spring movement, youth shall be an active force in building the nation (Art. 8).
- The state shall seek to achieve social justice, sustainable development and balance between regions based on development indicators and the principle of positive discrimination (Art. 12).
- The state commits to strengthen decentralization and to apply it throughout the country, within the framework of the unity of the state (Art. 14).

- Public administration is at the service of the citizens and the common good. It is organized and operates in accordance with the principles of impartiality, equality, and the continuity of public services, and in conformity with the rules of transparency, integrity, efficiency and accountability (Art. 15).

Title VII of the constitution (Arts. 131–142) elaborates on the country's new administrative structure and its characteristics:

- Decentralization is achieved through local authorities comprised of municipalities, districts, and regions covering the entire territory of the Republic (see Art. 131).
- Local authorities are headed by elected councils; the electoral law shall guarantee the adequate representation of youth in local councils (see Art. 133).
- Local authorities possess their own powers, powers shared with the central authority, and powers delegated to them from the central government (see Art. 134).
- Local authorities shall have their own resources, and resources provided to them by the central government, these resources being proportional to the responsibilities that are assigned to them by law (see Art. 135).
- Local authorities shall adopt the mechanisms of participatory democracy and the principles of open governance to ensure the broadest participation of citizens and of civil society in the preparation of development programs and land use planning, and follow up on their implementation, in conformity with the law (see Art. 139).

The new constitution thus entails a major public-sector reform program that aims at a complete overhaul of the country's public administration. This presents the country with an overwhelming implementation challenge, given the following features of Tunisia's public administration:

- **State-driven development.** In the 1970s Tunisia adopted a public-sector-led development model. It gave the state an active role in strategic economic sectors. Barriers to entry to large segments of the economy were imposed. Tunisia initially developed well during the 1970s as limited steps were taken to liberalize the economy, notably with the introduction of an "offshore"/privileged export regime, combined with pro-active government industrialization policies. However, when Tunisia was hit by a severe economic crisis in the 1980s, the limits of the state-led economic model started to emerge. The government reacted by opening up parts of the economy in the late 1980s and 1990s with an offshore sector under consolidation and as part of a process of greater integration with the European Union. However, the core thrust of the economic model remained fundamentally unchanged, as the state retained close control of most of the domestic economy. Today, more than 50 percent of the Tunisian economy is still either closed or subject to entry restrictions. Furthermore, state-owned enterprises (SOEs) hold between 50 and 100 percent of the markets for air transport, railroad transport, electricity, gas, and fixed-line telecommunication. Many SOEs act as monopolists in the production, import, and/or distribution of various goods (e.g., olive oil, meat, and sugar) (World Bank, 2014b).

- **The bloated scale of the civil service sector.** The size of the civil service sector reflects the important role of the state for the country's development. As universities have failed to produce graduates with the qualifications required by the local economy, the state has become an employer of last resort since the turn of this century. Public-sector staff numbers have almost doubled since 2000, with a total today of around 580,000 civil servants in public administration and around 150,000 in SOEs. This number increased more rapidly following the revolution, when municipal temporary workers "managed" to join the long-life employment of the civil service. To compensate people who had suffered from Ben Ali's oppression, they were offered employment in the government sector. In addition, the incoming Islamist party, Ennahda, tried to penetrate the system with its own followers (Brockmeyer, Khatrouch, & Raballand, 2014; Union Tunisienne du service public et de la neutralité administrative, 2016). The fiscal consequences can be seen in 2016's national budget, in which salaries represent 44 percent of total expenditure.

- **Corruption.** The omnipresent nature of the state, coupled with an excessively high number of poorly paid civil servants, reportedly creates a breeding ground for rent-seeking practices. According to a World Bank report:

  > The prevalence of corruption "to speed things up" in Tunisia is among the highest in the world by international standards. More than a quarter of all firms in the World Bank 2014 Investment Climate Assessment declared they have to provide some form of informal payment to accelerate some form of interaction with the administration. The prevalence of

corruption associated with the regulatory burden points to the importance of discretion and arbitrary application of the rules. Hence, in addition to the direct costs, the excessive regulatory environment also stifles competition by allowing inefficient firms to gain unfair advantages via privileges and corruption. These practices have a cost that goes beyond the corruption itself – they prevent the success of the best-performing firms and thereby lower the performance of the entire economy. (World Bank, 2014b)

Corruption as well as discretionary and arbitrary application of the law not only hold true for economic activity but can also be observed in each and every interaction of citizens with the state.

- **A centralized state.** Tunisia remains a highly centralized state, despite the fact that it had 264 municipalities and 24 regional development councils already under Ben Ali's regime. Assignments and resources for the local administrations were limited and dominated by the state. Although there were elections, political competition was rather limited. Municipalities covered only one-third of the country's territory, and one-third of the Tunisian population was unserved by a local administration. Today, municipal investments account for only around 3 percent of national investments, and municipal expenditures only for around 4 percent of total public expenditure (World Bank, 2015). Of Tunisia's 580,000 public servants, only 6,900 (i.e., 1.2%) work for the municipalities (Ministry of the Interior, 2016).
- **Risk-averse administrative culture.** Risk aversion and sector egoism are two more main aspects of Tunisian administrative culture. Barriers to reform are high as a result of a reluctance of staff to take ownership of decision-making, the poor communication about decisions made, the lack of information exchange, and that all decisions have to be approved by the highest authority. This is a result of a hierarchical structure that is typical of public administration but also particularly characteristic of the former authoritarian regime.

Sector egoism goes hand in hand with closed structures and vertical chains of command. Information-sharing, coordination, and cooperation between institutions is lacking. Examples of this include draft laws that are not coordinated between ministries, and monitoring data on public investment projects that is not shared between sectors.

The GIZ good governance project cluster to support public-sector reform

The German government responded to the Tunisian revolution with substantial and flexible project funding. In order to support the implementation of the new constitution, a GIZ project cluster on good governance was set up. GIZ was granted funding from several schemes for the following projects:

- Financed by the regional fund of the German Federal Ministry for Economic Cooperation and Development (BMZ) for the Middle East and North Africa (MENA) region, GIZ was implementing a regional project on municipal cooperation between Moroccan, Tunisian, and Algerian local governments prior to the revolution; initial contacts with the Tunisian Ministry of the Interior had already been established. After the revolution, this project (CoMun – Cooperation with Municipalities) would serve as a platform to host new funding; the first long-term staff arrived in September 2012.
- The German Federal Foreign Office's Transformation Partnership, newly created at the time of the Arab Spring, provided financial support for local democracy formats in selected Tunisian municipalities from mid-2012 onwards; it expanded the range of support for the CoMun project.
- BMZ's Open Regional Fund for Good Governance was managed by GIZ HQ in order to rapidly finance smaller projects (up to €1,000,000), as initiated by projects already under way; CoMun could thus gain funding to support Tunisia's local government association, the Tunisian National Federation of Cities (FNVT – Fédération Nationale des Villes Tunisiennes) and the Ministry of the Interior's decentralization school, the Centre for Training and Support for Decentralization (CFAD – Centre de Formation et d'Appui à la Décentralisation).
- Regional development and the capacities of regional administrations became the focus of a new bilateral project financed by BMZ from the end of 2013 onwards; Germany's technical support thus expanded from the municipal to the regional level.
- In 2014, BMZ started a new type of project funding via its special initiatives. The initiative, "Stability and development in the MENA region," extended the reach of the existing cooperation on regional and municipal governance and ensured funding for Tunisia's newly created International Academy for Good Governance.

After the revolution, GIZ's good governance portfolio in Tunisia had to start from scratch and reached a value of approximately €20 million after four years. The portfolio can be visualized as follows.

Table 1: GIZ's good governance portfolio in Tunisia

	Ministry of Development Started in 2013 • Methodology of regional development planning • Regional Development Strategy	Centre for Training and Support for Decentraliza-tion (CFAD) Started in 2012 • New training topics and formats • E-learning	International Academy for Good Governance Started in 2015 • Training of change agents • Coaching projects for change
NATIONAL LEVEL	Ministries of the Interior, Local Affairs, Finance, as well as other sector ministries Started in 2012 • Legal and institutional framework on decentraliza-tion and deconcentration	• Equipment **Tunisian National Federation of Cities (FNVT)** **Started in 2013** Capacity development for: • lobbying • service delivery • networking	
REGIONAL LEVEL	**Northwestern Governorates (Beja, Siliana, El Kef, Jendouba)** **Central-western Governorates (Kairouan, Kasserine, Sidi Bou Zid),** **Médenine** **Started in 2013** 1. Regional Governance Diagnostics 2. Capacity Development for Regional Development Structures 3. Regional Development Planning 4. Regional Development Project Fund		
MUNICIPAL LEVEL	**Municipalities of Ben Guerdane, Gabès, Gafsa, Jendouba, Kasserine, Menzel Bourguiba, Monastir, Siliana, Sfax, Sousse, Tunis, Le Kef, Kairouan, Beja, Sidi Bou Zid, Tozeur, Thala, Regueb, Sbeitla, Makthar, La Marsa, Testour, Kalaat Landlous, Bizerte** **Started in 2012** 1. One-stop shops/ *Espaces citoyens* 2. Participatory budgeting 3. Participatory planning 4. Young citizen's / Civil society participation 5. Women's participation 6. Municipal networking (Tunisia, Morocco, Algeria, Libya)		

How did this portfolio evolve? What is the strategy and what were the guiding principles? Why those projects, partners, and contents and not others? This story has to be told in three chronological strands that show how the three building blocks of the cluster came into being.

GIZ was working in Tunisia prior to the revolution. The CoMun project had begun to convince Tunisian authorities of the benefits of municipal networking in order to contribute to regional integration and constructive dialogue between the Maghreb countries at a local level. This idea had not been accepted prior to the revolution, but a good relationship was established among important decision-makers in the Ministry of the Interior, which created a good basis for sharing concepts.

The revolution opened up the country to international experiences and fresh ideas, and new cooperation was sought. Networking activities began through conferences in Tunisia and Germany, as well as study trips to the Netherlands and Germany regarding decentralization in those two countries. Following the multi-level approach of GIZ, those measures brought together municipalities and national authorities such as the Ministry of the Interior, CFAD, and FNVT right from the start. A policy dialogue thus evolved and – paired with the flexible funding mechanisms of the German government described above – projects became possible with two major multiplication actors: FNVT as the representative of municipal interests and a national platform for inter-municipal networking; and CFAD as the training institute for municipal human resources. Partnerships on a municipal and national level enabled capacity development in its three dimensions: 1) training for professionals on a pilot basis and its up-scaling via CFAD, 2) organizational development in municipal structures, 3) repositioning of municipalities in a more decentralized system due to the technical dialogue with the Ministry of the Interior, the constitutional assembly, and FNVT.

The second strand, concerning regional development, followed the insight that the marginalization of regions from the interior was a major trigger of the Tunisian revolution. The German government therefore accepted a request from the then Minister for Regional Development for cooperation. This started in 2013 with a focus on two macro-regions that had been agreed upon between the two governments. Here again, in order to shape this cooperation, a multi-level approach and GIZ's capacity-development understanding were combined.

The third strand – the project with the International Academy for Good Governance – started as a project financed by the German Federal Foreign Office and executed by the European Academy of Berlin, a private training institute for adult learning with a focus on European issues. From 2012 onwards, seminars were organized on good governance issues in Berlin. This model came to its limits for three reasons: 1) the academy was supposed to be relocated and based in Tunis in order to allow for more participants; 2) it was supposed to be integrated into existing training institutions in Tunisia; 3) individual learning could not be applied in structures that are not open to new ideas and new practice. In this situation, funding and execution changed: BMZ took over and mandated GIZ, due to its presence in Tunisia and its proven capacity to deal with capacity development beyond the training of individuals.

The portfolio of the cluster is thus the result of an adaptive cooperation management that responds to promising opportunities arising with partner institutions on different levels and builds on key individuals' receptiveness to change. It could not follow a roadmap or a consistent partner policy, as that does not yet exist. But it did follow GIZ's understanding of capacity development and the necessity to be embedded locally, regionally, and nationally, and to connect those three levels in a constructive way.

Tracing the implementation process

GIZ has not yet been able to measure the achievements of projects or policies because it is too soon after the revolution for reforms to have had time to take place. This is also due to our choice of the subject for this article: the implementation of Tunisia's new constitutional agenda on decentralization and good governance. We will therefore describe the processes, in which we are actors, and for which the results are yet unknown. For this purpose, we have selected four implementation processes that are representative of our portfolio in Tunisia. They demonstrate how we work on capacity development, combining the municipal, regional, and national levels.

The four implementation processes that we selected are:

1. Governance training for change
2. Making a sector ministry fit for decentralization
3. Transforming Tunisia's training center for decentralization
4. Municipalities acting for tomorrow: Bringing youth to the table

1. Governance training for change

Tunisia has a tradition of strong administration. This is not only due to French influence during the time of the "Protectorate" but also due to its roots, which go back to Ottoman rule at the end of the 19th century. Senior officials in Tunisian public administration, even today, regard themselves as being in the role of a "steward of the people's welfare," in the tradition of Kheireddine Pacha, a famous Tunisian reformer in 1871. For decades they steered the country's "modernization from above" on behalf of a highly centralized state and a strongly secularized and reform-oriented socio-economic elite. Although this approach and the related social model proved to be beneficial for Tunisia in the first decades following its independence, since the 1980s it has become less relevant. Even before the autocratic turn of Bourguiba's successor Ben Ali, public administration had lost its central role in economic and social development and become confronted with a much more complex and economically difficult environment. In the years of Ben Ali's ruling, the administration lost its credibility among the population due to corruption and nepotism. The result was a profound legitimacy crisis for the political-administrative sector and a deep lack of trust in the state and its agents. This was a cause of the 2011 revolution.

The consequences for the public sector are still being felt today. Public administration is no longer seen by the majority of Tunisians as a force of reform and development but, on the contrary, as a force of resistance, if not corruption. The public administration agents who face public repudiation feel highly disoriented and frustrated. In addition, they are struggling with their changed role in society. Initial and ongoing training in public administration is insufficient and does not address the needs of such a highly conflictual situation.

GIZ discussed this with its partners at the beginning of the process. GIZ supported the view of its Tunisian government partners that the concept of "good governance" – insofar as it de-centers the role of the political-administrative sector in society and stresses the need for collaboration with the private and non-profit sectors in accordance with shared principles and values – could constitute a valuable element of response to this challenge. This has consequences for the training of public officials as well.

Two questions had to be answered. The first one concerns the development challenge of our training project: *How to train Tunisian officials in order to build a modern, citizen-oriented public service based on the principles of good governance?* The second question concerns the implementation challenge: *How to find entry points for change processes in administrative structures and procedures?* Our experiences from other projects showed us that the dimensions, although they can be formally distinguished from each other, are in reality interrelated, so that the implementation challenge has to be integrated in the training process itself.

When we started at GIZ in the beginning of 2015 with the project, the project itself had already been in operation for three years and much experience had been accumulated. From 2012 to 2015, the project was entitled "Tunisian-German Academy of Good Governance," financed by the Germany Federal Foreign Office and executed by the European Academy of Berlin, a private-run institution for political education. The aim was to introduce practitioners from the Tunisian administration and related sectors to the concepts and methods of democratic governance following international standards as well as to give them a practical view of good practices in Germany. Therefore, seminars lasting between one and four weeks each were organized at the site of the European Academy of Berlin – a beautiful old villa in the Berlin quarter of Grunewald. In the three years, more than 270 people participated. All the participants of these seminars reported that not only had they learned a lot but that the vision of their job as a state agent had changed in a significant way. They were enormously impressed by what they had seen and learned in Germany and were impatient to put all this into action once they were back to Tunisia.

However, back in Tunis they found several obstacles to implementing change. Many of the participants' offices are in poor condition and badly equipped. Their supervisors were resistant to change, and their colleagues were demotivated. They had to work with dysfunctional old structures and procedures. The initial enthusiasm gave way to frustration.

This was the situation when GIZ took over the project at the beginning of 2015.[2] It was clear that it was necessary to readjust the concept of the project: How would it be possible to achieve changes, not only at the level of the knowledge and competencies of people, but also at the level of the so-called collective brain of the organizations these people were working in? In addition, the Tunisian partner, the Services of Good Governance at the Presidency of the Government, wanted more people to benefit from the training and for the Academy to be located in Tunisia. The Services of Good Governance also expected cooperation with the European Academy of Berlin and the study missions in Berlin to be maintained, as they had

---

2 This occurred when, for formal reasons, the project could no longer be financed by the German Foreign Office and was passed over to the BMZ.

had good experiences with it – thus the ties of trust between the directors of the academy and the Tunisians had been built.

When the decision was taken that the new academy would be located in Tunis, there arose another question: Should this Academy be an institution on its own or should it be hosted within an already existing structure? Two options were considered. The first, favored by GIZ, was to build a small but smart training institution with innovative methods in order to train a small number of people as change agents who had already demonstrated the capacity to achieve concrete changes at the organizational level. The second option, preferred by the Tunisian government, was to establish a more conventional training unit enabling a larger number of trainees to benefit. The first option was chosen, and it was decided to host the academy at the Tunisian National School for Administration (ENA) in order to make it operational as quickly as possible. In doing so, we profited from the experiences of GIZ in the domains of training and organizational development. We were able to benefit from the multi-level approach of capacity-building that is commonly used by GIZ.

Two factors enabled the government to follow GIZ's recommendation. Firstly, a Scientific Committee was established with about 20 members from several ministries, state agencies, civil society, trade unions and employers' federations, which helped to establish a constructive discourse among the different stakeholders about training for change. The second factor was that GIZ could refer to the proven experiences of such a small-scale training institute, the Academy for Leadership of Baden-Württemberg, the training institution for higher-level public servants in southwestern Germany. The particular characteristic of this institution is that it offers training courses for higher-level public officials of the region, coupled with organizational development of the region's public administration. The participants develop and implement a real change project ordered and mandated by the government of Baden-Württemberg. The way the state (*Land*) of Baden-Württemberg and the Leadership Academy have organized this process served as a practical inspiration for what we wanted to achieve in Tunisia. The concept for the new Tunis-based academy, now called the International Academy for Good Governance, was developed through a workshop with the members of the Scientific Committee in May 2015, in collaboration with the Academy for Leadership of Baden-Württemberg.

The first training program for "change agents" in Tunis was planned for autumn 2015 for a group of 25 to 35 participants from public administration, the private sector, and civil society. In July 2015 the Tunisian Ministry of Health mandated the first training program in the area of "Public procurement and management of conflicts of interest in the health sector" and undertook to support the change project that the trainees were to implement upon completion of the course.

This training phase of approximately seven months contained three modules: an introduction to the concept of good governance to international standards; procurement rules and practices in Tunisia; and the management of conflicts of interests in Tunisia and in other countries. Workshops were facilitated by international trainers on leadership, change management, and communication skills. There were two technical missions to Germany: one in cooperation with the Academy for Leadership, and one with the European Academy of Berlin.

Beside the Health Ministry, the Tunisian procurement agency was very much interested in this program. With the support of this agency and its trainers – who already had received a training of the trainers seminar financed by another international donor – it was possible to quickly realize a second program of high quality. A positive unintended side effect was that the representatives of the Health Ministry, who were skeptical regarding the application of Tunisian procurement rules to the health sector – insisting on what they called its "sectoral specificity" and asking for exceptions from these rules – entered into a real dialogue with their Tunisian colleagues from the procurement agency. The Academy was thus able to contribute, albeit unintentionally, to addressing one of the main deficiencies of the Tunisian administrative: its strong sectoralization and the lack of horizontal communication between and within different public services.

The 35 participants are now due to present their "change project" to the Tunisian Minister of Health. Thus, a new and interesting phase of cooperation begins – the action part. The change project contains concrete measures of reform concerning the Tunisian health administration – with indicators and a time schedule so that it can be evaluated. The implementation of this "change project" will be somewhat unpredictable, just as the academy project was, and will need a flexible and adaptive approach from the project managers and the Tunisian partners.

2. Making a sector ministry fit for decentralization

Regional inequalities were one of the triggers of the revolution. The interior regions are less developed than the coastal area, according to all indicators, including unemployment rates, school-dropout rates, and availability of medical services. To address this, granting the regions greater autonomy to make their own development decisions, using their own resources, is thus a major objective of Tunisia's decentralization policy, as enshrined in the 2014 constitution.

But this linkage did not seem to be evident to line ministries for several reasons:

- Since independence, regional planning and development has followed a top-down approach that has prioritized a sector focus rather than regional interests.
- There is skepticism by the central authority about the ability of the regions to make rational choices regarding their development priorities and investment projects. Officials in the center are still convinced that central planning is superior to "local irrationality."
- The implementation of the constitution is perceived as a long-term issue with many technical challenges that need to be addressed.
- The topic appeared to be owned by the Ministry of the Interior, a strong player that is not easy to cooperate with.

When GIZ began work with the Ministry of Development in 2013, its administrative system as a whole was paralyzed due to a lack of political leadership following the revolution. This was due to a rapid succession of new governments (there have been seven governments since the revolution in January 2011) and the dominance of overarching topics such as security, the constitutional process, the national dialogue, and the preparation of national elections for the end of 2014. The ministry itself has gone through several restructurings. Originally founded as the Ministry for Regional Development after the revolution, it then merged with the Ministry for Cooperation and International Development in February 2013, became part of the Ministry of Economy and Finance in 2014, and was reinstalled as the Ministry of Development, Investment and International Cooperation in 2015.

The ministry's five-year development plan was abandoned in the aftermath of the revolution. New initiatives such as a national consultation process in 2012 on regional development and the elaboration of a white book on the topic did not succeed in giving a new orientation to the sector's policy and structure, since they did not become national priorities.

This is the context in which the GIZ project began work on achieving its objective: the improvement of institutional conditions for more effective and participatory regional development. With the new constitution voted in 2014 and a unanimous discussion in the constitutional assembly on this issue, working on institutional conditions could only mean supporting the ministry's work on decentralization questions. The main implementation question thus was: *How to get a "disoriented" line ministry with centralistic habits to become an active proponent of more local and regional autonomy?* This is the implementation process we are interested in regarding our case study. We will look at it from three perspectives: a) tool adaptation, b) institutional reorientation, and c) policy-making.

a) Tool adaptation

Before the revolution, five-year planning was a top-down process dominated by line ministries and centered on a list of infrastructure projects. This practice stopped after the revolution. It was not until 2015 that the government would restart a new national development plan.

After the revolution, GIZ worked with the Ministry of Environment on a regional plan for the environment and sustainable development with four regions. It soon transpired that the regions wanted a new way of regional planning that would: be more participatory, integrated, and not sectoral; involve a thorough analysis of a region's comparative advantages; and propose projects and reforms based on a regional vision. GIZ developed such a methodology and, together with Swiss Cooperation, helped to elaborate and publish four plans. When the Essid government came to power in January 2015, the new minister for development asked GIZ to advise on the methodology of a new five-year plan. GIZ thus scaled-up its pilot experience and, together with United Nations Development Programme (UNDP), supported all 24 governorates in the development of a new regional development plan to link into the country's five-year plan for 2016 to 2020.

b) Institutional reorientation

The ministry requested staff training as a main focus of the project. A capacity analysis had been conducted in early 2012, financed by an international development bank. However, the results had not been validated and no activities resulted from the assessment. GIZ took this capacity analysis as a starting point and organized a participatory workshop to confirm the main findings. The workshop included representatives of the 24 regional development directorates, the four supra-regional development offices, and the ministry. It resulted in a working plan that envisioned capacity development based on participatory planning, local development planning, regional development data, socio-economic analysis, and group facilitation. Most of training sessions planned used an "action learning" approach and dealt with real-world issues, data, problems, and solutions. Although this was an unfamiliar approach for our partners, it was appreciated.

The 2012 capacity analysis hinted at structural problems that could not be overcome by the training of individuals alone. This included inefficient communication between different managerial levels, and the lack of consistency between procedures. The ministry also suffered from the weaknesses that plague public administration in general: overstaffing, hierarchical decision-making, risk-aversion, and over-bureaucratization.

GIZ therefore proposed training courses that were combined with public administration change projects, for which organizational development support would be provided by GIZ advisors. The ministry accepted the proposal. Representatives of all three levels of the ministry were selected to participate in a series of five training modules delivered by a Tunisian and a German expert. After the training, small-scale change projects on process management and decision-making were defined, with coaching support from the trainers. This was thus another training innovation with regard to the existing practice, as the issuing of a diploma does not mark the end of the training.

The capacity analysis and the validation workshop also highlighted problems with the ministry's external relationships – unclear task assignments and unclear relationships with the regional units of other ministries and the governorate administration. Moreover, the new constitution required that the ministries' deconcentrated structure would have to reposition itself toward the regions and districts as new levels of decentralization.

The ministry asked the GIZ project to finance a study on the issue. However, GIZ instead proposed a working group comprising of staff from the ministry and its regional structures. The group was selected by the Director General for Regional Development and met five times over several days. It commenced with an assessment of the current situation, worked on a new definition of missions, discussed international experiences that were made available thanks to a partnership with the Organisation for Economic Co-operation and Development (OECD) and the Forum of Federations, and laid down its recommendations in a final document for the minister ("*Rapport du Processus de Réflexion sur le Repositionnement des SDR: Les Structures de Développement Régional – Etat des lieux et perspectives de réformes*"). This format of an inter-organizational working group had several positive effects: It made representatives of the partner structure work on the future of their own organization, ensuring ownership of findings and recommendations; it permitted communication between the ministry, development offices, and regional development directorates; and, above all, it was a space to reestablish orientation in a difficult transition period.

The sequence of activities was probably not optimal. From an organization development perspective, it would be normal practice to begin with the redefinition of roles and missions, followed by addressing organizational issues. The training modules should have then been developed based on the requirements of the different posts. However, GIZ had to first demonstrate that it could meet the request of the ministry, which was training for individuals. Once the partner was convinced on the usefulness of the chosen approach and GIZ's capacity to implement it, the partner requested to work on roles and missions. With this experience, the ministry gradually agreed to follow the organizational development approach.

c) Policy-making for decentralization

Again the initial request from the ministry was for training only. However, again, GIZ proposed an action-learning approach through a working group. An interministerial group was established comprising the Ministry of Development, the Ministry of the Interior, and the Ministry of Finance and Equipment. The group was mandated to develop recommendations for the country's decentralization policy from a regional development perspective. It addressed development planning, territorial reform, task assignments and financing, citizen's participation, and restructuring of the ministry's deconcentrated structure. The working group was supported by an international expert and participated in a study trip to Germany to better understand regional development in a decentralized system. After several working sessions, the group produced a paper to describe the proposal of the Ministry of Development for the country's decentralization policy ("*Pistes d'orientation sur la décentralisation au service du développement régional. Synthèse des travaux d'un groupe de travail interministériel*"). The working group put an emphasis on the state's deconcentrated structure at the governorate level in order to make government action on regional development more coordinated and coherent.

A research project was conducted in order to improve understanding of the regional governance; the juxtaposition of the governors and their administrations; deconcentrated structures of national ministries and the regional council; planning practice; staffing; and the performance in development project management. It was conducted in 8 of the 24 governorates. The findings were discussed during a workshop hosted by the Ministry of Development, our project partner, and the Ministry of the Interior, lead manager in the field. The workshop concluded that line ministries would also have to be involved in decentralization issues since they should devolve responsibilities to local governments and strengthen their presence on the regional level with more consistent deconcentration. Another interministerial working group of 10 line ministries was therefore formed. It exchanged experiences on deconcentration. It mandated an international expert group to work on a charter of deconcentration and a new definition of the role of the governor.

This example reveals interesting implementation aspects:

- A constant and transparent dialogue with the strong Ministry of the Interior encouraged it to host a joint workshop with a rather weak Ministry of Development.
- This workshop started to open up the very closed Ministry of the Interior to other ministries.
- The ministries defined their needs for discussion and support together, thereby avoiding parallel and irrelevant studies or legal drafting.
- Based on the defined needs, an international expert group could advise on the rather delicate question of the state apparatus on the regional level and the future of the governor.

- German, Swiss, and Tunisian expertise facilitated the acceptance of the French expert, who was particularly interesting due to the common administrative legacy: France's reform process since 1983 and the country's outspoken practice on deconcentration.

3. Transforming Tunisia's Centre for Training and Support for Decentralization

With the mandate to train local authorities, CFAD should respond to the demands of municipalities. In the political turmoil of recent years, CFAD has not yet found its role in the transformation process and is currently facing a big challenge: to get closer to its local clients and to respond to the higher demands of cities, which want to be trained on conventional subjects, such as finance and IT, as well as on new themes deriving from the new constitution, such as local governance and public management.

To enable CFAD to improve its performance, qualifications, and responsiveness, it requested GIZ's support in adapting and decentralizing its training offers to meet the requirements of the municipalities.

The new constitution, adopted in January 2014, foresees a highly advanced, decentralized system and emphasizes that "local authorities shall adopt the mechanisms of participatory democracy and the principles of open governance to ensure broader participation of citizens and civil society . . ." Within this context, municipalities play a key role in the process of democratic transition and implementing the decentralization reform. The new legal framework offers a real opportunity to municipalities, but it is difficult for them to meet the new expectations and demands of citizens. Hence, the municipalities urgently need reorientation, awareness-raising, and tailor-made pragmatic tools. They must offer better municipal services, be open to participatory mechanisms, and implement new assigned competences focusing on self-governance.

The constitution requires further qualification measurements taking into account both new themes and new beneficiaries:

- It can be expected that a large number of civil servants at the national level will be transferred to the municipal level. At present, there are around 6,900 civil servants at the local level, compared with 570,000 at the national level. This will increase the need for training.

- The decentralization reform also needs to move along with deconcentration as the foundation for the new setup of local and regional structures. Again, information and training is required at both the local and national levels to better understand each role and support the reforms.
- Tunisia has recently created 86 municipalities. The new Ministry of Local Affairs has requested an emergency plan to train around four executives for each new municipality within six months.
- CFAD will also be a core trainer for around 7,000 municipal councilors and 300 regional councilors in the future. It will need to provide extended trainings to prepare the ground for local and regional elections in 2017.

CFAD is one of the key actors within the decentralization process. However, it currently lacks the information, personnel resources, institutional flexibility, and adaptiveness to satisfy this increased demand. CFAD has a yearly budget of roughly 900,000 Tunisian dinars (about €420,000) earmarked for operations. Although it therefore has the financial resources to undertake some reforms, a lack of staff capacities, centralism, and the absence of an internal strategy hinder change. Internal transformation and fruitful cooperation with other key national stakeholders will be needed to meet the current challenges of new and increased demands. CFAD needs to adapt its courses and internal organization to the new political context. The center also has to be open to making changes in the administrative and institutional cultures within its own structures to prepare for the upcoming tasks, foremost to accompany the local authorities in this transformation process. **To summarize, the center's implementation challenge is to develop mechanisms that will help with responding better to the existing challenges – but also to the new training requirements at the municipal, regional, and national levels – within this decentralized context, and to improve its outreach in the regions.**

To address the abovementioned challenges together, GIZ and CFAD developed their cooperation in different fields. The way the cooperation started illustrates a main approach in this partnership.

The first important entry point for change was to introduce new topics. When GIZ started working with the center in 2012, CFAD asked for awareness courses on "How to introduce participatory approaches" in order to cope with new municipal demands. Hence, the first step was to introduce these approaches to municipalities and anchor them in the annual curricula. This set the basis for the second step: to enlarge the cooperation and tackle sensitive issues such as analyzing the trainer pool and revising internal strategies with the aim of bringing the center closer to its beneficiaries.

CFAD, with the support of GIZ, held several workshops from June 2013 to October 2014 across the whole country, reaching out to large, medium, and small cities. The meetings provided a platform for exchanges on the participatory approach, the constraints of municipalities, and the establishment of participatory mechanisms. These awareness workshops highlighted the need to train local experts in this area in order for them to become mediators in each region. Selected according to specific criteria, candidates came from regions all over Tunisia with extensive field experience and local knowledge. Some of these new trainers were involved in following awareness workshops, and their experiences enriched the debates. This training of trainers was the entry point for CFAD to discover the importance of trainer pools, thus setting the basis for our cooperation in this field. The training and awareness course was supported by a handbook (French/Arabic) on "Local governance and citizen participation in municipal action." This manual was designed for CFAD trainers and was disseminated to all municipalities and civil society wishing to learn more about concepts, frameworks, and tools surrounding local citizen participation. In total, this course reached 225 municipalities (out of the former 264), and the handbook is still being used for follow-up courses on related themes, for example participatory investment plans.

Meanwhile, GIZ is supporting the center on three more aspects: strategy development to improve needs-identification and to respond to local demands, the reinforcement of the trainer pool, and the development of pilot modules. Tunisian experts provide technical advice, in tandem with Tunisian and European experts. They comprise GIZ experts; university professors from Tunisia, Germany, and other European countries; and external practitioners with long-term hands-on experience in the specific fields.

Regarding the first aspect, GIZ advised CFAD to focus on strategic development to regionalize the center and to introduce basic trainings, going beyond the conventional two to three days for advanced trainings. Taking into consideration the feedback of the regions and municipalities, the key questions for CFAD are how to better meet the expectations of the clients and how to bring the center closer to its beneficiaries in the field across Tunisia. CFAD, with the support of GIZ, conducted extended needs assessments in different regions and worked together on improving demand-mechanisms, evaluations, the establishment of a professions cata-log, and an overview of existing modules. Currently, two more joint stud-ies are in process: one on the regionalization of CFAD, another on how to shift from ad hoc to long-term basic courses. The GIZ project is also fos-tering exchange formats between different national institutions and train-ing providers (e.g., ENA and others) to overcome predominant competi-tion among national institutions on new roles and mandates. CFAD has started to think about solution-oriented partnerships between key stake-holders to solve the high number of upcoming tasks and requested the sup-port of universities for the ongoing studies.

The second component deals with reinforcing the CFAD trainer pool. It is based on an analysis of the existing trainer pool, which consists of about 150 temporary staff. Of the 150 trainers, only around 50 could be consid-ered as the *core nucleus*, that is, regularly available for trainings, mostly of administration modules. The study highlighted a lack of thematic diversity as well as communication and pedagogical skills among the trainers. Based on this, CFAD, with the support of GIZ, set up a strategy to develop and reinforce the trainer pool to bind them closer and to train them via "training of trainers" sessions in the field of communication, the concep-tion of modules, and pedagogical approaches. The goal is to set up a quali-fied and reliable trainer pool, a transparent evaluation system to reflect on the trainers' performance, and to facilitate a prestigious certification pro-cess to be recognized by the public sector as a main actor in the career of the civil servants.

Thirdly, new training modules are developed and disseminated on top-ics that include strategic urban planning, archive structures, and communi-cation and conflict management. A training course for general secretaries to become drivers of change when introducing municipal one-stop shops is now being offered. This is being done in close coordination with the GIZ Tunisia governance cluster.

In addition, GIZ supported the IT team of CFAD in the practical han-dling of "e-learning modules," which is a relatively new approach for the training institute. The IT team also received support in facilitating access to e-courses in remote regions.

To conclude, through this collaboration, CFAD has become more recep-tive to the introduction of new training subjects. It recognized the tremen-dous need for capacity development at the local level, as well as the grati-tude of the municipalities toward CFAD when responding to their needs.

This gave an enormous internal motivational boost, and the center is now approaching the necessary internal steps: the organizational development and regionalization of the center itself, hand in hand with the setup of a reliable and qualified trainer pool at the national and local levels. Consultations with key stakeholders on inter-Tunisian cooperation with other training institutes, such as ENA and universities, are in process. Staff members, including the Director-General himself, have participated in new pilot modules, thus discovering and experiencing modern participatory learning methodologies. We observed the beginning of an institutional cultural change by disseminating information, organizing regular team meetings, and realizing the importance of coordination with other national institutions to address the tasks together. So, CFAD is beginning to transform itself in order to better support local authorities with their necessary institutional and cultural changes toward a profound decentralization of the country.

4. Municipalities acting for tomorrow: Bringing youth to the table

More than half of Tunisia's population is under 30 years old, and it was mainly the country's youth who went to the streets to protest against the Ben Ali regime in January 2011. Six years after the revolution, they impatiently await the political reforms and tangible changes in their living conditions. From their point of view, social inclusion and the demand for more democracy are interlinked, as both topics were at the core of the Arab Spring movement.

Youth unemployment – one of the triggers of the protest movement in 2011 – continued to increase and was at 33.2 percent in 2013 for those aged 15 to 29, with numbers being even higher among young women and among young people in urban areas (World Bank, 2014a). The newly gained political freedoms led to an increase in civil society organizations in some places. However, other, more deprived parts in the west and south of Tunisia remain partially excluded from this development. Although the constitution (see Art. 8, Art. 131) explicitly stipulates youth participation, the direct participation of youth in politics is low overall, despite their leading role in the revolution and their strong presence in the burgeoning civil society.

The expectations of the young and well-educated Tunisian population toward the state are high, whereas their lack of trust toward institutions and political decision-makers remains unaltered. Moreover, the traditionally paternalist attitude toward young people as being those who "still need to learn" can make a fruitful dialogue complicated. This is particularly true for local politics. Young people are eager to shape their own futures and environments, and they can easily get frustrated when they feel that their concerns are not being taken into account.

The topic of citizen participation is increasingly attracting the attention of municipalities in post-revolutionary Tunisia under the pressure of the ongoing social uprisings. However, although the young people's demands for social inclusion and democracy were well received by the majority of the population, it often remains unclear to local authorities how to respond. Youth policy has not been among their assigned tasks, so far. Viewing citizen participation as an asset to local politics – and seeing young citizens as a major target group in this context – is a new and unfamiliar idea for mayors and municipal employees. **The development challenge we are dealing with here is creating a common understanding of what a "youth-friendly city" could look like and how different stakeholders could contribute to a local youth policy.**

Within this context, GIZ supports its partner cities to involve youth in developing their local environments. **The implementation challenge is to successfully pilot concrete formats of youth participation on site and to induce a reflection process among the involved partners.**

As a starting point, partner cities were supported to conduct a stakeholder analysis on the topic of youth participation in 2012. Among the main findings were a lack of belief in the capacities of young people to develop and implement meaningful projects, a lack of dialogue between local stakeholders, and a lack of funding and infrastructure for youth participation. Therefore, GIZ supported the partner cities in offering achievable, tangible, and visible measures in order to make young people feel that local politics have opened up and that their ideas and commitments for change are welcome.

- Idea competition for youth initiatives:
  The municipality launched a call for micro-projects and selected several of them in a transparent process. These selected projects were entirely led by young people, including budget responsibility, and involved other young people in a participative manner. Examples of winning ideas include blogging on civil society activities, election simulations, and internships at the municipality.

- Dialogue between mayor and young citizens:
  The mayor invited young people for dialogue and defined, together with them, which topics they wanted to tackle. Dialogue activities have taken place on youth-relevant topics on local radio, cultural activities have been created for the public space, and dialogues on environmental issues have been held, among other activities.

In order to facilitate practical exchanges, networking activities are offered in close cooperation with FNVT and CFAD. In this framework, stakeholders present their pilot projects on youth participation, capitalize on innovative approaches (e.g., by developing a guide on the idea competition for youth initiatives), and participate in study tours and training courses. The common training courses for municipal staff, youth center staff, non-governmental organization representatives, and young leaders aim at reinforcing capacities to set up local youth action plans. These are meant to be the beginning of a strategy on how to permanently and sustainably integrate young citizens into the process of building their local realities.

How did we steer the implementation process?

- A **multi-actor approach** has enabled stable cooperation with the partner cities. This is to prevent the risk of cooperation coming to an end due to changes in personnel at the partner level, and to integrate different stakeholders and different points of view. Local authorities suffer from a lack of resources and qualified staff, especially when it comes to new policy fields. Cooperation tends to depend on one person, who is already overburdened with other tasks.
- It has been a great advantage to work with **small-scale activities**, such as micro-projects and dialogue events on the local level. Typically, these are **low-cost measures**, which partners can easily put into place or replicate using their own scarce financial resources. Furthermore, small-scale activities lead to **quick and visible results**. Tunisian municipal councils are currently appointed and discharged for political reasons, and are therefore not able to engage in long-term planning. Additionally, young people are impatient to see tangible changes and might lose trust when these take time. Small hands-on measures, such as the idea competition for youth initiatives and the dialogue activities, respond to these requirements. Support measures with a longer time

frame, such as the preparation of the local youth action plan, need to plan longer-term practical implementation activities in order to keep everybody on board.

- It has been particularly important to identify **partners who are personally convinced** of the added value of youth participation **and committed to engaging in a dialogue that connects with young people**. As a consequence of the high degree of administrative centralization, local authorities are likely to understand their role as being an implementer of policies set at a higher level rather than as an actor for local change. Only in a longer relationship and with flexibility to support partners in a demand-driven approach could they **proactively promote their own ideas**.

- It has been crucial to start very **modest partnerships** on an activity or micro-project level and to accompany partners with clarifying roles and responsibilities. Due to sector thinking and "administrative habits," local authorities have little experience with engaging in partnerships with other local actors. Municipalities, youth centers, and civil society organizations within one city are typically not used to cooperating with those from another.

- The different stakeholders involved need to **overcome mistrust** – and even envy – before they really **commit to an action plan** and feel **ownership** of their common project. From a short-term perspective, it has been extremely motivating for them to manage an activity or a project together and to experience the added value of collaboration with partners from different backgrounds. Over the long run, the cities noticed a considerable improvement in the levels of trust between young people and municipalities, as well as the practical networking and ownership of the youth involved.

Lessons from the case study

Based on this description of four implementation processes in Tunisia – all aimed at putting the new constitution into practice – we conclude the following guiding principles for our work:

- **Trust allows for the identification of partners' needs**: Following the revolution and its aftermath, Tunisia is being confronted with issues that were hitherto completely unknown, such as creating transparency, citizens' participation, organizational development, and inter-agency cooperation. In this situation, partners can find it difficult to articulate their demands. They do not know what to ask for. Building trust and confidence is then essential to generate a discussion about needs and possible solutions, and this was the first step in all cases. Tunisia had never explicitly asked for a change academy, organizational development, a municipal youth policy, or for one-stop shops. Reacting positively and competently to the partners' requests for training set the stage for a deeper understanding of what partners needed and what international cooperation could deliver. It has been crucial to start very modest partnerships on an activity or micro-project level and to accompany partners with clarifying roles and responsibilities.

- **The ability to offer a long-term partnership** with key Tunisian partners proved to be an important element in building solid, trusting relationships, thus providing the conditions needed to tackle the "real" – often inner-institutional – challenges hindering reforms. Yet, a **long-term presence and commitment** were not only helpful for trust-building but also for other effects: They made it possible to pilot a new regional planning format that proved its feasibility and acceptance on the ground; the planning format gained the government's attention and was eventually replicated all over the country. A long-term presence also proves necessary when (cultural) changes take place gradually, as in the case of the municipal youth policy.
- **Action-training or training for change** makes real change more likely. Theoretical learning, in contrast, poses two transfer problems: Cognitively, participants do not learn to connect to real-world issues; and in organizational terms, the working environment can be hostile to knowledge application. This was the major insight, which drove the reorientation of the International Academy for Good Governance to an academy of change.
- **Change has to take place on the individual, organization, and system levels**. Only when qualified individuals, organizations that allow for change, and systems with well-placed organizations come together will capacity-development measures have a significant development impact. Working on these three levels has been possible with the Ministry of Development, as well as the training center, CFAD.
- **Participation was a main cooperation principle and proved to be essential for ownership, integration, and knowledge management**: Partners initially asked for studies and were not aware that their learn-

ing and decision-making cannot be substituted by external expertise. Multi-actor formats thus showed three advantages: Decisions remain with local actors, they bring about greater cooperation among the key players, and they use local knowledge. Examples from the case study include the Scientific Committee of the International Academy for Good Governance, the inter-agency working group on the future of Tunisia's development offices, the interministerial working group on deconcentration, the working group of training providers, and the municipal steering committees for one-stop shops.

- Finally, **cooperation with national and international expertise increases support quality and expands coverage**. The Academy for Leadership of Baden-Württemberg was useful as a living example of what an academy of change might look like; only by collaborating with UNDP could GIZ offer support to all governorates in regional planning; the OECD brought international experiences on regional development agencies; and, finally, a German training center shared with a Tunisian training center its experiences of training for decentralization.

References

Brockmeyer, A., Khatrouch, M., & Raballand, G. (2014). *Les systèmes de gestion des carrières et de la performance dans la fonction publique en Tunisie*. Washington, DC: World Bank.

Ministry of the Interior. (2016). *Etude sur la fonction publique locale*. Tunis: Author.

Union Tunisienne du service public et de la neutralité administrative. (2016). *Enquête – l'administration tunisienne au temps de la troika*. Retrieved from http://fr.africati me.com/tunisie/articles/enquete-ladministration-tunisienne-au-temps-de-la-troika-i-le-demembrement

World Bank. (2014a). *Breaking the barriers to youth inclusion*. Retrieved from http://w ww.worldbank.org/en/country/tunisia/publication/tunisia-breaking-the-barriers-to-y outh-inclusion

World Bank. (2014b). *The unfinished revolution. Bringing opportunity, good jobs and greater wealth to all Tunisians*. Retrieved from http://www.worldbank.org/en/count ry/tunisia/publication/unfinished-revolution

World Bank. (2015). *Note de d'orientation sur le financement des collectivités locales*. Retrieved from http://documents.worldbank.org/curated/en/549571467998495046/ Tunisie-Note-dorientation-sur-le-financement-des-collectivites-locales

Smart Implementation of Public Service Administration Reform in South Africa: Experiences from the Governance Support Programme

*Godje Bialluch, Lisa Hiemer, Ruan Kitshoff, and Tobias Tschappe**

Executive Summary

Cooperation between South Africa and Germany in the area of governance and administration reform started in 1994. Since then, a number of Technical Cooperation programs have been implemented by the Deutsche Gesellschaft für Internationale Zusammenarbeit (GIZ) GmbH on behalf of the German government.[1] In one way or the other, these programs targeted public service administration on the national, provincial, or local levels with the aim of supporting the reform of public-sector institutions and, eventually, the improvement of service delivery to the citizens of South Africa. In addition to focusing on the further development of technical capacities, emphasis was increasingly given to fostering cooperation and collaboration among government institutions over the years as well as between state and non-state actors as well as the private sector.

Available facts and figures prove that, overall, South Africa has achieved substantial results since 1994 with regard to improving public service delivery, especially for poor households, although one has to acknowledge that the existing service-delivery level was very low at the time democracy was implemented in 1994.

However, governance challenges remain evident. Among these, the lack of adequate collaboration and coordination between the different spheres of government and a certain attitude of "silo-thinking" continues to present obstacles for the government-wide, evidence-based planning and implementing of policies and strategies in a just, inclusive, and demand-oriented way for all citizens. The vision of transforming the public service

---

* The article is a joint effort of colleagues working in the initiatives that are described in the following text.

1 GIZ implements the program on behalf of BMZ.

151

administration into a responsive, transparent, and development-oriented service provider has not yet been achieved.

Our hypothesis, thus, is that the situation requires a partnership approach that focuses on forging alliances among stakeholders that aims at identifying innovative ways to address governance challenges related to the delivery of public services. Such an approach requires a high level of flexibility in project management and the willingness to take risks and endure setbacks. The core principle of engagement is to stay engaged with a wide array of stakeholders, to enable partner organizations to step outside their own limited spheres of jurisdiction, and to work with others on neutral grounds in order to find new opportunities or solutions.

This case study seeks to illustrate this management approach and philosophy by discussing examples in the area of governance and administration, such as (1) developing a common approach for a government-wide monitoring and evaluation (M&E) system, and (2) introducing community media support. The two examples portray the wide range of themes that technical cooperation supports in governance and administrative reform. In the following, we try to demonstrate that the content of cooperation changes, but that there are a few underlying principles of how the cooperation is molded that remain the same. We argue that these principles of engagement are crucial for overcoming implementation challenges and for achieving results.

In order to supplement the knowledge and experience of the national and seconded GIZ advisors working on the respective initiative, data and information from official sources is presented. In addition, limited interviews with former counterparts and national personnel have been conducted. All of them have had several years of experience in working with GIZ and are no longer actively involved in GIZ-assisted programs.

Extracting the lessons learned from the two examples, we put forward and conclude with five statements, which can give food for thought and guidance when supporting reform processes in the area of governance and administration and beyond. Although extracted from the specific experience of working in South Africa, this essence has indeed greater validity.

It might sound like a truism that the fundamental cognizance is to acknowledge there is no blueprint to support governance reform. Therefore, it is of utmost importance to understand the specific partner country context. A cornerstone of successful reform is mutual trust, and building this requires endurance. Flexibility is crucial, as is the ability to detect the right moment for change and to use it through the right incentives. Comprehensive challenges need comprehensive approaches, which include all levels and all relevant actors. Last but not least, the ability to create secure and neutral spaces where partners can engage freely with each other to explore new ways enables the fostering of trust.

Our comparative analysis of the two case examples reveals five principles of engagement that constitute smart implementation for us:

1. An in-depth understanding of the political and institutional context is paramount in order to accompany national stakeholders in change processes. Beyond understanding the context, advisors need to be able to operate and maneuver within it. This requires skills regarding adeptness to the context that go far beyond analyzing it.
2. A prerequisite to working with partners on transformative change processes is mutual trust and a long-term horizon of engagement.
3. Active presence in the partner's environment is crucial to detect the right moment for offering methods and instruments (e.g., workshops, dialogue series, technical advice, organizational development support) that can bring the process forward.
4. Openness and flexibility to include all relevant stakeholders at all levels is a requirement for creating new alliances that become change agents. The notion here is to be as comprehensive and inclusive as possible. Predetermined exclusions of actors or processes can jeopardize the effort and need to be negotiated. The established long-term trust relationship allows advisors to address such issues with partners.
5. Creating safe and neutral spaces for deliberation and for exploring new ways in addressing challenges is a unique and powerful offer that technical cooperation can provide to national change processes. The role of the advisor here is to be a neutral intermediary and broker of interests.

Introduction to the case study

The Governance Support Programme (GSP) is a partnership program agreed to between the Governments of South Africa and Germany. It is technical cooperation program jointly steered at national level in a partnership between the Department of Public Service and Administration (DPSA), the Department of Cooperative Governance (DCoG), the National Treasury (NT), the Department of Planning, Monitoring and Evaluation (DPME), and GIZ, the latter being responsible for the implementation of the German development contributions on behalf of the German Federal Ministry for Economic Cooperation and Development (BMZ). The GSP implements projects and activities at the national, provincial, and local levels and provides technical, policy, and process advice to support the South African government in addressing systemic shortcomings. The objective of the GSP is that public institutions have improved their service delivery, in cooperation with the private sector and civil society.

With the end of Apartheid in 1994, South Africa embarked on the mammoth task of transforming public service administration into a responsive, transparent, and development-oriented service provider for all citizens. The protagonists of the new administration took up their responsibility with high levels of energy but only limited hands-on experience in how to run a public service, let alone in how to transform a system based on racial segregation and discrimination into one that is inclusive, customer-oriented, and based on democratic values. In addition, the political pressure to address the overwhelming social disparities and deliver on such high expectations in due time was tremendous.

Development cooperation between Germany and South Africa in the area of governance and administration started in those early days, as a high-ranking counterpart recalls: "When Madiba[2] visited the foreign embassies in Pretoria asking for support, the Germans were immediately ready and offered to engage. They haven't left us since then."

Another common feature is the multi-level approach in program design. Most programs targeted public service administration at the national, provincial, or local levels, with a particular implementation focus in the two provinces of Mpumalanga and the Eastern Cape. The overall aim of engagement is to support the reform of the public administration and improve service delivery to the citizens of South Africa. During the last decade, support to strengthen cooperation between state and non-state actors as well as the private sector was taken aboard to enable achievement of the ultimate aim as a matter of joint effort.

Available facts and figures prove that, overall, public service delivery in South Africa has made substantial progress since 1994, especially for poor households. Access to formal housing increased from 65 percent to 78

---

2 The former South African president and icon of the struggle against Apartheid, Nelson Mandela, is commonly called Madiba.

percent, electricity from 58 percent in 1996 to 85 percent in 2013, and access to piped water and sanitation facilities from 82 percent to 90 percent, respectively (Statistics South Africa, 2011). However, unemployment rates, especially among young people, remain high: Officially, 25 percent of the workforce is unemployed, while at the same time employers complain about a lack of skilled workers (BusinessTech, 2015). The future holds even bigger challenges, since economic growth has slowed significantly since 2008 and only amounted to around 0.7 percent in 2016 (Statistics South Africa, n.d.). The general economic and financial forecast paints a quite bleak picture of South Africa impeding on the government's ability to provide more and better services to more people. At the same time, it can be observed that a number of major governance challenges remain, or even worsen, such as the political influence on administrative decision-making processes, the weakening of checks-and-balances mechanisms, inadequate collaboration and coordination between the different spheres of government (silo-thinking attitude),[3] and, consequently, insufficient government-wide, evidence-based planning, implementation, and monitoring of interventions. These governance and management challenges constitute major obstacles for implementing policies and strategies, and eventually contribute to undermining South Africa's endeavor for a just, inclusive, and demand-oriented service delivery to all citizens. The vision of transforming the public service administration into a responsive, transparent, and development-oriented service provider has yet to be achieved.

South African–German development cooperation operates in this space and has to deal with these challenges continuously. Our hypothesis, thus, is that the situation requires a partnership approach that can be characterized by a high level of mutual trust and the willingness to also cooperate on topics that are politically sensitive. Such a partnership requires a high degree of flexibility and the readiness to take the risk of being innovative in implementing projects while at the same time enduring setbacks and staying engaged, despite the fact that implementation might not yield immediate tangible results. It also needs the ability to forge new alliances by enabling partner organizations to step outside their own limited spheres of jurisdiction, engage with relevant stakeholders on neutral grounds, and think afresh. Finally, it needs creative thinking to identify incentives (i.e.,

---

3 The list does not aim to be comprehensive.

the right trigger points) that encourage partners to step out of their comfort zones and try different approaches. Such an approach requires trustful relationships on the personal as well as institutional levels in order to enable GIZ, as an external partner, to operate in a space characterized by the governance challenges outlined above.

This article argues that the role that GIZ has been playing over the last 20 years in South Africa as a true partner is not just due to acting as an appreciated partner that is valued for providing technical expertise when required, but in particular for its soft skills as a neutral intermediary and broker of interests between stakeholders. The importance of this partnership approach has been confirmed in interviews and discussions with counterparts, who have long-term, tacit knowledge in cooperation programs. As one partner concluded: "GIZ's partnership approach helped me, in the space I occupied as Deputy Director-General and Director-General, to grow professionally and personally."[4]

This case study seeks to explore the hypothesis highlighted above on the essentials of the South African–German partnership through two concrete examples gained from cooperating in the area of governance and administration. We have chosen initiatives that have been implemented during more recent years and are still ongoing: 1) the support of a common approach for a government-wide M&E system, and 2) community media support in the Eastern Cape province.

Although the two examples portray the wide range of technical cooperation areas in governance and administrative reform, we strive to prove that the approach and attitude to cooperation and means to overcoming implementation challenges remain the same, that is, the "what" might be different, but the "how" remains the same golden thread running through the examples.

Examples

The examples we have chosen illustrate the varied and rather technical challenges with which our partner organizations are confronted. However, although the subject matter ("hard issues") differs in each case, the con-

---

4 In the course of writing the article, we conducted interviews with counterparts who had been working with different GIZ programs during the last 20 years.

textual conditions ("soft issues") hindering progress are similar in both cases. Thus, the approaches applied for overcoming the individual challenges bear similarities.

(1) Support of a common approach for a government-wide M&E system

In 2005 the South African Cabinet approved the development of a government-wide monitoring and evaluation system as a "system of systems" drawing on existing M&E systems and data on the public sector and the country. The objective was to improve evidenced-based planning and implementation of policies for public service delivery. Nevertheless, by early 2011 it became apparent that the focus on M&E had caused a proliferation of systems and that coherence and integration among these systems was lacking. This lack of well-functioning monitoring systems and practices led to the deficient implementation of policies, which negatively affected the delivery of public services. Furthermore, in the absence of structured and planned program evaluations, it remained difficult to assess the impact of policies and make informed policy decisions. As a consequence, the effects of efforts to improve public service delivery, or the understanding of its strengths and shortcomings, remained unsatisfactory.

The above situation was exacerbated by contestation between different national ministries regarding mandates for the whole of government M&E system(s). For example, the DPME, the DPSA, the NT, the Public Service Commission (PSC), as well as the Offices of the Premier in the provinces individually monitored the ministries and required them to report. Municipalities had an added burden of reporting to the DCoG at the national as well as the provincial level. GIZ was a partner to all these departments as well as to the National School of Government – the state-owned public-service training institute – and received numerous requests to assist these departments in building their M&E capacities and systems.

Against this background, the need for consolidation and coordination around M&E was apparent, as was the need for GIZ to support this process in a manner that facilitated a common process toward M&E systems development. Soon it became evident that crucial "soft-issues" hindered the progress of developing government-wide M&E systems. These challenges were the competition for roles and mandates, a lack of communication and coordination between the different actors, as well as a lack of trust in the competence of others. As a consequence, this silo-thinking attitude was consolidated, that is, there was planning and implementation of individual initiatives without considering other stakeholders. These implementation challenges had to be overcome first to level the ground for the development of a joint vision and common approach.

The partnership approach of GIZ – following the principle of forging alliances among stakeholders aiming at identifying innovative ways to address existing challenges – proved to be key in this situation. As the case study shows, GIZ advisors engaged with a high level of flexibility in project management and with endurance. They acted as neutral brokers and, by doing so, created neutral grounds to enable partners to cooperate with each other outside their own limited spheres of jurisdiction. In other situations, they provided hands-on technical and/or process advice and, by doing so, furthered the decision-making process among partners. This mix of different roles was possible due to the high level of trust, which derived from the fact that the engagement was long-term.

When GIZ received the requests from its government partners to render support to improve their M&E systems, a first step was to convene a meeting with all parties involved to map already ongoing developments and compile the individual requests for support. The meeting took place at a GIZ office and was facilitated by a GIZ advisor. In this way, a neutral space was created that offered the actors an opportunity to engage freely and on eye-level with each other, without any of them taking a more prominent role or being inhibited by government protocol. The mapping exercise clearly revealed the fragmentation of the different M&E systems and, consequently, the need for a single department to take the lead in coordinating a harmonized approach was raised. But the meeting also revealed institutional challenges that needed attention in order to take the process forward, for example:

• There was uncertainty about which of the government institutions had the mandate to coordinate M&E for the entire public administration. The DPSA and the PSC "accused" the DPME of "mandate creep," that is, questioning the fact that the DPME holds the mandate to coordinate. However, after a facilitated discussion among stakeholders, the meeting designated that the DPME would lead the process going forward toward a coherent M&E system while respecting the particular mandates of other departments.

- Training programs of the National School of Government[5] were discredited as not being sufficiently tailored to the demands of public service and as being insufficiently aligned with the new outcomes approach introduced by the South African National Development Plan.
- GIZ had to acknowledge that it had itself contributed toward the fragmentation of the M&E system by previously supporting individual departments and provinces in developing their own systems. To address this problem, GIZ proposed to partners that, from then on, all requests for M&E support should be handled by a single body, which was called the "core group." Partners endorsed this proposal.

The meeting and decisions taken were an eye-opener and underlined the clear additional benefit for all actors to be able to engage with each other on a neutral platform and to think and work outside their own areas of jurisdiction ("think outside the box") about matters of common concern. At first sight, although individual partners might have lost their prior individual benefits, the new approach provided more transparency and coherence while still being flexible enough to accommodate individual demands in the core group. The major incentive, however, was that partners realized that, through the new approach, they would all benefit from the envisaged capacity-development support.

A matter of concern voiced by all partners centered on capacity-development needs in the area of M&E. Hence, the issue was discussed during the first meeting of the core group, and the stakeholders decided to develop an integrated capacity-development program on performance monitoring and evaluation and to establish the program as a formal and funded program of the DPME. This agenda was perceived to best create a collaborative spirit among actors and to provide a good incentive for other departments and provinces to join. Again the process to develop the outline and to agree on a framework for the program was facilitated by GIZ advisors. The main objectives of the core group were to obtain an agreed vision about collaboration and mutual benefit, ownership of content, and "acceptance" of the DPME leadership. Following this agreement, GIZ, endorsed by the core group, acted not only as facilitator but also provided complementary technical support, including:

---

5 The NSG was then the Public Administration Leadership and Management Academy (PALAMA).

- interviews with key officials and analysis of their operational plans as well as consultations with departments of the core group to define current and planned (over four years) performance monitoring and evaluation projects with budgets and identified capacity and resource shortfalls;
- development of an integrated capacity-development program on performance monitoring and evaluation that was refined and prioritized through sequenced workshops with the key stakeholders;
- development of an implementation plan for the integrated capacity-development program on performance monitoring and evaluation that was agreed to by all in the core group; and
- adaptation of the integrated capacity-development program on performance monitoring and evaluation to the format provided by the DPME in order to serve as a formal program of the department.

By constantly engaging bilaterally with individual partner organizations and at the same time offering space for group discussions on the strengths and weaknesses of each partner organization and joint learning loops to find the best way forward, GIZ was able to foster trust and mutual understanding among the stakeholders in the process. Furthermore, it was able to increase its own acceptance as a valued, neutral, and trustworthy facilitator.

In the first year, most activities under the program were supported by GIZ staff. GIZ advisors (both national and seconded staff) continuously provided opportunities for interdepartmental cooperation, sharing of knowledge, joint decision-making, and advocated for the inclusion of the DCoG, which is responsible for local government and had turned out to be an important but missing stakeholder. In this time span, the GIZ advisors, to a certain extent, stepped out of their roles as neutral facilitators and "honest brokers" and took a more active advisory role. The partner organizations appreciated this flexibility because they saw the immediate benefit of an invigorated group working together to spur the process. The services that the GIZ team offered served as oil in the machinery, allowing the negotiations and coordination process to run smoothly. This was possible due to the high level of flexibility in project management and the willingness of GIZ advisors to smoothly switch between the different roles of facilitator and advisor providing hands-on support. The risk that partner organizations might feel offended was regarded as being minimal in this case because of the high level of trust between advisors and counterparts.

As the program was adapted to the DPME format, it automatically became a permanent (three-year) program of the DPME and, as such, was included in the DPME budget process, ensuring its financial and institutional sustainability. M&E capacity-development activities took place through and in the program. The core group met on issues of program implementation and its monitoring. As a practical example: Training programs of the National School of Government were reviewed by the core group and adapted according to the combined needs of core group departments. New training programs for the induction of senior managers on monitoring and evaluation methodologies were developed jointly. Thus, a feeling of ownership and responsibility in DPME was fostered.

Until today, the core group continues to exist under the leadership of the DPME, with GIZ as an observer. The focus of GIZ's support now lies on the development of supportive software ("Cloud"), which will enable partners to compile and utilize data based on agreed quality standards. In the development of the government-wide M&E system, the initial focus was on national and provincial government, and the integration of local government data into the system lagged behind. Currently, GIZ is supporting its partners to harmonize M&E systems with a particular focus on the monitoring of local government performance, governance, and service delivery.

The provision of technical expertise, currently with a focus on software development, continues to go hand in hand with on-the-job training for counterparts on how to use and maintain these systems and utilize the software. The current role of GIZ advisors is rather that of "classical" technical supporters. Emphasis nevertheless continues to be given to fostering the exchange, joint learning, and joint decision-making between the different spheres of government and policy-making national departments.

In conclusion, it becomes evident that the inclusive partnership approach, combined with a high level of flexibility in project management and endurance over a long period, was key to success in this case. The engagements of long-term national and international experts who ably translate state-of the-art expertise to the South African context were a further key factor for success.

(2) Support to improve communication between the state, the media, and citizens in the Eastern Cape province

In South Africa, gaining access to information for citizens is a tricky matter. Print media is predominantly privately owned, and the media market is highly commercialized. Newspapers range from major weeklies and dailies to regional and local papers. Their common denominator is that they are owned by major media houses. In this context, the space for democratic transformation faces two main challenges. Firstly, commercial pressures skew content in mainstream media. Alternative voices of marginalized groups are thus highly underrepresented, and the relevant information for socially excluded groups to participate in the democratic processes of the country is lacking. Secondly, the relationship between the government and the media has deteriorated and is encapsulated by the disputes about the media's roles, expectations, and norms in South Africa's transformation process. The narrative is moving toward "media being anti-government," and thus is facing real potential policy changes in the areas of media freedom and media regulation. In recent years, South Africa has thus deteriorated in its status from a "free" media system to a "partly" free system (Freedom House).

Community media remains a powerful tool to negotiate and maneuver in the space outlined above. Mostly owned by individuals having an interest to "plough" back into their community, these small newspapers often publish in vernacular and focus on stories from and in the local space. Yet, also on the local level, the relationship between the small community newspapers and local municipalities remains strained. Any perceived negative reporting by newspapers was "punished" by withholding government advertising, or the threat of such actions. Municipalities did not generally see the often vernacular style in newspapers as being a way for meaningful engagements with citizens. If at all, the communication from municipalities through the newspapers was for announcing big meetings, events, or council schedules. Considering the above-listed challenges in the broader media market, the relationship between the community media and local government, in a way, also missed a point: It was a real opportunity to increase information access for citizens in impoverished communities.

In the Eastern Cape, GIZ has supported community papers for many years to improve their professionalism, ability to engage communities, and to report on local governance and civic matters. Much of this support was channeled through the Eastern Cape Communication Forum (ECCF), a civil society organization providing training and advisory services to community journalists.

The objective of the GSP is to improve the service delivery of the public sector, in collaboration with the private sector and civil society. This objective necessitated that capacity development be provided to public, private, and non-state organizations. Since 2013, GIZ has, against this background, adapted its strategy and shifted the focus of its support solely to community media to improve meaningful engagement between citizens and municipalities, where local newspapers are key instruments for this engagement. However, it is obvious that core "soft-issue" challenges hindered this shift to fostering meaningful engagement and that these hindrances had to be overcome first. These hindrances include the lack of existing and open communication channels between the different actors; a lack of understanding between newspapers and government communicators of each other's working environment and decision-making processes; a lack of understanding of how a sound relationship can assist in advancing each other's objectives; and outright mistrust between the different actors.

Having in mind the "soft-issue" challenges, governmental partners and newspapers sought GIZ support to focus cooperation on the following objectives:

- support to local newspapers to improve on professional content reporting while seeking innovation and efficiency in operations;
- engagement with municipalities, particularly among municipal officials responsible for communications, to see the opportunities of working closely with regional and community newspapers to engage citizens;
- support to newspapers and municipalities to develop mutual trust and cooperation arrangements; and
- implementation of a pilot project on improving communication with citizens in two municipalities in the Eastern Cape, using newspapers as well as new information and communication technologies.

Realizing the potential of using media more effectively to communicate and ensure accountability, partners called for a shift by GIZ toward strengthening the work of newspapers, the ECCF, as well as municipalities to support improvement of the communication function in municipalities and capacity development for relevant officials as well as professional journalism by newspapers. Support to the ECCF thus continued, and community journalists were trained in understanding municipal processes, procedures, and relevant legislative framework.

The initial idea of a strategic move toward bringing government communicators and media closer together and improving accountability through a pilot project was developed in conceptual discussions between the provincial Department of Cooperative Governance and Traditional Affairs (CoGTA), the South African Local Government Association (SALGA) and GIZ. At that time also, the national Department of Cooperative Governance (responsible for systems and structures in municipalities) had proclaimed its new program on "Back to Basics," which had a strategic and prominent focus on service delivery and a central focus on citizens and civic affairs. In this context, the momentum and the window of opportunity for a concrete support initiative on communication and accountability in this highly contested space arose.

The first obstacle to master was to get the buy-in and steering from provincial and municipal partners. Situated in the interface of communication and governance was the Provincial Communications Core Team consisting of Communications Managers of CoGTA, SALGA, and the Government Communication and Information System (GCIS), the latter being a new partner to GIZ.

In the first discussions, it became quite clear that the GIZ approach of linking state and non-state actors on governance and accountability was new to the provincial office of the GCIS. Firstly, the GCIS demonstrated a certain level of suspicion and criticism toward community media. Secondly, they brought forward the objective of using this pilot project as a means to "get the positive stories" about governments' achievements to communities. From the beginning, the initiative was thus situated in a difficult space, whereby the main provincial partners showed signs of the above-listed challenges. During the course of planning and implementation, the GIZ advisors were required to continuously stay engaged by raising concerns and opinions. In essence, this space allowed GIZ to engage in a way that is emblematic of the broader situation in terms of state–media relations. What was clear was that provincial government partners recognized the need for improved engagement, but that the "how" of engagement was not understood.

In this context, GIZ decided to also engage directly with the national GCIS officer responsible for the GCIS coordination of all the provinces. The GIZ advisor met with the national officer personally and explained the approach and the intention of the pilot project to him in detail. The national officer communicated his support to the initiative to the provincial GCIS office. Through GIZ's engagement with the national level at the right point in time, the pilot project received the necessary endorsement from higher-level authorities and the go-ahead for practical implementation on the provincial and local levels.

Moving forward, the details of the pilot project on improving communication were conceptualized and agreed upon in the Provincial Communications Core Team. The GIZ advisor was invited to its meetings on a regular basis, and thus was able to become an accepted and trusted partner. In this space, GIZ and core provincial government partners agreed on two selected pilot municipalities. The pilot project sought to address how media, community development workers, and municipalities can better educate, empower, and engage communities, without harming the authority of municipalities and independence of the media.

The first activity in making the agreed upon pilot initiative operational was to lay the foundation for better interpersonal relations between municipal officials and community journalists. GIZ staff suggested carrying out a joint exposure and study trip to Germany for participants from the municipalities and the media. The idea was supported by the Provincial Communications Core Team. It was agreed that implementation of the pilot project would commence upon returning from the study tour.

In the planning phase of the study tour, the abovementioned contested space of media and the state became obvious on a practical level. To ensure a balanced approach toward bringing the two actors of government communicators and community journalists together, GIZ decided on a particular selection process for delegates. Non-state delegates, that is, community journalists, were selected in collaboration with relevant sector organizations such as the ECCF and the Association of Independent Publishers in a competitive application process. This ensured that participants were selected using fair and transparent criteria with independent input, thus obviating the perception of "driving an agenda" through arbitrary selection. Representatives from the state side, that is, government communicators, were discussed with the Provincial Communications Core Team and directly nominated.

However, a setback in the process was experienced when government officials contested the selected community journalists, particularly a senior journalist who was perceived to be hostile toward the provincial government. GIZ decided to meet this contestation with an open discussion between partners on the objectives and principles of this initiative, namely to create space for frank and professional discussions on differing views, to bring participants out of their comfort zones and to challenge preconceived perceptions by discussing new and different perspectives, and eventually to form new relationships based on trust.

As a means to introduce the underlying objectives of the initiative to the delegates, GIZ hosted preparatory workshops where all delegates had the first opportunity to engage with each other. In the very first discussions, both sides already touched on the very points that often hindered collaboration on a day-to-day basis. These included accusations of bias toward anti-government "agendas" by newspapers, the threats by government to withhold advertising (and thus revenue), and the distribution of local newspapers in the communities. The atmosphere for new, creative thinking during the study tour was set once GIZ also presented a case study on media in Germany and the experiences of a German journalist who had worked in a number of countries. The study tour created a space in which both parties felt they were on neutral ground. Discussions were always very open, and a deeper understanding of each other's work circumstances was created.

The study tour was successfully completed, and new alliances between actors on the local government level were forged. Upon return, GIZ moved toward the practical implementation of the agreed upon pilot project in two municipalities.[6] The personal links created with delegates who operate in the geographical area of selected municipalities, either as journalists or responsible government communicators, helped to access the municipality. Nonetheless, GIZ advisors had to still facilitate the buy-in of the political leaders (the mayor, speaker, and whip) of pilot municipalities. This required the GIZ advisors – together with representatives from both parties – to present the project ideas to members of the Municipal Council. During this process, it became obvious that anchoring the initiative in the Provincial Communications Core Team had its limitations, as this was a bit removed from the daily operations of – and differences in – procedures in municipalities. GIZ adapted its strategy and established a Project Committee – consisting of participating municipalities and representatives from SALGA and GCIS – responsible for the specific municipalities and

---

6 In further engagements, one of the two selected municipalities displayed an increasing lack of commitment and ownership. Despite various attempts to resuscitate a previously stable relationship, GIZ and provincial partners decided to reduce the number of pilot sites to one.

surrounding areas on the operational level. With their inputs on the operational decision-making process, the pilot proceeded.

Multi-stakeholder engagement remained a core principle in getting the pilots off the ground: Citizens in respective municipalities were engaged through a data collection (survey) process, in which they indicated what kind of information they required most in their municipality, in which form they preferred this information to be presented to them, and through which channels they would like to receive it. At the same time, the municipality was engaged through an assessment of the status quo of communication practices. Through interviews with various municipal officials and Community Development Workers (officials who interface with communities on an ongoing basis on service-delivery matters), institutional bottlenecks in the flow of information were identified and recommendations on how to address them developed. In the interview process, community media in the respective geographical areas were asked to assess their levels of capacity and reach, potential challenges, and existing links to the municipality. Furthermore, relationships to other international partners supporting freedom of the media in South Africa were established, for example to Hivos, an international organization that, through its program "Making All Voices Count," addresses the very same challenges of citizen-media-state relationships. Using this opportunity, GIZ brought together one of the pilot municipalities and Hivos through its South African implementing partner MobiSAM (Mobile Social Accountability Monitor). By implementing a mobile-based communication mechanism, Hivos and MobiSAM will further continue GIZ's already concluded work and thus increase sustainability. The new relationship between these actors and the pilot municipality rests upon the trust and understanding that GIZ had established.

How does the selected mode of operation make for smart implementation?
Lessons learned from the case studies

The two case studies depict different cooperation areas in governance and administration reform in South Africa. In the first example, the provided support led to the development of a government-wide monitoring and evaluation system for improved planning and implementation of public services, and the second fostered cooperation between municipalities and community media for better public participation. Also, the partner landscapes of both examples differ, as do the technical challenges that the partner organizations face. Finally, the technical expertise GIZ provided to support its partner organizations was quite distinct and very much depended on the matter at hand as well as the concrete partner requirements. Despite these differences, one can, however, detect similarities, which run like a golden thread through both cases. It is the contextual conditions, referred to here as "soft issues," that hindered progress in both examples, which are similar. Thus, the approaches applied to overcome the individual challenges also show similarities.

There is a tendency of a rather inward-looking and delimiting attitude of partner organizations. This hinders cooperation and coordination with actors who are not part of the sphere of jurisdiction or in the structural group (e.g., ministry, unit, or state versus non-state). Sometimes this is further aggravated by a behavior of compliance. Duties are accomplished because the order was given, although the wider meaning, benefits, or risks as well as consequences are probably not understood. Together these factors promote silo-thinking of stakeholders. In addition, this constitutes a restriction, which makes innovative thinking and exploration of new avenues difficult. In more pronounced circumstances, this might even lead to feelings of mistrust, which undermines the chance to find common ground and develop joint approaches to shared challenges. This might be the case, even though the goals that the different actors or stakeholder groups pursue are quite similar. The examples on the difficult interactions between the local media and municipalities in the Eastern Cape and the challenges of initiating a joint monitoring framework speak to this. These characteristics are not exclusive to the South African context. They can rather be detected in most partner countries, although obviously with differing degrees and nuances. The advisors confronted with such settings and corresponding attitudes and behaviors of stakeholders, however, have to be aware of them and understand them to be as important as the technical challenges, capacity constraints, and know-how deficits that might exist on the side of partners.

Considering the two cases described above, the following essence of how to best support governance processes can be extracted and translated into generally applicable practices on how to support and implement reform processes in a "smart" way. We feel that these lessons learned are not unique to the South African context, but can be used in a general way when supporting governance and administration reform as well as reforms in different sectors in partner countries.

There is not one blueprint to transformation and reform. It might sound like a truism, but it cannot be taken seriously enough. There is no such thing as a one-size-fits-all approach. Supporting transformation and governance reforms will, as in any other sector, not be successful if it follows a linear approach. Rather, the support provided has to be iterative and flexible and has to allow for repeated learning loops to account for the fact that transformation and reform are long and non-linear processes.

While working on developing country-wide M&E systems, it became obvious that the smart implementation approach had to be found through a concerted effort by all partner organizations involved. GIZ became a learning partner, too, and had to understand that only by adapting its own approach – from supporting several individual partners simultaneously to supporting one joint program (the "single mechanism") – could it promote progress. This shift in mindset enabled a joint learning process, which fostered ownership and mutual understanding.

In the example from the Eastern Cape, GIZ adapted its project steering structure several times to overcome bottlenecks, accommodate partner needs, and foster ownership, that is, from steering together with the ECCF as the only partner, to steering with a "loose" group of partners on the provincial level (CoGTA, SALGA), to using an existing government structure (i.e., the Provincial Communications Core Team), and finally to establishing a project steering committee on the implementation level.

It is important to note that what at first might have looked like a trial-and-error approach of learning through mistakes and successes was rather a deliberate choice to be flexible and to adapt the approach whenever it was necessary in order to stay close to the situational requirements and responsive to the partners' demands. Partner organizations appreciate this as a counterpart, retrospectively reflected in more general terms during the interviews for this article:

> GIZ's approach was not as such selling one model or one approach. It was much more trying to work through the "mess" in the most supportive and thoughtful ways, which were context-sensitive and trying to traverse the space between the politics that were there and the international relationships and the expert issues. Requests were accommodated in the concepts always, and initial nets spun wider to bring something in which did not fit in initially.

Understanding the country and reform context is key. Each transformation and reform process needs to be grounded in the particular context in which it takes place. Content issues of reform might be comparable among countries, but the politics in negotiating them and thus their process or outcome is not. Advisory services can only add value to these processes if they are grounded on the specific context in which a partner organization operates. The fact that GIZ combines international and national advisors in its program teams allows for insider and outsider perspectives in understanding this context. It enables the teams to utilize tacit knowledge of the partner countries' challenges and cultural sensibilities, augmented with international experiences. In this way, the teams are better prepared to see the whole picture of the partner countries' socio-economic and political context. Furthermore, this knowledge can be maintained beyond the lifespan of one program cycle (i.e., approximately three years), because national advisors often stay employed with GIZ in their own countries, whereas international advisors tend to change posts more frequently.

The perspective of a long-term engagement enables advisors to be there, to first listen and observe, and then to advise. A former national advisor captured this attitude by explaining how GIZ employed a partner-oriented approach:

> More room was created by just relaxing on time frames and making deadlines a bit more open. By giving this space, partners became aware that we are of support. Partners began seeing us as the only ones understanding their context. We were not coming in the room saying "Our matrix says we have to do xyz," but we came and said "So what is the big picture here?" Partners came with tasks from the minister and asked us to help them think through. They wanted our "thought processes." We supported them in finding their feet with regard to the task at hand. In a nutshell: It is creating space and having the right conservations.

Building trust is a long-term affair. Building a trustful relationship with counterparts and the partner organization as such requires continuous and long-term engagement and support. As shown in the examples, GIZ's cooperation is designed as a long-term affair that centers on direct engagement between advisors and partners. The examples show the huge benefit of advisors working closely and continuously with their counterparts. By doing so, they can flexibly follow the demand, give hands-on support if needed, and either engage bilaterally or create space for group exchanges and learning. At the same time, they are able to build the level of mutual trust and recognition necessary for effective partnerships. As one counterpart who participated in the development of a joint M&E framework recounts while looking back: "The additional benefits were that I developed personal relationships with the advisors. They were sound-boarding through their own experiences and perspectives. They carried global experience and understood the bigger picture."

The ability to build trust among partner organizations also requires a certain attitude of openness toward the demands of the partner organization and counterparts as well as flexibility in accommodating these and mastering unforeseen challenges. As a counterpart summarized it while looking back on her working experience with GIZ advisors:

> I always could pick up the phone and ask for insight. The advisor became a very trusted person. The GIZ colleagues were always approachable and did not behave in a high-handed way. They were extremely supportive always and flexible to accommodate the uncertainties and changes, because it always was unpredictable, and things did not work in "ZOPP"[7] blocks.

Use windows of opportunity and set the right incentives at the right time. If the partner countries' context is properly understood and cooperation is grounded on a trustful relationship, the identification of the right point in time to utilize an opportunity is not rocket science. In the example of supporting a joint M&E framework, the shared experience of being stuck in a rather unsatisfactory situation (i.e., a multitude of uncoordinated M&E approaches) created a push (window of opportunity) for all partner organizations involved, despite their reservations. The fact that all actors also had similar capacity needs was then turned into an incentive by creating a joint program on capacity development. This eventually brought different actors together to jointly steer the program (the "single mechanism") and contributed to their ownership.

Multi-level and multi-actor approaches allow for seeing the whole picture and fostering ownership. In the Eastern Cape example, the challenge was clearly located on the municipality level. However, the GIZ advisors from the beginning engaged provincial institutions and at times even national institutions in the project. They worked with different spheres of government and with state and non-state partners simultaneously.

Cooperation and communication with institutions on different levels were crucial to overcome bottlenecks in the implementation process. It enabled the advisors also to understand the broader context and relate this

---

7 "ZOPP" is the abbreviation of "Zielorientierte Projekt Planung," a planning method developed in the 1970s by the then GTZ, that is, one of GIZ's predecessor organizations.

to the individual initiative they were working on at a specific point in time. It gave the advisors the ability to make connections, as recalled by a national advisor on a similar case:

> Often, national government partners were designing and rolling out a process. And then we often discovered that there is a time-lack in communication and orientation of the provincial partners. But we could do the translation, because we were connected to both the national and provincial partners. We could take up the role as a translator taking the national policy into the implementation space. So it is this skill: to understand the broader context and the specific issues on the level it needs to be translated to. That is the important skill.

Create a secure space where partners can engage freely. If trust and mutual understanding is lacking and creating bottlenecks in the process, it proves to be worth the effort to create a situation in which they meet with each other beyond their own limited areas of jurisdiction and on neutral ground.

As described in the example on supporting the cooperation between community media and municipalities in the Eastern Cape, a crucial element of success was to create common ground on which diverse partner organizations could interact with each other and overcome their prejudices. A joint study trip became the icebreaker, as counterparts were taken out of their own comfort zones and explored unknown space together.

Beyond the mere educational effect of increasing "technical" knowledge, study trips foster personal relationships. This is especially fruitful if people traveling together come from different spheres of the partner landscape, for example media and public service, civil society, and government. Study trips create joint learning opportunities, in which partners can experiment and get to know each other outside their normal spaces. As one counterpart recalls: "Exposure trips to Germany were powerful. They were a way to make people think outside the box and allowed people to ask questions. It was the right people traveling together doing hard work together and learning together."

References

BusinessTech. (2015, January 21). *South Africa unemployment: 1994–2015*. Retrieved from https://businesstech.co.za/news/general/77737/south-africa-unemployment-19 94-2015/

Statistics South Africa. (2011). *Census 2011 statistical release – P0301.4*. Retrieved from http://www.statssa.gov.za/publications/P03014/P030142011.pdf

Statistics South Africa. (n.d.). *Economic growth*. Retrieved from http://www.statssa.go v.za/?page_id=735&id=1

FOCEVAL – Promoting Evaluation Capacities in Costa Rica: Smart(er) Implementation with Capacity WORKS?

Sabrina Storm

Executive Summary

The National Monitoring and Evaluation System of Costa Rica and its corresponding laws were established during the 1990s. Since then, the country has endeavored to implement monitoring and evaluation (M&E) activities as part of its public policy framework. Nevertheless, hardly any systematic evaluations had been conducted, and monitoring activities had been reduced mainly to the institutional self-reporting of implementation compliance. Persisting regional disparities and growing levels of inequality among the population raised the level of pressure on the government to present reliable information on the effectiveness of public interventions. Hence, results-oriented evaluations were promoted by some Costa Rican departments as tools that would support evidence-based policy-making while also increasing public-sector accountability.

This paper focuses on the strategies and steps pursued by the Costa Rican government – and supported by the Deutsche Gesellschaft für Internationale Zusammenarbeit (GIZ) program Strengthening Evaluation Capacities in Central America (FOCEVAL)[1] – to improve evaluation capacities within the public sector between 2011 and 2014. Mistrust and a lack of dialogue and communication between different units and departments were some of the challenges GIZ faced. Also, academic and political discourse on evaluation was detached from public-sector conditions. Soon, the program team had to learn that the initial operational plan – which included proposals for large-scale impact evaluations – was overambitious and that a much more incremental approach was needed. Commitment, alliances, and common understanding needed to be developed before pilot evaluations could be successfully executed. It is shown how creating space for communication, co-creation, and learning fostered a

---

1 GIZ implements the program on behalf of BMZ.

joint and feasible approach for implementation within the cooperation system. GIZ's management model Capacity WORKS – with its integral concept of capacity development and systemic orientation toward the success factors of strategy, cooperation, steering structure, processes, and learning and innovation – provided a framework for creating this space. The case study is structured around Capacity WORKS, and thus exemplifies how the management model of GIZ can provide support.

Introduction

When Costa Rica's former Minister of Planning Roberto Gallardo left office in 2014, he was asked in an interview: Which were the five most important issues he would like to hand over to his successor? Evaluation of public policies and programs was one of the topics he chose to put in this list of priorities. "For policy-makers, it is of vital importance to count with information that allows them to understand and assess an ever more complex reality" (Gallardo, 2013).

In the two years preceding this statement, the Costa Rican Ministry of National Planning and Economic Policy (MIDEPLAN[2]) had just executed the very first strategic evaluations within the framework of the National Monitoring and Evaluation System. It had developed and harmonized guidelines for results-oriented planning, monitoring, and evaluation; had overhauled the compilation process and methodological setup of the National Development Plan; and the ministry's evaluation unit had trained dozens of planning officials from sectorial ministries and agencies. Results-oriented evaluations were promoted as tools to address some of the persisting development barriers of the country more effectively. However, MIDEPLAN needed to align many stars in order to move closer to its vision of an institutional M&E practice, which would not only be technically sound but also useful for learning, improvement, and strategic decision-making in public administration and government.

Costa Rica's national M&E system is composed of an institutional network of at least 100 agencies in 14 government sectors. Although the system had already been created in the mid-1990s, hardly any systematic evaluations had been conducted, and monitoring activities had been

---

2 See http://www.mideplan.go.cr/

reduced mainly to institutional self-reporting of implementation compliance. Standards, procedures, and orientations for planning, monitoring, and evaluation – set out by the Ministry of Finance, the Supreme Audit Institution, and the Ministry of National Planning – were incoherent and caused frustration and confusion within the sectorial and institutional planning units. Persistent misconceptions and a highly diversified understanding of evaluation and its objectives could be observed, with "evaluation" often being used as a synonym for auditing, scrutiny, or control.

This paper focuses on the strategies and steps pursued by the ministry – and supported by the GIZ program FOCEVAL – to strengthen the evaluation component within the National Monitoring and Evaluation System (Sistema Nacional de Seguimiento y Evaluación – SINE) between 2011 and 2014. In 2009 the Costa Rican government, along with the University of Costa Rica, presented a proposal to the German Federal Ministry for Economic Cooperation and Development (BMZ) for a cooperation project to improve evaluation capacities in the country.

FOCEVAL's first phase (2011–2014) was implemented by GIZ on behalf of BMZ and funded via a supra-regional cooperation fund for Evaluation Capacity Development, which had been set up as a response to the international agreements on aid effectiveness (i.e., mutual accountability and results-based management) in Paris and Accra. The first phase, which will be analyzed in this paper, focused on Costa Rica and regional knowledge-sharing; its objective was to improve institutional conditions for evaluations of public policies and programs. It was the first Evaluation Capacity Development (ECD) program of its kind within German cooperation and had a total budget of €3.3 million over the three years.

GIZ's management model Capacity WORKS provided a structured approach for the project's implementation process. Capacity WORKS was used

- as a framework for joint reflection and discussion within the cooperation system;
- as an organizing set of principles that helped to define the shape of the program;
- as a management toolbox; and
- as an orientation for internal and external communication.

This paper aims at illustrating how a deliberate approach toward Capacity WORKS' five "success factors" (strategy, cooperation, steering structure, processes, learning and innovation) supported adaptive management and results-oriented implementation.

Contextual conditions

The Republic of Costa Rica is one of the most stable democracies of the Americas. The Constitution of the Republic of 1949 and its political implementation by the respective governments fostered the provision of broad-based access to education and healthcare, as well as a robust system of checks and balances. Political stability and the successful transformation from an agrarian-based economy into a service industry provided the basis for the necessary investments in basic social services, while a good endowment of human capital and natural amenities has further contributed to socio-economic progress.

In recent years, a number of socio-economic challenges, together with the fragmentation of the political system and the public administration, have been putting pressure on the country's governance mechanisms and have resulted in decreasing levels of trust in public institutions (OECD [Organisation for Economic Co-operation and Development], 2015). Costa Rica's public administration is characterized by an important number of subsidiary bodies of central government ministries and a large, institutionally decentralized sector (e.g., semi-autonomous and autonomous bodies, state- and non-state-owned enterprises). As a recent OECD governance review (OECD, 2015) points out, the country's public administration has limited steering capacity by the center of government and limited accountability mechanisms. The center of government is composed of the Ministry of the Presidency, the Ministry of National Planning and Economic Policy, and the Ministry of Finance. Persisting regional disparities and increasing levels of inequality among the population require reliable information on the effectiveness of public interventions for evidence-based policy-making.

MIDEPLAN's primary duties include the preparation of the National Development Plan; the verification that public investment projects across government entities are aligned with the priorities set forth in the National Development Plan; and the approval of investment projects of public agencies when such projects are externally financed or government approval is required. The ministry is also responsible for the setup and coordination of SINE. Through these functions, the ministry gives technical and political advice to the Presidency of the Republic and other public institutions while it formulates, coordinates, monitors, and evaluates the strategies and priorities of the government.

Development challenge

The National Monitoring and Evaluation System of Costa Rica and its corresponding laws were established during the 1990s. Since then, the country has endeavored to implement M&E activities as part of its public policy framework. Critics contend that no efforts were undertaken to strengthen SINE as an institutional support network for research and strategic analysis, and that no systematic evaluations of public programs were carried out. Thereby, the national M&E practice transcended into a bureaucratic follow-up and institutional self-reporting system for the government's principal political agendas. Thus, although it served basic accountability needs, it was hardly used for decision-making, learning, and strategic management or the design and development of new policies (Sanchez & Storm, 2016).

Implementation challenges and hypotheses

FOCEVAL's objective was to create improved institutional conditions for the evaluations of public interventions. This paper focuses on how the program developed, executed, and adapted a joint approach with its national counterparts to deal with the following implementation challenges.

1. The Ministry of Planning was considered to be weak and as having limited steering capacities as well as being rather isolated within Costa Rica's highly fragmented public administration. Inside the ministry there were conflicting views on the institutional mandate toward monitoring and evaluation, and there was generally little dialogue and coordination between the different units and departments. In the wider institutional context, evaluation was perceived as an instrument for scrutiny and control that manifested in resistance and fears of personal scapegoating. The demand from civil society and parliament for evaluation results as a basis for evidence-based policy-making was still low, and evaluation was perceived as an additional administrative cost rather than as an instrument enhancing transparency or public adminis-

tration performance. Planning and reporting mechanisms were focused on activities and lacked results-orientation. Institutional information politics were restrictive, but evaluations that are only accessed by policy-makers provide a very limited kind of transparency – inwards and upwards. In this context, the challenge to be tackled was: How to create an enabling environment for a reform process that would require changes in organizational behavior and mindsets from a multitude of actors?

2. Many consultants and public servants had already been trained in evaluation methods but had no practical evaluation experience, and the actual public-sector programs did not match the classroom conditions. Academic discourse on evaluation was detached from public-sector conditions. Program theories and detailed objectives often needed to be reconstructed ex post; in cases where the data from monitoring systems or other statistics was available, it was often not reliable, incomplete, or impossible to disaggregate, posing difficulties for effect and impact-oriented evaluations. Inter-institutional processes and procedures for strategic evaluations as well as their setup and utilization were not yet in place. Officials in MIDEPLAN had no experience with managing evaluations and guidelines, standards, as well as the processes and steering mechanisms that needed to be established. Hence, the second implementation challenge for the program was: How to design, select, and set up pilot evaluations that, for them, become catalysts for greater interest and acceptance of evaluations in the public administration and among civil society and parliament while matching international standards?

The program's hypotheses of how to best approach these challenges were as follows:

a) Establish an integral approach to capacity development that addresses the individual, organizational, and political levels simultaneously by combining training and sensitization on an individual level with organizational development and changes on a policy level.

b) In order to create an authoritative environment for reforms, the program needs to create alliances with – and gain broad support from – political decision-makers, in particular. Also, strategic alliances between academia and public-sector institutions are considered important to enhance the relevance and usefulness of national training offers on the one hand, and the legitimacy of evaluation processes on the other hand.

c) As a pilot program, with little available information on what had worked where and why elsewhere, the program's success is dependent on tight feedback loops involving information and perceptions from a variety of stakeholders and allowing room for reflection, deviance, and adaptation. Hence, an incremental and results-based approach needed to be part of the design in order to achieving the program's objective.

These hypotheses remained relevant throughout the implementation process, but the program had to adapt its specific approaches and strategic responses during the course of implementation. GIZ staff and program stakeholders discussed the logic and strategy of implementation ("how" are we going to work and implement the program and "why") on a regular basis. GIZ's management model Capacity WORKS – with its integral concept of capacity development and systemic orientation toward the success factors of strategy, cooperation, steering structure, processes, and learning and innovation – provided a framework for these reflections and enabled discussion and decision-making within the cooperation system. The main themes of the five success factors are (GIZ [Deutsche Gesellschaft für Internationale Zusammenarbeit], 2015)[3]:

Strategy: The cooperation system will succeed if and when the cooperation partners agree on a joint strategy to achieve the negotiated objectives. This requires an investment of time and resources in a communicative and social process of strategy formulation with partners.

Cooperation: Trust, the negotiation of appropriate forms of cooperation, and clearly defined roles form the basis for a good cooperation. Only when the participants in a cooperation system acknowledge that they are all dependent on each other and play their parts can the system be successful.

Steering structure: A development project has to take decisions daily about management and needs an adequate structure to do this. The cooperation systems is guided by agreements on how the actors involved will go about jointly preparing and taking the decisions that affect them.

---

3 Please see the paper from Neill Hatton for further details.

Processes: Successful cooperation systems include a clear understanding of effective ways of delivering outputs, for which new processes are established or existing processes modified. The management (change processes) of the project as well as the permanent processes in the sectors and countries where the sustainable change is to take place need to be analyzed, designed, managed, and improved.

Learning and innovation: The cooperation partners create an enabling environment for innovation by boosting the learning capacities of the actors involved. The systemic concept not only focuses on learning needs on an individual level but also interdependencies and learning needs on an organizational and policy level as well.

Tracing the implementation process

This section aims at illustrating how decision-making and adaptive management took place and which lessons were learned with regard to the program's hypotheses and implementation challenges. It does this with reference to the three hypotheses identified above as being particularly relevant: (a) integral capacity-development strategy, (b) promoting coalitions and alliances, and (c) feedback loops and adaptive management. Although the mentioned success factors – as they are associated and interconnected – are all relevant throughout the analysis, the first part has a particular focus on strategy and processes, the second on cooperation and steering structure, and the third on learning and innovation as well as cooperation.

Strategy development

Implementation of FOCEVAL began in July 2011. One of the first activities GIZ and MIDEPLAN agreed upon was to set up a strategy process that included a series of short workshops with stakeholders from different institutions and sectors. The purpose of this process was to:

1. increase MIDEPLAN's visibility as a lead agency for the national evaluation system;
2. enhance understanding and information about barriers and existing good practices with regard to evaluation in the public sector;

3. shape the capacity-development strategy and the operational setup of the program;
4. promote the project and identify cooperation allies.

A core team was identified that was comprised of staff from GIZ and MIDEPLAN, which organized the strategy process. The process was conceived as a joint learning process, during which each of the team members assumed responsibility for specific tasks and topics. Impressions and hypotheses derived from the events were discussed within the team, and each member carried a learning diary. During this process, it became obvious that the project needed to address not only the supply side (technical capacities) – as it was established in the project offer (training, pilot evaluations, M&E systems) – but also the demand side (support and demand for evaluation from policy-makers and civil society representatives) in order to achieve its set objective, which was to create improved institutional conditions for evaluations of public interventions. The dimension of responsivity toward evaluation and evaluation results by stakeholders in order to use the instrument of evaluation to facilitate change was underestimated by the appraisal team. However, the leeway given a GIZ program to adapt to changing circumstances during implementation allowed for the inclusion of this dimension in the operationalization of the program. The program was promoting a systemic approach toward capacity development that considered interventions at the individual, organizational, and societal levels. The table below illustrates how such a conceptual understanding of a systemic approach to capacity development is operationalized and leads to the identification of core activities for the program.

Table 1: FOCEVAL: Generic capacity-development strategy

ECD	Supply	Demand
Individual	Training of evaluators Training the trainer – formats Trainings on evaluation management for commissioning organizations Learning by doing formats	Sensitization of political decision-makers Advocacy directed at members of parliament and representatives of civil society organizations
Organization	Conduct pilot evaluations Harmonization of concepts and terminology (manuals, seminars) Adapt training offers to local demand and context and anchor them at local training providers	Establish incentives to develop and use M&E systems (e.g., quality award) Promote dissemination and accessibility of evaluation results and dialogue between civil society and the public sector on M&E results (e.g., monitoring reports: National Development Plan)

Cooperation and networks	Promote strategic alliances between public administration and academia Promote professional exchanges among networks of evaluators and national and regional professional associations (Community of Practices) Promote and support of inter-institutional evaluation projects	Foster civil society networks / NGOs working on transparency and accountability Promote knowledge-sharing with other national M&E authorities (Colombia, Mexico, El Salvador, Ecuador)
Political and societal conditions	Foster the evaluation component within the national M&E framework Foster the role of the executive M&E authority (MIDEPLAN): coordination mechanisms/steering groups, standards	Foster principles and mechanisms of accountability that are based on evidence and evaluation results Ensure institutional budgets for evaluations

Source: FOCEVAL/GIZ (Strengthening Evaluation Capacities in Central America/ Deutsche Gesellschaft für Internationale Zusammenarbeit, 2012a)

The joint strategy process fostered team spirit, trust, and communication within the core cooperation team. As a result of it, as many observers from other organizations commented, MIDEPLAN was viewed as taking a very different role than usual: asking questions, facilitating discussions, and listening to concerns. Overall, the strategy process was crucial for developing a joint understanding of context and specific challenges, promoting a systemic understanding of the implementation challenges, and establishing the foundations for the program's cooperation strategy. It also strengthened the role of the leading agency, MIDEPLAN, vis-à-vis other agencies in the public administration, and thus raised the likelihood that MIDE-PLAN could deliver the task it was mandated with. The process had fulfilled its purpose as an initial strategic loop within the implementation process.

However, though most of the identified intervention areas and change projects remained relevant throughout the project, assumptions and specific approaches had to be tested and developed while moving along with the implementation process. Although the strategy process helped to shape an understanding of the key processes that the program had to address within the institutional setup as well as gain clarity on the process map, the key change, strategy, and support processes within the program sequencing of – and entry points for – change initiatives could not be fully understood through analysis and discussion alone. Through learning by doing and joint reflection within the cooperation system, the program gained an increased understanding of the underlying barriers and stabilizing factors for existing processes and could allocate its resources more efficiently. Shifting forces, interests, and coalitions in the wider institutional context needed to be assessed and monitored on a regular basis. Retrospectively, the initial change model and operation plan of the project were far too complex and overloaded with measures and indicators. A more iterative, flexible "learn as you go" approach while testing the temperature and staying open to strategic changes and alternatives would have been more appropriate. Also, it took a lot more time "to work the territory" than initially planned before concrete, feasible evaluation projects could be identified and initiated. Relationships and trust needed to be established, institutional contexts assessed, and political and technical support ensured. One of the initially foreseen evaluation projects had to be cancelled in the end because these factors had not been taken into account properly.

Building alliances

The operational plan and objectives for the first year contained numerous initiatives and change projects. The elaboration and publication of a manual for strategic evaluations by MIDEPLAN had been an important milestone. Now it had to be put into practice and prove its usefulness in real evaluation processes, but this process moved slowly. Health had been selected as a sector for an evaluation pilot. MIDEPLAN had received a formal request from the Costa Rican Department for Social Security to support the enhancement of the institutional M&E system. The background for this request was a report from the Supreme Audit Institution. However, discussions about an evaluation of primary healthcare were conflictive and, after a series of meetings and several months, it was still not possible to agree on the scope and purpose of evaluation. Other activities/ change projects were still more on a level of general proposals and required a considerable amount of clarification, discussion, and negotiation on how to approach them. After a year of back and forth without breakthrough, frustrations and worries among the program team increased concerning the achievement of visible progress, particularly with regard to concrete evaluation projects.

These worries were reiterated in a workshop with the wider group of stakeholders, who had been invited to serve as a sounding board to the project: The lack of national evaluation cases that could be used to promote evaluations and serve as good examples was seen as a big problem by all stakeholders. Promotional activities remained rather theoretical without national "show cases" that could demonstrate the benefits and challenges of evaluation.

The project team discussed the implementation strategy by making use of the five Capacity WORKS success factors and asked for feedback. The main recommendation that emerged from the workshop was: Create more spaces for inter-institutional discussion and coordination; allow more actors to take an active role in the program, not only as beneficiaries of program activities but also as active change agents; and improve communication on program activities and their intended results.

The GIZ team discussed these recommendations and their impressions and hypotheses internally and with MIDEPLAN. Supported by the feedback from the stakeholders' meeting and seeing the need for more inclusive inter-institutional coordination, MIDEPLAN agreed to the revision and adaptation of the program's steering structure.

There were concerns that flexibility and promptness of decision-making could be lost if more voices were to be heard and included. Final decision-making should remain within MIDEPLAN and GIZ, whereas the steering structure should serve as a platform for strategic consultation and mutual information, and an advisory board for improved coordination and implementation. The coordination group included representatives from public administration, academia, and civil society (see below for details). Most of the participants were familiar with the program and had been involved in specific program activities. Monthly meetings were set up and hosted by GIZ and MIDEPLAN in the FOCEVAL facilities. The coordination group became an important motor for innovation and joint activities within and outside the scope of the program. Seminars and presentations were promoted and organized together. Representatives from MIDEPLAN and the Ministry of Finance engaged actively in the preparation and development of new training offers at the Training Center for Public Administration. The discussions facilitated a common understanding and language with regard to evaluation. Naturally, every organization also brought its particular interests to the table and looked for opportunities to benefit from the program's resources. However, through joint discussion, these became more transparent, resources could be pooled, and synergies (e.g., joint trainings, disposition of rooms, equipment, facilitators) could be identified more easily. In other contexts, a lean steering structure might have been the most efficient one: In this context, the coordination group was not only a means to an end for improved implementation but also an intervention that addressed deficits of inter-institutional communication and lack of coordination. It facilitated a common understanding of the challenges and objectives and strategic alliances with regard to a new and controversial issue.

One of the first joint activities became the promotion of an "evaluation challenge" and the subsequent selection of pilot evaluations.

The following chart of the FOCEVAL steering structure illustrates the multiple purposes the steering structure had, next to decision-making: The steering structure became an important instrument for building understanding of the issues among a wider group of stakeholders and forged alliances among stakeholder groups via its focus on consultations.

Figure 2: FOCEVAL – steering structure

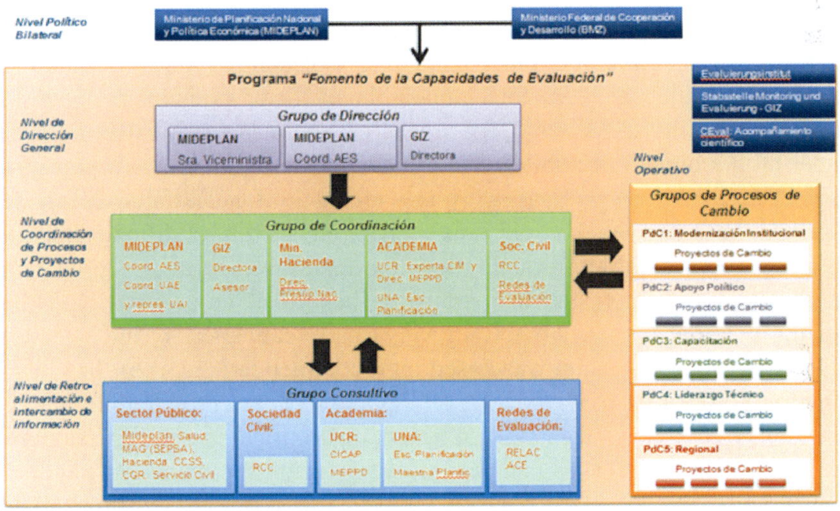

Source: FOCEVAL/GIZ (2012b)

Learning by doing, learning from failure, and learning from data

A tracer study conducted by the program reviewing the professional development of graduates from postgraduate training courses in evaluation and the University of Costa Rica's master's program on the evaluation of projects and programs confirmed the existence of a significant gap between "theory and practice." Hardly any graduate was able to apply his or her acquired evaluation knowledge in the job they obtained after their degree. There was no demand nor opportunity to apply these skills. The organizational conditions were not yet in place. Though most graduates of specific evaluation courses confirmed the usefulness of the content learned, overall, the longtime capacity-building activities had not manifested in institutional M&E practices. No systematic evaluations that had been executed or commissioned by public institutions could be identified or were publicly available. In addition, many graduates also expressed the need for further training and did not feel prepared to design and conduct evaluations of public policies, plans, or programs.

One of the program's conclusions in light of this situation was that the program needed to promote institutionally embedded evaluation pilots that would allow for learning by doing under "real life" conditions, and thereby enhance individual and organizational evaluation capacities. The health pilot had not been a good choice in that sense. The topic of primary healthcare was extremely complex, with lots of controversies, conflicting views of a multitude of actors, and high levels of political and public attention. The Costa Rican Department of Social Security was already under high amounts of public scrutiny at the time the evaluation was discussed, and it had been shaken by several institutional affairs. It can be assumed that the evaluation was perceived as an additional threat. Although considerable resources (predominantly in terms of time and energy) had been invested in getting the health-sector evaluation to the starting point as a pilot, the activity was finally cancelled by the Minister of Planning. This decision was based on recommendations from the working group on healthcare evaluation and FOCEVAL's steering committee. It was followed by an exchange of tense institutional notes. Frustrations among all involved actors had accumulated during the tenacious negotiation process. On the other hand, it allowed for important learnings. The program team discussed the lessons learned and how they should be considered in the following evaluation pilots: 1) The evaluation should be voluntary and not imposed externally. Participating institutions should have the opportunity to present themselves as "early movers" and models, with an interest in learning and transparency. 2) A clear commitment from technical staff and leadership was needed. Institutional representatives should be involved in the whole evaluation process.

FOCEVAL decided to organize an evaluation challenge. Organizations were invited to compete to "win" an evaluation by presenting proposals for evaluations of public programs. Criteria were established beforehand

and included: relevance, evaluability, as well as political and technical support. The selection process gave MIDEPLAN and GIZ the time and opportunities to assess the viability and context of the evaluation proposals – which had been a significant deficit in preparation of the healthcare evaluation.

The challenge was promoted through the steering groups and the networks the project had developed during the first year of implementation. It led to about eight proposals from different ministries and agencies. The proposals were assessed by a team from MIDEPLAN and GIZ. Two proposals from two different sectors seemed eligible and were selected. Both were handed in from former participants of FOCEVAL trainings: one from the Institute of Social Support, one from the Ministry of Education. The selected proposals were presented in a press conference with participation of the institutions leadership and the Minister of Planning. Formal inter-institutional agreements were signed, making detailed notes of roles, contributions, and responsibilities of each organization and the commitment to publish and discuss evaluation results.

Now that pilot evaluations had been identified, the according processes needed to be designed in a way that would generate individual and institutional learning experiences and allow for practicing roles and processes. FOCEVAL proposed to follow a highly participatory learning-by-doing approach: Each evaluation team consisted of functionaries from the Ministry of National Planning, GIZ advisors, and the institution responsible for the program that was evaluated. Technical quality was ensured via external Costa Rican evaluation consultants and backstopping from the Centre of Evaluation from Saarland University in Saarbrucken, Germany. Representatives from the involved organizations discussed and developed the evaluation design jointly with the evaluation team and were informed regularly on evaluation progress which ensured transparency and continuous feedback during the whole process. Conflicts and disagreements were treated in a steering committee that had been set up for each evaluation. Though MIDEPLAN was not supposed to execute evaluations itself, it was considered important that the staff, who were supposed to coordinate, commission, and ensure the quality of evaluations in the future, be involved to gain detailed insights into the whole evaluation process. Thus, officials from MIDEPLAN formed part of the evaluation teams throughout all stages of the evaluation process, including data collection and analysis.

By the end of 2012, several pilot evaluations were on their way: MIDE-PLAN had decided to lead by example and was preparing a strategic evaluation of the methodological setup and compilation process of the National Development Plan. A team from MIDEPLAN, GIZ, and the Ministry of Agriculture was working on a feasibility study for an impact evaluation of a large irrigation project. People from different areas of MIDE-PLAN had begun to discuss and align their concepts and guidelines for planning, monitoring, and evaluation, and they used the experiences from the pilot cases to adapt its manual for strategic evaluations.

There was one last area of concern the program had to address at this point. Though the GIZ team had established a close cooperation with its main counterpart, MIDEPLAN, and engaged in regular conversations and joint reflections, tensions in the cooperation became apparent: Feedback from interviews that had been conducted after the first year of implementation revealed that misunderstandings and frustrations regarding roles and cooperation had arisen within the ministry. In a two-day workshop organized and facilitated by the GIZ team, GIZ and MIDEPLAN discussed these findings and their mutual impressions. In the first part of the workshop, the group reflected on what they had achieved so far and what had worked and why. In a second part, the teams from MIDEPLAN and GIZ made their difficulties with cooperation visible in a drawing: MIDEPLAN chose to draw a football stadium with an ongoing game as a symbol for the cooperation. On the field were players from MIDEPLAN and GIZ – however, it was not always clear if they were playing on the same team or competing against each other, nor what the exact rules of the game were. Meanwhile, there were a lot of spectators at the margins – watching, cheering, and relaxing, and occasionally throwing new balls onto the playing field – representing other institutions/stakeholders of the program, but also staff from MIDEPLAN's other areas.

The teams realized that they were in danger of reproducing the patterns and becoming part of the problems they were trying to solve: competition, miscommunication, and lack of coordination. They decided on a series of measures. These included explicit agreements on roles and rules of the game. For example, in all project activities or change projects, one person was appointed as the official coordinator or focal point, who would serve as the entry point for requests from other institutions and shared all information within the team. The team also organized Q&A sessions within the ministry and improved communication with – and the involvement of – other areas from MIDEPLAN.

As a program that was working on accountability, transparency, and organizational learning, the program itself tried, and needed, to be a model in how it gathered, processed, and made information and data available. The project paid much attention to the setup of its own monitoring system, which was supposed to serve as a good practice in itself. The program's M&E system consisted of various elements:

- process- and results-indicators assessed by different methods such as focal groups, surveys, document analysis, etc.;
- a comprehensive study that consisted of a series of in-depth interviews with relevant stakeholders, external observers, and experts. Interviews were conducted by an external independent consultant and designed as a panel. The interviews focused on implementation progress/results but also on the project setup and internal functioning. They included an analysis and visualization of actors and relationships within the wider institutional system;
- regular assessment and evaluation of Capacity WORKS "success factors": Where do we stand with regard to the five success factors? Which success factors require our attention? Which modifications are necessary in order to achieve our objectives/results more effectively?

Feedback that was obtained by different means and from different sources was shared and discussed within the steering group. Lessons learned in all components were discussed and documented on a regular basis. An important source of feedback was the panel study, which included not only interviews and perceptions from stakeholders and beneficiaries but also external observers and independent experts as well. Critical observers, who were not directly involved in project implementation and had no immediate stake in particular activities, were an important source of information to assess blind spots and biases of the project team. Regular joint reflection within the cooperation system – combining evidence from external data with internal perceptions, lessons learned, and hypotheses – were important loops for shaping the implementation process.

By the beginning of 2014, all four pilot evaluations had been finalized and results were discussed and published. Institutional management responses and plans were developed. MIDEPLAN set up a national evaluation agenda for the upcoming years.

The coordination group organized an international knowledge-sharing event in March 2014. All actors of the coordination group assumed a very active role during the preparation and execution of the conference. During this event, the Minister of Planning officially submitted the reports of the country's first strategic evaluations to the corresponding authorities, and MIDEPLAN presented its achievements and learnings together with a group of committed allies.

An evaluation of FOCEVAL, conducted in September 2013, came to the following assessments (GIZ, 2013): In comparison with other comparable technical cooperation programs with similar funds, the program achieved to position the topic in the sector in a relatively short time; the good cooperation with the Ministry of National Planning and the commitment of other stakeholders affected the cost-effectiveness relationship positively. The connection of the program with its political counterpart was exemplary. The Ministry of National Planning has actively pursued the institutionalization of strategic evaluations.

Conclusions

Was FOCEVAL's implementation process smart? In retrospect, many of the program's decisions were not smart. The decision to engage in the health sector evaluation was not smart. However, there appeared to be good reasons for it at the time. In other countries (e.g., Mexico), large-scale, strategic evaluations that received broad public attention had served as icebreakers for developing national evaluation capacities. Nevertheless, the evaluation case, its implication, and its context needed to be assessed and understood, and the decision was made – and announced – too early (due to political pressures from different sides). Strategic evaluation was introduced as a new process to the public sector; roles and procedures – though existing on paper – needed to be practiced. Practice requires room for detours, delays, and possible failure. The pressure that built up with regard to the first evaluation was counterproductive and tied up too much of the program's attention for too long.

The strategy process can be considered as being somehow smart – it served different purposes, increased ownership among counterparts, and helped the program to establish the foundations and contacts for program implementation – but the outcome (operational plan and results model) was overambitious. The program team and their counterparts would have been wise to listen to more critical voices initially. However, as it can happen when a new project is set up (and especially when most of the people involved have a strong planning and/or evaluation background), the team fell into a planning illusion and believed it had to identify only the right paths and patterns. From today's perspective, the advice of the program team would be to start small, think big, and grow as you go. The initial illusion was that the program could tackle all relevant processes at the same time and began with the most audacious challenges (healthcare evaluation).

Probably the smartest thing about FOCEVAL was that the project was able to attract and include an increasingly large number of diverse voices over time and to build a platform for collective learning and impact. This did not happen by chance – it was supported by structured reflections and also by making use of tools from Capacity WORKS. The project identified and approached cooperation partners deliberately and opened options for their participation and involvement (e.g., through the steering structure). Spaces and processes for reflection, learning, and cooperation were created. However, a high level of intensity of cooperation and a multitude of actors often imply high levels of conflict as well. A cooperation system has an underlying set of different organizational logics, interests, and cultures at its base, with different needs and requirements for more or less formalization, communication, or information. This has been a recurring issue in the program. The lesson learned is possibly that there is no optimal outcome that will satisfy all but rather only an approximate good compromise. In the course of the program, it was important to reflect on when and where it was adequate and eligible to change the visible and invisible rules of the game, and where it was necessary to enforce and not inadvertently undermine them, for example by establishing temporary, parallel structures and processes. For example, it was considered crucial that MIDEPLAN was – and was perceived as – the owner of the pilot evaluations and set the rules for them.

There is no one-size-fits-all approach for a cooperation system and steering structure. Different means and options – and their advantages and disadvantages – should be considered. In the case of FOCEVAL, the coordination group was not only a means to an end for improved implementation but also an intervention that addressed deficits of inter-institutional communication and the lack of coordination. Also, there were no other relevant donor activities in the sector; therefore, no other coordination and transaction costs were imposed on program staff and counterparts. The discussions and joint activities within the coordination group improved the common understanding of challenges and objectives as well as strategic alliances with regard to a new and controversial issue. In this context, it was a crucial catalyst for the other success factors of learning and innovation, strategy development, and cooperation.

Finally, did Capacity WORKS make FOCEVAL's implementation process smart(er)? Capacity WORKS was an integral and important part of the program's management approach. It provided orientation and helped to facilitate a joint learning process within the cooperation system, which enhanced trust and enabled critical discussions over time. It was furthermore helpful to establish a common language and approach in order to discuss implementation challenges within the cooperation system. This required resources (time and space) and commitment, as well as a high level of interaction. It was an enabling factor that there were people among the program's main counterparts who felt immediately attracted to the systemic ideas underlying the model and who assumed visible leadership and supported its joint application throughout the implementation process. In the end, any management model can only be as smart as the people working with it.

References

Gallardo, R. (2013, July 20). Columna de opinión. *El financiero*.

FOCEVAL/GIZ (Strengthening Evaluation Capacities in Central America/Deutsche Gesellschaft für Internationale Zusammenarbeit). (2012a). *ECD strategy*. Internal documents. Costa Rica: Author.

FOCEVAL/GIZ. (2012b). *Steering structure*. Internal documents/workshop documentation. Costa Rica: Author.

GIZ (Deutsche Gesellschaft für Internationale Zusammenarbeit). (2013). *Informe de evaluación. Programa FOCEVAL*. Internal documents.

GIZ. (2015). *Cooperation management for practitioners. Managing social change with Capacity WORKS*. Wiesbaden: Springer Gabler.

OECD (Organisation for Economic Co-operation and Development). (2015). *Costa Rica. Good governance, from process to results*. Retrieved July 29, 2016, from http://www.oecd.org/countries/costarica/costa-rica-good-governance-from-process-to-results-9789264246997-en.htm

Sanchez, S., & Storm, S. (2016). Political use of evaluation results in Central America. In R. Stockmann & W. Meyer (Eds.), *The future of evaluation. Global trends, new challenges, shared perspectives* (pp. 204–213). London: Palgrave Macmillan.

Safe Enterprises: Implementation Experiences of Involving the Private Sector in Preventing and Fighting Violence Against Women in Peru

Christine Brendel, Franziska Gutzeit, and Jazmín Ponce

Executive Summary

> A medical representative was absent on Monday – one of many occasions – but the reality was that she was not merely absent, she had been killed by her husband who then committed suicide. No one could have foreseen the fateful event. (General Manager, Laboratorios Bagó, Peru)

The general manager of Laboratorios Bagó in Peru depicts this as being the turning point that prompted the lab to start a program to combat violence against women. Yet, it should not have required the death of an employee to deliver a wake-up call. Estimates show that 30–50 percent of women in Bolivia, Peru, and Ecuador are subjected to physical violence by their partners (World Health Organization, 2013). If warning signs such as the repeated absence of a medical representative are noticed, such fateful events can not only be foreseen, but prevented.

The Laboratorios Bagó case is just one example of the many reasons that the "Combating violence against women in Latin America" (ComVoMujer) program was initiated; the team pushed through the obstacles in their way to prevent cases such as these. This case study aims to outline the implementation strategies, experiences, challenges, and successes of the ComVoMujer regional program involving a new actor – the private sector – in preventing and fighting violence against women (VAW) in Peru. The study answers three main questions:

- Can the private sector be an important partner in preventing VAW?
- Will the private sector take ownership, despite the fact that VAW is perceived as not being their concern?
- Will governmental institutions recognize the engagement of the private sector and work together?

ComVoMujer was launched in 2009 and was prompted by the commissioner, the German Federal Ministry for Economic Cooperation and

Development (BMZ), to include the private sector into its activities by creating ownership and encouraging cooperation with governmental and non-governmental actors. Although faced with challenging circumstances, ComVoMujer was able to manage obstacles mainly by understanding the nature of the private sector and using its logic to create innovative measures.

As VAW is an extremely multifaceted and widespread problem, it was also important to reduce complexity while focusing on prevention and intimate partner violence against women in order to successfully carry out decisions and steer the program toward a fruitful implementation. Clearly structured internal-steering processes and permanent supervision were also vital. Additionally, it was helpful to count on knowledgeable and multidisciplinary staff with experience in the field and valuable contacts to important and relevant external partners.

An important counterpart was the Peruvian Ministry of Women and Vulnerable Populations (MIMP[1]), which signed a work agreement committing formally to include the private sector in its work after having been convinced of the advantages of a multi-sectorial and multi-stakeholder approach. In order to win over the private sector and connect all sectors involved, the program elaborated a conception framework and indicators for safe businesses as well as carried out various research studies on the economic consequences of VAW for companies with the University of San Martín de Porres (USMP). Especially the empirical evidence of the financial impacts of VAW provided a very useful argument.

Along the way, the program also learned other valuable lessons that it took into consideration for future actions: It became evident that it was necessary to always count on the approval and involvement of the upper management of possible partners in the private sector, as only in this way could a sustainable partnership be guaranteed. Additionally, alliances were always helpful as door-openers. Exchanging best practices and mutual learnings was not only a great asset but also a very effective scaling-up strategy. It was also of utmost importance to involve the media to spread knowledge and information and to generate further interest.

Looking back at the three main questions before implementation, all can be answered with a "yes." This proves that the strategies applied by

---

1   The ministry was known until 2012 as the Ministry for Women and Social Development (MIMDES), and thereafter as the Ministry of Women and Vulnerable Populations (MIMP).

ComVoMujer worked: Having started with zero enterprises to work with, the program is now working intensively with 100 companies, 4 business associations, and has collaborated with about a further 400 companies.

After having been convinced of the effects that VAW has on them, companies took ownership by conducting campaigns, carrying out further studies on the effects of VAW, training their employees – both through workshops and online certifications – and implementing special management models to prevent VAW.

State institutions are increasingly recognizing the work that has been done by the private sector. The MIMP, for example, launched the certification "Safe enterprise without violence and discrimination against women" in order to encourage more businesses to implement preventive measures. Even the USMP and other representatives from the academic sector carry out – and will continue to carry out – research on the effects of VAW by analyzing, for example, which consequences VAW has on students' productivity.

Introduction

Gender-based violence against women is one of the most widespread human rights violations: It is an expression of the unequal power relations between genders and hinders social and economic development. Violence against women not only affects individuals, it also has consequences for families, communities, nations, and the global community at large, as well as generates high costs for both the public and private sectors.

Development challenge(s)

Combating violence against women poses unique development challenges in Latin America, as it takes place in a socio-cultural environment in which the concerns of women are subordinate, and in which violence against them is tolerated. Despite international attention and the progress achieved, the number of victims of violence is still alarming. The main shortcomings are in the implementation of measures for prevention, but when it comes to counseling and assistance, punishment and compensation measures are also lacking.

As VAW is particularly widespread in Latin America, BMZ saw that it would be useful to set up a regional program to prevent violence against women and commissioned the Deutsche Gesellschaft für Internationale Zusammenarbeit (GIZ) to create a program to tackle this particular issue. The program was to directly support the implementation of international and regional human rights conventions such as the Millennium Development Goals (especially MDG 3), the Convention on the Elimination of All Forms of Discrimination Against Women (CEDAW), and the Convention of Belém do Pará, as well as the development agendas of the partner countries and BMZ.

Implementation challenge(s)

The program was not based on an explicit demand from one partnering country, but an answer to a severe regional problem. As there was no regional state organization dealing with violence against women, after a long discussion of who might be the best lead partner for the program, the regional network for women's rights, the Comité de América Latina y el Caribe para la Defensa de los Derechos de la Mujer (CLADEM) was chosen, as they were the only regional organization that explicitly dealt with the topic. However, the partnership came to an end after only one year due to irreconcilable differences on the implementation of the program. One of the problems was that CLADEM did not really want – due to their ideology and principles – to work with the private sector, which complicated cooperation significantly. Since then, the program's political lead partner has been the MIMP, which had been previously considered but did not have a regional interest, which they later developed.

In the program's first phase (2010–2013), the emphasis was on indigenous women and the private sector. Focusing on the private sector seemed like a risky initiative at the time, as so far there had been few examples of cooperation dealing with human rights – although the German development corporation had been focused on working with the private sector since 1999. Yet, because the program was drafted as a pilot, BMZ was willing to take the risk and include the private-sector component.

All partner countries have committed themselves to preventing, combating, and punishing violence against women. They have also ratified major international agreements, put in place laws on protection from violence, and developed action plans to tackle gender-specific violence. How-

ever, the limited exchange of information and experience between countries and the lack of dialogue between public-sector, non-governmental,
and private-sector stakeholders make it difficult to implement existing
laws and action plans, and even more difficult to realize prevention strategies.

Additionally, one challenge in implementing the program was that civil
society, the state, and the private sector showed no major interest in working together on the prevention of violence against women, as they did not
consider the others to be relevant partners for them. As a matter of fact,
the only actor that was truly active in the field of human rights was civil
society. This made it even more important to encourage cooperation
between the sectors. Yet, the deep split and mistrust between the three parties at the beginning of the program made it very difficult to get them all
involved to exchange information and experiences.

These splits and levels of mistrust have an historical background: These
actors generally work independently of one another, and there have been
few common socio-political interests. In Peru, civil society movements are
usually left-wing and seen as being a very strong opposition to the profit-
oriented private sector as well as to the government. On the other hand,
the relationship between the Peruvian government and the private sector
has always been very volatile, as it heavily depends on the political orientation of the current administration. Therefore, cooperation between the
sectors has been difficult and, in some cases, when achieved, it has only
been selective and never long-lasting.

The program's implementation challenges ranged from finding and successfully working with the right lead partner to involving the private sector, communicating between and within countries, as well as cooperating
between sectors. The decision was made to focus on the private sector in
order to gain a new player to increase the possibility for change. The fact
was that there had been hardly any work done in Peru, and the private sector did not consider VAW at all as an issue that affected them. Only a single company had done some basic work on the topic. The program at the
time did not have an entry point for collaboration with the private sector
and could not count on its support.

Implementation questions

The main concerns and questions as program implementation began were therefore:

- Can the private sector be an important partner in preventing VAW?
- Will the private sector take ownership, despite the fact that VAW is perceived as not being their concern?
- Will governmental institutions recognize the engagement of the private sector and work together?

In the following pages, the contextual conditions of the case study will be elaborated in further detail, including the strategies used to convince partners when there was very little interest in collaborating, and especially how things got started when, at first, it seemed there was nothing to get started with.

Contextual conditions of the case study

This case study mainly focuses on Peru due to the fact that the first activities to involve companies in the prevention of violence against women were initiated there. Peru is a presidential democracy divided into 25 regions with a business-friendly policy framework that encourages further economic growth. The main economic activities are mining, manufacturing, agriculture, and fishing, with a very strong informal sector (more than 50%).

The political landscape is marked by weak institutions, time-consuming bureaucratic procedures, a low-skilled workforce, and precarious infrastructure. Private-sector influence in the political sphere was – and is – very strong. In contrast, the general interest in political issues as well as political participation of Peruvian citizens is very low: 8 percent according to El Comercio and Ipsos Apoyo (2014). This is especially true when it comes to VAW.

VAW is a widespread problem due to unequal power relations, strong patriarchal structures, and machismo. It is tolerated and barely considered a public concern, which translates into little political interest and a strong societal indifference to preventing and combating it. Even though the prevention of VAW is included in Peru's development agenda and the country has a strong normative framework, many of these norms and laws are not properly implemented. The country ratified conventions such as Belém do Pará and CEDAW. Additionally, the MIMP has a National Plan[2] as well as a National Program against domestic and sexual violence: "Programa Nacional contra la Violencia Familiar y Sexual" (National Program Against Domestic and Sexual Violence). However, these plans and programs are not as effective as they should be for different reasons – one being that they focus mostly on addressing violence when it occurs and rarely on prevention.

Furthermore, one of the most important weaknesses in the eradication of VAW in Peru is a nearly non-existent budget in comparison with the dimension of the problem. The limited budget that MIMP has, compared with other ministries and even other social programs, has resulted in a poor and weak presence in all regions. All this adds up to why – despite the government's efforts over the last decades – VAW has not been notably reduced.

In the case of the private sector, due to the socio-economic development of Peru and the influence of globalization in the last decade, companies have started to include social measures in their actions. At first, this was done through philanthropic intentions, which later developed into a corporate social responsibility (CSR) approach, in which sustainability and the generation of capacities in society are required principles. ComVo-Mujer used CSR as a door-opener for the prevention of VAW as well as the wide range of implementation possibilities within companies' action plans because CSR initiatives have to produce a positive impact on employees, clients, and the community.

On the other hand, even though companies do not have specific budgets for programs to prevent VAW, they normally have a general one for CSR. This means that VAW competes with numerous other social themes, as well as the fact that it is mainly considered a private matter. For that reason, it was very important to develop arguments demonstrating the economic impacts of intimate partner violence for companies.

In summary, even being conscious that the relationship between state institutions and the private sector has had its ups and downs, it was of utmost importance to develop a multi-sectorial approach in order to pre-

---

2 Up until 2016, this National Plan was known as "Plan nacional contra la violencia hacia la mujer 2009–2015" (National Plan to Fight Violence Against Women 2009–2015). Now the plan has been renamed "Plan Nacional Contra la Violencia de Género 2016–2021" (National Plan Against Gender-based Violence 2016–2021).

vent resistance to a program that specifically fights against VAW. The program was therefore challenged to achieve a sustainable alliance between the government and the private sector and overcome some obstacles.

The program was designed based on a few assumptions, which did not all play out in reality. One assumption was that companies would have specific demands and be interested in engaging with the topic of VAW. Another assumption was that finding a regional partner would be easy. Yet, at the beginning, there was no explicit demand for the program and finding a reliable partner for the whole region proved to be difficult. On the one hand, this posed some serious challenges when it came to enlisting enough partners in time, but on the other hand, it gave program coordinators the freedom to choose who to work with and ensure that chosen partners had a strong level of ownership and were highly motivated to succeed with a new theme under difficult circumstances, as described above.

When making the decision about whom to work with, the program based its choice on several criteria. First, the political, legal, and economic contexts within the countries and on a regional level were analyzed. Second, the potential partner's interests, capacities, strengths, and weaknesses were considered. Third, the resources they could allocate and the level of pro-activeness they demonstrated in preventing and combating VAW were assessed. Finally, their openness to cooperate with entities from other sectors was analyzed. This was done while always remembering that, in order to come to a successful collaboration, the combination of potentials, experiences, contacts, financial resources, etc., needed to be mapped out well – within one partner but also between different partners.

This process demonstrated the importance of not only analyzing potential partners, but also potential opponents or possible risks or disturbances. The main criteria while making decisions focused on potential-seeking criteria rather than problem-solving ones, meaning the program selected partners that were interested in combating VAW and did not have to be convinced to do so – a task for which the ComVoMujer lacked the means and time.

To formalize collaborations, ComVoMujer negotiated with each partner a legally non-binding memorandum of understanding (MoU), the perfect instrument for this working context. Why? Because it allows for the strengthening of ownership through a specific and incremental implementation of interventions; opens space for iterative proceedings, experiments, and learning; and gives partners the required flexibility to move forward and the feeling of importance. Very often partners used the act of signing the MoU for public-relations exposure.

For the program, tracing the dynamics in the landscape of its partners is an ongoing process. The results of monitoring that is based on facts were used for making further decisions, as a means to stay on track with a specific chosen partner, for adapting or re-orientating the work in a new direction, or ending collaboration. For example, the need to re-orientate the work was necessary once the partner gained experience working with the topic; their engagement was institutionalized into their politics; and processes were incorporated into their value chain. The intensive phase of working together is completed and then only occasional advice is required. In contrast, when the partner changes its CSR priorities and VAW is not a main concern anymore, it is necessary to end the collaboration.

As elaborated above, because of existing challenges in trying to implement a sustainable program and connect – in this case especially – the private and public sectors, a reflexive management approach was chosen. This means there has to be a process of continuous searching and questioning, disputing conclusions, devising alternatives to setbacks, and helping to open up new possibilities for action by allowing deliberation from the middle ground between skeptical and overly optimistic approaches. It also means recognizing that every intervention has consequences on all management processes.

Tracing the implementation process

Connecting the private and public sectors and using existing interest in the country was seen as another helpful strategy to gain traction for the initiative. The question was: How to find this interest? The very first idea that came to mind, which seemed like a logical step, was to undertake a baseline study. The study was commissioned to determine the Peruvian companies and business sectors to start working with and to have local information on the issue. It was a difficult process that received a lot of resistance from companies. They showed no interest, refused to set up meetings, or stated that VAW was not an issue within their company. The baseline research nevertheless enabled the creation of specific criteria that showed which companies were suitable to work with and how to best approach them.

An important side effect that we did not anticipate at the time – but which served us in the long run – was that the information garnered about the local Peruvian context additionally helped to approach the MIMP, as they had not previously had such a baseline available. It was an important step, as the government holds significant sway in Peru and, as such, would help to open doors to corporations.

Integral to this process was having a Peruvian project team member. She had previous experience and connections to the government and knew how ministries worked and how to implement new policies. She contacted the director of the National Program in the ministry, signaling that GIZ was very interested in collaborating within the priorities of the National Program, one being the inclusion of the private sector.

Some branches of the ministry were initially skeptical as to why the government should do something for enterprises, when these have a bigger budget than the ministry. The resistance was also political, as the government feared garnering the image that it was getting too involved with the private sector – at the time, the government had also been privatizing many former state-owned entities. The answer that quieted the doubting voices was that combating VAW required a multi-stakeholder and multi-sectorial approach, as was evident by the fact that, despite the government's efforts over the last 15 years, VAW had barely declined in Peru.

After several meetings and workshops, the Peruvian project member from ComVoMujer arranged with the ministry to use businesses as new allies for the prevention of violence against women. This result was reached by simply asking questions and letting the MIMP draw their own conclusions, as this seemed to be the most sustainable form of communication and exchange.

The MIMP signed a work agreement in 2010, committing themselves to championing a prevention initiative against VAW, which was to be implemented along with the private sector. This document was particularly important, as it showcased a formalized commitment of a state agency to collaborate with the private sector. The collaboration and resulting work agreement were helpful in different ways: The slowly developing relationship with the MIMP (still called MIMDES at that time) gathered strength, as demonstrated through formalized agreements, which are particularly important in a context of high informality, as is the case in Peru.

With the support of the MIMP now acquired, a set of strong arguments was needed to convince the private sector, yet the information that was needed to formulate those arguments was sparse. As there was no data available on the subject of VAW and the private sector in the region, the initial investigation – conducted in collaboration with the Gender Program of the GIZ headquarters in Germany – was based on research done world-wide in order to outline arguments for the private sector.

The results of this investigation demonstrated that most of the work done worldwide had been realized in Western, Anglophonic countries and focused on CSR. Study results and arguments were presented in a conceptual framework. Once the conceptual framework was finished, it became clear that – since there had been so little previous regional research on the subject – having an academic partner involved would help deepen the subject matter and create proper data for the region. Scouting for academic partners, the manager of the program reestablished her contacts from a former work stay in Peru with the USMP. Their business management faculty showed interest and, as a first action, jointly published the previously elaborated framework.

At this stage of implementation, the overall strategy evolved so as to include all counterparts in approaching the private sector, as opposed to solely focusing on the private sector itself. First, the focus was on establishing contacts and creating trust between the program and the individual actors. Now those actors also had to be connected with each other, with ComVoMujer serving as the connecting piece.

The program was therefore willing to work with whoever showed real interest, involvement, and commitment, as demonstrated through time, money, and human resources pledged. It became clear that keeping an open mind, understanding the logic and rationality of the private sector, and finding different approaches was imperative to open doors. At the time, the program mainly used the personal relationships of its two senior technical advisors to achieve the necessary contacts. To build on solid arguments, it was necessary to create scientific academic evidence regarding the effects of intimate partner violence against women on the private sector.

Multi-stakeholder business breakfasts held to start a conversation on VAW with companies

Directly confronting company representatives had previously proven not to be very successful, as they did not believe that VAW affected them, and additionally felt accused of ignoring violence that affected employees within their companies. It was therefore seen as necessary to create a more open, non-confrontational space or platform to enable enterprises, the state, universities, and civil society to exchange opinions and experiences about the role of companies to prevent VAW. To achieve this, GIZ came upon the idea of holding business breakfasts. Simultaneously, the program tried to strengthen the bond between different actors, which is why the government and civil society were also always present.

One company, BELCORP, was invited to present their experiences at the first business breakfast. This decision was made in order to start a dialog and because the work BELCORP had done was the only experience available in Peru. The results of the breakfast were mixed: Direct feedback was not really received, some queries came from companies, but most of the interest came from state and civil society representatives. The breakfasts were successful in the sense that they exposed companies to the topic of VAW, but they did not have the desired effect of creating cooperation and partnerships with them. So the question remained about what to do to really motivate businesses to get involved in the prevention of VAW.

At that point, companies in Peru were already using CSR certifications to prove their social commitment and image. The program manager of ComVoMujer took advantage of this and came up with the idea of developing concrete indicators for VAW that businesses could use to fulfill part of their certifications, such as ISO 26000, the Global Reporting Initiative, etc., and/or existing laws and norms by implementing measures against VAW in their own organizations and within their communities.

These indicators were then developed in collaboration with Peru 2021 – a business association that focuses on CSR – and the USMP. The decision to partner with Peru 2021 was made because it is a well-recognized and well-regarded entity by corporations, and it would help to give the indicators more political weight. Additionally, Peru 2021 was very interested in the work and provided some interesting new perspectives about the elaboration of the criteria.

Simultaneously, the program ended up partnering with its first enterprise, TASA – one of the biggest Peruvian fishing companies. Contact with their human resources department was established through a team member of ComVoMujer Peru. The first activities were the elaboration of an informational leaflet and the organization of workshops for male employees along the coast.

An effort was also made to implement activities in the frame of a public–private partnership (PPP) project with TASA. After investing the necessary time for meetings on the elaboration of the PPP, it turned out that, although middle management had been successfully working together with ComVoMujer and the work was well-received by employees, the head management was not well-informed about the collaboration. So when it was time to sign the document, they stated that they were not interested in the prevention of VAW and pulled out. This once again confirmed for the program and its members that for a successful cooperation, an agreement with the head management had to be in place. Fortunately, this was not the end of the road with TASA: After bringing the collaboration to a halt for two years, TASA renewed its commitment to working together.

At the same time, ComVoMujer explored a new avenue and came across the idea of expanding its network by joining forces with other GIZ programs. The manager of ComVoMujer asked several directors of other programs, but the main answer was the same as with businesses: They did not think that violence against women was something that affected their work. But there was one exception: The GIZ water program in Peru had a lot of cooperating enterprises and good ties with them, so it was an ideal partner to work with. Initially, they were also reluctant, but the manager of the water program was willing to start a small survey on the ground and discovered that 11 of the 14 representatives he had in the field confirmed that VAW was a relevant topic – so the collaboration could continue.

An advantage was that the water program's communications officer was simultaneously the gender representative for GIZ in Peru. He was imperative for the cooperation in general, and specifically in creating an effective campaign. He orchestrated for the ComVoMujer manager to present the VAW project at the water provider's annual meeting. The manager was slated to hold the presentation at the end of the half day. This could have been a disadvantage but ended up being a boon, since the communications manager was able to use the time beforehand to convince the Arequipa provider to sign on – they were not only hosting the meeting that year but also celebrating an anniversary and looking to do something special. Being able to say the water provider in Arequipa and some other companies had already signed on during the manager's presentation greatly helped to push the other companies that were present to follow suit.

The reason why this event was more successful than the business breakfasts was due to the lobbying work done before and during the event within their association and among their members. Additionally, the chosen approach focused on their core business, with a strong connection to VAW: The slogan was "Turn off the tap against violence against women" (*Cierra el caño contra la violencia hacia las mujeres*). And third, the water companies were offered three options to get involved: Print the previously designed slogan on their November invoices, send a calendar with messages against VAW along with their invoices, and/or hold workshops about VAW for their employees. In the end, 37 companies signed on, allowing the VAW message to reach more than 3 million households, equal to 15 million people – or 49 percent of the Peruvian population.

A government seal to reward companies' efforts

At the same time, the implementation of measures with the MIMP was concretized: The "Seal for safe businesses free from violence and discrimination against women" – elaborated by using the indicators developed with Peru 2021 and the USMP – was finalized and launched at the end of 2010. The seal certifies companies that have taken measures to prevent violence against women. This was an important step to connect the different parties (state, private sector, and civil society as their service providers).

Unfortunately, national elections were held in 2011 and the change of government paralyzed the ministerial approbation of the seal. However, some of the permanent staff members of the MIMP lobbying and negotiating to maintain the seal succeeded, and the new government only changed parts of the design, but luckily not the content. That same year, the seal was finally approved with a ministerial decree, which converted it into an official government policy instrument, deepening the ownership of the ministry and making it more sustainable and public. This drawn-out process is symptomatic of any process that deals with government entities in Latin American countries – there are always unforeseen delays in getting ventures off the ground, which can be problematic because projects are only slated to take place for a limited amount of time.

In 2012, the MIMP relaunched the seal on March 8, International Women's Day, by presenting some prior results of the Peruvian study on the effects of intimate partner violence against women on businesses in Peru and inviting companies to participate. This proved to be very effective, as the surprising cost of VAW in terms of financial loss encouraged even more companies to take part and served as a very strong argument to implement preventive measures for VAW.

The seal was received well and 33 companies signed up, including big international companies such as IBM. After a process of assessment and evaluation, 23 companies qualified, from which 16 received honorary recognition and 7 received the seal. The MIMP followed up with companies that received honorary recognition and encouraged them to gain the necessary qualifications to be awarded the seal.

This initiative exemplified that the processes of competition as well as awarding committed companies correspond very well with the competitive character of the private sector. The seal helped make their social engagement marketable, which meant they could use their "unprofitable" extra work to improve their image. This instrument helped to place violence against women on the CSR agenda and make it more visible. This experience underlined the importance of working together with the state. One can also not disregard that, although previous ventures such as the business breakfasts might not have been as successful as desired, they did establish a good base that could be built upon with the seal.

A further supporting factor for the seal was the press coverage and interest generated by the research project between ComVoMujer and the USMP on determining the economic costs of intimate partner violence against women for businesses in Peru. At the time, there was no research available on the economic impacts of VAW on businesses in Peru or even Latin America, and, as already mentioned, local companies did not feel that VAW had any bearing on them, so a Peru-specific research study acted as a strong motivator. In addition, the MIMP successfully leveraged the study results as a marketing tool to gain public attention. The process of how the USMP and the MIMP involved the media and the public was an important lesson learned by ComVoMujer – a lesson that led to ComVoMujer deciding to hire a communications professional.

Using research to prove to companies that VAW is a critical matter

Understanding the nature of the private sector and its need for economic arguments, the investigation idea was presented to the USMP through previously established ties. The Director of the Research Institute of the Business Management School, Dr. Vara-Horna – an open-minded and innovative researcher – expressed interest in conducting the study. It is also

209

important to note that the investigation would not have been possible without the financial support of the sectorial GIZ Gender Program, which has its headquarters in Germany.

For Dr. Vara-Horna, his team, and the team of ComVoMujer, it was a steep learning curve at the beginning – although the USMP was enthusiastic about the study, the team did not have a gender background, and the ComVoMujer team did not have the necessary economic one. Quite a number of meetings, discussions, and reviews of the research were necessary in order to become versed on the subject before the actual study began. Of course, this was also an ongoing process, and it was imperative to maintain a balance between gender and women's rights and the economic perspectives as well as to guarantee the use of gender-sensitive language. Dr. Vara-Horna and his team proved to be extremely cooperative and always faced the program's feedback head on.

The combination of the professor's passion for the project coupled with the USMP's network of alumni enabled the involvement of 211 companies in the research – something the program would have never been able to achieve on its own. It was still a challenge to gain this pool of companies in order to have a representative sample for the survey, but the university's backing greatly aided in the process.

One success factor for the investigation was to include the private sector, civil society, and state during the initial design of the study as well as to make them part of the discussion once the results came in. This ensured that all sectors felt included and valued, which not only resulted in a better study but also guaranteed their support.

Another important factor was that, because of the experience and knowledge of the ComVoMujer team concerning gender-based violence, a challenge that needed to be addressed was revealed when the research was designed: If victims of VAW create higher costs for a company, this could be translated into the argument that women in general are more costly employees compared to men and should not be hired. Such a message would be very counterproductive to the overall purpose of the program's women's right agenda, that is, the social and economic empowerment of women. Dr. Vara-Horna therefore suggested including the costs generated by aggressors as well. This idea had very positive effects, and in the end it proved that aggressors in some areas generated greater costs than victims.

There was also some pushback from the ComVoMujer team internally to accept "capitalist theories" and to work with companies, as these did not necessarily represent the values of some team members. Up to this day, this resistance is part of the continuous learning process of ComVo-Mujer as a team, but it does not affect its work, as it is made clear in meetings and conversations that the cooperation with the private sector does not replace the rights-based approach but rather complements it. Furthermore, certain criteria have been established, such as not working with blacklisted companies or dealing with the topic always in the frame of CSR. The little to no knowledge about the work with the private sector also played an important role in the resistance of the team, which is why team members were trained in order to feel more secure when dealing with the topic. In the end, an agreement could be reached that companies were valuable allies for achieving the overarching objective.

After a year and a half, the results were in: VAW in Peru generates an annual loss of more than $6.7 billion due to 70 million missed working days. This remarkable number is equivalent to a loss of 3.7 percent of gross domestic product. These results had a big impact, in large part because Dr. Vara-Horna also continually involved and interacted with the media, thereby gaining exposure for the study. The study in itself, of course, merited this attention – it was the first of its kind, not only in Latin America, but worldwide, and it offered a huge amount of primary data that opened up a lot of new research aspects.

This research delivered the needed arguments to create interest within companies, as it demonstrated how VAW economically affects them. The broad distribution of the results also generated great interest in all sectors and enabled the establishment of VAW as a business matter in Peru.

Advising companies on implementing campaigns and educating staff

In 2011/2012, still trying to expand its network, ComVoMujer started working with Laboratorios Bagó, a pharmaceutical company that was very interested in the prevention of VAW. One of its employees was murdered by her partner, who then committed suicide – an event that left management in shock and very much committed to preventing VAW. They contacted ComVoMujer with a specific goal: They wanted to specifically sensitize and educate their 14- to 24-year-old customers about VAW through one of their products, Anaflex Mujer – a medication that helps to alleviate menstrual pain. They already had a young soap opera actress on their payroll who they wanted to use to produce informational video clips to be disseminated online. The program's role was to provide assistance to the writer, be present during filming, and establish a connection between Laboratorios Bagó and the MIMP in order to tie-in that young women could contact the MIMP's chat, making it a win-win situation for all parties.

Laboratorios Bagó continues to spearhead its own campaigns, occasionally bringing in ComVoMujer to consult. But by and large, it has autonomously continued to champion the cause, thereby exemplifying an ideal result: that technical assistance is provided to companies for them to get acquainted with a topic and how to deal with it, enabling them to take on the cause as their own, even after the support has ended.

On the scientific side, although the study had been thorough and successful, a number of new research questions had emerged that could not be answered solely in one study. There was some room for new research, but there was no budget to fund another large-scale project. Dr. Vara-Horna came up with the idea to start a scholarship fund to support students who would write their research projects on the topic. Additionally, the inclusion of VAW in their academic career meant that these future employees would be aware and educated on the topic, transferring their knowledge to their future workplaces.

With the study on economic costs, the involvement of state institutions and civil society, and the concrete work done, there were convincing arguments for more companies to get involved in the prevention of VAW. Now ComVoMujer was able to offer them different options of participation, such as capacity-building, technical assistance when applying for the seal, inspiration while developing campaigns for employees or clients, guidance to develop projects within the community, and then custom-tailoring their choices. This was the most fitting approach because companies did not want to take part in a standard program – they wanted to know the options that they could choose from and then adapt them to their own needs and timelines.

A handbook to support training in companies

However, the offer of instruments or concrete products to use for preventing VAW within businesses was not yet completely accomplished. Although programs had been tailored to companies' needs, there was still a request for a specific guide. Therefore, in 2013, ComVoMujer developed a handbook with training modules for businesses that served to develop capacities of employees and management, and one training module specifically developed for men. This instrument has proven to be an important part of a constructive solution to the problem, a tool to reduce the effects of VAW.

Once the handbooks were created, it was necessary to teach trainers who could instruct companies' personnel. It was necessary to establish a network of trainers who could educate other trainers in order to have enough qualified human resources. Additionally, everyone that took part in the training program committed to holding two free workshops so that it would not remain just a theoretical goal.

The continual problem – also with this training program – is that there are people specialized in the topics of VAW and gender, and then there are those who specialize in dealing with companies and human resources. But it is difficult to bridge the gap between the two in order to have fully trained people in both specialties who are able to train others.

Now that the work with companies had started and first results could be seen, something was needed when approaching a new company that did not just appear as GIZ trying to convince them, but also to have them hear from their peers. Although GIZ has a very positive image in the region, it is simply not part of the private sector. Therefore, a video was created in which companies shared their experiences when participating in the program, and it turned out to be a great motivating factor when companies heard directly from others about their positive experiences.

Different reactions in different countries

Although the work in Peru was fairly successful, the progress with companies in Bolivia and Paraguay was rather slow. The problems were the same as in Peru initially: Although the study was interesting, companies did not feel the findings applied to them. A logical next step at this point was to duplicate the study in Bolivia and Paraguay, to confirm the findings applied there as well, and have local discussions.

The role of the government was different in both cases, compared to Peru's. In Bolivia there was little interest from the government in participating. In Paraguay the replacement of the government meant having to rebuild a previously established relationship with the Ministry for Women's Affairs. Fortunately, at least in Paraguay, cooperation has thrived and the ministry has given the program better access to companies.

Dr. Vara-Horna conducted the study in Bolivia, and a consulting company was hired in Paraguay that was, however, still trained and supervised by Dr. Vara-Horna. In Bolivia the Bolivian-German Chamber of Commerce supported the work to reach companies, and in Paraguay it was the Global Pact. Originally, an exchange between the University of Asuncion in Paraguay and the USMP in Peru was planned. But at the last minute, there was a change in management at the Paraguayan university and the exchange fell through, as the new director's goal for the administration was for it to differentiate itself from the previous one, so the agreed cooperation was cancelled. The necessary human resources and time that were needed to convince the director were not available in Paraguay at the time. Luckily, the relationship with the Global Pact, which had initially been part of the exchange efforts, could be maintained. In Paraguay, the desired positive uptake in interest was achieved, yet in Bolivia – despite the study results being the most harrowing of the three countries – there has been little movement, which is currently being investigated.

The idea behind the scientific studies was not only to advise companies to take reactive measures against VAW but rather to show them the greater effects of proactive measures. The USMP elaborated a "Model of Management," in which companies would see the return on investment when dealing with VAW proactively. It is hypothesized that for every dollar invested, the return would be around $24.50 in four years.

In order to go beyond theory, the validity of the model is currently being tested. ComVoMujer had built a relationship with the Bolivian-German Chamber of Commerce and was acting as a consultant to the PPP that the chamber had set up with INTI, a big pharmaceutical company. The implementation of the Model of Management is part of this deal. Dr. Vara-Horna is jointly overseeing this challenging process with ComVoMujer, and there certainly are more lessons to be learned. To ensure that knowledge about VAW and the private sector is maintained as well as further distributed, the USMP, with the assistance of ComVoMujer, is elaborating a master's degree on equitable management.

Main results

ComVoMujer works in a triangular relationship between the private sector (which takes the view that VAW is not a relevant topic for them), the state (which has a normative framework regarding VAW but executes it poorly, be it because of a lack of resources or other priorities), and civil society, or more accurately, women's rights organizations (which have a reduced implementation radius).

With a view toward long-term political-strategic goals, ComVoMujer takes steps that emphasize the common goals shared with counterparts – even as they differ for each sector – and provide them with the evidence and technical tools needed for them to create a framework based on their individual visions and missions. This converts counterparts into agents of change, generating a value of their own, which in turn drives them to continue implementing measures against VAW, thus ensuring the program's sustainability.

Sustainability is further ensured not only by working with counterparts in all four countries, but also by fostering cooperation between the sectors while implementing new measures into their daily work. It is also important to concentrate on replicable measures and to distribute tasks to the team as a whole, not individuals. This allows each team member to contribute their strengths, and thus maximize the use of available resources.

The general response to the work with the private sector could be qualified as being surprisingly positive, as evidenced through its additional outcomes in the governmental and academic sectors as well as other international development agencies beyond Peru. There are new strategic partnerships (public–private, public–public, and public–private–social) in the region to prevent and fight VAW.

The progress made has matched or overcome the good practices of the Anglophonic countries that first inspired the work, which at this time is seen as an international example when it comes to knowledge-transfer about intimate partner violence against women and its consequences for companies, for example in the "Guide for Companies: Companies Free of Violence Against Women" of the United Nations Development Programme and the Spanish Agency for International Development Cooperation. Four of ten case studies demonstrate the work of ComVoMujer with the private sector. ComVoMujer additionally receives many national and international invitations to present its work with the private sector.

Having started working with the private sector in 2010 with no enterprises on board, the project's goals were more than surpassed when, in 2015, ComVoMujer had worked intensively with 100 companies, 4 business association, and collaborated with about a further 400 companies. Thanks to the scientific evidence elaborated, now enterprises not only know that intimate partner violence against women leads to the loss of 70 working days and \$6.7 billion per year (3.7% of GDP) in medium- and large-sized Peruvian companies, they also know that VAW is not a private issue and that it is a problem affecting all companies – and as such, it is a human resources management issue. This includes companies with a majority of male workers – for them, monthly presenteeism costs are \$100 higher than for victims.

Companies are also clear that prevention of VAW improves the work atmosphere, leads to higher motivation, loyalty, and personal commitment, and results in less turnover, which means improved staff performance and capability. It also helps to improve the public image of the company, which leads to greater consumption and use of their products and services. Another outcome is that around 300 enterprises wanted to know what is going on in their own businesses and carried out studies to measure the costs of violence against women in their companies.

To ensure information and capacity-building, new instruments have become available, such as: training modules for employees, managers, and a specific one for men; online certification; and a management model to prevent VAW in companies that was completed by an actualized conceptual framework, now with best practices of the region.

Concerning the outcomes in state institutions, the following should be noted:

* The Peruvian Ministry of Women and Vulnerable Populations (MIMP) is launching for the second time the certification "Safe enterprise without violence and discrimination against women." The initiative was replicated by the Ministry for Women's Affairs in Paraguay.
* The MIMP asked ComVoMujer to conduct a national study on gender-based violence against female owners of small and micro businesses and showed interest in a study concerning the costs of VAW for the government.
* ComVoMujer's work with enterprises has likely contributed to the creation of the Department of Entrepreneurship and Development in the MMIP.
* GIZ was invited to present the investigation results during the APEC Women and the Economy 2016 forum "Breaking Barriers to the Economic Integration of Women in the Global Market" in order to promote similar studies and measures in other Asia-Pacific economies.
* BMZ sees and uses the work done as a good practice.

There are also some very important outcomes regarding the academic sector:

- The study has been undertaken in Bolivia and Paraguay, and there are demands for more investigations in other business areas.
- Interest in the methodology of the study is spreading worldwide, for example the National University of Ireland is using parts of it in order to do surveys in African and Asian countries, and there is knowledge-exchange with Canadian, American, and European universities.
- Studies of the International Finance Corporation, the World Bank, and the Inter-American Development Bank are inspired by the new aspects of the Peruvian studies.
- New lines of business research as well as scholarship contests in the region are being created, and an MBA program is in development.
- In Paraguay, ComVoMujer is currently undertaking an investigation that has not been carried out before in the American continent or in Europe. It concerns the costs of intimate partner violence against women, which include costs for the government, the costs for the private sector, and the costs for households and their interrelations.

The work conducted by ComVoMujer is anchored in existing structures and mechanisms, allowing for its continued sustainability, even after the program's end. For example, when elaborating the quality seal, it was intentionally designed as a "national-owned label" rather than one imposed from the outside, since the goal was for it to become national policy.

The approach taken was that working on VAW is an investment, and that integrating measures to prevent it into corporate policies and action plans – combined with strong ownership – fosters sustainability, since companies tend to want to secure their contributions. Last but not least, the feeling for which measures could be sustainable is a very important skill for program teams to have to ensure continued success upon completion.

Lessons from the case study

Focusing on **key implementation lessons**, let us come back to the questions posed at the beginning of the program's implementation. *Can the private sector be an important partner in preventing VAW? Will the pri-*

vate sector take ownership, despite the fact that VAW is perceived as not being their concern? Will governmental institutions recognize the engagement of the private sector and work together? These questions could definitely be answered with a yes, as long as one takes into account the following points:

- A political understanding of the implementation requires asking to which extent traditional and modern political theories – such as the distinction between the public and private sectors, manufactured categories that have become fundamental in our thinking – are imbued with traditions of sexual order. This results in VAW being relegated to the private-life sphere and the communal responsibility being assigned to the state, which further strengthens stereotypes. Rather than combating this problem head on, it is important to focus on the potential, as ComVoMujer did with the seal. Since the private sector values governmental recognition, this hierarchical setup is not viewed as a problem but converted into an opportunity to motivate the private sector to combat VAW.
- Conducting initial context research and focusing on potentials, not problems, is important to gain a good entry point – in this case intimate partner violence and its consequences for companies, using the framework of CSR instead of VAW in the workplace.
- Alliances (personal connections, other GIZ programs, the USMP, the MIMP) are needed to open doors when introducing a new subject matter.
- Exchanging best practices and mutual learning is not only a great asset but also a very effective scaling-up strategy. The exchange of knowledge and capabilities between the academic, private, and public sectors as well as civil society is very important to develop strong actions for the prevention of VAW. For example, business conventions and meetings are very useful to disperse relevant information about the issue and link businesses that have good practices and experiences.
- To involve companies and state institutions in the prevention of VAW, it is necessary to generate empirical evidence, thereby making the effects and costs of VAW visible.
- It is, however, also necessary to involve the media to spread the knowledge and generate broader interest, as evidence-driven argumentation works very well. Concrete, easy-to-understand messages are therefore needed.

- (Re)orient and sequence the collaboration according to the conditions, new demands, and capacities of companies and state institutions, for example TASA, the seal.
- Minimize the project's visibility as much as possible. This might at first glance seem counterintuitive, but ComVoMujer found that smart implementation in this case meant establishing partnerships, starting discussions, and providing support – but ComVoMujer itself should never be the center of attention.
- The commitment of higher management is necessary in order to guarantee adequate implementation and sustainability.

The above points combined to form a certain code for ComVoMujer when it came to rules of engagement, namely "goals before personal opinion" in some cases. The goal of the program is for change to take root in society, and although ComVoMujer plants the seed, change should flourish even without its help.

Principles of managing and steering implementation

Within the requirements of human and women's rights (conventions, treaties), the implementation is driven by counterparts. Their demands, priorities, and mechanisms (national and sectorial politics, CSR) as well as existing instruments (action plans, business policies) and multi-sectorial relationships at all levels are at the forefront of management. The exploitation of opportunities, flexibility, the timely adaptation of strategies, consideration of the motivations and logic of counterparts as well as their operative capacities and possibilities of cooperation are mandatory.

The reduction of complexity for a subject such as VAW – focusing on prevention and intimate partner violence against young women – was the right choice and as important as designing strategies from a regional perspective based on sound competition between countries and sectors. The generation of evidence accompanied by appropriately timed dissemination and exchange – tailored for the particular needs of every group of actors – is a door-opener and fosters learning at the personal, organizational, and political levels.

For the abovementioned aspects, clearly structured internal-steering processes and permanent supervision are necessary. This means having memorandums of understanding with counterparts to define technical and financial responsibilities. It means acting like a competent "knowledge broker" supported by professional information management.

Last but not least, it means building a multidisciplinary team that is committed and works together well to face all these challenges to bring about permanent change.

References

Diario El Comercio. (2014). *Los peruanos somos poco solidarios y apolíticos*. Retrieved from http://elcomercio.pe/lima/ciudad/peruanos-somos-poco-solidarios-y -apoliticos-noticia-1717227

World Health Organization. (2013). *Global and regional estimates of violence against women: prevalence and health effects of intimate partner violence and non-partner sexual violence*. Geneva: Author. Retrieved from http://apps.who.int/iris/bitstream/1 0665/85239/1/9789241564625_eng.pdf

Rule of Law in Public Administration: Building Up an Administrative Legal System in the South Caucasus

Franziska Böhm and Christopher Weigand

Executive Summary

After the demise of the Soviet Union, the governments of the newly independent states had to transform their societal frameworks in order to enable the development of a market-oriented economy and the rule of law. The transformation process included extensive legislative reforms with a clear orientation toward Western models. The Deutsche Gesellschaft für Internationale Zusammenarbeit (GIZ) supported these efforts by advising Armenia, Azerbaijan, and Georgia on legal reforms starting in the early 1990s.[1] Although in the beginning the priority was the reform of civil laws, the focus shifted quickly to administrative law, as the need for a public administration based on the rule of law as a requirement for positive societal development was becoming increasingly obvious. However, the legacy of the Soviet Union posed challenges to the project. During soviet times, the citizens were treated as mere objects of the administration without individual rights in the administrative process and without the possibility of appealing an administrative decision before an independent court. Consequently, the general relationship between the citizens and the state had to be readjusted. Furthermore, almost all essential parts of an administrative legal system were missing and had to be built up from scratch.

Although the implementation processes varied according to the different reform dynamics within the countries, the approaches of the project were similar in all three countries. The starting point was to provide support for the creation of the administrative law framework. Additionally, the project supported the establishment of legal institutions, with a primary focus on administrative courts and judges. Besides that, the project – in collaboration with civil society organizations – informed the citizens about the new laws and their rights. Complementary to the bilateral

---

1 GIZ implements the program on behalf of BMZ.

efforts, the project adopted a regional approach to enhance the professional exchanges among the three countries and to create synergy effects.

By examining three critical junctions (short timeframe in the legislative process, resistance from within the administration, and radical political change), this case study illustrates what strategies were applied by the project to overcome impediments during the implementation process. It demonstrates the importance of closely accompanying and supporting the countries constantly throughout the process of establishing the rule of law. The project invested in individual agents of change from within the partner countries and created personal alliances between them and the project staff, which prepared the ground for the cooperative implementation of the administrative law reforms. A politically backed, long-term engagement and a continuous presence in the partner countries were important prerequisites to overcome unforeseen opposition to the reforms and, therefore, were crucial for the success of the project.

Introduction

Georgia 1998: Giorgi is an ambitious and talented young man of 27. After studying social science in the Soviet Union, he is not able to find a job in his profession and does not see any chance of working in the public sector due to a lack of contacts. Eventually, he decides to start his own car repair business in Tbilisi. He drives to the nearest administration building to find out about the necessary requirements to obtain a business permit. In the administration office, nobody provides Giorgi with the necessary information about the exact requirements for opening up his business. On the contrary, the public official behind the counter keeps on asking for additional documents each time Giorgi returns to the administration office to present the requested documents. Even for the "service" of providing information, the officer requests a small informal fee. Alternatively, Giorgi is told, he could pay 500 GEL to "speed up the process," but Giorgi does not have the money and therefore leaves the office frustrated and without a permit. An independent judiciary where Giorgi could file a complaint does not exist. The next day, Giorgi meets his cousin, who is the owner of a gas station. He offers Giorgi to start his business in a garage next to the gas station "without all this official paperwork." Giorgi accepts the offer gratefully, but he is aware that an illegal business startup under the roof of his cousin's business makes both entrepreneurs more vulnerable to arbitrary harassment from government officials.

As this story exemplifies, administrative corruption is a big obstacle to development. Bureaucrats deliberately obfuscate and increase the number of rules, procedures, regulations, and fee-paying requirements to induce the public into offering more bribes, thereby hindering individual citizens like Giorgi from opening up businesses and enhancing the development of the country (Karklins, 2002, p. 25). In contrast, a citizen-responsive and effective administration is based on the principles of efficiency, transparency, and accountability.[2] The first and foremost purpose of the administration is to act in the interest of the general public and to secure the rights of the individual citizens. The objective of administrative law is to provide a legal structure that is based on the rule of law for the relationship between the state and the citizen. Ideally, the necessary information for administrative procedures is easily accessible to citizens, and it is possible for them to apply for a judicial review before independent courts if they do not agree with the decision.

This contribution shows how – and with which strategy – the GIZ program implemented an administrative law system based on the rule of law in the three countries of the South Caucasus: Armenia, Azerbaijan, and Georgia.

Contextual analysis

After the demise of the Soviet Union, it quickly became clear that the newly independent states inherited a historical legacy that posed a severe challenge to the state-building efforts of Georgia, Armenia, and Azerbaijan. A deteriorating economic situation with rapidly increasing poverty rates was exacerbated by political turmoil. In Georgia different regions demanded independence from Tbilisi. Local warlords and organized criminal groups were challenging the state's monopoly of power. Simultaneously, the country drifted into poverty as its GDP dropped by 73 percent between 1991 and 1994 (De Waal, 2010, p. 134). A similar economic breakdown happened in Armenia, where the struggle for statehood was aggravated by the ongoing Nagorno-Karabakh conflict and the aftermath of the devastating earthquake that hit the country in 1988. The Azerbaijani-Turkish blockade of the country led to a severe scarcity of

---

2 See http://ec.europa.eu/civil_service/admin/index_en.htm

goods, which fostered widespread corruption and a widening division between a small, wealthy, and politically connected elite and the larger, more impoverished general population (Bertelsmann Stiftung, 2016a, p. 3). In Azerbaijan, after democratically elected Abulfaz Elchibey was overthrown by a military coup in 1992, Heydar Aliyev seized the opportunity to take power. Aliyev managed to bring stability to Azerbaijan by negotiating a ceasefire with Armenia, appeasing Russia, and cracking down on local warlords (Bertelsmann Stiftung, 2016b, p. 7).

Under these circumstances, the states' capacities to rule via administrative and judicial institutions were weak. The public perceived these institutions as being corrupt, incompetent, and interspersed with clientelism and arbitrary rulings. Administrative corruption and bribery for administrative services were not uncommon in the former Soviet Union (Waters, 2004, p. 43). However, following the demise of the Soviet Union, corruption began to affect virtually every aspect of daily life in the newly independent states of the South Caucasus (Sandholtz & Taagepera, 2005, pp. 109–131). Public officials understood that this regulatory vacuum allowed them a high degree of discretion in administrative decisions and actions that could lead to additional sources of income. In this situation, citizens had to rely on bribes to get any administrative issues addressed. In order to enhance democratic development and economic growth, the governments of Georgia, Armenia, and Azerbaijan wanted to transform their legal and institutional frameworks to establish market economies and the rule of law. The transformation process included extensive legislative reforms with a clear orientation toward Western models. This general orientation toward Europe was evidenced by the accession of the three countries to the Council of Europe. Georgia became a member of the organization in 1999, Armenia and Azerbaijan in 2001. The Council of Europe is an international organization that focuses on promoting democracy, human rights, and the rule of law. By becoming members of this organization, the three states committed themselves to uphold these principles.

GIZ supported these efforts by advising the three countries on legal reforms starting in the early 1990s. The former German Foreign Minister Hans Dietrich Genscher and the former President of Georgia Eduard Schewardnadse had a close and friendly relationship and agreed that Germany would support the transformation process of Georgia through technical assistance on legal and judicial reforms. GIZ sent Prof. Rolf Knieper as an expert – he had previously been active in legal reform projects in Africa. Prof. Knieper went to Georgia to meet with the Justice Minister, and both agreed upon reforming the civil law system to create a framework for a market economy. In the mid-1990s, the idea to include more countries in the reform process was introduced, and a conference with all post-Soviet countries and different donor organizations was organized in Bremen. At this conference, all participants – the post-Soviet countries as well as the donor organizations – committed themselves to the reforms of the legal systems.[3] Subsequently, GIZ set up bilateral programs with different countries. The programs were coordinated from Bremen – under the supervision of Prof. Knieper – but additionally every country had its own national coordinator. These coordinators were hand-picked based on their individual legal qualifications and professional potential. Prof. Knieper wanted to ensure that qualified individuals who could become long-term partners for the projects were in these positions. Many of these coordinators later made successful careers in their respective countries. One example is Lado Chanturia, from Georgia, who was the first Minister of Justice before becoming President of the Supreme Court and who is now the Georgian ambassador to Germany in Berlin.

Although in the beginning the priority was the reform of the civil laws, in the late 1990s the focus shifted to the public law framework, as the need for a judicial overview of administrative actions and decisions as a requirement for a positive economic environment was becoming increasingly obvious. As a consequence, the idea of administrative law reform was introduced more frequently in the regular debates with GIZ's partner organizations in the three countries. Georgia was the first of the three countries that started to work on the reform of administrative law in 1998/1999 and adopted the code on administrative court procedure (CACP) and the code on administrative procedure (CAP) in 1999. Both laws entered into force in 2000. In Armenia, the drafting process for both laws started in 2001. Although the CAP was adopted in 2004 and entered into effect in 2005, the CACP was adopted in 2007 and came into effect in 2008. In Azerbaijan, the drafting process started in 2002, but the laws did not enter into force before 2011.

---

3 Rolf Knieper, Interview, June 22, 2016.

Development challenge

The legacy of the Soviet Union posed a difficult task to the project organizers. It was especially problematic that the general concept of a citizen-responsive, transparent, and accountable administration was totally unknown in these countries. Although a civil law tradition existed and debates in Europe about civil law were followed closely in these countries since the 19th century, the situation was very different in the area of administrative law. Not only was there no tradition of an administrative law, but in fact the administration during soviet times was governed by principles diametrically opposed to those that characterize administrative law today (Luchterhandt, Rubels, & Reimers, 2008, pp. 15ff.). The citizens were treated mostly as mere objects of the administration without individual rights in the administrative process. Administrative decisions therefore were made without taking the opinions or motives of individuals into account. Rather, only the needs and reasons of the state were taken into consideration. The individual citizen was powerless to protest in the face of an all-powerful bureaucracy. Only the code of civil procedure contained some possibilities for the citizens to appeal against administrative decisions. However, this played a very marginal role in practice. Hence, in the Soviet Union, administrative law was neither a separate field of law nor did courts exist that had jurisdiction over administrative decisions. The only law that addressed administrative regulation was the law for administrative offenses. This setup reflects the implied relationship between the state and its citizens: It was a repressive regime that enabled the state to take the necessary steps against its citizen. Administrative law in that sense emphasized the obligations of the citizens and treated them as objects of state power.

As a consequence, the administrative law system had to be built up from scratch, as all the essential parts were missing. In essence, administrative laws did not exist and had to be drafted. A systematic review and reorganization of administrative agencies and proceedings was necessary for each body, section, and level of public administration. At the same time, the courts needed to be reorganized and budgeted for the new task. New judges had to be selected, appointed, and trained. Administrative law had to be introduced as a subject in the universities' curricula, and legal experts needed to be found who were able to teach the new legal concepts. Legal literature about administrative law was a prerequisite for that matter. Furthermore, lawyers, NGOs, and the media needed to obtain information on the reform concepts as well. Finally – and most importantly – the general relationship between citizens and the state had to be readjusted. The citizens had to be convinced to overcome their distrust of the courts and the state institutions in general, and to make use of their rights against the administrative bodies confidently. On the other hand, state employees had to change their attitudes toward the citizens and help them to put their rights into practice and, at the same time, accept judicial oversight of their actions and decisions.

Approach of the project

The approach of the project was similar in all three countries. However, the implementation processes varied according to the different reform dynamics within the countries. The starting point for the project was to provide support for the creation of legal texts for administrative law that would capture a citizen-centered approach and provide clarity in administrative procedures. All the partners involved unanimously agreed without further discussion that the creation of legal texts was the prerequisite for any further development of the administrative law system because written administrative laws strengthen the position of the citizens against the administrative bodies. Legal texts give the citizens the possibility to inform themselves about their rights in the administrative process, the legal obligations of the administrative body, and the legal possibility to appeal against an administrative decision. The strategy of the program was to enable local jurists to take the reform process into their own hands. Therefore, the program invested in capacity-building for the local experts and trained them in the concepts of the new administrative laws. During the legal drafting process, the program coordinators provided expert advice to guarantee high-quality legal texts and the orientation on international standards.

Additionally, the program supported the establishment of legal institutions, with a primary focus on administrative courts and judges. New administrative courts and special chambers for administrative complaints were set up. At the same time, the program provided trainings for the administrative judges. This was an especially difficult task because the vast majority of the local jurists had previously not been educated in administrative law and had little background knowledge about guiding administrative principles.[4] The program focused on the establishment of administrative courts and the training of administrative judges because of their relatively small number in comparison to the amount of administrative personnel. Therefore, the idea was to use the administrative courts as leverage to introduce a transparent, rule-based administrative system. The underlying assumption here was that judges in administrative courts would oversee administrative actions and decisions, and thus secure the law-abiding behavior of public officials. Additionally, well-educated and self-confident administrative judges would resist outside influences – for example, bribes or attempts of political influence – and would therefore gain the trust of the population in the new administrative system and encourage the citizens to make use of their new rights.

Besides that, the program supported the efforts to restore the trust of the population in the courts and other legal institutions. In collaboration with civil society organizations, it informed the citizens about the new laws and their new rights. This was done, for example, through the production of TV and radio shows, newspaper advertisements, and the distribution of flyers. Moreover, in recent years the program has supported collaboration with around 80 schools in Georgia, Armenia, and Azerbaijan, and introduced civic and legal education in the schools' curricula.

Although at first the support was provided by three bilateral projects, soon a regional perspective was promoted to enhance professional exchanges among the countries and create the potential for synergies. This broadening of the projects' perspectives and approaches was based on the observations and experiences of the project staff during its work on the ground. It became increasingly clear that all three countries faced similar conditions and problems in their transition process toward the establishment of the rule of law (Knieper, 2004, p. 22). This regional perspective was reinforced when the German Federal Ministry for Economic Cooperation and Development (BMZ) launched the Caucasus Initiative in 2001. The goal was to "foster cooperation between Armenia, Azerbaijan and Georgia, and to support economic, social and political development in the region, thus helping to defuse conflicts" (Bundesministerium für wirtschaftliche Zusammenarbeit und Entwicklung, n.d.).

---

4 Gerd Winter, Interview, June 5, 2016.

Implementation challenge

The regional approach was based on the assumption that all three countries faced similar conditions and challenges in the transformation process. However, the challenges for the program varied in the different countries because of changing political situations and different reform dynamics. Especially in Georgia, over the course of the program the political landscape shifted several times. In the 1990s, young progressive politicians – with the backing of President Schewardnadse – wanted to move the country closer to Europe. The program coordinators supported these efforts and worked closely together with these young reformers. Yet, the haste of the reform process – in combination with the will to make use of favorable political circumstances – put the legal drafting process under enormous time pressure.

These young reformers came to power after President Schewardnadse was toppled during the "Rose Revolution" in 2003. Under President Mikhail Saakashvili, they pushed radical constitutional amendments through parliament and changed Georgia from a parliamentary republic into a strongly presidential one (De Waal, 2010, p. 194). Their goal was to strengthen the Georgian state, to crack down on corruption, and to transform the economy. Even though the reforms were partly successful, especially the fight against petty corruption in the law enforcement agencies, these goals were reached through legally dubious methods. The new government saw the country in a post-revolutionary phase that legitimized these constitutionally problematic methods. A common phrase of the leading politicians at that time was: "We have to break the law to establish the rule of law."[5] The methods that were used to carry out the reforms gave reason for vocal criticism and posed problems for the program, as they affected the justice system as well. Many judges were removed with questionable justifications and replaced by politically favorable judges. For example, disciplinary law was used to replace unpleasant judges with ones affiliated with the ruling party. Additionally, government-friendly state prosecutors were appointed as administrative judges. These replacements of judges had an effect on the independence of the administrative courts. Court-monitoring reports show that before the change of government in 2012, the administrative courts heavily favored the state party. In 2011 and

---

5 Zeno Reichenbecher, Interview, June 17, 2016.

2012, the state party was entirely successful in 85 percent of the monitored cases in 2011, and in 79 percent of the monitored cases in 2012 (Transparency International, 2014, p. 3). Moreover, "in cases of significant public interest, judges appeared to not only render decisions favorable to the state party, but also to violate procedural regulations in favor of the state party" (Transparency International, 2014, p. 3). After the parliamentary elections in October 2012, a new government came into power. Since then, a positive trend has been observed, and the success rate of the state party has declined significantly. In 2013 the state party was entirely successful in 58 percent of the monitored cases, and in 2014 the percentage dropped to 53 percent (Transparency International, 2014, p. 3). Furthermore, the perception is also that "courts have become more independent and judges can act more freely."[6]

The political development was different in Armenia and in Azerbaijan, where the reform forces were weaker and less numerous than in Georgia. On the other hand, forces from within the public administration were more influential and put up resistance against the reforms. This was because the goal of the reforms was to make the administrative procedures more transparent, predictable, accountable, and less susceptible to corruption. In consequence, this meant a loss of power for the administrative bodies because their actions and decisions would be controlled by an independent judiciary. Additionally, many public servants lost a source of revenue because a transparent administrative procedure made it more difficult to ask for bribes.

Finally, the political tensions between Armenia and Azerbaijan because of the ongoing tensions in the Nagorny Karabakh region posed a serious challenge to the regional approach of the program. The main concerns and questions for the program were therefore:

- What is the best way to deal with time pressure during the drafting process?
- How can the program overcome resistance from parts of the administration?
- How should the program react to unlawful measures taken by the partners?

---

6 Olika Shermadini, Interview, June 22, 2016.

- How can the regional approach be applied when the relationship between Armenia and Azerbaijan is conflict-ridden and shaped by mutual mistrust?

Tracing the implementation process

As mentioned before, the strategy of the program was to start with the drafting of the new administrative laws, because this was seen as a prerequisite to any further implementation efforts.

From the beginning of the drafting process, the program coordinators worked together and established relationships with reform-oriented jurists (*agents of change*) from the respective partner country. The program focused on these individual agents of change because there was very little expertise on administrative law among the jurists in the partner countries. Therefore, the program invested in these agents of change to increase their legal capacities with regard to administrative law. This was seen as a precondition of a fruitful working relationship between the program and the partner countries, because this knowledge enabled the agents of change to hold discussions with international experts at eye level and to actively steer the reform process. Thus, considerable time and funds were spent introducing them to the concepts, principles, and standards of modern administrative law.[7] This was done during intensive trainings in Germany and in the respective partner country.

At the same time, working groups were set up that consisted partly of local jurists and partly of international experts. Whereas the international experts provided the legal expertise on international standards, the local jurists contributed knowledge about the societal conditions of the country and the respective legal system. However, the idea was that the process should be steered by the local jurists and that it should be their responsibility and task to draft the legal texts. The head of the working group acted as a link to the political level in each of the countries. The details of the laws were discussed and drafted within the working group without the involvement of other actors. A broader participation of different stakeholders was not pursued, either by the national stakeholders or the program, because a wide public debate was perceived as being politically too risky for the

---

7 Gerd Winter, Interview, June 9, 2016.

reform intention. Besides the individual agents of change, who had been intensively trained, there was hardly anyone capable of assessing the implications of the administrative reforms, not to mention the capacity of proposing alternative legislative solutions. When the drafts were finished, different stakeholders were involved to discuss and comment on the results. Through this process, the drafted laws gained legitimacy. However, participation was mostly limited to presenting and explaining the new laws to selected individuals representing the government, the judiciary, and the media.[8] It must be borne in mind that universal standards and concepts exist in the area of administrative law, and therefore a broader debate about the general concepts is not an indispensable part of the reform process. In fact, all three countries are members of the Council of Europe, which provides clear guidelines for aligning the administrative laws of the different member states.

Critical junction I: Short timeframe in Georgia

Georgia was the first country in the region to start with the reforms of the administrative law system. This can be explained by the political dynamics at that time. Georgia had active civil society organizations as well as young reformers who were pushing for reforms. Through the codification of the administrative laws, they hoped to gain stability in the country as well as recognition and solidarity from European countries. Because the program had been involved in the legal reform process since the beginning of the 1990s, it had already established a good working relationship with these agents of change. Lado Chanturia, who used to be the program coordinator for Georgia and in 1998 was Minister of Justice, acknowledged the need for the introduction of a transparent and citizen-responsive administrative law. Mikhail Saakashvili, who would later become president and was the chairman of the legal affairs committee in 1998, was also in favor of the reforms. The program – together with the Council of Europe and others – supported the reform efforts of the national agents of change. Saakashvili and Chanturia – next to other representatives of Georgia – participated in seminars organized by the Council of Europe in which advisors from France, the Netherlands, the United States, and Germany pro-

---

8 Hryar Tovmasyan, Interview, April 16, 2015.

vided insights into their respective administrative law systems. As a result, a working group was set up in Georgia under the guidance of the legal affairs committee of the parliament with the mandate to elaborate the two basic administrative laws. The drafting process was a joint project between Germany, the United States, the Netherlands, and Georgia. The working group consisted of two Georgian jurists and one expert from each country, with Prof. Gerd Winter from the University of Bremen being the expert for the program. Prof. Winter was asked to join the project since a cooperation agreement exists between GIZ (then known as GTZ), the judiciary, the Bremen Chamber of Commerce, and the University of Bremen, and he was already active in the international cooperation on administrative law. The experts provided legal texts that were analyzed and evaluated by the Georgian jurists before they discussed the details with the experts and drafted the laws in Georgian. This draft was translated into English and was discussed again with the experts. During the drafting process, the two Georgian jurists spent several weeks in Groningen and in Bremen. During their time at the University of Bremen, they were able to study intensively the concept of German administrative law and were in close contact with Prof. Winter. This time in Bremen shaped the working relationship between Prof. Winter and the Georgian lawyers profoundly, and it was increasingly based on mutual trust and respect. Another factor was that Prof. Winter was the only expert who was attending all the seminars in which the legal drafts were being discussed (Winter, 2010, p. 412). This personal relationship helped to overcome some difficulties in the drafting process. The most problematic part about the drafting process proved to be the short timeframe available for the consultations.

The drafting process in Georgia was under time pressure from the very beginning, because the reformers wanted to use the political momentum to pass the laws through the parliament before the parliamentary elections in October 1999. They argued that the composition of the parliament at that time guaranteed a smooth adoption of the drafted laws, and they did not want to risk failure of the reforms due to any possible changes in the parliament's composition and power structure. After the General Administrative Code was written, there was not much time left for the Administrative Procedure Code because of the approaching parliamentary elections. A lot of time was lost because, on the advice of the Dutch expert, the Georgian jurists drafted a complete code that neither took the civil process code of Georgia into consideration nor the fact that Georgia had decided not to introduce separate administrative courts.

The problem was that there was not enough time left to draft a completely new version of the code. In this situation, the Georgian counterparts followed the advice of Prof. Winter to adopt a simpler and shorter version of the law with references to the civil procedure code. Because of the shortage of time, the general approach of preparing the texts with local experts had to be left aside, and Prof. Winter wrote parts of the draft himself with little coordination with the other participants (Winter, 2010, p. 412). The established trust between the counterparts in the working group made it possible for the Georgian jurists to accept Prof. Winter's relatively short draft, which had only 35 articles. This draft later passed through parliament without major discussions.

The drafting process and the outcome were not ideal. The rudimentary law caused problems in its application, therefore it was amended 22 times between 2000 and 2010 (Winter, 2010, p. 413). However, the drafting process as well as the outcome were the best *possible* solutions and the consequences of particular historical circumstances. The possibility to plan the legal drafting process ahead of time is generally very limited. Moreover, it is a process that is shaped by uncertainties and unexpected turning points. As Prof. Winter expressed it:

> Legal transfer is not only an exchange and a mutual learning process, it is as well a political process, where imbalances of power, disparities, cultural differences, strategic behavior and last but not least rational discourse interact. It is a process of "muddling through" and the search for second best solutions. (Winter, 2010, p. 431)

Because of the process-based character of the legal consultations, the experts and their working relationships with the counterparts are central to the success of the process. As the Georgian example clearly shows, this enabled the program coordinators to react quickly and flexibly to changing situations. This is only possible if the expert has been given enough discretion from the program and enough trust from the partner side. In Georgia this trust was on the one hand gained by the continuous efforts and dedication of Prof. Winter, and on the other hand by the long-term engagement of the whole program. Furthermore, the process of drafting the laws without broad participation but through a small group of lawyers was also due to the specific historical situation. Very few people in Georgia had experience with the concept of a transparent and citizen-responsive administrative law. Therefore, the program's strategy was to work with a handful of jurists and enable them, through trainings, to actively participate and steer the implementation process.

After the laws came into force, the program continued to support the reform process by training administrative judges as well as providing assistance to Georgian jurists to write two textbooks and a commentary on the administrative laws. Subsequently, trainings for administrative personnel were conducted as well. After 10 years, the program started a project to review and overhaul the administrative laws. Working next to two Georgian administrative judges and one professor from the State University of Tbilisi, Prof. Winter was again the program's expert. The working group proposed comprehensive draft amendments and presented them to the ministries and to the Georgian parliament, but due to the absence of political will, the reforms were not carried out. Prof. Winter – with the approval of the program – used his personal relationship with the Ministry of Justice to promote the reforms, which led to two expert panels, in which the reforms were discussed and Prof. Winter acted as moderator (Winter, 2010, p. 414).

However, because of other political priorities, the amendments have still not been adopted by the parliament. This shows the dependency of the program's success on the reform dynamics in the partner country. Currently, the program is preparing the ground for subsequent reforms by setting up another working group in consultation with the Ministry of Justice in order to be ready to act if a window of opportunity appears.

Critical junction II: Resistance from the administration

The resistance from within the administration against the reforms was stronger in Armenia and in Azerbaijan. In Azerbaijan, the traditionally strong and centralized administration was opposed to the idea of judicial oversight of their administrative acts. As one program expert expressed it, "to impose a rigid legal framework on the administration and to limit the administrative decision-making scope must have appeared as an alien concept."[9] However, there was no open resistance from the administration because the reforms had the approval of the president. Here, the regional perspective of the program contributed toward fostering the initiation of the reforms and convincing national decision-makers to support the administrative law reforms. After the administrative laws had entered into

---

9 Thomas Melzer, Interview, May 12, 2015.

force in Georgia, in 2002 the program organized a regional conference in Bremen. It supplied the legal texts of the Georgian administrative laws, which provided the opportunity for the delegates from Armenia and Azerbaijan to learn about the Georgian experience with the administrative reforms as well as discuss different issues about administrative law. This was probably one of the key factors for convincing Armenia, and subsequently Azerbaijan, to follow the reform path. Considering the political tensions between Armenia and Azerbaijan, it is remarkable that high-ranking officials came together to discuss different aspects of the administrative reforms. This was just possible because the program focused exclusively on legal issues and left out all political aspects that could have caused tensions among the participants from the different countries.

In a speech during the conference, the Minister of Justice of Azerbaijan praised the courage of his Georgian colleagues for their reform efforts (Deutsche Gesellschaft für Internationale Zusammenarbeit, 2002). At the same time, he showed his commitment to an administrative system based on the rule of law and his willingness to reform the legal system. From that moment onward, the government supported the administrative law reforms, and there was no open resistance against the process from within the administration. Because the program had already been active in civil law reforms in Azerbaijan during the 1990s, it was asked that the administrative law reforms be supported as well.[10] Thus, the involvement of the program in the administrative law reforms was a direct consequence of its broad approach to legal reforms as well as its previously established alliances and good personal working relationships with the Azerbaijani government.

In Armenia, the program found a strong ally in the Minister of Justice, David Harutunjan. Under the auspices of the Ministry of Justice, a working group for the drafting process of the administrative laws was founded and included the program's country coordinator, Wartan Poghosyan, on the Armenian side. However, the situation in Armenia was different because forces from within the administration resisted the reforms more strongly. Opposition against the Administrative Procedure Code built up after the laws were drafted. The parliament had adopted the General Administrative Law in 2004. At that time, the working group was already working on the Administrative Procedure Code. It was planned to submit

---

10 Sayyad Karimov, Interview, April 7, 2014.

the draft to the parliament in early 2004 so that both laws could become effective simultaneously on January 1, 2005. However, it took another three years before the Administrative Procedure Code was finally adopted by the parliament. This delay was primarily due to growing resistance within the administration, to which the parliamentarians were reacting. This was partly a reaction to the information events and training seminars that were conducted by the program after the General Administrative Law was adopted in 2004. Administrative authorities started to realize the implications of the administrative reforms and understood in greater detail how the new law restricted administrative procedures and decision-making in general.[11] Because of this resistance, the reform process was stalled.

Even though there was a valid decision in principle from the parliament in favor of the new General Administrative Law, it did not take any legislative action to enact the new law. This situation was problematic for the program, as it had – on request of the Minister of Justice – already trained 20 Armenian judges at great financial and personal expense, which raised expectations on the side of BMZ.[12] Because of approaching general elections in Armenia and the possibility of a change in political majorities, there was a risk that all the program's efforts would have no effect and that the administrative reforms would not just be postponed but suspended completely.

The program coordinators believed that one possibility to overcome the stalled reform process was the direct intervention of President Robert Kotscharjan. The program coordinators had heard that the president was still in favor of the reforms. This was consistent with his past statements in favor of reforms in "the spirit of the Council of Europe."[13] Additionally, he had already supported a constitutional reform a year earlier.

An opportunity arose when the president was on a visit in Germany and had a meeting with Chancellor Angela Merkel. The program expert, Prof. Otto Luchterhandt, who was already a central figure throughout the drafting process, informed the German government about the stalled reform process and asked to include the issue of the administrative law reforms in the government consultations. In his letter to the government, Prof. Luchterhandt underlined the importance of the administrative reforms for

---

11 Wolfgang Reimers, Interview, April 27, 2015.
12 Letter from Otto Luchterhandt, November 10, 2006.
13 Letter from Otto Luchterhandt, November 10, 2006.

the further convergence toward European standards and the legal development of Armenia in general. He encouraged the government officials to stress the fact that the German government expected its investment in development aid to have an effect. Otherwise, this would have consequences for further development cooperation between the two countries. This letter led to the inclusion of the topic in the governmental consultations. Shortly after his return, the president intervened in the process and the law was passed through the parliament.

This intervention shows the importance of individual members of the program as well as of their long-term involvement in the reform process. It is not enough to give legal advice during the drafting process of the laws. Moreover, it is important to accompany and closely monitor the implementation of the reforms and to support the reformist side within the country. A requirement for this approach is a close working relationship between the program coordinators and the local agents of change.

Through its long-term engagement in Armenia, the program was familiar with the peculiarities of the situation and knew the political decision-makers who were important for the success of the reform process. Having this insight about the current reform process, the program coordinators were able to influence the process positively by reminding the partners about the benefits of the reforms for their country. The commitments that the countries had made due to their accession to the Council of Europe were helpful for the program coordinators to substantiate the line of argumentation in favor of the reforms.

Critical junction III: Radical political change

The cooperation and the personal relationships between the program coordinators and the national agents of change went beyond the drafting process and also had an impact on the implementation and the further development of the laws. In Azerbaijan, Mr. Sayyad Karimov was the program's counterpart who had developed a good understanding of modern administrative law and who was one of the driving forces of the reforms from the Azerbaijani side. Because of his expertise and his convincing character, the program employed him as a short-term expert to perform trainings for the administrative personnel. He was sent to different towns together with a co-trainer to give one-day training seminars to a wide range of participants. The personality of Karimov proved to be essential for the success of the trainings because of his dedication and persuasive-ness.[14]

In 2010, the Armenian president appointed Hrayr Tovmasyan as the new Minister of Justice. Mr. Tovmasyan had interacted with the program and worked on the legal reform program for many years. Having a close collaborator who became a key government decision-maker, the program was in an ideal position to advise on new legal reforms and thus move the reform agenda forward. This was, for example, one of the reasons why the program was included in the working group for the constitutional reform process.

In the drafting process for Georgia, one of the two jurists was Zurab Adeishvili, who spent many months at the University of Bremen during the drafting process and worked closely with program expert Prof. Winter. After President Schewardnadse was toppled in the "Rose Revolution" in November 2003, Adeishvili became – among other posts – Minister of Justice and Prosecutor General under President Saakashvili. As described above, the government replaced critical judges with government-friendly ones, even though these methods were unconstitutional and an infringe-ment of fundamental legal principles. Adeishvili was a clear supporter of these actions.

Ironically, by supporting this course of action, he ignored the laws he previously helped to create and that were partly written by him.

This political maneuvering caused severe problems for the program, as it affected core principles of engagement. The problem for the program was twofold. The first question was how to react to the obviously unlaw-ful methods. Then there was the problem that a lot of the trained personnel were replaced. Nonetheless, the program coordinators decided to continue with the trainings. The idea was that even though the participants would not work as judges, the expertise on administrative law would still remain in the country. Many of the trained judges later worked as lawyers or in other legal professions in Georgia, thereby still raising the quality of the administrative law system in the country as a whole.

Besides that, the program coordinators decided to stay out of politics and to focus exclusively on legal issues. The strategy was to stay neutral in political affairs but at the same time to "carry a backpack of values."[15]

---

14 Thomas Melzer, Interview, May 12, 2015.
15 Zeno Reichenbecher, Interview, June 17, 2016.

This policy put a limit on the support of governmental actions. Political decisions were not actively opposed, but any kind of collaboration was avoided. Because of the long-standing involvement of the program in the reform process of the different countries, this was a strong and clear statement. Consequently, the program withdrew its support for Adeishvili and terminated the cooperation. Taking a neutral standpoint on politics and focusing exclusively on legal issues proved to be beneficial in the long run. It helped in establishing mutual trust with the leading politicians and gave the program leverage to bring about change in the society. This can be seen in the current situation in Azerbaijan. Due to the current government policy, most NGOs have withdrawn from the country. However, the program is an exception and is still active in the country, promoting and strengthening the rule of law in public administration. This is because it takes a neutral standpoint toward politics and focuses exclusively on legal issues.

Baseline: Continuous investment in people to establish long-term working relationships between the program and the national agents of change

As the example of Georgia shows, not all the investments in individual agents of change proved to be beneficial. That is a risk the program had to take. On the other hand, when the program invested in the right people, the outcome was very fruitful and opened up new possibilities for the program to support the reform process in the country.

The general approach of the project was very broad and not limited to a specific area of law. The reform of the administrative law was embedded in a wider project covering different areas of the legal system. This approach gave the project flexibility and the possibility to continually be involved in new reform projects and work on the legal system as a whole. The long-term engagement in the region was made possible by the political support from different parties during different German administrations since the 1990s.[16] Across all party lines, the political decision-makers agreed that the establishment of a legal system based on the rule of law was a project that could take decades. This political backing gave the program the planning security it needed and was the prerequisite for taking

---

16 Rolf Knieper, Interview, June 22, 2016.

such a broad approach that went beyond the reform of a single area of the legal system.

Through the establishment of good working relationships with national agents of change, the program was – and continues to be – seen as a partner in the reform process of the country. These working relationships are built up through personal connections between the local jurists and the program's employees. That is why continuity in the program's personnel is so important. This counts for the program's experts, the country managers, as well for the program's local staff.

All the program's experts were involved in the reform processes for more than a decade. This long-term engagement enabled the experts to make personal connections with the local jurists and develop a sense for the reform dynamics in the different countries. This allowed the program to follow up on the reforms and help with the implementation process. However, the experts were just involved in the program from time to time. Therefore, it is crucial to ensure continuity between the program and the local agents of change through the project managers, as they worked in these countries continually for many years. Their role was to keep contact with the local jurists and the political decision-makers and to establish new relationships, especially after a change of government. Additionally, the local program employees form the basis of the program and ensure a consecutive working relationship with the local partners when the project managers are exchanged.

Furthermore, the program not only worked with the current agents of change but also invested in future generations. Therefore, for example, the program started the regional network "Transformation Lawyers" to create a professional dialogue among young lawyers of the three countries, and thus to establish the basis for future working relationships with the next generation of agents of change.

Lessons from the case study

To be able to draw some lessons from the case study, we come back to the implementation questions from the beginning: *What is the best way to deal with time pressure during the drafting process? How should the program react to unlawful measures taken by the partners? How can the program overcome resistance from parts of the administration? How can the regional approach be applied when the relationship between Armenia and Azerbaijan is conflict-ridden and shaped by mutual mistrust?*

- **Alliances and good personal working relationships are crucial to overcome difficulties in the drafting process:** The legal drafting is shaped by specific circumstances of the country, and it is not always possible to have an ideal process. Rather, it is beneficial to use windows of opportunities – for example, favorable political power balances in the parliament – and push the reforms forward. Under time pressure, it might even be useful for the program to take a stronger and more proactive role in the drafting process. A good working relationship with the partner based on mutual trust is a prerequisite for this approach.
- **Taking a neutral standpoint on local politics and focusing on legal issues helps to maintain a good relationship with the partner and to increase the influence of the program:** It proved to be positive for the program to take a neutral standpoint on local politics and to focus exclusively on legal issues. However, the program still had a values-based approach. In consequence, the program did not actively interfere with any unconstitutional methods of the government nor actively supported any governmental decisions that were incompatible with the values of the program, especially the rule of law. Therefore, the program ended the cooperation with former partners who supported unlawful actions.
- **It can be useful to use government consultations to apply political pressure to overcome a stalled reform process:** Introducing administrative laws in a country implies a difficult reform process with different stakeholders and varying interests involved. Political support should be given to the reformers' side, and political pressure should be applied to different levels of political decision-makers, including the president.
- **A clear focus on legal issues creates common ground for professional discussions between the countries:** An exclusive focus on legal issues also helps to overcome political tensions and mistrust between countries. The program made it clear from the very beginning that political issues would be left out of the discussion. For this reason, it was possible to gather high representatives from the three branches

of government of the different countries and to have productive discussions.[17]

Principles of managing and steering implementation

Under the particular circumstances of the reform process, a *multi-stakeholder approach* had to be adjusted. When the process for developing the reforms of the administrative laws in the three countries began, there was no tradition of a transparent administrative law system and the vast majority of the population – including the jurists – had little understanding of the underlying principles. That made the broad participation of different stakeholders problematic, because very few were able to contribute to the drafting process. As the case of Armenia shows, the involvement of too many stakeholders can even be harmful to the reform process. Therefore, a small group of local jurists drafted the laws with the help of international experts, and only afterwards were different stakeholders involved to discuss and comment on the drafts. Through this involvement, the drafts gained legitimacy from broader segments of the society. Hence, the involvement of different stakeholders – and thus the multi-stakeholder approach – was not abolished by the program. Rather, it was postponed to a later moment in the reform process.

An *interdisciplinary and multi-sectoral approach* is beneficial but requires a process that is ridden with prerequisites. Because no expertise existed in modern administrative law, the program had to start educating local jurists and building up legal capacity so these jurists could support the newly introduced laws. Because of the sheer amount of people affected by the administrative law reforms – especially within the administration – it proved to be beneficial for the program to focus initially on just one sector. The courts were chosen for two reasons. First of all, it was because of the relatively small number of administrative judges in comparison to administrative workers. Second, because the courts oversee administrative actions and decisions, they could be used as leverage to implement the laws by encouraging the administration to follow the laws. After the administrative courts were established and the administrative judges were trained, the program could expand its agenda and include

---

17 Zeno Reichenbecher, Interview, June 17, 2016.

other disciplines and sectors. To sum up, the program did not turn its back on the *interdisciplinary and multi-sectoral approach* but rather chose a gradual approach. First it invested in one sector – the administrative courts – and later expanded its reach to different disciplines and sectors: the administrative personnel, lawyers, universities, journalists, and the general population.

A *long-term engagement* of the project is indispensable when administrative laws in a post-soviet state are introduced. It is a long-term process because it is not enough to just write new laws and reform the legal institutions of the state – the relationship between the citizens and the state also has to be readjusted. The project can guide and facilitate this process by sensitively monitoring it and offering advice to the jurists and political decision-makers. Therefore, the long-term engagement should not just be understood in temporal terms but also apply to the personal level. This includes investment in individual agents of change as well as potential future leaders from the partner countries. Personal relationships between these individuals and the program have to be nurtured. That is why a long-term engagement of the program experts and the program managers is important. Lastly and just as important, consistency has to be ensured through local experts who are working in the program.

Every country is different, and a *context-specific and incremental implementation of interventions* is important. However, in the area of legal development, universal legal standards exist and will only be moderately modified to the specific context. The Council of Europe provides clear guidelines in the area of administrative law. Context-specific legal development means adjusting the universal legal concept to the specific reform process of the country while at the same time taking into account the existing legal system and its legal traditions. Again, the program did not abandon the approach of context-specific and incremental implementation of interventions. Rather, it modified it to the implementation of legal reform projects.

References

Bertelsmann Stiftung. (2016a). *Armenia country report*. Bertelsmann Transformation Index. Gütersloh: Author.

Bertelsmann Stiftung. (2016b). *Azerbaijan country report*. Bertelsmann Transformation Index. Gütersloh: Author.

Bundesministerium für wirtschaftliche Zusammenarbeit und Entwicklung. (n.d.). *Caucasus initiative*. Retrieved July 14, 2016, from https://www.bmz.de/en/what_we_do /countries_regions/Central-Eastern-and-South-Eastern-Europe/kaukasus/index.html

De Waal, T. (2010). *The Caucasus: An introduction*. New York, NY: Oxford University Press.

Deutsche Gesellschaft für Internationale Zusammenarbeit. (2002). Conference report. Bremen: Author.

Karklins, R. (2002). Typology of post-communist corruption. *Problems of Post-Communism, 49*(4), 22–32.

Knieper, R. (2004). *Juristische Zusammenarbeit: Universalität und Kontext*. Wiesbaden: Universum Verlag.

Luchterhandt, O., Rubel, R., & Reimers, W. (2008). *Leitfaden zum allgemeinen Verwaltungsrecht*. Yerevan: Deutsche Gesellschaft für Technische Zusammenarbeit.

Sandholtz, W., & Taagepera, R. (2005). Corruption, culture, and communism. *International Review* of *Sociology, 15*(1), 109–131.

Transparency International. (2014). *Overview of three-years of monitoring on administrative cases*. Tbilisi: Transparency International Georgia.

Waters, C. P. M. (2004). *Counsel in the Caucasus: Professionalization and law in Georgia*. Leiden: Springer Science + Business Media.

Winter, G. (2010). *Verwaltungsrechtsentwicklung und ihre ausländische Beratung in Transformationsstaaten. Das Beispiel Georgien*. Verwaltungsarchiv, 408–436. Retrieved from http://www.gerd-winter.jura.uni-bremen.de/vwrentwicklung.pdf

Strengthening the Eastern Partnership in Azerbaijan: Challenges in Implementing a Civil Service Training Capacity Program with a Focus on EU Affairs

Melanie Wiskow

Executive Summary

The EU co-funded project "Support to civil service training capacities with a focus on EU affairs" was implemented in cooperation with the Civil Service Commission under the President of the Republic of Azerbaijan (CSC). The project had the objectives to support the development of the national civil service training strategy and its implementation and to strengthen the capacities of the CSC to deliver regular, standardized trainings.

The institutional setup of EU (co)financed projects left limited room for changes and adaptation. The project strived to use the small amount of room available to move within these areas and deviate in time, quality, and format from the initial implementation path, but not from the objectives. The political context of the project changed during its implementation, but the project team had to explain and make clear to the CSC that one had to stay within the framework of the agreed objectives, results areas, and activities, even if other areas were more interesting or important for the CSC. The focus on the CSC as the only project partner required implementing activities at the pace of the CSC and in accordance with its views on what was appropriate.

Maybe the greatest hindrance to the implementation of this project as initially planned was the short duration of the project. Due to the limited amount of time, the project team had almost no time to really change the approach to activity implementation; rather, it had to find quick and pragmatic solutions once implementation problems occurred. In GIZ projects, especially in this field of public administration reform, the duration of projects is planned with more realistic timelines, including substantial time spent on the preparation of the project.

Background and context of project

The project "Support to civil service training capacities with a focus on EU affairs" was co-funded by the European Union (EU) and the German Federal Ministry for Economic Cooperation and Development (BMZ). The project was implemented by the Deutsche Gesellschaft für Internationale Zusammenarbeit (GIZ) in cooperation with the CSC. The project duration was 28 months: from December 2013 to March 2016. Like all projects that utilize EU grants, the basis of the work was the description of action, including a logical framework (logframe) and a corresponding budget. Any changes to the activities or other elements of the logframe or to the budget had to be communicated to the EU – depending on the extent of the change, it might have necessitated a formal amendment to the contract.

Cooperation between the EU and its Eastern European partners, which include the Republic of Azerbaijan, is a crucial part of the EU's external relations. Human capacities and institutional reforms are being addressed under the Comprehensive Institution Building (CIB)[1] program of the Eastern Partnership (EaP).[2] The EaP provides for the possibility of gradual integration into the EU economy with enhanced economic and trade relations between partner countries and the EU by establishing a Deep and Comprehensive Free Trade Area (DCFTA) in the framework of a future Association Agreement (AA) once the necessary conditions are met. The CIB program was agreed upon by the European Commission and the Azerbaijani government. Based on the Framework Document, Institutional Reform Plans (IRPs) were designed for selected institutions in 2010 in

---

1 The CIB is a framework jointly developed and implemented by the EU and partner countries. It is specifically intended to help partner countries address the conditionality linked to concluding an Association Agreement and, where relevant, starting and concluding the negotiations on a DCFTA in the framework of the Association Agreement and make progress toward visa liberalization as a long-term goal as well as meet the related commitments.
2 The EaP was launched in 2009 in Prague. It was a new initiative to strengthen relations between the EU and six partner countries: Armenia, Azerbaijan, Belarus, Georgia, the Republic of Moldova, and Ukraine. The EaP seeks to bring partners closer to the EU and promote stability, good governance, and economic development. This initiative is based on shared values such as democracy, the rule of law, respect for human rights and basic freedoms, market economy, and sustainable development. For more information, see: https://eeas.europa.eu/topics/eastern-partnership

partnership with government representatives and EU member states interested in contributing to the CIB program. With the IRPs, multiannual programs have been identified that bundle and focus support in three priority areas.

It could be observed that the context of the project changed during its implementation, since in June 2014 Azerbaijan suspended the AA negotiations that had started in July 2010. The issue is that the AA – with its objective to achieve closer political relations and gradual economic integration between Azerbaijan and the EU – built a platform for the implementation of the CIB program and IRPs in the country, and thus provided the general framework of this project. Consequently, at one point, the project found itself operating in a new framework. However, in practice, the direct environment of the project did not undergo noticeable changes and continued to be conducive and enabling.

Project objectives

The project addressed the second main objective of the IRP3, which is one of the three Institutional Reform Plans defined for Azerbaijan according to the three priority areas. This project, together with a second project that is being implemented by the United Nations Development Program (UNDP), jointly contributed toward achieving the same overall objectives, which are

> [t]o strengthen the capacities of the Civil Service Commission under the President of the Republic of Azerbaijan (CSC) with regard to management and coordination of civil servants training and professional development function across state bodies and leading the development and implementation of training strategy and training policies.

Contributing to the achievement of the same overall objectives and addressing all three specific objectives of the IRP3 made the overall intervention quite complete and comprehensive. Good cohesion of the two launched projects became a precondition for the successful implementation of the entire intervention.

The project had two specific objectives, which were (i) to support the development of the national civil service training strategy and its implementation (monitoring and evaluation mechanisms and training of the Human Resources Management/ Human Resources Development staff of state bodies) and (ii) to strengthen the capacities of the CSC to deliver regular training by providing support to the development of standard training modules for priority crosscutting areas supporting the adaptation of state bodies to European standards. In order to achieve the specific objectives foreseen, the project defined three key results as being the most relevant areas for support, with a view to the needs and constraints of the beneficiaries:

1. developing a national civil service training strategy and initiating its implementation,
2. developing and validating standard training modules in EU-related and selected priority areas,
3. establishing a pool of certified trainers who would be able to conduct training in the priority areas.

Their delivery was to strengthen the CSC's capacities to organize and deliver training and provide the basis for the sustainable management and coordination of civil servants' training and professional development across state bodies.

Links and synergies with other projects or programs

The project retained continuity with the EU Technical Assistance to the Commonwealth of Independent States program "Support to reforms in the field of civil service" (2003–2004), which significantly contributed to the creation of the CSC. Furthermore, the project benefited from the existing collaboration of GIZ with the CSC-SIGMA[3] cooperation in the development of a national civil service strategy of Azerbaijan. Furthermore, the project built on previous successful bilateral cooperation between the CSC and GIZ in the field of the reform of civil service (September 2009 to June 2013).

---

3 SIGMA (Support for Improvement in Governance and Management) is a joint initiative of the Organisation for Economic Co-operation and Development and the European Union. Its key objective is to strengthen the foundations for improved public governance, and hence support socio-economic development through building the capacities of the public sector, enhancing horizontal governance, and improving the design and implementation of public administration reforms, including proper prioritization, sequencing, and budgeting.

The overall objective of the "Reform of civil service" project was the following: "The conditions for transparent and 'citizen-oriented' performance of civil service in central government bodies of Azerbaijan is improved and thus supporting Good Governance." The key methodological elements were technical and organizational advisory services to the CSC. The project contributed to overall public administration reforms in five fields of intervention, namely: (1) strengthening the organizational capacity of the Civil Service Commission, (2) development of a training and qualification system for civil servants, (3) improvement of communication mechanisms between the Civil Service Commission and its clients, (4) improvement of the merit-based recruitment system for civil servants, and (5) advisory services on strategies and legal provisions for civil service reform.

Today, the CSC has successfully introduced itself as an important player in shaping the future of the civil service. It has earned the CSC a reputation of being a modern organization that is able to achieve significant improvements in the civil service.

Framework for project implementation

The project "Support to civil service training capacities with a focus on EU affairs" was implemented by GIZ in cooperation with the CSC as the single partner of the project. It was not foreseen to involve other institutions in the decision-making processes about activities or to implement activities separate from the CSC with other institutions. The project was a stand-alone project and not attached to an ongoing bilateral or regional project. The initial project duration (from December 2013 to March 2016) had been planned to last for 24 months, with the possibility to be extended one time for four more months.

Like all projects that utilize EU grants, the basis of the work was the description of action, including a logical framework (logframe) and a corresponding budget. Any changes to the activities or other elements of the logframe or to the budget had to be communicated to the EU – bigger changes may have necessitated a formal written amendment to the contract. This structure is very different from the flexible approach that projects financed by BMZ have. BMZ-financed projects can react quickly to a changing political environment and adjust the methodology and activities. Co-financing by the EU leaves limited room for maneuver and restricted freedom of action and adjustments for the project during implementation. This constraint affected both GIZ and the CSC as the implementing agencies as well as the CSC as the main beneficiary of the project. The EU made it clear from the beginning that they wished to see the agreed objectives achieved by implementing activities in the three defined results areas.

For success, the commitment of the CSC – at the top management and working levels – as well as the involvement and participation in the formulation and implementation of all project activities was crucial. This approach ensured full transparency for the CSC, and thus increased the ownership in the CSC and the sustainability of the achieved results. With the help of an implementation agreement, it was agreed when and how the CSC would be involved in the project activities. One of its guiding principles read as: "All project activities will be implemented in cooperation and with the consent with the Civil Service Commission under the President of the Republic of Azerbaijan." In practice, this agreement meant, for example, that for every agreement, the Terms of Reference (ToR) or other specifications were jointly developed and agreed upon by GIZ and the CSC. Bid and application evaluations on each ToR were done by a panel comprising a CSC representative taking into account the protection of data privacy. Contracts were only awarded based on prior written agreement by the CSC (email). Contracts were only finalized after the quality of the services had also been confirmed in writing by the CSC.

This process ensured full transparency of the project implementation. Such an approach also takes time, and the implementation of project activities had to be adjusted to the capacities of the CSC staff assigned to this action, who were also involved in the regular operations of the CSC.

Challenges in project implementation

According to EU rules for the awarding of contracts, the potential grant recipient has to prepare a set of documents to serve as the project proposal. Subsequently, the description of action for the project was prepared by GIZ and closely coordinated with the CSC. This happened by sending drafts for comments to the CSC. Comments were delivered orally in meetings. *The person in the CSC responsible for the preparation was replaced by a new person at the beginning of the implementation period.* The new person in the CSC was not involved in the detailed planning of the project proposal and, therefore, had to become familiarized with the logic of the project planning. In the beginning of the project, a stakeholder analysis was jointly conducted, and the operational plan (as the operationalization of the logical framework/logframe) was discussed with the new project manager of the CSC. Because the new person responsible had his own ideas and perspectives of how to best implement the project, some adjustments to the sub-activities had to be made. For example, regarding activities under results area 2, it was decided to limit the scope of the Training Needs Assessment (TNA) in order to define topics for curricula development not only based on results from TNA and to shape the process of the identification of learning objectives differently. The initial plan was to conduct activities under results area 2 in the following chronological order: prepare TNA methodology → conduct nationwide TNAs → identify from TNA results the topics for curricula development → establish thematic expert groups to advise the curricula development → identify experts for curricula development → draft curricula and preliminary approval → pilot training modules → revise curricula and approve final versions.

The implementation period of the action started officially on December 1, 2013. Due to open questions regarding the administrative implementation, the project became operational only in April 2014. Therefore, *activities that had been planned to be implemented consecutively had to be implemented in parallel.*

Development of TNA methodology

After a preparatory mission of the TNA experts and meetings with representatives of training centers in other state bodies and selected HR departments, it became clear that *TNA as an instrument was largely unknown.* So far, such an assessment instrument had not been applied in Azerbaijan. On the basis of the meetings during the fact-finding mission, it was decided that the first TNA should be rolled out not on a national level but with a selected number of pilot institutions. As the TNA methodology was only in a final draft stage, it was impossible to gain the necessary trust among recipients: There was a big fear that the results would be negative and therefore shed a negative light on the institution. After consultation with the experts and the project teams, two state institutions were selected for piloting the TNA. This process was very intensive and took more than three months. One of the two pilot institutions was the CSC itself; the other one was not really relevant (as its area of responsibility was very narrow, and results from the TNA would not be representative for other state institutions), but *it was not possible to identify a more relevant and central state institution* that was willing to participate in a TNA.

The goal was to develop a TNA methodology that would be available to all state bodies and identify crosscutting training needs as well as sector- or organization-specific training needs. A first draft of the TNA methodology was sent by the TNA experts at the beginning of January 2015 and served as the basis for the first training[4] on TNA at the end of January. The results from the TNA pilot, which covered two organizations, were analyzed in a workshop with the experts in April 2015. The two pilot TNAs were conducted by the local TNA expert (a member of the team of TNA experts who developed the methodology) and a representative from the CSC. A final draft of a TNA methodology to assess needs in the Azerbaijan civil service was prepared by July 2015, with TNA instruments having been localized to the country context. This final draft had been with the CSC since August 2015 for a final revision. It was planned that once the final Azerbaijani version of the TNA methodology was ready, it would be printed and distributed to state bodies, together with further trainings. It was also planned that the final version would be translated into English to allow the CSC to present and discuss it on an international level with colleagues from other civil service institutions. *Due to the delay on the final draft (the main reason for the delay was the limited personnel resources allocated to the project from the CSC – one person had to manage both (GIZ and UNDP) projects), it was not possible to print and promote the methodology within the timeframe of the EU-funded project.* It was agreed with the CSC and UNDP that the finalization and promotion of the TNA methodology will be supported by the UNDP project, as TNA is an integral part of the standard operation procedures of the future training center. For the CSC's ownership of the methodology, it is essential that the final product be revised by the institution itself. Of course, it would

---

4   The CSC invited 15 civil servants from nine different state institutions to participate in the training held by one of the international experts and the Azerbaijani expert. Among the participants were representatives from the CSC, the Ministry of Transport, the Ministry of Economy and Industry, the Ministry of Taxes, the State Committee on Property Issues, the State Statistics Committee, the State Social Protection Fund, and the Science and Learning Center of the Ministry of Finance.

have been possible to finalize and print the methodology without a final okay from the CSC's side, but it was to be expected that, in this case, the final product would have been less well accepted.

Development of training modules

With support of the EU-funded project, information on existing training modules and the status of the training materials for these modules were compiled in a comprehensive list. Based on that list as well as on the *list of training needs predefined in the EU call for proposals,*[5] it was discussed in a meeting between GIZ and the CSC that, besides the expected results from the TNA, there were topics already known for which modern curricula needed to be developed or updated. Five thematic areas for curricula development were specified and agreed with CSC management. With this approach, it was possible to start the process of curricula development in parallel to the TNA methodology development and piloting process. Otherwise, it was feared that the delay in the TNA process would lead to the fact that no – or not enough – training curricula could have been developed within the project.

The learning objectives and main content of the trainings were defined by the project team, agreed with the CSC, and specified in the ToR for the development of the training curricula. The project team, together with the CSC, developed a document defining the elements of standard training that had to be followed by all experts developing training curricula for the CSC. This way, it was ensured that all materials were homogenous and met the same high-quality standard.

---

5 These topics were identified by the EU during the process of preparing the tender for this grant. Information was collected by experts by conducting a brief training needs analysis. A combination of the most relevant methods was used. In order to get a complete picture from several sources and viewpoints, analysis of existing written materials and documentation was combined with semi-structured and in-depth, face-to-face interviews. Semi-structured interviews provided both quantitative and qualitative information for identifying the training needs of different target groups, as well as allowed the interviewees to provide evidence and describe their ideas regarding the needed training interventions. These interviews with the targeted authorities served also for verifying and updating the information obtained from the written documents.

Consultants developed the training curricula for the five identified subjects. For all five topics, complete sets of training curricula and all supporting materials were discussed, adjusted, and approved before piloting them in June/July 2015. The CSC undertook to validate the materials. After the successful pilots, revisions to the curricula and the training materials were done by the trainer with the support of the CSC. The final set of training toolkits (curricula and supporting materials) were submitted to the CSC and were applied widely thereafter within the project.

Response of the project team to implementation challenges

In reality, the order and scope of the activities had to be adjusted, but due to the limited room for changes with regard to planned activities defined under the results areas of the logframe, any necessary adjustments could only result in a deviation from the planned path to reach the objectives. It was never an option to change the objectives or results areas. The only options were to deviate from the initial plan with regard to time, quality, and format of the activities.

As one example of a necessary deviation during the project implementation, the following situation should be further analyzed: It had been planned to apply the newly developed Training Needs Assessment methodology in a large sample of institutions, but in reality it was only applied in two pilot institutions.

Fact-finding phase

The project had a difficult start. Only after initial administrative problems were solved could the project team start implementing activities. The lengthy process of solving the administrative problems led to mistrust by the CSC in the capabilities of the project team. As a measure that could be implemented very quickly, it was decided to organize a study tour and an international conference as the first activities because they were strongly requested by the CSC. However, because only limited personnel resources were available to GIZ and the CSC, everyone's capacities were greatly reduced due to the preparations for these two events. This further delayed starting the development of the TNA methodology and implementing the nationwide assessment of training needs in the civil service.

In the description of action, it was elaborated and later reconfirmed in inception meetings with the CSC that the essential preparatory step to identify the most relevant EU-related training areas for which training modules for civil servants were needed was to conduct a comprehensive TNA on a national level in the civil service sector. Because the trainings foreseen under this action sought to address training needs that were relevant for all state bodies – excluding sector- or organization-specific training needs – the focus had to be on crosscutting training fields with relevance for target groups related to the negotiation and the implementation of Azerbaijan-EU agreements.

During the fact-finding mission of the TNA expert team, meetings with selected HR managers from different stakeholder organizations were conducted in order to understand their current approaches, processes, and tools. The CSC scheduled meetings only with a selected number of institutions, namely the Azerbaijan Diplomatic Academy University, the Training Center of Ministry of Finance, the HR Department of Ministry of Labor and Social Protection of Population, the HR Department of the State Committee on Statistics, the Baku Appeal Court, and the Coordination Unit for World Bank-financed projects in the Ministry of Education. These institutions were considered "friendly" institutions by the CSC with counterparts open for initiatives from the CSC. Other institutions that were more central, such as the Ministry of Economy, were not considered for interviews. There was no opportunity to influence the selection process, which was decided by the chairman, head of the CSC. It became evident during these meetings that these institutions had little experience with tools to identify training needs, but also that none of the institutions expressed an interest in conducting – or a need to conduct – such an assessment in their institution.

Preparation for implementation

In the intensive working sessions with experts during the mission, the person in the CSC responsible for project implementation said that, actually, the top management of the CSC was not confident about exposing itself on a national level affecting all state bodies with an untested methodology that is not based on a current decree from the Cabinet of Ministers or the president. There was no other TNA methodology available in Azerbaijan that could have been used instead for this purpose. Without the consent of

CSC management, the plan of a nationwide TNA could not been pursued any further. The only possibility was to use the drafted materials on a smaller (less comprehensive/threatening) scope and to make use of the concept of an existing methodology by adapting it to the context of Azerbaijan and its political landscape.

Decision-making phase

During discussions in a regular working meeting, it was jointly decided not to conduct a TNA on a national level but to implement the methodology on a pilot level in a few selected institutions. The alternative would have been to postpone the TNA implementation until after the methodology had been finalized and promoted, or to cancel the activity completely.

The first alternative was not really an option, as it was clear from the quality of the first draft methodology that its revision would take time, and implementation of a pilot after the approval but within the time span of the project was not realistic.

Furthermore, there would have been no other options, for it was realized that the CSC does not have the organizational and human resources available to approach all institutions in Baku and in the regions – the number of CSC staff was very limited (35 civil servants), and most of the time they were busy conducting recruitment interviews (one of the main tasks of the CSC).

Instead, it was decided that piloting one to three selected tools from the methodology in two to three different organizations would be useful to allow for an in-depth assessment and the combination of several instruments. The decision was taken in a meeting between the CSC, GIZ, and TNA experts, and was backed by CSC management.

Identification of pilot institutions

This resulted in a deviation in nature and format of the planned activity. The initial concept had to be realized with the full involvement and ownership of the CSC. The decision to have a pilot implementation in a few institutions at least offered an opportunity to try the instruments within a local environment and produce authentic results for the second training/workshop with the experts focusing on analysis of the TNA results.

The identification of these selected pilot institutions still proved to be very difficult for the CSC, although the process was started right after the fact-finding mission. The factors for these difficulties related both to the general motivation of organizations to conduct TNAs, their relationships with the CSC, and their organizational configurations.

In the time between the fact-finding mission in October 2014 and the first training on the TNA methodology in January 2015, it was the task of the CSC to use their relationships with other state institutions to identify relevant pilot institutions. They did not want visible support from GIZ in this task. GIZ provided support to the CSC as the partner organization in fulfilling its responsibilities, but it was not to act on behalf of the organization. The CSC, together with GIZ, drafted a concept paper describing the piloting process of TNA tools. In this concept, there was great emphasis asserting that the assessment was not to be regarded as a test of the capacities of the institution but of the applicability of the developed tools in Azerbaijan. The objective of the pilot was to test several tools of the TNA to evaluate their effectiveness in organizing the targeted training of civil servants or other civil service employees in Azerbaijan. Those organizations that participated would not only gain experience with the specific tool but also they would be able to directly use the results of the assessment to develop their own training or staff development plans. The concept offered the prospect that some of their training needs would be directly covered by the CSC training center within the project.

The concept paper was sent by the CSC to the selected state bodies from whom they sensed a general interest. The CSC chose to approach selected state bodies on a personal level (by phone and email). With this approach, the CSC expected to get quicker and more honest feedback on their proposal, as official letters tended to be answered with long delays or vague answers.

Pilot application

Finally, one of the two pilot institutions became the CSC itself. The other pilot institution was the State Motor Transport Service of the Ministry of Transport of the Republic of Azerbaijan. However, it was clear from the beginning that the results of the TNA from the second institution would only be partially transferable to other civil service institutions in Azerbaijan. It was impossible to identify a more relevant and central state institution that was willing to participate in a TNA.

Again, the decision had to be made about whether to continue with the activity, even if the quality of the results deviated from what was initially planned. It was jointly decided to continue, because at least some of the instruments could be tested in a real-life situation. As prior experience with the application of TNA instruments in Azerbaijan largely did not exist, any test or real-life application provided an added value. One could have thought of mounting an awareness-raising campaign about the benefits of TNAs and attempted to gain the interest of more relevant institutions. But the tight time schedule would not permit these activities.

The actual pilot implementation of the TNA faced some critical problems:

- The interviews (interviews and tests were the selected TNA instruments to be tested) could not be delivered in an open-minded way. The selected institution was unprepared for a TNA process, and its top management tried to keep information a secret. It seemed that the institution did not believe in the confidentiality of the pilot and could not see the identification of needs as being an opportunity that could help to improve the capacities of the staff, but rather as a sign of failure of their service delivery. As it is common in Azerbaijan that the president dissolves institutions overnight, the institution's fear of making itself vulnerable was understandable.
- The questionnaires only partially followed the advice of the handbook and, therefore, had partially poor results.

Relevance of results from pilot

From a learning perspective, the results were relevant, and they were summarized. The consolidated results were discussed in a joint workshop at the end of April 2015 in which TNA experts, GIZ, the CSC, the other pilot institution, as well as other state bodies attended. The workshop especially aimed to build capacity in the area of interpretation of TNA results and to draw the right conclusions. As the next step after the finalization and printing of the methodology, further trainings and other promotion activities on TNA implementation with government officials will be conducted by the UNDP project. The TNA is one crucial part in their development of standard operation procedures for the future CSC training center.

Maybe the greatest challenge for the implementation of this activity as initially planned was the short duration of the project: 24 months plus four additional months agreed in June 2015 were foreseen to implement this complex project in the field of institution-building and public administration reform. Due to the limited time and the knowledge that no extension was possible according to EU regulations, the project had almost no time to really change the approach to activity implementation but rather had to find quick and pragmatic solutions once implementation problems occurred. This can lead to deviations in format, quality, and time of implementation of activities. Nevertheless, the project was finished on March 31, 2016, on a very positive note and praised by the CSC, the EU Delegation, and the German Embassy. Even if in some areas there were substantial implementation problems, in general the project was successful in achieving the targeted objectives in the three defined results areas.

Bibliography

Bertelsmann Stiftung. (2016). *Azerbaijan country report*. Bertelsmann Transformation Index. Gütersloh: Author.

Deutsche Gesellschaft für Internationale Zusammenarbeit. (2015). *Project "Support to civil service training capacities with a focus on EU affairs."* Retrieved from https://www.giz.de/de/downloads/giz2015-en-civil-service-training-capacities-azerbaijan.pdf

Government of Azerbaijan. (s.a.). *Civil service commission under the President of the Republic of Azerbaijan*. Retrieved from http://dqmk.gov.az/aze/downloads/Beledci/CSC%20brief%20brochure%20draft%20v 7110711.pdf

Implementing Change Processes for Inclusive Social and Economic Development in Situations of Conflict and Fragility: Lessons from the Philippines

Yvonne Müller and Stephanie Schell-Faucon

Executive Summary

This paper presents a case study illustrating the approach adopted by the Philippine–German Conflict Sensitive Resource and Asset Management Program (COSERAM), which was implemented in Mindanao by the Deutsche Gesellschaft für Internationale Zusammenarbeit (GIZ)[1] with a broad range of Philippine partners from the state level, civil society, and the private sector.

Taking as an example the support provided to Butuan City from 2011 to 2014, the case study analyzes how to assist government agencies in designing and implementing a complex change process that fosters inclusive and sustainable socio-economic development in an extremely volatile conflict situation. The development challenges described are representative of various parts of Mindanao. Parts of the approach that were successfully developed and implemented by the City and its partners are currently being replicated in other areas.

A huge asset and precondition for the case study project was the newly elected leadership of Butuan City, which entered office with a strong will, a commitment to good governance, and a vision to transform the City's poorest conflict-affected communities, which were largely neglected by public services and influenced by non-state armed groups. Both the absence of government institutions and legitimacy in the area as well as a precarious security situation called for something other than standard approaches to socio-economic development. The case study shows which strategy was developed and how it could be implemented successfully – despite several setbacks.

---

1 The program was implemented on behalf of BMZ.

For four years the COSERAM Program provided the City and its partners with a broad range of tailored political, procedural, and technical advice and financial support. The implementation of this change process – hereinafter referred to as "the inclusive co-management project" – was carried out in three phases. The paper illustrates how the level of leadership and responsibility for the implementation of the project of the City was gradually and continuously increased. With the City becoming the "face of the project" vis-à-vis the affected communities, direct interventions by GIZ decreased.

Although the project experienced a number of setbacks throughout the process (including violent incidents and difficulties in providing secure land tenure), it has successfully improved the socio-economic situation of the population in the project area. Government services and financial support through various development schemes are now available. Two years since this project has ended, the communities are developing their land in collaboration with the City and national agencies, and the vast majority are confident that the local and central governments will further assist them in doing so. The positive response by the local communities to the transparent and participatory approach also prompted the neighboring province to replicate the approach of conflict-sensitive reentry and participatory planning in other areas.

The case study shows how fundamental approaches and principles of GIZ's common practice were successfully integrated into a change process driven and managed by the partner. The paper's analysis shows that three sets of principles were instrumental for the successful implementation. First, sustainability and risk mitigation require continuous monitoring of both the political economy and conflict situations as well as an adoption of a context-specific, incremental approach of multi-sectoral dialogues. Second, a clear distribution of responsibilities and roles between main actors enables the leadership of the major partner. Lastly, conflict-sensitive management is needed that involves a highly flexible modus operandi, the provision of safe spaces, as well as reflexive management.

In relation to smart implementation, the case study illustrates GIZ's long-term, sustainability-oriented approach to strengthen the partners' capacities to realize complex change processes in a holistic and context-specific manner.

Introduction

The Philippines is marked by numerous violent political and social conflicts. Inequitable access to its wealth of resources and assets is at the core of these conflicts. Conflicts over land use, monopolistic land ownership, poor governance, and dysfunctional institutions all contribute to the exploitative use of resources and constitute a major challenge to development. The consequences are weak economic development and the increasing impoverishment of several population groups, primarily Indigenous people, women, and young people.

Despite its vast natural resources (in particular mineral resources and forests), the region of Caraga in the northeast of Mindanao is one of the poorest regions in the country. A fact-finding study commissioned in 2008 by the German Federal Ministry for Economic Cooperation and Development (BMZ) and the Philippine government confirmed that the inequitable access to natural resources and land is one of the main causes of violent conflicts in Caraga. For decades, this situation has been fertile ground for non-state armed groups, in particular the New People's Army (NPA), which is the armed wing of the Communist Party of the Philippines and historically has had its stronghold in Caraga.

In order to prepare for a joint development program in Caraga that is agreed upon by the Philippine and German governments, five core peace and development needs were identified for the region in 2009: (1) land classification and demarcation; (2) processes of regulation and enforcement; (3) management and utilization of natural resources; (4) human security, need for local conflict transformation and livelihoods; and (5) access to services. These needs were the basis for the elaboration of the Philippine–German Conflict Sensitive Resource and Asset Management Program (COSERAM), which started in 2011. Its **overall objective** was to ensure the governance of land and natural resources in selected areas of the Caraga region in a peaceful and sustainable manner, thereby benefiting the community.[2]

The COSERAM Program, currently commissioned until end of 2018, is steered by a National and a Regional Program Steering Committee, both consisting of five government agencies of the Philippines: the Department of Environment and Natural Resources (DENR), the Department of Inte-

---

2 COSERAM Conceptual Framework and Proposal to BMZ.

rior and Local Government (DILG), the National Commission on Indige-nous Peoples (NCIP), the National Economic and Development Authority (NEDA), and the Office of the Presidential Adviser on the Peace Pro-cesses. The COSERAM Program is implemented by the Deutsche Gesellschaft für Internationale Zusammenarbeit (GIZ) GmbH in coopera-tion with various local, regional, and national partners from the state level, civil society, and the private sector.

This paper presents one of several approaches developed and piloted by GIZ with its Philippine partners in the context of the COSERAM Program in Caraga.

A huge asset of Butuan City when approaching GIZ for support in 2011 was its newly elected leadership with a strong political will and a vision for inclusive socio-economic development.

Although it appeared to not be so difficult to find interested investors of various kinds, the City government initially had underestimated the com-plex character of this endeavor.

- The area was, in fact, not accessible for government officials, since relations with the local population had been disrupted. The communi-ties felt threatened by the idea of external investors being given land use rights for the land they occupied partly. The non-state armed groups were alarmed and tried to incite the communities to reject the City government's efforts.
- Relations between the formal partners for the co-management of the area, that is, City government and DENR, were complicated and strained due to the very diverse interests in the area. Hence, the steer-ing and management structures were dysfunctional.
- There were high expectations and political pressure on the City gov-ernment to show results, as promised in the electoral campaign. It was expected that the City fosters economic development by entering into concessional agreements and resolving the unclear land tenure situa-tion.
- At the same time, "backstage" power relations and economic interests were influencing key stakeholders and increasing the conflict escala-tion potential.

Recognizing the huge levels of defiance as well as the weak capacities of the City government itself, the City's mayor requested the support of the COSERAM Program. The COSERAM Program Steering Committee agreed to provide the assistance through GIZ. They saw this case as a good learning opportunity for partners on all levels, as the development challenges of this particular forestland in Butuan City and the questions of how it could be best co-managed in collaboration with DENR while involving the residents are representative of challenges in various areas of Mindanao. Many local and national government agencies are confronted with similar problems, such as the inaccessibility of an area for government officials, overlapping claims on land rights, as well as powerful informal actors with incompatible interests.

Although the COSERAM Program Steering Committee initially expected this support to last no longer than two years, it turned out to be a lasting four-year collaboration of GIZ with Butuan City and its partners. In the following, we refer to this whole change process as "the inclusive co-management project," according to its main objective.

The COSERAM Program through GIZ provided the City and its partners with a broad range of political, procedural, and technical advice as well as financial support. The case study shows how fundamental approaches and principles of GIZ's common practice were successfully integrated into a change process driven and managed by the partner.

Context

More than half of the 2 million hectares of land in the Caraga region is classified as forestland. Butuan City, with a population of approximately 270,000, is the biggest city in the region and has been a center of the regional and national wood industry since the 1950s; 26,800 hectares – or 33 percent of the whole territory of Butuan City – is classified as forestland.

The inclusive co-management project of the City and its partners focused on an area comprising more than 10,000 hectares of classified forestland. The area is spread over eight different local government units, so-called *Barangays*, led by elected *Barangay* Captains. This land used to be managed by the Nasipit Lumber Company Inc. under a timber license agreement issued by DENR. The company ceased its operations in the mid 1990s due to allegations of human rights violations, especially regarding the treatment of their labor force and unsustainable management of the forest. It left behind idle land that no one managed or controlled.

As is quite common in the Philippine context – which is defined by high population growth and the regular movements of internally displaced people, either due to natural disasters or violent conflicts – the abandoned area quickly became occupied by various groups using the land and claiming tenure rights over time. Initially, the land was mainly occupied by former workers of the lumber company who had lost their employment. Partly they remained because they had been promised an allocation of land in return for outstanding salaries. Many also stayed despite the absence of alternative employment opportunities due to the decline in the traditional wood industry and also due to a number of concessions being withdrawn in other parts of the region and country. Over time, settlers from other parts of Mindanao moved in as well. Most households engaged in different agricultural activities for subsistence. This happened with and without tenurial instruments, formally and informally.

Additionally, the same land was and is home to Indigenous communities. They had been forcibly displaced when the lumber company started operations in the early 1950s. Some of them returned, and a claim of the Indigenous communities to parts of the land as their ancestral domain added to the complexity of conflicting tenurial claims. According to the Philippine Indigenous Peoples Rights Act of 1997, these Indigenous communities can be granted ownership rights to a territory that they can prove as their ancestral domain in a defined process led by NCIP. However, in this case, the legitimacy of the claim was not clear. Although the national laws on the rights of Indigenous people is one of the most progressive worldwide, it is also often misused to exploit the vast natural resources for the economic benefit of influential individuals and land brokers. Fears and uncertainties of settlers as well as authorities on the implications of such claims on their rights and mandates fueled conflicts between settlers and Indigenous communities.

The complexity of the context of the co-management area of Butuan City reflects the region's history of conflicts over access to natural resources and land use with various human rights violations – be it in terms of the people's socio-economic, cultural, political, or civil rights. It led to an exploitation of land, creating wealth for very few while impoverishing the majority over many decades and providing fruitful grounds for recruitment activities by the NPA, the armed wing of the Communist Party of the Philippines.

During the 1980s and 1990s, the forest area of Caraga was a refuge for the NPA. They closely cohabited with the Indigenous communities; still today, the NPA is known to recruit heavily from Indigenous communities. This is partly possible because the Indigenous communities feel – and actually are – extremely alienated by government services, which neither reach them in remote areas nor reflect their specific needs. This was further aggravated through various disruptions of the lumber companies' operations by the NPA while simultaneously making it difficult for government agencies to access the concession area. Sometimes education and health services were provided by the companies, but these also ceased to exist when the companies left. The area of Butuan City, where the Nasipit Lumber Company Inc. had operated, was a crucial home base from where the NPA had started recruiting and spreading their activities in the region. Incidents of violence occurred also in Butuan City when officials tried to enter the co-management area, for example shootings and harassment through the confiscation of technical equipment by armed groups.

This fragile situation of land insecurity and the increasing tensions due to more people continuously settling down persisted also after the timber license agreement had been officially cancelled in 2003 and the agreement of the Butuan City with DENR to co-manage the area was signed in 2004. Such co-management agreements with local government entities are a tool for DENR – the authority legally mandated to manage public lands and natural resources – to share competencies and management functions for a particular piece of public land with the respective local government. In the case of Butuan City, the agreement was signed, but the structures defined for co-management (especially the Co-Management Steering Committee, technical working group, co-management office) were never established. Neither the former City government nor the relevant government agencies such as DENR had made a firm attempt to fulfill their mandates and provide public services. One reason certainly was that the area was known as being influenced by the NPA.

The combination of all these factors (i.e., settlers with unclear tenurial claims, overlapping land claims, military groups, and lacking management structures) led to a complete absence of public service delivery by government agencies in the area for many years. One of the aggravating negative effects was that, in 2010, the majority of the population in the area lived below the poverty threshold of $2 per day and profoundly mistrusted any intervention by the government through both local government and national line agencies. Tensions and suspicion also existed between and amongst the communities – with some of them being more closely affiliated to the NPA than others, and some families perceiving to have more legitimate rights on the land and its use than others.

DENR and the City government disregarded the area more or less until 2010. In 2010 a new City mayor was elected based on a campaign promising good governance and socio-economic development for the poor in general, and in conflict-affected areas of the city in particular. In line with these general principles, he actively searched for appropriate investors. With the new dynamics of the City, domestic as well as international investors showed high interest in the area.

The mayor, however, quickly realized that the unclear tenurial arrangements and weak management structures as well as the tense security context for government officials were severe constraints for sustainable socio-economic development of the area. Entering into agreements with investors without a transparent process and the consent of the local population would provide grounds for armed groups to engage in violent conflicts. This would significantly affect the potential operations of any investor in the area. The developments in the neighboring province Agusan del Norte provided a warning, in which a timber license agreement for 60,000 hectares directly adjacent to the project area was issued without proper consultation and information processing. In such a scenario, neither the local population nor the City government or the investors would benefit.

In this situation, the City mayor requested support via the COSERAM Program through GIZ. The main objective was to "open" the area or to prepare the grounds allowing for peaceful and sustainable socio-economic development, thereby benefiting the communities.

Given the above context, the inclusive co-management project faced several major implementation challenges to accomplish its objective:

- How can a multi-stakeholder cooperation be set up and facilitated toward aiming at building new trust among stakeholders and allowing for deliberation and negotiation if stakeholder groups in the project area are inaccessible?
- How can a pragmatic local approach be established to resolve overlapping land tenure claims that touch upon the mandates of various line agencies such as DENR (which has the mandate to manage forestland) and NCIP (which is mandated to protect the rights of Indigenous people)?
- How can the interests of powerful players – that is, investors – be managed so that they do not jeopardize the conflict transformation and dialogue process?

At the outset, four particularly critical issues or development challenges were revealed that would require specific deliberation in the strategy of the project.

The government has no "face" and no safe entry in the project area

The project area was not accessible to government officials and GIZ personnel for security reasons. Also, GIZ staff could not offer to act as an external broker between the government and the local communities. Hence, it was crucial to first explore the question of which actor would be acceptable to the majority of the local communities and be able to gain their trust. This intermediary would, of course, also have to be trustworthy for the City government so that it actually would be able to act as an independent broker. Eventually, the intermediary would prepare the ground for the government officials to take up their role as a reliable service provider and become the "face" to the local communities. The risk of this approach was that the intermediary could be perceived as the "face" substituting governmental services, which would further weaken the government's legitimacy in the area. Thus, particular strategies needed to be developed in order to avoid this effect, including an exit strategy of the intermediary from the outset.

Interrupted relations between the two key partners

The relations between the two main governmental partners, jointly responsible for the management of the area, were strained and more or less dysfunctional at this point. At the time, DENR had a reputation of taking intransparent decisions and was often accused by the population of being partly corrupt. This could potentially endanger the City government's attempt to establish a positive reputation. Nevertheless, the inclusion of DENR was mandatory due to its constitutional mandate as the primary agency for the management of public lands and natural resources, and its formal role in the management structure of the project area according to the 2004 co-management agreement between DENR and the City government. The challenge here was how to mitigate the risks and come to joint commitments.

Political pressure on the City mayor

Although the City mayor was committed to an inclusive and collaborative process that would not want to put at risk long-term peace and security, he was under severe pressure by brokers and investors to enter into concessional agreements for the area, fulfilling his promises to foster economic development through increased private investments. These stakeholders had high levels of political influence and could exercise power on the mayor to act swiftly, which could jeopardize the change project at any time and, in a worst-case scenario, cause the conflict to escalate. However, (re-)establishing trust and relations with the local communities would need time. The different expectations among parties on priorities and pace created a politically dangerous situation for the mayor that needed to be managed with considerateness. Therefore, strategies allowing the Mayor to appease and reassure these stakeholders for a certain period of time needed to be found.

Unclear legitimacy of claims by local settlers and Indigenous people

The legal situation on land use and tenure rights in the area had a high degree of uncertainty. Some settlers possessed certificates on (private) land use and tenure rights in the area, which, according to legal standards, should not exist in an area classified as public forestland. This opened opportunities for misuse by "backstage" power players driven by personal economic interests. Clarifying which claims were legitimate (i.e., which of the tenurial instruments were obtained in an official procedure), was a necessary but highly sensitive issue. As the shooting of a government official in 2010 illustrated, this undertaking would only be possible in cooperation with – and with the support of – the local population. Another particularly sensitive subject was a specific claim by a group of Indigenous people. The legitimacy of claims to ancestral domains are usually hard to establish and require a complex verification process that lasts several years, often causing fear and conflicts in non-Indigenous communities. Verification would include questions such as: Were these people truly indigenous or just claiming to be so in order to obtain access and rights to land? Have these people perhaps been influenced by land brokers or other individuals, misusing the progressive national laws on the rights of Indigenous people to get access to the forest resources for economic exploitation?

Continuous reflection on these challenges and their changes over time guided the design and implementation of the project.

Tracing the implementation process

The implementation of the inclusive co-management project can be broken down into three phases:

1. Vision and project design for the inclusive co-management project
   (April to September of 2011)
2. Re-entry of the government into the co-management area
   (October of 2011 to March 2012)
3. Realization of the inclusive co-management project with the communities
   (April 2012 to beginning of 2015)

The following sections outline each phase along its most important milestones.

Phase 1: Vision and design for the inclusive co-management project

This initial phase was implemented between April and September 2011. Its main objectives were:

- to identify the stakeholders needed for socio-economic and inclusive development in the co-management area and define a joint vision for the co-management project;
- to agree on principles of cooperation and to develop a concept for how the identified main challenges could be addressed.

A small team consisting primarily of personnel from the City's offices most relevant for the management of the forestland (planning, investment promotion, and agriculture) and appointed by the City mayor and GIZ staff of the COSERAM Program prepared an initial project design.

As a first preparatory step, the team took part in a training course on multi-stakeholder dialogues and cooperation. This is a core principle and methodology in conflict transformation, and GIZ wanted to emphasize from the beginning that a holistic approach was needed and had to include various sectors, agencies, and the communities – be it Indigenous people or settlers. The training enabled the participants to understand the relevance and benefit of multi-stakeholder cooperation in a protracted conflict context. The team was introduced to various tools of analyzing the current situation and designing a comprehensive approach (e.g., stakeholder analysis, conflict analysis, time line, influence power grid, levels of decision-making). It established hereby a common understanding on all relevant stakeholders and resulted in an initial strategy on how to cautiously and gradually involve additional actors.

The team realized in the course of this process that the implementation of a multi-stakeholder approach in this particular forestland area urgently called for the (re-)vitalization of the dormant Co-Management Steering Committee (CMSC). As determined in the co-management agreement of 2004, this committee was the central body formally mandated to steer the management of the area. According to this agreement, DENR and the City were the co-chairs of the committee. Further members were the regional directors of the following six government agencies: the Department of Agriculture, the Department of Agrarian Reform (DAR), the DILG, the Department of Social Welfare, the Department of Trade and Industries, and NEDA. With this setup, the team acknowledged that, as co-chair, DENR was to be brought on board first before any Co-Management Steering Committee could be convened. This was particularly crucial, as DENR – due to a lack of working relations with the City at the time – had not been involved in any trainings and preparations so far and could easily feel sidelined.

The outcomes of the training were presented to the City mayor, who approved the general direction and agreed to discuss the project with the regional director of DENR. To flank this effort, GIZ simultaneously briefed the COSERAM Program Steering Committee on the proposed next steps and the need to revitalize the steering structure of the co-management area. Since the regional directors of DENR, DILG, and NEDA were members of both Steering Committees and had formerly approved the support of GIZ to the co-management area through the COSERAM Program, the shared responsibility for the success of this comprehensive change process became very obvious.

As a result and first milestone, a meeting of the CMSC took place in May 2011. The CMSC approved the suggestion to jointly foster socio-economic and sustainable development in the area through a comprehensive and incremental multi-stakeholder process and cooperation. It was decided to establish a Technical Working Group (TWG) composed of relevant staff from all member organizations to ensure the implementation of the process. The TWG was led by the representative of the City, the head of the City planning office. Additionally, the City government was authorized to establish a Co-Management Project Office for the operational activities. GIZ was requested to facilitate the further conceptualization process with the TWG. It was also recommended to formalize the cooperation of the City with GIZ through a Memorandum of Understanding.

The TWG needed time to find its role, to get into an open exchange, and to trust each other with different institutional backgrounds and – at times – overlapping mandates. However, they realized rather quickly that they themselves and their institutions lacked information on the actual situation in the co-management area in general, and Indigenous people in particular. They were not sufficiently aware of the Indigenous leadership structures, customary laws and practices on land ownership, and use of these communities. This information was – if at all – only known to NCIP. Although it was impossible to consult the Indigenous communities at this point in time of the project, there was also no institutional link of the TWG with NCIP. NCIP was not a member of the CMSC structure agreed in 2004 and consequently was also not represented in the TWG.[3]

To address this gap, GIZ again made use of the COSERAM Program Steering Committee, where NCIP was a member. Hence, GIZ could easily approach the regional director of NCIP. In July 2011, GIZ hosted an informal exchange between the TWG and the regional director of NCIP – dubbed as "*Kapehan*" (meaning "fireside chat" in an Indigenous language). The event provided a safe space for an open dialogue of the local government agents with NCIP, which had been rarely in contact so far.

This informal exchange prompted greater awareness of, and acceptance toward, the rights of Indigenous people by the members of the TWG. The most important and tenable output was the formal request of the TWG to

---

3 NCIP was established under the Indigenous Peoples Rights Act in 1997, but it had been hindered in its operations for many years due to a petition filed before the Philippine Supreme Court challenging the constitutionality of the Act. Even though the Supreme Court eventually upheld its constitutionality in 2003, the constitutional dispute between the jurisdictions of DENR for the management of public lands (i.e., all classified forests, mineral reservations, national parks) and the Indigenous claims under the Act remained unresolved.

NCIP to assist in the implementation of the inclusive co-management project. As a first follow-up measure, a discussion with traditional and customary leaders of the Indigenous tribe to which the group claiming the area belonged was facilitated by NCIP. It aimed at generating their support for the engagement of the local Indigenous community into the co-management project.

By August 2011, a vision with the main objective and basic concept for the inclusive co-management project was developed (see Figure 1). It formed the basis for the respective Memorandum of Understanding between Butuan City and GIZ signed in the same month. For the development of the vision for the inclusive co-management project, the TWG additionally sought the advice of two local non-government organizations (NGOs) that were experienced in working with Indigenous communities and had a good reputation in community work. They enriched the discussions with their community perspective.

Figure 1: Vision (goal) and components of the inclusive co-management project

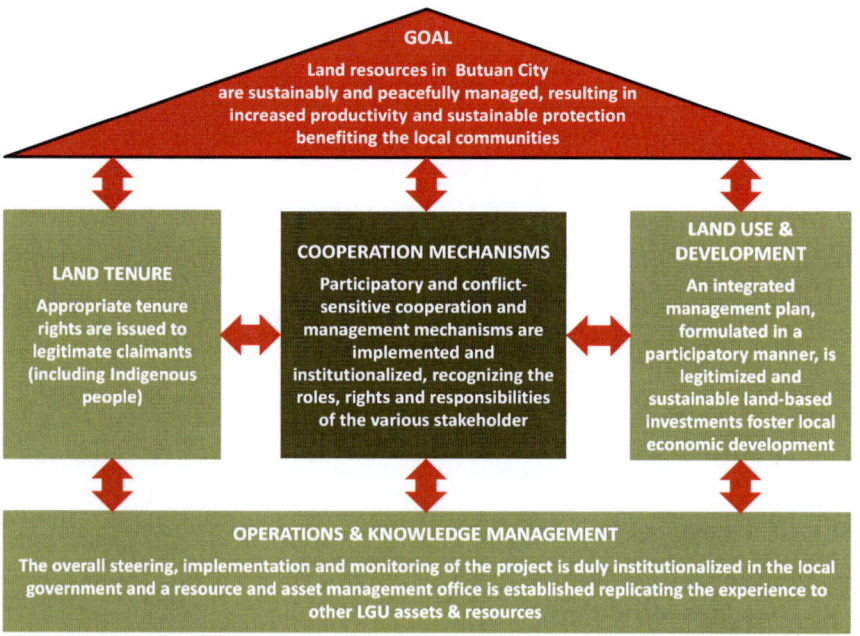

Source: Authors

276

Conflict sensitivity appeared as a cross-cutting issue in the whole concept. It also contained strategies on how to address the implementation challenges initially identified, which are described below.

- Inaccessibility of the project area by government agencies

A gradual process was envisaged with (1) collection of in-depth information about the situation and concerns of the population through an NGO as intermediary; (2) re-entry of the co-management partners facilitated by the intermediary; and (3) gradual establishment of direct cooperation mechanisms between the governmental partners and the local communities.

- Strained relationships to DENR and other line agencies

Establishing inclusive cooperation and management mechanisms was at the center of the whole strategy, recognizing the relevance of each stakeholder with its rights and responsibilities. Due to the special role of DENR in the steering of the co-management area, strengthening the cooperation of the City and DENR was a particular focus. A first success in the cooperation with the line agencies was their acknowledgement that NCIP had a crucial role to play and thus was invited as a regular member of the TWG.

- Political pressure on the mayor to facilitate new concessions with investors

The consultative re-entry process into the area via an intermediary was to be accompanied by a parallel process of defining criteria for the assessment and selection of potential investments in the area. These criteria were to be developed in an inter-disciplinary manner involving government agencies, academia, civil society, and the private sector. This process was designed to inform potential investors that a transparent assessment of investment proposals was envisaged. It was also meant to ease the pressure a bit and provide more time for the preparation of an inclusive decision-making process on investment projects.

- Unclear legitimacy of the claims of local settlers and Indigenous people

Financial and technical support for the verification of the claims was prioritized and a close cooperation with NCIP envisaged. Clarification of land tenure through a participatory and transparent process and issuance of appropriate tenurial instruments to legitimate claimants – both settlers and

Indigenous people – was incorporated as a main pillar into the projects concept.

Overall, several objectives were to be pursued with these strategies: (1) committing the Co-Management Steering Committee to a structured, transparent process of decision-making; (2) sending positive and clear messages to residents as well as to potential investors that the City and DENR were committed to looking for sustainable investments only; (3) gaining time to establish consultation and cooperation mechanisms with the local communities in order to involve them in the decision-making on investment projects and the overall management of the area.

A good indicator for the significant progress made already in the course of this initial phase was the visit of the Chairperson of the Committee on Economic Cooperation and Development of the German Parliament at the end of August 2011. Only five months after the project had taken off, the City mayor felt safe and confident enough to invite the German delegation to visit a cooperative of local farmers at the periphery of the project area under the protection of the local communities.

In September 2011, the CMSC formally approved the overall concept and a comprehensive work plan for each project component for the inclusive co-management project.

Altogether, the conceptualization phase was characterized by the strong role of GIZ in designing and facilitating activities, providing conceptual inputs, and clarifying roles and cooperation mechanisms between the main implementing partners.

Phase 2: Re-entry of the government into the co-management area

The second phase of the project was implemented between October 2011 and March 2012. Its main objectives were:

- to establish initial direct contact between the City and the local communities of all eight *Barangays*;
- to support the TWG working as a team that constructively makes use of the diversity of its member organizations with its different – and at times overlapping – mandates.

Establishing direct contact would be done through engagement of a local NGO as an intermediary, tasked to act as a "door opener" and facilitator of first contact for the City government and its partners. Beforehand, the

TWG and GIZ deliberated the pros and cons of cooperating with a local NGO to establish access of the government actors to the local communities. The hypothesis was that established trustful relationships of the local communities and the NGO would be a helpful basis for the City government to reconnect with the communities and be introduced as a development partner. Finding an NGO willing and able to play this role was, however, a challenge. Finally, a well-established NGO with a good reputation among both communities and government agencies was found.

The main tasks of the NGO were: a) improving information for the City and raising awareness with the local communities on the objectives, structure, and current state of the Co-Management-Project; b) identify members of the local communities who potentially could become part of a community-level counterpart body to the formal co-management structures; and c) prepare and facilitate the initial direct contact between the City government and its partners with the local communities.

It was clear that this strategy involved the risk of further undermining the already weak government structures and legitimacy on the ground: If the NGO's activities were not sufficiently linked back to the governmental implementing partners, an NGO would be established as the "face" of the project and service provider. Important for the selection of the NGO was the credibility of the staff, the reputation as being a neutral party, and their access to the communities of the area.

It was strategically decided to contract the NGO formally through GIZ for the initial tasks. Above all, it was a risk-mitigating measure for the staff of the organization: Through the engagement of GIZ – as an international organization perceived as a neutral broker in the region – the NGO staff did not have a formal line of responsibility to the City government or DENR, both of which were still perceived by the local population and the armed groups as conflicting parties.

The staff members of the NGO successfully established close contacts with the local communities. The information collected by the NGO were used to design information events in each of the *Barangays*, in which the City government and its partners presented and discussed the general objectives and concept of the inclusive co-management project to the local communities. This phase culminated in the conduct of public information and consultation events.

Part of the preparation for the information events was the formulation of key messages to be communicated by the City mayor and TWG members as well as anticipating how to respond to questions and issues that might be raised by the local communities. Those messages were based on the grievances, allegations, and concerns of the local communities collected by the NGO's community workers. For instance, it was confirmed that legal recognition of existing claims and land tenure instruments was the key issue for the local population.

In February 2012, with exception of one *Barangay*, the information and consultation events were successfully conducted, reaching a critical portion of the population in the area. The delivered key messages proved to be well prepared and were well received by the communities. The mayor and the TWG members who were present managed to keep the discourse with the local participants constructive and avoided entering into confrontational arguments. However, in one of the *Barangays*, almost no participants came to the announced event. Reportedly, armed groups prevented the greater part of the local community from participating. This concerning information led to intensive reflection and discussion within the TWG, the NGO, and GIZ on its implications and potential strategies to redress the situation. Since obviously the local community was interested in joining the event, it was decided to proceed with the information events as scheduled in the other *Barangays* and to repeat the one in the concerned *Barangay* a few days later. Finally, the information event was successfully repeated on another date.

This was the first time in many years that government officials had entered the area seeking a direct exchange with the local population. The events, thus, were the initial step to (re-)establish the confidence and trust of the local communities in the seriousness of the City's intentions to prepare the ground for the pro-active and constructive engagement of the local communities in helping the project to progress.

To sustain the positive initial effect of the information events, the TWG ensured that there was follow-up on several agreements between the City mayor and the local communities on short-term resolutions for urgent concerns. For instance, a disputed auction on the portion of land where the processing plant of the old timber company was located was stopped to clarify legitimacy of the auction. Also, an impassable farm-to-market road was rehabilitated in the weeks following the information events.

The conducting of successful information events was an important test for the acceptability of the developed concept by the local communities. With its strong presence, the City government presented itself as the committed driver of the project. Also, it was a strong push for the self-confidence and motivation of the TWG as a team, showing that they could successfully manage a very critical situation.

An unexpected but very important by-product that the NGO was able to compile due to the established trustful relationship with the local population was detailed data on the population (settlers and Indigenous people), various land tenure instruments possessed by some residents, and existing local governance structures in the area. The data on a variety of tenurial instruments included also relatively recently issued certificates on granted land use rights by several government agencies – including members of the CMSC. Although it was not the result of a representative survey, this data challenged the previous assumption that most settlers illegally occupied parts of the project area and raised questions on the practice of certain authorities in issuing tenurial instruments. It also indicated that resolving the land tenure conflicts in the area might develop into a more complex and legally challenging issue than expected. The findings even revealed that one particular individual, a well-known land broker, possessed up to 800 hectares of land within the area – whereas legally a maximum of only 5 hectares would be possible. Other reports of local communities on the intensive activities of well-known land brokers in the area – confirming investigations conducted by NCIP – stressed the need to approach the land tenure issue comprehensively and with priority.

In order to further foster the work of the TWG as a team, in October 2011 GIZ conducted a team-building activity. This included also the joint assessment of important capacity development needs of the TWG members with respect to the implementation of the different components of the project. Additionally, the process to develop criteria for the assessment and selection of potential investment projects was started in December 2011. The initial workshop involved the TWG as well as additional participants from academia, the private sector (e.g., farmers associations), NGOs, other governmental agencies, and members of the City's investment-related council commissions. With this wide range of participants, the involvement of all relevant actors and bodies in this crucial and sensitive process was ensured.

The end of this preparatory phase constituted the signing of a Financial Agreement in March 2012 between Butuan City and the COSERAM Program with the support of GIZ concerning the implementation of the project. The Financial Agreement also incorporated capacity-development measures for the TWG, as identified in the joint assessment in October 2011. GIZ committed to provide 48 percent of the planned total costs of the project over a period of two years. The remaining funds would mainly be covered by Butuan City, manifesting the mayor's high commitment and also his personal political responsibility to the project. DENR committed to 5 percent of the total planned costs.

GIZ's role in this phase was still a very strong one in terms of conceptualizing activities and reflecting on new information and developments. However, the TWG was brought into a successively more pro-active role, slowly taking over the preparation and facilitation of meetings and activities, for instance.

Phase 3: Realization of the inclusive co-management project with the communities

The actual implementation phase with the communities started in April 2012 and ended at the beginning of 2015. The main objectives were:

- to establish sustainable structures and mechanisms for the steering and management of the project, including the refocusing of the TWG to its original task as a support and advisory body of the CMSC;
- to implement the inclusive co-management project according to the agreed vision and components, fostering an inclusive socio-economic development of the co-management area.

The full-fledged start of the implementation, however, was hampered by the fact that the inclusive co-management project did not yet have a strong operational body to implement project activities: Although already authorized by the CMSC to establish a so-called Co-Management Project and Program Office (CMPPO) in May 2011, conflicting opinions of the City council members on the administrative anchoring of the office within the City administration delayed the establishment of the CMPPO for months. This hampered the implementation schedule for the inclusive co-management project from the beginning and remained a significant challenge throughout the implementation. As a result, the TWG facilitated the establishment of a Project Implementation Team (PIT) as an interim solution to partly compensate for the resulting lack of personnel resources for the implementation of the project until the formal appointment of staff for the CMPPO. However, since the PIT members were still the regular staff of their respective agencies and offices, their resources for the implementation of activities under the inclusive co-management project were limited. Thus, the implementation of the project significantly gained pace only after the approval of the CMPPO at the beginning of 2013.

Although the information events in the re-entry phase initially (re-)established the contact with the local communities, the relations were still fragile. Due to the absence of a strong operational body for the project, i.e. the CMPPO, which could drive forward the further trust-building and shaping of the cooperation mechanisms with the local communities, it was decided to continue utilizing the NGO to engage with the initial re-entry for this task. Due to its successful work establishing close contacts and trust with the local communities, the NGO was in a good position to organize the local communities and support the establishment of community-based cooperation structures. Based on the strategy to establish the City government as the "face" of the project, the City government directly contracted the NGO. With this, the NGO was now acting as a service provider directly on behalf of, and steered by, the City government. Only after a couple of months and mutual complaints by the NGO and the City government did it become obvious that both the City and the NGO had not yet fully adapted to this change in roles. The City government was not yet able to administer, steer, and monitor service contracts. As a consequence, the work of the NGO in the area was not sufficiently linked and coordinated with other work packages of the inclusive co-management project, with the NGO implementing its own agenda on development of the area. Under the facilitation of GIZ, finally the main contractual and procedural issues were able to be resolved, but the relations between the City and the NGO never completely recovered until at the end of the contractual relationship. As a positive outcome of this experience, the TWG and PIT / CMPPO staff realized that they needed to engage much more directly in relation-building with the local communities and that the administrative part of the implementation required equal attention and resources. Also, supported by the respective capacity-building measures provided by GIZ, the City government reacted with internal structural and procedural adjustments.

The political pressure on the City mayor and the CMSC to enter into agreements with investors continued to be a constant threat to the project. As a mitigating measure, GIZ intensively lobbied to approach the development of criteria for the assessment and selection of potential investment projects in a two-staged process. To show the City councils and investors that existing investment proposals were being taken seriously, investment proposals were to be checked against a set of criteria. These criteria could be developed in a rather quick process and approved by the CMSC and City council. To ensure that only investment projects that promote sustainable socio-economic development would be approved, relevant international standards and principles for land-based investments (e.g., the UN Food and Agriculture Organization's Voluntary Guidelines on Tenure of Land and Natural Resources, or Principles for Responsible Agricultural Investments of the FAO, the International Fund for Agricultural Development, and the World Bank) were used as reference for the development of the criteria. Investment proposals successfully passing this first-level check, however, would need to obtain the approval of the potentially affected local communities before any agreement could be signed. Although the TWG, in principle, agreed on this two-staged process, the political pressure through the City council and the CMSC was huge, and the Mayor and the TWG were able to prevent action on decisions made by the CMSC or the City's Investment Board on concrete investment proposals several times, but only at the last minute.

The political sensitivity of the issue and complexity of the approach caused several delays, diversions, and loops in the formulation of the criteria for assessment and selection of investment projects. After a rather tedious process, the criteria were finalized and approved by the TWG only at the end of 2015. Adoption by the CMSC is still outstanding; however, the City agricultural office and the public–private partnership office are applying them today.

As also the information events confirmed, effectively approaching the land tenure and land development issues was a key concern and success factor for the whole inclusive co-management project. As a precondition, a detailed stocktaking of the actual land use and tenurial claims in the project area was necessary. However, any attempts of DENR to survey the area in 2010 and earlier resulted in harassments and even killings because such activities were interpreted by the local communities as preparatory actions to oust them from the area and prepare the entry of external investors. To avoid previous mistakes and resolve the fears of the population, a highly participatory process of elaborating land use plans was set up, including a participatory approach on stocktaking of the area. Through intensive consultation and dialogue activities with the local communities, the PIT explained the participatory approach toward the land tenure issue and land use planning anchored in a principle of close community involvement. This finally enabled the conduct of a perimeter survey for the whole co-management project area in June 2013. The peaceful conduct of this survey, in cooperation with the local communities, was a very important milestone and success for the inclusive co-management project. Although the co-management agreement was signed already in 2004, only now were the exact borders of the co-management area clear to all stakeholders.

Perimeter survey of the co-management area in cooperation with the local communities

In an intensive process over several months, GIZ capacitated the PIT (later the CMPPO) in implementing the participatory land use planning. This included exposure to GIZ-supported project sites in other regions of the Philippines, in-house trainings, training-on-the-job, and back-stopping of the multi-sectoral and multi-agency team. The team finally conducted the participatory planning exercises in all eight *Barangays*, including a detailed recording of existing land uses and tenurial claims, but also of conflicts over land use and development priorities of the local communities. Meanwhile, it was also clarified by NCIP that the claims of Indigenous people in some parts of the area did not qualify for an Ancestral Domain, that is, a certificate of communal ownership of this Indigenous group in the area. Thus, the very particular Indigenous planning and management regime did not apply, but the Indigenous population within the project area needed to be treated in the participatory planning process as a special group of the local community. In order to effectively involve them,

NCIP advised and facilitated particular processes and tools that were in accordance with the Indigenous governance system and customary laws for the involvement of this community.

In order to support the ongoing trust and confidence-building between the City government and the local communities, the local communities should already see visible positive effects of the improved relations with the City government and its partners in the phase of shaping and deepening the cooperation mechanisms and preparing for the participatory planning process. A first measure in this regard was the delivery of the immediate actions promised by the Mayor during the initial information events. To provide initial tangible results, the project concept earmarked funds for further small-scale infrastructure projects with immediate effect on improvement of the living conditions of the local communities. Being the result of a consultative process, the CMSC approved the implementation of six small-scale and quick-impact projects enhancing the water supply in the eight *Barangays*. In order to avoid the creation of additional conflicts as well as anticipating the results of the participatory land use planning exercise, the CMPPO ensured that only those projects were selected that were unanimously supported by the whole community. In the intensive consultations with the local population, awareness was also raised about the participatory formulation of land use plans, which was to start concurrently with the implementation of the small-scale and quick-impact projects. Memorandum of Understandings between the CMSC and the respective *Barangays* formalized the agreements and the mutual contributions in October 2013.

The final outputs – land use plans at the *Barangay* level – were adopted at the beginning of 2015. Although their integration into land use and development plans at the City level is still ongoing, they provide the official bases for the land use and development direction of the inclusive co-management area.

As already indicated in the re-entry phase, the situation on tenurial claims was highly complex. The existence of several types of presumably legally issued tenurial instruments that were, however, not in accordance with legal standards created doubts that the situation could be resolved within the capacity of the co-management partners alone. To provide support and potential avenues to engage national-level agencies, GIZ once more utilized the COSERAM Program Steering Committee. Through the facilitation of GIZ, the Caraga offices of DENR and NEDA, together with Butuan City, jointly commissioned a legal study on land rights. The co-

Participatory planning session in Barangay Dulag, facilitated by the PIT

management area of Butuan City was one of the two areas for which the study was to assess the possibilities for resolving the tenurial overlaps and recommend tenurial instruments that could be issued to the local population. Besides other recommendations, the study emphasized the potential of using a little known Joint Administrative Order of DENR, NCIP, and DAR on outlining basic steps on how to resolve overlapping tenurial issues.

The backbone and cross-cutting task for the sustainability of the inclusive co-management project was the continuous strengthening of the functioning of the CMSC, its TWG, as well as the CMPPO as the operational unit. To support this, GIZ provided constant strategic advice and coaching to the CMSC and the TWG. Additionally, the PIT and (later) the CMPPO were the recipients of various trainings and intensive coaching on cooperation management by GIZ staff – besides capacity development on technical issues. Whereas, for instance, the involvement of NCIP in the project could be institutionalized at a very good level, it remained challenging throughout the inclusive co-management project to obtain the full support and commitment of DENR, both in the steering and in the implementation. However, communication and cooperation mechanisms between the implementing partners and the local communities were successfully institutionalized, resulting in a sustainable, positive impact on the relations with the local communities. As a result of an intensive dialogue between the CMPPO, local communities, and GIZ, community-based co-management structures (so-called Co-Management Area Coordination Centers) were established. To be effective, they were linked both to the formal co-management structures as well as to the *Barangay* Development Council as the formal governance structure at the local level (see Figure 2).

Despite those successful developments in trust-building and establishing coordination mechanisms with the local communities, there were several setbacks at several instances throughout the implementation phase. In 2013 and 2014, Caraga, including the project area, witnessed a heightened general security situation with the movement of armed groups and so-called counter-insurgency measures of the armed forces. This hindered the implementing partners and GIZ staff from entering the project area, resulting not only in delays of the implementation but also allowing for rumors to circulate quickly on the real intentions of the City. Although there were no direct threats against the government agencies or GIZ, threats to community members were not unusual, and it was often unclear as to what extent they were related to the project.

In order to better monitor those security risks and the development of conflicts in the project area, a system to monitor the conflicts in the co-management area was established. Furthermore, the City developed a comprehensive communication strategy to ensure that the communities would be well-informed about the plans and next steps of the City and the progress of the project. The system for collecting and analyzing information on the security and conflict situation involved sources from the local communities and provided useful information for the joint reflection and adjustment of measures of the co-management project. The *Barangay* Captains and member of the communities supported the CMPPO in the continuous monitoring and analysis of the security and conflict situation. They were also an important backbone to the communication strategy, ensuring that the progress of the project was also broadly known in the communities.

Figure 2: Amended management structure of the project linking formal steering structures to governance structures at community level (new features in red circles)

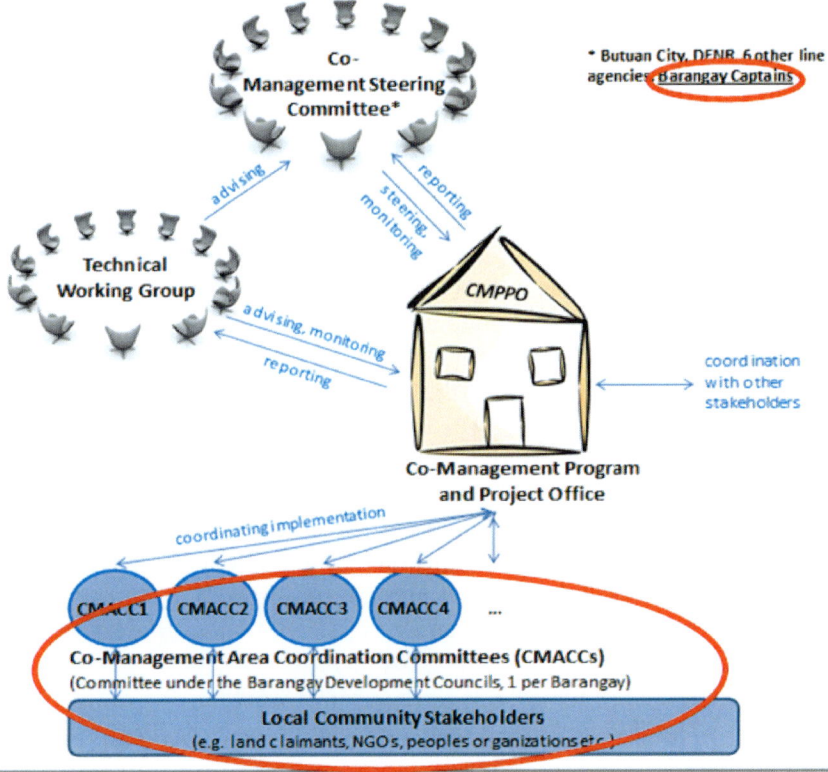

Source: Authors

GIZ's support in this implementation phase focused on coaching and strategic advice to the City mayor and the Project Implementation Team. GIZ was generally invited as an observer (e.g., to the Co-Management Steering Committee meetings), but the leading role was with the City. Technical expertise was mainly provided for the setup of the local conflict-monitoring system and the communication strategy.

Lessons from the case study: Achievements and principles that guided the project implementation

The results achieved by the inclusive co-management project were considerable, despite a number of setbacks in the course of the implementation (including violent incidents and difficulties in providing secure land tenure).

Violent conflict has not ended in Caraga and Mindanao, but the number of conflicts in the inclusive co-management project area have declined. Since 2014 the social and economic situation of the affected population has steadily improved. Government services and financial support through various development schemes are now available. Among them are a 36 million pesos (approx. €675,000) fund from the National Greening Program of DENR, benefiting close to 2,000 families and including 600 families from a part of the co-management area that was most affected by violent conflicts and the presence of the NPA. Another huge fund of 360 million pesos (approx. €6,750,000) from the Philippine Rural Development Program is geared toward the support of those areas most severely affected. With this support, the communities are developing the land with cash crops (cacao, coffee) and industrial trees (falcate and rubber), and farm-to-market roads are being constructed or improved. Interviews and focus group discussions conducted by GIZ confirmed assessments of the City government that the vast majority of people are confident that the local and central governments will assist them further.

The institutional achievements of the project went beyond more effective and efficient administrative structures and procedures. Huge progress was to be observed in the change of attitudes of government officials. The positive response of the local communities on the transparent and participatory approach convinced not only the City but also prompted the neighboring province to replicate the approach of conflict-sensitive re-entry and participatory planning in other areas.

Three sets of principles were instrumental for the successful implementation of the project:

- principles guiding the implementation process and its design
- principles guiding the responsibilities and roles of the main actors
- principles guiding the support provided by GIZ

Principles guiding the implementation process and its design

The fact that today both the City and the local population of the project area are benefiting from inclusive socio-economic development is first and foremost a result of the process that was applied in the project. The following principles guided this implementation process:

• Do No Harm and conflict sensitivity to mitigate risks, ensure context-specific and culturally sensitive processes, and achieve sustainable development results

At the center of the whole implementation process were the principles of Do No Harm and conflict sensitivity. To mitigate security risks and to avoid other unintended negative impacts in the course of the project implementation, an in-depth analysis of the situation by the partners themselves was required and had to be reviewed on a regular basis. This context analysis had to take into account the interests, anxieties, and relationships of all stakeholders and the conflict dynamics over time. The causes of the conflicts and potential factors that could further escalate or de-escalate the levels of violence had to be identified in order to decide on an appropriate conceptual approach.

As the case study indicates, such an analysis is not easy to establish and starts with a process of raising awareness about potential risks. Thereby, the government officials realized that they were not familiar enough with the area to ensure that their analysis included all actors and interests. Support by various partners – particularly NCIP and local NGOs – was needed to better understand the history and dynamics of the co-management area. The context (as described in the "Context" section above) was not fully clear from the outset but is the product of a continuous analysis of the partners involved.

In the course of the implementation, the partners of the inclusive co-management project experienced several setbacks, which also included violent attacks on community members who engaged in the process. Although some of these incidents were claimed by the NPA, others were related to individual disputes. Regardless of the motives, each time the partners of the project realized that they were again lacking information and that continuous monitoring – but also transparent information on the progress of the implementation process – was a must. It was only in 2014 that the City government set up a conflict-monitoring system together with the communities and developed a comprehensive communication strategy.

Over time, all methods, tools, and instruments applied – be it for land use planning or conducting quick-impact measures for small-scale livelihood support – were discussed with the partners in terms of their conflict sensitivity. The following principles are the result of this conflict-sensitive lens.

• Multi-stakeholder approach to ensure participation and inclusiveness

The success of a change project in volatile conflict situations cannot be guaranteed, but prioritizing efforts in engaging all relevant and affected stakeholders – leaving no one behind – is a key in striving toward sustainable results. Multi-stakeholder dialogues and multi-sectoral cooperation are crucial approaches for such settings and based on the principles of participation and forming partnerships.

As the case study shows, reaching out to a variety of different actors of civil society and at the state level allowed the government agencies not only to re-enter into the co-management area but also to improve the cooperation and efficiency of the agencies. For instance, the urgent need to address illegitimate claims of land brokers misusing Indigenous people's rights resulted in a new alliance of the City with NCIP. Sharing the same interest of promoting legitimate claims on land, this cooperation enabled a relatively quick verification of the claim at hand. The fact that this particular claim was found as not qualifying for ownership rights under the Indigenous Peoples Rights Act eased a lot of anxieties on the side of the settlers. But it also required the development of sound strategies on how to adequately involve the Indigenous people as a stakeholder group with particular customs and needs. The latter was only possible through the support of NCIP and the close cooperation of the City and NCIP.

Multi-stakeholder cooperation is, however, a very demanding approach. It is rarely smooth and linear and requires time and patience. To be successful, government agencies and officials needed training and coaching on how to set up and "orchestrate" such a process. They had no prior experience of involving so many different partners, nor were they very confident working in networks and building alliances with state and civil society actors. It was a very new experience to engage with the communities at eye-level and form real partnerships, which resulted, for instance, in joint conflict-monitoring and land use planning processes. After the initial hesitation of some crucial government officials, those same people became the most committed persons in the participatory processes over time. The increased openness and capacities to reach out to settlers as well as Indigenous people as equal partners were key enabling factors for the actual implementation of the project, resulting in the formalized involvement of the local communities in the co-management of the area.

Engaging with all relevant actors and ensuring inclusiveness, of course, always raises the question and challenge of how to deal with powerful agents who pursue incompatible goals and try to influence the project and/or the communities – be it non-state armed groups using the means of violence or influential economic stakeholders, such as the abovementioned land brokers. To address these challenges, the following principles were of great relevance.

• Incremental process to steadily increase ownership of all stakeholders

The case study is a good example that, in highly disputed contexts, incremental implementation is required. The higher the potential of violent escalation of a conflict, the more caution is needed when bringing stakeholders of various backgrounds and affiliations together. At an early stage of the process, huge roundtable discussions, for instance, would have run the danger to just serve as a welcome platform for the most vocal and influential stakeholders. Trust-building processes of this kind require, first, the identification of change agents within the communities and agencies that can become credible voices and supporters of the project. It was a learning process for Butuan City and the other involved government agencies to understand that partnerships had to be forged in a careful process of stepwise increasing the number of stakeholders in line with growing levels of trust and ownership for the project. But even after the government agencies had access to the area, they still had to design their approaches slightly differently from *Barangay* to *Barangay* within the co-management area. For example, in some parts of the co-management area, the first public consultations were well attended; in others the process failed and afforded time for reflection on what the missing link was and what contacts, data, or information was still needed.

For an incremental process to work out and to increase a sense of ownership, it is of utmost importance to *start the project initially with those change agents that are highly motivated, have the political will, and are ready to invest in the process.*

The investment can be quite different according to the partners' capacities, but in all cases it means making significant additional efforts beyond business as usual. In the case study, it is implied that the City leadership backed up its lip service with financial commitments in the annual budget. The sincere commitment of Butuan City manifested in a counterpart of more than 50 percent to the financial agreement with GIZ. This counterpart was further increased in the course of the process, with additional funds being added for the implementation of more small-scale investment measures for livelihood support to the communities.

Other stakeholders who increasingly were enrolled in the process also needed to invest. This is particularly true for the communities in the co-management area. For the *Barangay* Captains and all involved community members, investment meant time and active participation in planning and management processes – while also needing to earn their livelihoods. Even more importantly, it required the courage of the communities to safeguard and lobby for the project, especially when being approached by stakeholders with other incompatible interests in the area. The reaction of influential power players, and especially of non-state armed groups on such developments, cannot be predicted, of course. It was always clear that the project could be perceived as a threat, especially to the NPA, and might trigger violence. At the same time, there was also a certain probability that those groups would be careful to strongly oppose or disrupt interventions if the local community saw those developments as being beneficial for them. Especially the NPA, claiming to fight for the rights of marginalized communities, would take the risk of losing the support of its constituencies.

- Develop and implement strategies to mitigate "backstage" actions of influential stakeholders with interests incompatible with the objectives of the project

"Backstage" power-plays of influential stakeholders challenging the development vision of a change project cannot be circumvented but need instead to be analyzed with, and by, key implementing partners in order to determine adequate strategies on how to deal with them. It is neither helpful to scapegoat, sideline, or ignore these stakeholders, nor can it be of interest to provide them too much space and voice to interfere with the project. Butuan City and its partners had to either find ways of constructively engaging these stakeholders in the process or – if this was impossible – at least mitigate the harm they could do to the process. In their case, these actors were stakeholders urging for land-based investment. As a strategy to ease the political pressure and appease the potential investors, the formulation of transparent assessment and selection criteria for investment projects was started right at the beginning. Although this process was not finalized for a long time, the premature signing of agreements with investors could be prevented. Although the investment selection criteria have not yet been adopted or applied at the level of the City, several City departments have applied them, including the City agriculture and public–private partnership offices.

- Targeting short-term milestones while keeping the long-term vision in mind and keeping the long breath

The case study also demonstrates that complex change processes need time and perseverance by all involved. The "long breath" is normally not to be expected from the beginning. It needs to be nurtured throughout the process by highlighting achieved milestones and transparency on challenges encountered. Though this seems rather obvious for most agencies supporting good governance, conflict transformation, and comprehensive development processes, it cannot be emphasized often enough, as it might not reflect the perspective of the main change agent and partners. As the case study shows, the City had initially hoped that the process would perhaps need a year. The COSERAM Program Steering Committee saw the support by GIZ limited to two years. When eventually entering into a financial agreement with GIZ at the end of 2011, the partners already foresaw a further implementation period of two years. Finally, it needed a bit more than four years before GIZ was able to withdraw its support to the partners and allow them to continue on their own.

When there is a lot of political pressure and high expectations from the population, it is particularly difficult for the actors involved to accept that so much time will be needed. Hence, emphasizing as an external advisor from the beginning that a process might need many years could even heighten the temptation to opt for quick solutions, like those that seem to have been offered by the land brokers. Therefore, it is helpful to clearly think in terms of milestones and communicate successes achieved on the way. In the case study, significant milestones were, for example, the reactivation of the Co-Management Steering Committee, the signing of the Memorandum of Understanding with GIZ, the alliance with NCIP, the request by the neighboring province to learn from Butuan City and join the process of training local government officials in conflict-sensitive land use planning or the implementation of first quick-impact measures supporting the livelihood of communities. Butuan City reported many of these milestones and achievements on its website, in the media, and also in the communities. Successes as well as setbacks encountered were regularly discussed in the respective Co-Management Steering Committees as well as the COSERAM Program. This allowed all partners to understand the dynamics better and to maintain their engagement.

Principles guiding the responsibilities and roles of the main actors

Transparency on the responsibilities and roles of all stakeholders involved in a change process is generally of great importance, but even more so if the aim is to re-establish the legitimacy of government agencies in situations of fragility and conflict. As responsibilities and roles may shift during the course of implementation, regular clarification is needed throughout the cooperation. Although this is also not a new lesson to most agencies supporting good governance, conflict transformation, and comprehensive development processes, the case study offers some insights on the interplay of government and non-governmental agencies as well as external advisors.

Ensuring the leadership of the main change agents

Although GIZ had initially a very active role in bringing together different stakeholders of the project, the preparatory activities were already designed in a manner to enable the City government and its core partners to take the leading role and be the "face" of the change project. Despite several critical moments and varying levels of success regarding the degree of commitment and involvement of the different governmental stakeholders, the City managed to take the lead in the implementation of the project and institutionalized – with the support of other government agencies – comprehensive steering and cooperation structures and mechanisms involving local communities. The publicity of successes achieved had to be associated with the main change agents and the associated Philippine government agencies. This also meant that GIZ as well as the NGO that assisted as an intermediary had to sometimes subdue their own legitimate interest of promoting their own organization.

Trust-building with the support of intermediaries

In situations of fragility and conflict, the population often loses trust in governmental institutions and services and/or they perceive the state as being a conflict party. Hence, the collaboration with non-state actors, for example local NGOs, can be crucial, if not indispensable. Provided that these intermediaries are able to gain the trust of – or already enjoy the confidence of – the population, they may act as brokers and facilitate the process of (re-)establishing disrupted state–society relationships. However, in order to ensure that this actually strengthens state legitimacy and leads to a robust cooperation mechanism between the state and society in the long run, a clear strategy to sequentially reduce and readjust the role of intermediaries is essential. The non-state actor has to be able to re-establish its dissociative role as the watchdog of the state; on the other side, the state needs to prove itself to be trustworthy in order not to undermine the role and reputation of the intermediary either (GIZ [Deutsche Gesellschaft für Internationale Zusammenarbeit], 2015, pp. 20f.).

In the case study, this worked out to the benefit of the City. It even prompted the City to continue work with the support of other civil society organizations. The process also did not harm the role or reputation of the NGO. The potential risks implied for the intermediary were, however, also not reflected by the project in its full scope. The co-management partners and even GIZ had a certain governmental bias when reflecting upon the roles.

GIZ as external broker and advisor

As described, in situations of conflict and fragility, local capacities, resources, and trust among actors – especially between the state and citizens – are often scarce. At the same time, enhancing capacities and rebuilding trust in the state and among various sectors of society is a long-term process. To respond to urgent needs, external expertise and resources may become necessary to fill capacity gaps in managing public resources and to support the (re-)establishment of structures to ensure public service delivery (GIZ, 2015, pp. 11f.).

GIZ is an implementing agency of the German development cooperation that supports partner countries to set up and implement change processes for a limited and target-bound time. Hence, GIZ needed to ensure its role as an external advisor and facilitator throughout the whole process. It is clear that GIZ can play an important role in facilitating new alliances and supporting cooperation management among diverse partners. In particular in conflictive contexts and interrupted relations, GIZ often serves as a neutral broker, bringing together different actors. However, this engagement needs to be carefully reflected. GIZ itself has – as an implementing agency of the German government and acting upon bilateral agreements among states – a slight bias toward government agencies. To work toward sustainable results, GIZ always has to pay attention to not become an implementing party itself that substitutes tasks of other stakeholders in the partner system. In contexts of fragility and conflict, this risk is particularly high, as the conflicting parties often have weak capacities and/or could use the support by GIZ as a vehicle to indirectly voice their stands and positions. Although the latter has not happened in the case study, there were numerous situations in which the City and its partners would have preferred that GIZ take the lead. Allowing this to happen would only create dependencies on GIZ as an implementing partner. Therefore, it is important to keep in mind that, eventually, a conflict cannot be solved by external actors. It requires first and foremost the will and interest of the conflicting parties, who likewise need to be capable of handling change processes and emerging conflicts over the long term.

Principles guiding the support provided by GIZ

The above principle – "GIZ as external broker and advisor" – already indicates that there were also a number of principles that guided the support GIZ provided to the implementing partners.

Comprehensive support for key actors to increase their capacities and maintain their commitment to the project despite setbacks and delays

GIZ provided the City and its key implementing partners with a broad range of tailored political, procedural, and technical advice as well as financial support. This included strategic and methodological advice as well as capacity development at all levels: strengthening human capacities, organizational development, networking, and cooperation as well as the development of an enabling framework for local policies. The measures ranged from the provision of technical expertise to the strengthening of administrative and managerial capacities of the institutions.

Through this comprehensive support, the partners understood the challenges at stake and the approaches needed. Thereby, they underwent change processes in their own institutions, which impacted also on policies. It resulted, for example, in the capacity of the local government, in particular the City mayor, to engage in national policy dialogues on the guidelines of co-management areas.

Comprehensive support also implied that GIZ had to understand the political commitments and needs of the main implementing partners beyond the project context. Within the mandate of the COSERAM Program, GIZ involved the City mayor and the regional directors of DENR and NCIP repeatedly in other initiatives not directly related to the change project in order to strengthen their position and to foster alliances with heads of other governmental agencies. For instance, upon the initiative of GIZ, the City jointly commissioned a legal study on potential solutions for resolving overlapping land rights with the regional offices of DENR and NEDA, the strongest government agency.

Providing time and space for trust-building and ensuring monitoring through reflection and feedback loops

Especially in the beginning of the process, GIZ strategically supported relationship- and trust-building between various groups and individuals. Without developing trust, all the feedback loops and reflection would not have led participants to bring up the critical issues that needed to be addressed. GIZ regularly facilitated informal encounters to ensure that there was a constructive atmosphere that provided a safe space for exchanges. For instance, the *Kapehan* of the NCIP regional director and informal meetings later with Indigenous leaders allowed the staff of the implementing agencies to get to know each other and better understand different points of view. This reduced anxieties about the "other" and their intentions and provided space to jointly identify possible solutions to conflicting interests and risks of the work. This was underpinned by special measures to foster more exchanges on the leadership level, in particular between the City mayor, the DENR regional director, and the NICP regional director. One of the highlights that prompted more direct contacts afterwards was a joint learning visit by the City mayor and the NCIP regional director to Germany (the DENR regional director was intended to join as well, but was not allowed to travel by the DENR national office). Another connector was the abovementioned land rights study, which was jointly commissioned by the City, DENR, and NEDA, and provided recommendations for the local, regional, and even national levels.

Open and critical reflection was made possible due to the increased levels of trust. Initially, GIZ facilitated regular feedback loops at different levels of the project. This was always done after crucial activities with the local communities (e.g., the public consultation events). Reflection sessions with the technical level generally also included direct feedback from the TWG to the mayor and a discussion with him on the conclusions. Altogether, effective steering and management by partners requires a well-established reflection-and-monitoring system of the partners. The case study shows that partners can be supported in establishing conflict-sensitive monitoring systems if the benefits of such a system are understood.

Keep your vision in mind but maintain flexibility and openness to readjust strategies and support measures

Long-term planning in situations of conflict and fragility is often challenged by dynamics on the ground, requiring adaptation, capability, and flexibility in order to come up with adequate responses. At the same time, development partners legitimately require an agreed upon framework and set of indicators to ensure that chosen approaches and activities serve the situation on the ground as well as the envisioned objective(s). Although the envisaged (mid- to long-term) objective is clear, approaches may vary, according to the dynamics and corresponding emerging opportunities in a given setting (GIZ, 2015, pp. 28f.).

The intensity and type of support provided by GIZ in the presented case study varied according to the implementation phase, but prompt and flexible reaction to the needs of the partners was practiced throughout the whole project. As the case study shows, some capacity-development measures had to be added when an unexpected lack of capacities became apparent. Numerous – and at times administratively cumbersome – adjustments had to be made.

Altogether, the tailor-made and flexible provision of advice and specific capacity-development measures, combined with regular reflection and planning exercises, enabled the implementing partners to make use of emerging opportunities and also to adjust strategies and operational plans to delays and the changing environment. The overall vision and goal remained the same throughout the process and guided the numerous changes.

References

GIZ (Deutsche Gesellschaft für Internationale Zusammenarbeit). (2015). *Capacity development in situations of conflict and fragility. German approaches and lessons learnt by GIZ*. Eschborn: Author.

Challenges and Opportunities for Implementing Financing Mechanisms for Climate Change Mitigation Guided by Principles of Good Financial Governance: The Case of Indonesia*

Tim Auracher and Heiner von Lüpke

Executive Summary

Indonesia is ranked consistently among the top 10 global greenhouse gas (GHG) emitters. This is mainly due to land use conversion processes (from forest land to agricultural crops and plantations as well as forest and peat fires) followed by emissions from fossil fuel combustion. At the occasion of the G20 meeting in Pittsburgh in 2009, the Indonesian president declared an ambitious commitment to reduce GHG emissions in Indonesia 26 percent by 2020, compared to a "business as usual" scenario. Although this target ought to be capable of being achieved using only domestic resources, a 41 percent reduction was announced to have been achieved with international support. International donors quickly stated their willingness to make contributions while Indonesia transformed the president's commitment into framework regulations in 2011.

The specific challenge of financing climate change mitigation gained momentum due to the president's commitment as well as national and international responses. Several national ministries claimed their stakes in steering, monitoring, and managing funds for climate change mitigation. The initiatives on individual funding mechanisms that evolved were neither based on a comprehensive implementation strategy nor were they always compatible with the existing national budgetary procedures and transfer mechanisms to subnational governments. The challenge was to

---

* This case study refers only to advisory processes related to climate finance in the area of the reduction of GHG emissions (mitigation), not to the adaptation of climate change. This is not implying that one topic is more important than the other one, but is due rather to the specific focus of the GIZ technical assistance programs involved.

develop and implement such a strategy and combine it with a coherent funding and transfer system for climate change mitigation with many powerful stakeholders who would each defended their own interests. The Ministry of Finance of Indonesia (MoF) – not a major player until then – realized that it had to play a more prominent role in shaping policies instead of only executing them; financing climate change mitigation is as much a question of public financial management as it is of climate change mitigation policy.

The Deutsche Gesellschaft für Internationale Zusammenarbeit (GIZ) has been supporting the Indonesian government for several years in the focal areas of "environment and climate change" as well as "decentralization and local governance" regarding German development cooperation.[1] This case study explains how the dynamics within a reform process required an advisory approach that could offer technical and organizational development advice to different partner institutions involved in climate finance in order to forge agreement on a financing mechanism that would be effective and sustainable. For this, GIZ gathered climate change policy and fiscal decentralization experts from different GIZ programs and developed tailor-made approaches to support and accompany the MoF and other stakeholders in this process. The aim was to substantially contribute to the establishment of financing mechanisms for climate change mitigation that would also fulfill criteria for good financial governance.

The case study discusses opportunities and challenges within a bilateral development cooperation agency to offer ad hoc, multi-sectoral advisory services to partners, as well as discuss its limitations within a real-time reform process in Indonesia. The case study furthermore gives examples of different approaches to providing support as a policy advisor, and thereby displays the importance of flexibly shifting between providing technical expertise, facilitating between differing interests among stakeholders as an honest broker, and providing platforms for knowledge-exchange. It illustrates the case by reflecting on two processes: first, the development of policies and regulations on the appropriate financing mechanisms for GHG emission reductions; and second, by addressing the highly politicized policy on fuel price subsidies that, if abolished, would have a notably positive impact on GHG emission reductions. The support needed for developing policies and regulations required rather technical

---

1 GIZ implements these programs on behalf of BMZ.

expertise and facilitation skills. Addressing fuel price subsidies, however, was only feasible by providing platforms for evidence-based discussions between Indonesian stakeholders.

Introduction

One of the 2030 Agenda's guiding principles is the "integrated and indivisible" (United Nations, 2015) character of its goals and targets. Hence, besides improving the ecological dimension of sustainable development, Goal 13 on "combat[ing] climate change and its impacts" must also consider the economic and social dimensions. And building "effective, accountable and inclusive institutions," as claimed by Goal 16, should be pursued as a means to improve the social, economic, and ecological dimensions at the same time. This is undoubtedly ambitious, and there are no clear concepts yet on how to implement and verify such demanding principles.

Between 2011 and 2013 – that is, long before the adoption of the 2030 Agenda – teams from several GIZ-supported programs in Indonesia tried working in a more integrated way. They supported the Indonesian administration in considering principles of good financial governance in climate change mitigation and integrating financing mechanisms for climate change mitigation into the existing fiscal decentralization system. At the beginning, this happened more by coincidence than by design. But soon the interdependence between climate finance and fiscal decentralization became obvious to all stakeholders involved. Later, also the green economy dimension increasingly played a role in the integrated advisory approach.

This case study describes how GIZ advisors on climate policy and their colleagues, who were specialized in fiscal decentralization, developed an integrated approach to support their counterparts in the Indonesian administration, and how they tried to overcome obstacles on the way. Smart implementation, according to this case study, is the flexibility to work across sectors in an integrated manner and to quickly adapt advisory approaches to opportunities and circumstances. But, as this case study also shows, flexibility also has its flip side and needs to be balanced with the right degree of formalization.

Setting the scene: Description of the context

Relevance of climate change mitigation in Indonesia and its impact on the world

Although Indonesia's GHG emission rates have fluctuated over the years, the country is ranked consistently among the top 10 global emitters (World Resources Institute/CAIT, 2016). To a great extent, those emissions stem from the processes of land use, land use change, and forestry, amounting to approximately 65–70 percent, according to the latest official inventory data of 2010. Land use conversion processes (from forest land to agricultural crops and plantations as well as forest and peat fires) rank highest among the factors leading to these GHG emissions. The second most important sector in terms of GHG emission rates is the energy sector, including power generation, transportation, and industry. Waste management still ranks relatively low in its share of GHG emissions, but it is nonetheless of high importance for local development in Indonesia.

Substantially reducing these GHG emissions requires significant changes in land use policies and their enforcement as well as investments in the renewable energy and energy-efficiency sectors, transportation, industry, and waste management. Institutions have to be fit for purpose, equipped with the right level of capacities, and the private sector and civil society need to be engaged in order to address these challenges, as the mitigation of climate change is an urgent matter.

Political commitments from President Yudhoyono and governmental response

In the context of the 13th Conference of the Parties of the United Nations Framework Convention on Climate Change (UNFCCC COP13), hosted by Indonesia in December 2007, the group of developing countries declared for the first time in history that they would be ready to undertake nationally appropriate actions to reduce GHG emissions. Following the COP13, President Yudhoyono took political action by declaring a national target for the mitigation of climate change during the G20 meeting in 2009. The declared target was set, which required a reduction of GHG emissions by 26 percent by 2020 utilizing only domestic resources and efforts; this could be increased to 41 percent by 2020 if international support were to be made available to Indonesia. However, the reduction was calculated not in absolute terms but in comparison to a "business as usual" scenario.

Following the national GHG mitigation targets, announced in 2009, two regulations were enacted by the Indonesian president in 2011: one on the preparation of national GHG inventories (#71), and a second on the implementation of the National Mitigation Action Plan on GHG emission reductions (RAN-GRK) (#61).

Presidential Regulation #61/2011, regarding the National Mitigation Action Plan (RAN-GRK), delineates the reduction of Indonesia's national emissions by 26 percent (or 41% with international support) by 2020. The RAN-GRK provides a policy framework that outlines GHG mitigation actions in five sectors: agriculture; forestry and peat land; energy and transportation; industry; and waste. At the national level, all relevant ministries and institutions were tasked to implement RAN-GRK mitigation activities, monitor them in their respective fields, and report on progress to the State Ministry of National Development Planning (BAPPENAS). At the provincial level, the provincial offices (governors) had to develop Regional Action Plans (RAD-GRK) based on the RAN-GRK policy framework and according to the implementation guidelines developed by BAPPENAS. The compilation of all provincial RAD-GRK and their contributions to the national GHG emission reduction targets have been facilitated by BAPPENAS and the Ministry of Home Affairs. BAPPENAS has been mandated to coordinate the evaluation and review of the RAN-GRK and to report the results to the Coordinating Ministry for Economic Affairs, which then reports to the president of Indonesia.

Estimated financial needs to achieve the GHG emission reduction targets

Estimates of overall financial needs to fund climate change mitigation actions and to provide related investments varied significantly, according to different studies and documents. Whereas Indonesia's Medium Term Development Plan 2010–2014 estimated that around $925 million would be required annually during the years 2010–2014 to master the target, the National Council on Climate Change estimated in 2009 that around $19.26 billion would be needed annually between 2010 and 2030. Instead, the Climate Public Expenditure and Institutional Review (Republic of Indonesia Ministry of Finance, 2012) indicated financial needs on the order of magnitude of about $7–9 billion per annum. These estimates refer to national funding needs, whereas the only source indicating needs from international sources is found in the area of reduced emissions from deforestation and forest degradation in developing countries (REDD+) ($10 billion per year).

The diversity of estimates about financing needs shows that their underlying assumptions on financing needs differ substantially. The fact that not a single governmental finance needs-assessment study was available is one explanation for this phenomenon, pointing to missing benchmarks and guidance on the government's side.

The MoF calculated the actual flows of finance through the established governmental transfer mechanisms to be $1.67 billion in 2012. However, according to the MoF's estimations, this amount would only contribute to 15 percent of the set GHG emission reduction target. This confirmed concerns that were raised after the enactment of the RAN-GRK and the RAD-GRK in 2011, that is, that effective and efficient channeling and disbursement mechanisms are required, as well as potential new sources of finance in order to fully deliver on the GHG emission reduction targets of the government. Although international development partners announced they would provide significant amounts to support GHG emission reduction actions in Indonesia, they actually disbursed funds very reluctantly due to insufficient regulatory and procedural clarity and a lack of transparency.

Indonesia's complex state administration

Indonesia features a very diverse range of landscapes, ecosystems, and cultural spheres that spread across 7,000 islands on an east-west longitudinal stretch of more than 5,000 km. The country is the fourth most populous nation worldwide – almost 260 million inhabitants reside in 34 provinces, which are in turn divided into 491 districts.

Considering this diversity and complexity, it comes as no surprise that the administrative system in the decentralized government is facing challenges. These challenges are also reflected in the policy implementation cycle of the RAN-GRK: Regional Action Plans (RAD-GRK) are developed at the provincial level while implementation of the mitigation actions takes place at the district level. With close to 500 districts, it is a real challenge to keep track of and monitor the implementation progress. The authority-sharing between the local and central governments adds to the complexity, especially when considering that five sectors are included in the RAN-GRK, posing significant challenges for both intersectoral and local–central governmental coordination. Climate change mitigation on an economy-wide basis, such as in the case of Indonesia, requires coordination and implementation across sectors. For example, in the case of emissions related to land use change, processes between forestry, energy, and mining and agriculture need to be coordinated and managed. Coordinating energy supply and demand for industry and transportation is another example of such cross-cutting topics.

The main implementation challenge was that policies that would allow for more effective implementation of mitigation actions addressing structures, mandates, and processes had not yet been developed. The initiatives on individual funding mechanisms that evolved were not always compatible with the existing national budgetary procedures and transfer mechanisms to subnational governments. Furthermore, the national ministries and agencies, as well as subnational governments and services that were primarily involved in the RAN-GRK implementation, were tasked with the development, supervision of implementation, and monitoring of mitigating actions with relatively few additional financial and human resources, which strained already stretched capacities further.

The challenge was to develop and implement such policies and combine it with a coherent funding and transfer system for climate change mitigation with many powerful stakeholders involved – each defended their own interests. A clear regulatory framework for funding procedures and clearly defined roles and responsibilities of Indonesian stakeholders would have made it much easier to attract the much needed international funds for GHG emission reduction actions.

The institutional setup of bilateral German development cooperation with Indonesia

In 2011, the bilateral technical cooperation between Indonesia and Germany was structured in three priority areas: a) good governance and decentralization, b) climate change, and c) private-sector development. This opened a wide range of possibilities for GIZ to address the above-mentioned challenges for the financing of climate change mitigation from various angles, such as public-sector instruments and policies (equitable, efficient, and inclusive); resource efficiency; and a favorable business climate in private-sector development and climate change policy development. In addition, sector-specific issues were targeted, especially in the areas of renewable energy, energy efficiency, waste management, and forestry. This framework provided the option to offer advisory services to the government of Indonesia that emphasize a cross-sectoral approach on climate finance, creating synergies and fostering collaboration among involved entities.

Within this framework, the challenges of climate change financing were addressed from the specific perspectives of each of the three priority areas.

The Policy Advice for Environment and Climate Change program (PAKLIM) worked extensively with BAPPENAS on development, implementation support, and monitoring concepts for the RAN-GRK, both at the national as well as subnational levels, including cities and industries, partnering with municipalities in Java and the Ministry of Industry, respectively. One area of activity was related to the development of finance mechanisms and concepts for the funding of the RAN-GRK actions.

The Forests and Climate Change Programme (FORCLIME) advised its main political counterpart, the Ministry of Forestry,[2] on integrating climate change mitigation policies into sector-strategic plans at the national and subnational government levels. In particular, the RAD-GRK financing in the forest sector, as well as the question about what type of funding mechanism might be most suitable for REDD+ financing made it necessary to involve the MoF.

The Decentralisation as a Contribution to Good Governance program (DeCGG) had no direct link to climate change financing issues. However, one component supported the MoF on matters regarding fiscal transfers and local taxes and charges, which constitute the institutional setting for climate finances at sub-national levels.

---

2 Before the presidential elections in 2014, won by Joko Widodo, successor to Susilo Bambang Yudhoyono, two important ministries relevant to climate change policies existed separately, namely the Ministry of Environment and the Ministry of Forestry. These two ministries were merged in October 2014 following the elections. Up to 2014, Indonesia also had a National Council for Climate Change, which hosted the UNFCCC focal point and organized the delegation for the international climate change negotiations. Furthermore, the country had a specialized agency responsible for the oversight of the implementation of the UNFCCC's REDD+ scheme, which is now integrated as a unit into the Ministry of Forestry and Environment.

Sudden acceleration: Kickoff of a transformation process

Changing role for the Ministry of Finance

Sometime in early 2011, the MoF realized that it had little influence in an increasingly important policy domain. The president had set the scene with his international commitment at the G20 meeting in Pittsburgh in 2009, international development partners were increasingly making substantial financial pledges, and other key ministries – such as Planning, Environment, and Forestry – were busy carving out the necessary national policies and procedures to achieve the climate targets. However, with all the national and international financial attention, it became obvious that the MoF had to play a more prominent role. It had to start shaping policies instead of only executing them.

The Fiscal Policy Office – an influential policy department within the MoF – took on the charge and created two institutions in mid-2011: a 12-member expert team on climate change mitigation (*tim astistensi perubahan iklim* – TAMPI) tasked to directly advise the finance minister. TAMPI was to consist of renowned experts from academia and representatives from several ministries (Finance, Forestry, Energy, and Planning). Thereby, the MoF clearly made its claim to enter not just as one player among others, but as the coordinator. A division within the Fiscal Policy Office (the Center for Climate Change and Multilateral Policy, *Pusat Kebijakan Pembiayaan Perubahan lklim dan Multilateral* – PKPPIM) was created to act as the secretariat to TAMPI.

The MoF already had a policy paper to position itself: a Green Paper, published in 2009, and several follow-up papers (2011), developed by the Australian–Indonesian Partnership Program. The papers advocated, among other things, for a Regional Incentive Mechanism for fiscal transfers to the subnational levels to finance Nationally Appropriate Mitigation Actions in Indonesia.[3] In September 2011, the pressure to act rose considerably for the Indonesian administration, as the president enacted Regulation #61/2011 on a National Action Plan for GHG emission reductions (RAN-GRK). This regulation was the first concrete translation of the ambitious GHG emission reduction targets – already announced interna-

---

3 In the UNFCCC context, countries' mitigation actions are called Nationally Appropriate Mitigation Actions, which in Indonesia corresponds to the RAN-GRK.

tionally – into a binding national regulation. It thereby served as a kickoff for the Indonesian administration to put this declaration into action.

From reactive to proactive: GIZ's response to the changing institutional environment

In search of advice on how to breathe life into the newly founded institutions, TAMPI and the PKPPIM turned to the GIZ advisory team on fiscal decentralization (DeCGG/FD team). GIZ's FD team had been based in the Directorate General for Fiscal Balance (MoF) since 2009. The FD team had some insider knowledge about the functioning of the influential expert team on fiscal decentralization (*tim asistensi desentralisasi fiscal* – TADF), which was identified as a potential model for TAMPI. Besides the institutional setup, TAMPI and the PKPPIM sought advice on operationalizing the concept of the Regional Incentive Mechanism. Actually, TAMPI and the PKPPIM not only contacted the GIZ FD team but also a broad range of development partners. The PKPPIM also got in contact with GIZ advisors from PAKLIM.

Both teams used the flexibility given by the mandate of their existing commissions from the German Federal Ministry for Economic Cooperation and Development (BMZ) to seize the opportunities of cooperating with the MoF on climate finance. For PAKLIM, the mandate was straightforward because financing mechanisms for climate change mitigation obviously play a crucial role in achieving objectives, as determined in the commission, especially with regard to implementing the RAN-GRK. The link to the mandate given by the commission for the DeCGG program was less obvious, but nevertheless plausible for two reasons. First, the potentially important amounts from national and international sources challenged the existing fiscal transfer system. A revision of the law that regulates the fiscal transfer system was about to be prepared in the MoF. This constituted a window of opportunity to shape some fiscal transfer funds in order to make the fiscal transfer system compatible with climate finance while safeguarding the overall architecture and its principles. Second, getting the Directorate General of Fiscal Balance (DJPK) and the PKPPIM to work together was already an important step for more coherence within the MoF. For several other reasons, GIZ submitted a proposal to BMZ to alter the existing commission for the DeCGG program in August 2012. At that occasion, the support for climate finance as part of the support for fiscal decentralization was included into the commission, thereby fulfilling the necessary formal requirements to the commissioner.

Obviously, the PAKLIM and DeCGG/FD teams coordinated their responses to the requests from the MoF. Soon it became clear that a strategic choice had to be made: Either each team responds to the requests of their respective partner in the MoF while making sure that support would be complementary, or both teams develop a more coherent response that would go beyond reacting to specific requests and offer a more integrated approach of support. The second option implied that both teams needed to develop a joint support strategy, identify synergies, and develop innovative ideas and approaches compared to the vast expertise on offer by various other development partners. In short, the second option required a considerable investment in time and effort.

Both teams were more or less drawn into the second option for the following reasons. Different rationales among the PAKLIM and FD teams became apparent when support measures began to be loosely coordinated. It was quickly realized that both teams had different viewpoints and understandings about what the desired outcome of the support to the MoF should be. The PAKLIM team focused on getting funds to where they were needed to implement effective measures for GHG emission reductions. Furthermore, their aim was to make sure that planning and accounting standards for the RAN-GRK and the RAD-GRK would meet international standards in order to be recognized as Nationally Appropriate Mitigation Actions. Instead, the FD team focused on the importance of a coherent, rules-based, predictable, and fair transfer system for subnational levels, with climate change being just one of several sectors to be considered. Parallel funding mechanisms seemed a pragmatic option for the climate experts but a red rag to a bull for the fiscal decentralization team.

However, discussions among both teams showed that these differences could be turned into added value for the partner institutions. If approaches that consider the existing fiscal transfer system could be developed with the MoF while responding to the (international) requirements for climate finance, solutions might be more complicated in the short run, but results might be more sustainable in the long run.

A second challenge soon became obvious: An integrated approach would mean working with all institutions involved in climate financing in Indonesia simultaneously. It proved to be much more difficult to develop coherent approaches to climate finance with all key ministries and concerned governmental institutions together. Even progressive cooperation among actors such as the MoF, BAPPENAS, the Ministry of Environment, and the Ministry of Forestry turned out to be close to impossible. Despite having renowned academic experts, TAMPI could not live up to its intended role as a coordinating expert team with relevant representatives from the abovementioned ministries. It was soon overrun by the PKPPIM, which was originally created to be its secretariat but quickly became the major driving force in developing climate finance strategies within the MoF.

A joint support strategy from PAKLIM and FD teams – often also joined by advisors from FORCLIME – allowed for offering support beyond mere technical expertise. The three GIZ teams had developed over the years a trustful cooperation with their Indonesian counterparts and a good understanding of the specific organizational culture within each institution. The FD team was based in the Directorate General of Fiscal Balance of the MoF; PAKLIM had teams with the Directorate of Environment in BAPPENAS and the Ministry of Environment; while FORCLIME was based in the Ministry of Forestry. These teams were able to mobilize their counterparts to join work processes on climate finance. In the end, this did not change fundamental shortcomings in the collaboration culture within Indonesian administration. However, mobilizing stakeholders from these different institutions made a helpful contribution by providing opportunities for fruitful exchanges among them, sometimes at quite a high level of decision-making. The MoF's Directorate General of Fiscal Balance, for example, is the responsible institution for steering and monitoring fiscal transfer funds and subnational taxes and charges. However, it had not been actively involved in policy discussions about climate finance. Due to different meeting formats, facilitated by GIZ, it finally began to play an active role, thereby opening the door for reforms to the existing fiscal balance system in order to allow for integrating climate financing mechanisms. On the other hand, the Directorate of Environment in BAPPENAS – responsible for steering and monitoring the RAN-GRK and the RAD-GRK planning processes – was at first reluctant to discuss the financial aspects of these plans with the MoF but then became actively engaged at the director's level. These exchanges were necessary – though maybe not sufficient – to develop sustainable financing mechanisms for climate change mitigation.

Based on the above analysis and experiences, the offered support strategy to the MoF had two cornerstones: first, technical and organizational development support to the PKPPIM for developing financing mechanisms that integrate and enhance the existing system of financial relations between the central government, the provinces, and the districts; second, facilitation of multi-stakeholder deliberation that brought key players together from central ministries and the presidential monitoring unit – called the President's Delivery Unit for Development Monitoring and Oversight – in order to forge agreement on new or contentious issues that were required to move the agenda of an integrated approach to climate financing mechanisms forward.

A quite successful test run for this support strategy was the development of a policy brief on *Instruments and Mechanisms for Financing of Greenhouse Gas Emission Reduction Programs in the Land Based Sector.* The purpose of this paper was to respond to the existing uncoordinated accumulation of funding and transfer mechanisms for GHG emission reductions and to develop ideas on how to integrate them into the existing budget and fiscal transfer procedures. Requested by the PKPPIM in September 2011, the multi-sectoral GIZ team (consisting of climate change and fiscal decentralization advisors from the abovementioned programs)[4] tried to respond with a more thorough result than just technical expertise. Although the policy brief did not deliver fully detailed proposals for implementation and focused only on the land-based sector, it addressed a major challenge: namely, how to integrate, in a coherent manner, two worlds that had been separated until then – international climate finance and financial relations between the national and subnational levels. The policy brief's main message was that various national and international funding sources could be channeled properly through budget mechanisms, and then – according to purpose and responsible recipient institution – channeled through existing or new but compatible transfer mechanisms. It explained how a coherent system of funding and transfer mechanisms could basically look and suggested next steps to reform the system. The relevance of the paper was clear to all stakeholders: An estimated $4.4 billion of financial support from development partners for GHG emission reductions needed to be absorbed properly. Funds would only be transferred if financing mechanisms were clearly regulated, efficient, and transparent.

---

4 Subsequently, the case study will refer to this multi-sectoral GIZ team just as "the GIZ team."

The process of developing the policy brief was as important as its main message: The GIZ team carefully orchestrated the process of developing the policy brief. It started with the strategic selection of the consultant team. One expert had a strong professional background in fiscal balance and local taxation and was proposed by GIZ's fiscal decentralization advisors, whereas the second consultant's background was in climate finance and proposed by GIZ's climate change advisors. The first expert had been renowned and respected by the DJPK and a member of TADF; the second expert was well known and respected in BAPPENAS and the Ministry of Environment. The trust that the leading parties had in the consultants aided communication with all sides enormously. Representatives of the concerned ministries paid attention to the consultants' analysis and conclusions. The PKPPIM steered the process of developing the policy brief. With support from GIZ, it organized several "focal-group discussions" with representatives from the MoF (Fiscal Policy Office and the DJPK), from BAPPENAS, and from the Ministry of Environment. Using this format to forge agreement did not always work out well. Not all invited parties participated in the discussions, or they sent low-level representatives. The latter could neither take decisions nor did they have the authority to share their opinions openly in front of a larger audience – a well-known phenomenon in Indonesia. However, it integrated important stakeholders at an early stage, and hence increased the prospects of agreeing on a coherent financing mechanism for climate change mitigation actions.

Shortly after discussing the final draft in a focal-group discussion in December 2011, the PKPPIM published it in January 2012 as a policy brief on its own initiative. It thereby positioned itself among national government institutions that have a say in climate finance. The policy brief helped the MoF to play a more proactive role in shaping policies for climate change mitigation. It formulated a vision for a coherent architecture for funding and transfer mechanisms. This supported the MoF's interest of avoiding a situation in which a confusing multitude of partially incoherent, or even counterproductive, funding and transfer mechanisms coexist.

The policy brief did not go into much detail, but the PKPPIM used it as a basis for further steps to develop more detailed procedures and regulations. To do so, it continued to cooperate with the GIZ team. Hence, throughout 2012 and 2013, the two-pronged advisory approach was repeated to develop a concrete proposal for a regulation on how to finance local action plans for GHG emission reductions (RAD-GRK) based on the national plan (RAN-GRK). This approach also helped to develop policy proposals on "Financing REDD+ through a Trust Fund Mechanism."

In short, combining multi-sectoral technical expertise with facilitation between different interests as honest brokers actually turned out to be helpful as long as the identified problem required technical expertise and agreements among decision-makers. However, during GIZ's cooperation with the PKPPIM and other stakeholders from involved ministries, the significance of another challenge to climate change mitigation in Indonesia rose steadily: Fuel price subsidies increased significantly due to rising international fuel prices. The impact of cheap fuel on climate change is obvious. But because providing technical expertise was not an appropriate response to the challenge, it became something like the elephant in the room.

The elephant in the room: Fuel price subsidies

Fuel price subsidies have been heatedly debated in Indonesia for some time. Because of rising fuel prices in the international market throughout 2011, 2012, and 2013, it has increasingly become a topic of very high political priority. In 2012 fuel subsidies accounted for more government spending than education and health combined, or 12 percent of total national expenditures. However, several studies revealed that these subsidies largely missed their goal of protecting the poor since they were provided according to the number of liters consumed rather than being based on consumer income. Only 3 percent of the subsidized fuel had been used for public transportation, compared to 53 percent for privately owned cars. Furthermore, low fuel prices were an incentive for many households to purchase private vehicles, resulting in even more traffic congestion and GHG emissions. The fiscal and environmental consequences of subsidized carbon-emitting energy consumption and transportation were enormous. A policy change on fuel price subsidies was the untapped potential to reach the set targets for reducing GHG emissions.

However, the issue was highly politicized, and it became difficult for external advisors to address without them being accused of interfering in matters that were considered internal political affairs. Especially in a self-confident middle-income country such as Indonesia, international development cooperation is constantly viewed with a good amount of suspicion.

One obvious answer would have been to provide technical expertise to precisely analyze the problem, its impacts, and (technical) options to solve it. That, however, had already been done by many other development partners, nationally and internationally. All facts and figures were known, and all available numbers had been crunched several times. At that point, providing further technical expertise would not have made any difference.

After some discussions, the GIZ teams and the PKPPIM developed an idea on how to approach this challenge differently in order to make a useful contribution while maintaining good relations with the political level. Although data was available and fiscal and environmental simulations were allowed for evidence-based scenarios, the level of public awareness on the environmental impact of subsidies was low. Understandably, the fear of many citizens of having to bear the direct and personal consequences was more important than the impacts themselves, which appeared to be of a more general and impersonal nature. Of course, there were debates about the issue of fuel subsidies, but there were rarely open exchanges on the subject; rather, polarizing presentations with opposing positions on the matter were the norm. Consequently, creating a level playing field for all participants was a precondition for a discussion forum to be credible, especially on such a politicized topic. The purpose of such a format was to openly discuss the advantages and inconveniences of fuel price subsidies, to raise awareness about the subsidies' many consequences, and to discuss options on how to address these consequences. However, this potentially conflicted with the fact that the MoF had clearly positioned itself in the public as an opponent of fuel price subsidies. As the initiator and host of a discussion forum, it would not have been credible to many. And even if a third party had hosted such a debate, the amount of people reached would be quite limited. Another challenge was that the potential scope of debates about fuel subsidies is nearly endless, be it on the various (financial, environmental, congestion) consequences, or on policies to reduce subsidies and appropriate compensation matters. If the topic is too large, a public debate would not come to conclusions; if it is too narrow, it would become a rather boring discussion among experts.

To address these challenges and obstacles, the GIZ team agreed with the PKPPIM to facilitate the organization of dialogue fora on the matter, allowing for the exchange of key facts and figures in a moderated discussion. To address the risk of polarization, the dialogue format was to allow a fair and free exchange of arguments from all standpoints. The right mix of Members of Parliament and representatives from public administration, the private sector, and civil society would allow for more nuanced discussions. An audience of about 100 to 200 participants could raise questions and challenge viewpoints of the panelists. As neither the MoF nor GIZ could be an impartial host, it was decided that universities should play that part, not only in terms of providing a location but also to act as organizers. Indeed, in Indonesia, a university campus is highly respected as a space for open academic exchange. To increase the potential outreach, the idea was to invite established media institutions and to use alternative channels such as video-sharing websites. Given the vast scope of potential specific topics related to fuel price subsidies, the GIZ team and the PKPPIM agreed to initiate not only one debate but a small series. The first debate was to look at the topic in a comprehensive way. A second forum could then target a more specific issue, ideally the one that turns out to be the most challenging in the first round. The third forum could then build on the conclusions of the former, leading to a progressive discussion.

Three of the most highly renowned universities showed their interest in running this experiment. The first dialogue forum took place at the University Gadjah Mada in Yogyakarta on June 22, 2013. The auditorium was full with around 150 participants and a highly diverse panel with opponents and supporters of fuel price subsidies from the political sphere (a Member of Parliament), public administration, civil society, and the private sector. The location turned out to be the ideal place for the panelists to speak more openly than they would have within the walls of one of the protagonists. The whole debate was put on YouTube, and some radio stations aired broadcasts with summaries and commentaries. Reactions were very positive, especially because the debate was results-oriented and fact-based and not simply the exchange of politically heated standpoints.

On September 17, 2013, the second forum took place at Sriwijaya University in Palembang, South Sumatra province. It was important not to organize all events on the island of Java, although clearly the most renowned universities are on this central – and by far most populated – island of Indonesia. The forum went equally well and allowed for a more focused debate on transportation issues, as this turned out to be the most crucial issue in the first forum in Yogyakarta.

The third and final forum took place at the University of Indonesia in Jakarta in November 2013. Based on positive feedback from the prior events, trust in the format increased and high-level participants were easier to mobilize. TV and radio stations aired broadcasts with summaries, commentaries, and interviews. The outcome of the debates was surely not a policy master plan on how to resolve the issue, but in many ways it was a useful contribution on the matter. It raised public awareness, and it allowed for key stakeholders to approach the challenges in a less polarizing way, allowing for a better understanding of the motives behind each standpoint.

The impact of these dialogue fora cannot easily be measured beyond anecdotal evidence. It would not be serious to pretend that it directly contributed to President Widodo's bold decision in December 2014, shortly after his election, to scrap diesel subsidies and considerably reduce gasoline subsidies. It may have laid the groundwork for better public acceptance of the decision, though. The widely discussed issues created public awareness that something might change.

It was of fundamental importance for the GIZ team to adapt its approach and to entirely slip into the role of a provider of platforms for evidence-based discussions between Indonesian stakeholders. This role required a different self-concept than the role of the technical advisor. Whereas the technical advisor works on content matters directly with one or several counterparts, the provider of discussion platforms focuses on the space provided to others. This role is actively taking place in the background, and the biggest challenge is to refrain from coming in with one's own positions. For this change of roles to be credible, it was also important to give the actual convener – the selected university faculties – enough space.

From three to seven: Increasing coordination challenges

It could be taken as a proxy indicator of a successful approach, or as a failure because it overburdened the system: The truth is probably a bit of both. The successfully close cooperation between GIZ advisors on fiscal decentralization (DeCGG program) and on climate change policy (the PAKLIM and partially FORCLIME programs) triggered the awareness that actually a much larger coordination effort would be necessary. Not only DeCGG, PAKLIM, and FORCLIME programs dealt with climate finance issues, but also four other GIZ-supported programs. All in all, there were seven programs from three focal areas (good governance; climate change and environmental protection; private-sector development) as well as a regional program supporting ASEAN:

- Policy Advice for Environment and Climate Change (PAKLIM)
- Decentralisation as a Contribution to Good Governance (DeCGG)
- Least-Cost Renewables (LCORE-INDO)
- Local and Regional Economic Development (RED)
- Forests and Climate Change Programme (FORCLIME)
- German – ASEAN Programme on Response to Climate Change (GAP-CC)
- Sustainable Urban Transport Improvement Project (SUTIP)

The challenge became apparent when the PKPPIM initiated the organization of a large conference on "Charting the Way to a Green Economy through Fiscal Policy Reforms: A Role for the Ministry of Finance," which was held in October 2012. The conference involved all of the abovementioned GIZ-supported programs. All of these programs worked with the MoF on aspects of climate finance, be it on matters of promoting a green economy, financial incentives for a green energy policy, or investments for an ecologically sustainable urban transportation policy. It would not be possible to coordinate GIZ's cooperation with the MoF in the same informal way advisors from PAKLIM, DeCGG, and FORCLIME had worked together hitherto.

Hence, a more formal agreement between GIZ and the MoF was necessary, involving all concerned programs. The initial idea to call it a "Memorandum of Understanding" was quickly dropped, as this term has clear legal implications, so it became a "Cooperation Agreement." Drafting it took quite some time – a finalized version was only signed in October 2013 by the GIZ country director and the head of the PKPPIM. It outlined key objectives of the cooperation between GIZ and the PKPPIM, responsibilities and contributions, as well as organizational matters on operational planning, monitoring, evaluation, and reporting. The involved GIZ advisors were convinced that, without any tangible coordination mechanism, the agreement would remain just a (toothless) piece of paper. They therefore agreed to create the post of a senior national advisor with the task of coordinating collaboration with the MoF among all these programs.

The intention was good and necessary, but in the course of implementation, limits became apparent with regard to what could be achieved. The coordinator started to work in November 2013, so all in all the whole process took more than a year – from the initial idea during the conference in October 2012 to the implementation of such a mechanism. Furthermore, the mandate of that coordinator was not defined clearly enough and not sufficiently clarified with all programs involved, so he ended up being caught performing several roles. The ambition to manage a meaningful coordination mechanism between so many different programs was probably too high, and the effort to do so turned out not to have a meaningful relation anymore with the outcome.

Conclusion: Smart, but not smart enough?

The best way to quickly evaluate an initiative you were responsible for is to ask yourself "*Would I have done it the same way if I had the chance?*" As the involved GIZ advisors from the initial core team, we, the authors of this case study, come to the conclusion that, in principle, yes, we did the right thing, but we apparently underestimated some of the challenges when setting our goals. We identified the added value that our joint support could provide, and we had the right ideas on how to design and implement support measures. We contributed measurably to a coherent positioning of the MoF with regard to climate finance. The financing mechanisms proposed by the MoF were developed jointly between the Fiscal Policy Office (especially the PKPPIM) and the DJPK, thereby considering the principles of the existing fiscal balance architecture. Furthermore, we contributed to fact-based and solutions-oriented exchanges between key stakeholders, be it as focal-group discussions on specific technical issues or as open fora on a more political level.

Arguably, in terms of measurable achievements, a different story could be told. Technical expertise provided by GIZ supporting the MoF and BAPPENAS to draft regulations has not yet produced the desired effects of them being passed. Although many discussions took place, complications remain for the MoF and BAPPENAS to agree on how funds for RAD-GRK implementation should be transferred and which institution would have which responsibilities in the process. The MoF still has legal concerns with regard to using the International Climate Change Trust Fund. And proposals to adapt transfer funds of the existing fiscal balance system (in particular the transfer fund for earmarked transfers (Dana Allokasi Khusus – DAK), and the one for shared revenues (Dana Bagi Hasil – DBH)) are being blocked because the underlying law – under revision since 2009 – has been submitted to Parliament but not yet passed.

Some of these aspects are beyond the reach and influence of development cooperation, such as the blockade of the law revision on fiscal balance. Others show that accompanying a government's reform agenda involving highly political issues takes time. As programs and their focus had shifted by the end of 2013, other teams – in a different setup and with slightly different mandates – continue to provide advisory support on climate change financing so that more measurable changes might be visible at a later stage.

But as a more generalized conclusion of the experiences we made, we may state the following:

- A cross-sectoral approach can help to change perspectives and find new approaches for solutions. This is especially the case when adding a governance perspective to another sector. To really release its potential, however, cross-sectoral approaches must be based on a true understanding of each side's underlying motives, goals, and priorities. Often, multi-disciplinary teams are a group of experts who do not speak each other's language. It is important to invest sufficient time and effort to establish a common language.
- A tailor-made approach to one challenge that proves successful may not be appropriate for another challenge, even if both challenges are closely linked to each other as part of one process. Smart implementation, to us, also means understanding that an advisor has several roles to offer: provider of technical expertise, honest broker between different actors (and interests), and provider of platforms for knowledge-exchange. What makes for smarter implementation is the capability to know which role is required at which point in the process and to quickly change roles when necessary and appropriate. It is crucial to constantly monitor and evaluate support measures and to anticipate challenges ahead in order to develop and adjust approaches accordingly.
- The advantage of seizing windows of opportunity at the working level is that you are quicker and more responsive compared to institutionalizing a process at a higher level first. Furthermore, first tangible results may convince decision-makers more easily to shift priorities. The risk is that the initiative develops such momentum that any effort to institutionalize the cooperation always lags behind. When this risk becomes apparent, it is important to reshape the intervention strategy and define milestones. A formalization of the advisory approach can take place, including agreement on specific objectives and indicators to make the approach more binding. These may help to synchronize the technical

support and institutional setup by putting the former on hold while investing time and effort in the latter.

References

Republic of Indonesia Ministry of Finance. (2012). *Indonesia's first mitigation fiscal framework*. Retrieved from https://www.unpei.org/sites/default/files/e_library_docu ments/Indonesia_MFF_report.pdf

United Nations. (2015, September 25). *Transforming our world: The 2030 Agenda for Sustainable Development*. United Nations General Assembly Resolution 70/1, preamble and reiterated in § 71. New York, NY: Author.

World Resources Institute / CAIT PINDAI. (2016). Indonesia Climate Data Explorer – PINDAI. Retrieved from http://cait.wri.org/indonesia

Synthesis

Smart Implementation in Transformation: Findings and Outlook

Pauline Heusterberg, Renate Kirsch, Elke Siehl, and Albrecht Stockmayer

The guiding framework for development cooperation in the coming years is the 2030 Agenda for Sustainable Development, which promotes a conceptual shift from "aid" to "global goods," and from development work to international cooperation. Achieving this vision as well as the set goals and targets requires new forms of cooperation and implementation of our programs with our partners. In this final chapter, we take stock of how the Deutsche Gesellschaft für Internationale Zusammenarbeit (GIZ) governance programs are implemented, discuss identified strengths and weaknesses, and review if we are prepared for the upcoming challenges. In the second part of this chapter, these findings are then related to the discussion on Doing Development Differently (DDD) and the Problem-Driven Iterative Adaptation (PDIA) initiative. We do so from the perspective of an implementing agency owned by the Federal Republic of Germany and established with the purpose to promote international sustainable development by implementing measures in the field of capacity development for German ministries and international donors.

IMPLEMENTATION IN GIZ GOVERNANCE PROGRAMS: EXPERIENCES AND FINDINGS FROM NINE CASE STUDIES

Based on nine case studies, we present key findings for smart implementation in GIZ programs. We further examine if elements for sound implementation identified by other practitioners and scholars are supported by these findings or not and if additional lessons can be drawn. Teams were asked to explain *how* they implemented programs rather than describe what they did. The focus is on explaining the unpredictable and unexpected parts that caused deviations from the original design and planning.

The case studies reveal a very rich and diverse picture of implementation experiences. At first glance, the chosen instruments and approaches vary considerably, and comparisons between cases are not readily apparent. The governance programs also have little thematic overlap and vary in topics, from extractive industries, decentralization, public-sector reform, and rule of law to gender. However, regarding the five questions posed in the introductory chapter to smart implementation, the cases can be compared and commonalities identified. The following analysis is structured along these five questions, which we asked program teams to address and which are listed here again.

- What kinds of challenges occurred during program implementation? What did working in uncertain, unpredictable, complex, and political environments mean in your case?
- How did program teams and partners orient themselves in complex and unpredictable environments?
  - Which principles, instruments, or approaches were referred to or adopted?
  - What kind of analysis was used? How was insufficient information handled?
  - How did teams and partners learn?
- Were there tensions between achieving predefined results and adapting to changing circumstances? How were they handled?
- Which frame conditions (at the level of the development organization and in country) were conducive or hindered implementation in complex environments?
- What aspects of implementation were transferrable between contexts and countries, and what was context-specific and needed to be newly created?

Tackling implementation challenges

The first question posed to program teams asked what working in uncertain, unpredictable, complex, and political environments meant to them and what implementation challenges they faced.

The array of implementation challenges portrayed in the case studies is broad. They range from unexpected political developments; resistance to changes from staff within organizations who are needed to implement reforms; mistrust among actors avoiding cooperation; visions for change that were still so vague that they lacked common understanding and agreement on central elements among actors to operationalize them; capacity and resource constraints; and the institutional environment not providing sufficient flexibility for programs to adapt to changing local circumstances. Working in uncertain, unpredictable, complex, and political environments was often referred to as "challenging." The following pages describe how teams addressed these challenges in more detail.

Most implementation challenges are political by nature

Political challenges were mentioned most often as the reason why programs deviated from their plans. All of the case studies mention how vested interests, power struggles, and exercised influence affected the implementation of the programs. They led to irritations, for which the programs had to find answers (Melia, 2016; see also Organisation for Economic Co-operation and Development, 2015). The following description illustrates what kinds of political issues arose and how they were addressed.

In **Liberia**, vested interests of decision-makers were affected when the introduction of a new mine licensing system was proposed. The new system (called the Mining Cadastre and Revenue Administration approach) addressed the highly unregulated mining economy by putting a set of rules in place that prevent the individual allocation of mining licenses and enables the government to monitor fiscal and social license compliance. The program team invested in the regional exchange of experiences demonstrating the benefits of the new regulation and how individual concerns can be answered.

Overcoming vested interests of influential and powerful middle-class voters regarding potential cuts to fuel subsidies was one of the challenges the team in **Indonesia** faced. Government partners from the Ministry of Finance and GIZ team decided to tackle the issue by convening broad public consultations. This issue was only partly related to the program's objective to develop new approaches for financing climate change mitigation. Cutting fuel price subsidies would have a notable positive impact on greenhouse gas emission reductions, but it was only one aspect in the wider set of options. The public concern over potentially raising fuel prices dominated the discussion so strongly that it needed to be addressed first in order to advance the broader agenda on climate change mitigation. In this instance, the Ministry of Finance deliberately decided not to be the convening party in the consultations but left it to universities to convene the deliberations while the ministry itself just participated as one of several institutions defending its point of view. This effort contributed toward creating sufficient political space for a new incoming government to reduce the fuel subsidies.

In the case of the **Philippines**, resistance to change came from one of the conflict parties: Armed groups prevented the local population from taking part in information events organized by the program and its partners to start a communication with city officials on socio-economic development in an area they controlled. The program team rescheduled the event to avoid further confrontation and made sure that interested communities had multiple ways to express their points of view.

In contrast to the above, in some cases political dynamics could be used to excel the implementation process and leapfrog ahead. In the case of **Tunisia**, GIZ had tried to convince authorities of the benefits of municipal networking and regional integration prior to the revolution, without much success. The Arab Spring led to a change in the government's priorities on these ideas, and the government asked for assistance in reviewing options for decentralization in Tunisia.

Yet another perspective is provided in the case of **South Caucasus.** The program team decided to deliberately take a neutral standpoint on local politics and focused on legal issues when the dynamics were such that legal boundaries were pushed. This helped to maintain a good relationship with the partner and to increase the influence of the program as a trustworthy facilitator over time. Still, the team needed insights into the political dynamics to be able to assess the situation correctly and to decide upon this move. Staying out of local politics does not mean that the program can take up an apolitical position.

Solutions need to be crafted to fit the local context

Most of the case studies present problems to which solutions were not readily available but had to be found. These local problems often led to junctures, thereby changing the course of the envisaged implementation path. In responding to these problems, teams often started the search for options or solutions. This was done either by experimenting or by retreating to experiences and available knowledge in the form of best practice examples, international standards, or previous program applications. However, previous knowledge only provided a first entry point. Each of these ideas had to be crafted to fit the local context and needed modulation to achieve the required accuracy necessary to fit the local situation (Andrews, 2015; Levy, 2014). The case studies stress that trust among partners and advisors is essential to work in this manner. Trust was even considered a precondition for identifying partner needs and problems – let alone solutions. It was argued that, without trust, partners hardly allow an inside perspective to the real issues that the support structure is suppose to help address.

The case studies explain how they came to context-specific solutions, which were then tested incrementally.

The **Indonesia** case study outlines in detail how the program used international and regional experiences of climate financing and combined them with local knowledge on instruments for fiscal decentralization to come up with a proposal that would fit the purposes and interests of the government. They used this information also to address political sensitivities.

The team in **Costa Rica** recalls internal discussions on how to best strike the balance between maintaining international evaluation standards when developing capacities in ministries while also addressing the interests, culture, and needs of the collaborating ministries involved in order to build their commitment for more transparent, accountable, and evidence-based information at the institutional level. The team realized that this balance had to be constantly reassessed and re-established. Frequent reflection sessions allowed for reviewing when it was adequate to accept context-appropriate evaluation designs and when there was an opportunity to demand higher standards and more progress in institutionalizing them.

The **Peru** program aims at reducing and preventing violence against women. It advocates and promotes a policy agenda that leads to a different program design. For example, they were able to independently select their partners and choose their focus area. This case is thus an example that portrays what it means to uphold a policy objective while still having to find local solutions to see changes in attitudes and behaviors in a specific context. The program identified the private sector as a societal entity that could assist in changing attitudes and prevent violence against women. The program started out wooing the private sector to become a partner in advocating for the cause and taking action to prevent abuse and violence in the workplace and at home. Knowledge of the local context and contacts of the national program staff helped identify options for cooperation. Yet, it took several "experiments" to find the right hook that caught the attention of businesses to get them involved: It was a research program that calculated the monetary effects of partner violence for businesses, which caught the most attention. Thereafter, local businesses started to engage in awareness-raising and training.

The most illustrating description on how local solutions are being crafted is given by the quote of a counterpart in the **South Africa** case study, who stated:

"GIZ's approach was not as such selling one model or one approach. It was much more trying to work through the "mess" in the most supportive and thoughtful ways, which were context-sensitive and trying to traverse the space between the politics that were there and the international relationships and the expert issues. Requests were accommodated

in the concepts always, and initial nets spun wider to bring something in which did not fit in initially." The team says that identifying the right time to use opportunities and to set the right incentives is not rocket	science when the partner's context is properly understood and the coopera- tion is grounded on a trustful relation- ship (see the South Africa case study from Godje Bialluch et al. in this pub- lication).

Instruments and principles that facilitate implementation

The second question asked which principles, instruments, approaches, and analysis provided orientation to teams when faced with insufficient infor- mation in complex and unpredictable environments.

Multi-stakeholder approaches are a craftsman's hammer for smart implementation

The instrument most often mentioned in the case studies for facilitating implementation was stakeholder consultations and adopting a multi- stakeholder approach, with particular attention to bringing stakeholders together that had not interacted with each other before. It was the instru- ment of choice for addressing conflicts, overcoming bottlenecks, and find- ing locally relevant and legitimate solutions that make sustainable change more likely. The case studies mention that the instrument helped to tackle several implementation challenges:

- first and foremost, a multi-stakeholder approach allows for the partici- pation of stakeholders, making it a core cooperation principle that can build trust and ownership as well as support learning. Stakeholders provided valuable information, whereby actors saw the process at present and how things would develop;
- the focus on working jointly with as many parties as possible supports the coordination of interest groups, even donor agencies, around a local problem;
- activities that are performed simultaneously by different actors could be connected, and then new lines of communication, options for coop- eration, and alliances for change could be created;

- stagnancy could be tackled by portraying opposing views, conflicts of interest, and vested interests, and subsequently by identifying space for agreement and compromise among actors;
- consultations provided space for reflection and learning and influenced opinions that addressed social patterns and behavior;
- it was also mentioned that decisions remained with local actors and that ideas for solutions that evolved from consultations took local aspirations, traditions, dynamics, and know-how into account;
- multi-stakeholder approaches support inclusion and participation, which in turn builds confidence and trust among actors and strengthens cooperation. This is often the basis for developing or trying out new options and solutions within a complex change process. The initiated cooperation can facilitate joint action that drives the process forward.

The following three case study examples show how stakeholder consultations shaped the implementation process.

The inclusion of multiple national stakeholders through a round of consultations was crucial in **Liberia** to obtain support for the establishment of a data exchange system. The consultations helped in clarifying and setting priorities for the system. The data exchange system itself improved data availability – a quick-win approach the team chose in order to foster confidence among actors and broader support for the reform on mine licensing.

The GIZ team in the **Philippines** opted to handle the volatile conflict situation through an inclusive and participatory approach ("leaving no one behind"). Engaging all relevant and affected stakeholders through dialogues, workshops, and overall transparency enabled the team and its partners to deal with powerful economic background interests. At one point, the program was pushed by influential stakeholders exercising their power to a critical juncture they did not foresee: The peace-building efforts between Butuan City and the precluded communities in the forest areas had shown first encouraging results. This occurred when investors and brokers exercised pressure on the mayor to enter into a concessional agreement for the area, which would allow for economic investments in the forest areas. Responding to these demands would have violated the principle of inclusion and common agreements and put the peace-building efforts at risk. Yet, these powerful actors could not be ignored either. Referring to the commonly agreed principle of consultation and joint decision-making, the mayor asked the investors to become responsible for developing criteria for concessions and economic operations in the restricted area. The negotiation process was tedious, and it took several years before an agreement among all parties involved could be made. This bought time to strengthen the

peace-building process between the City and the forest communities. On the other hand, the GIZ team in **Azerbaijan** encountered challenges due to the fact that they were confined to working with only one partner institution, which set the pace on	implementing activities and did not support broader consultations. Later on in the process, it was not possible to gain support from a broader group of stakeholders to broaden perspectives and options.

Working incrementally allows for gradual adaptations during implementation

All programs implemented their activities incrementally instead of rolling out predefined activities on a large scale; it seems to be the principle of choice in uncertain and hard-to-predict environments with insufficient information. Experimenting with new rules, approaches, or activities in an incremental manner allows teams to closely evaluate their fit to the specific context at every step. Short feedback loops help to detect failures and inadequate fits early on and provide for readjustments and changes that are gradual and not abrupt. The iterations between planning and implementation as well as between activity and adjustment are short, which provides flexibility to stay tuned to a changing environment. The quick adjustments improve the accuracy of an intervention's fit to the specificities of the local context. The approach is even more useful when several experiments run in parallel and effects can be observed in comparison. Incremental implementation also helps teams to achieve quick wins, which boosts stakeholders' confidence that results and successes can be reached and presented. Confidence and trust in the process and the cooperation form the basis on which more difficult aims can be tackled. Furthermore, working incrementally also helps to manage and reduce risks (DDD Manifesto Community, 2014; Wild, Andrews, Pett, & Dempster, 2016). Cooperation is an effective tool to work in this manner. However, bringing incremental results to scale is a challenge for GIZ programs.

The case studies present various examples how ideas, approaches, or solutions were implemented incrementally.

The program in **Costa Rica** assisted the government in utilizing evaluations better to enhance evidence-based policy-making. The first evaluations were selected via a competition. However, time pressure and competition among different ministries proved to be counterproductive for creating a collaborative environment among stakeholders. Trust, rather than competition, was the incentive for more cooperation among ministries. Collaboration among these actors was required to achieve the overall objective to conduct evaluations in public agencies consistently. Once the team realized that the chosen instrument did not serve the purpose well, they changed to a joint selection procedure for evaluations.

The program in the **Philippines** carefully planned how to re-engage with communities in the land management zone. They had to act cautiously, focusing on being trustworthy to people who perceived city representatives as enemies. Working incrementally in this case meant relying on a non-governmental organization (NGO) that entered the region offering assistance with socio-economic needs but eventually facilitated the contact between the two conflicting parties.

The team in **Peru** conducted several experiments on a small scale to identify the best avenues for engaging the private sector in a joint agenda to combat violence against women. These included a series of business breakfasts, training programs in selected companies, and introducing a government seal to praise active companies. The activity that spurred the most reactions and engagement was a research program with the university that showed the costs of domestic violence for businesses.

A multi-level program design assists in addressing implementation hurdles and risks

A multi-level program design provides flexibility when operating in complex systems. Systems theory acknowledges non-linearity in social change processes, with ruptures, blockages, reversals, and accelerations happening simultaneously in different parts of the system. A multi-level program design is a way to deal with these overlaps during implementation. It enables teams to support issues where the energy or opportunity for progress exists, while only preparing or nudging subjects along that need to be addressed but where there is little dynamic for change. Different routes and speeds of progress can be accompanied with different measures and levels of intensity. A multi-level program design provides sufficient flexibility to shift attention among topics if a target has been met or new opportunities arise. The interdependence of different levels is used to drive the reform process forward as a whole. How GIZ designs programs at different level has been briefly explained in the introductory chapter. The case studies illustrate how multi-level program designs were used to maneuver implementation in complex environments.

In **Liberia** the GIZ governance program supported the introduction of a new licensing system in the mining sector. Strong vested interests caused resistance and delays at the policy and institutional levels. Developing the capacity of technicians in the new administration system was a low-risk entry point to which general support from all stakeholders was ensured. This set of activities enabled the team to show movement in one area of the reform process. Simultaneously, the setup of an inter-agency task force for better data-sharing on mining revenues was facilitated, which improved transparency and cooperation among ministries. Members of this task force identified issues that needed response from the policy level. This signaled a need for change at the level where resistance was strong. Here, the multi-level program design made it possible to use the interdependence between the institutional and policy levels in the mining sector to induce catalysts for change at the levels where progress was slow. The program supported the signaling by providing additional impetuses (e.g., via the exchange of experiences with the mining program in Sierra Leone, where a similar reform was successful, and expert study tours to forge alliances for change among leaders) to create momentum for opening a debate on new rules for awarding mining licenses in Liberia.

The challenge to enhance understanding and communication between the media, citizens, and the government in the case study from **South Africa** was an issue that arose mainly at the municipality level. However, the program facilitated awareness-raising and discussions between the government communicators and community media for factual and just media reporting simultaneously at the provincial and national levels. It worked with these government institutions and non-state agencies because all of these actors influenced how the media would be perceived in the Eastern Cape province. This approach was easy to convene due to a multi-level program design that provided the opportunity to engage national-, provincial-, and local-level stakeholders in a process with only moderate political attention at the upper levels.

Short, quick, ad-hoc information collection and analysis is needed to still the constant demand for information

Context and political economy analysis are crucial for program teams to determine their position within the system and for identifying which contributions fit best when, where, and how. The need to conduct sound context analysis at the outset to inform program appraisal and design has been stressed in development cooperation for several years now; many development organizations, including GIZ, have raised the bar on formalizing and consistently integrating this type of analysis into their program cycles (Fritz, Levy, & Ort, 2014; Booth, Harris, & Wild, 2016; GIZ [Deutsche Gesellschaft für Internationale Zusammenarbeit], 2015). Yet, problem-driven political economy analysis (called "context analysis" in GIZ terminology), which is a standard tool in the Capacity WORKS repertoire, has only been mentioned in four of the nine case studies as an instrument that provides orientation for implementation. Some programs mentioned using available analysis published by universities, research institutes, and other development agencies to detect options and inform decision-making. Some programs also mentioned their performance-monitoring system as an important source of information to steer the program. Upon inquiry, it became apparent that the analysis of day-to-day implementation issues is considered inevitable in order to maneuver a program, and thus it is an integral part of project management. However, formal, systematic analysis with long preparation time does not seem to be the right fit for program implementers. Instead, quick, short, light-handed, problem-specific, and ad-hoc analysis on technical and political economy issues that have a very specific purpose and an immediate application provides the information that can be absorbed and utilized. This seems to be even more the case if a program has been running for several phases and the team's knowledge on technical, sector, and political issues has been built over time. In this case, new research is incorporated in due course during regular adaptations. Wild, Booth, and Valters describe a similar use of analytical work during program implementation at the United Kingdom's Department for International Development (DFID). More attention is given to what they call, with reference to Hudson et al., "everyday political analysis," which involves the ongoing questioning of incentives, space, and capacity for change (Hudson, Marquette, & Waldock, 2016; Wild, Booth, & Valters, 2017, p. 20).

The case studies also reveal that analysis is used as an instrument for providing advisory services. Teams invest in generating new analysis to underpin the relevance of an argument with local evidence, to inject new information into a debate, or to start a discussion with a new constellation of actors. Here, analysis is used to direct the cause of implementation.

The team in the **Philippines** continuously analyzed the interests, concerns, and stakeholder dynamics with rapid appraisal methods. This information was used to assess security risks, monitor conflict dynamics, and identify the scope for cooperation and peace-building. Sharing all available data and analysis without exception among all stakeholders was used as an instrument to enhance transparency and generated trust and peace-building during implementation.

In **Tunisia**, the team conducted short capacity analyses to develop a strategy for how to transform a ministry with an unclear mandate and centralistic habits into an active proponent of local and regional autonomy. The analyses hinted at structural problems that required the training of individuals combined with organizational change in the public administration.

The team in **Indonesia** used the rich amount of available information on benefits and costs of fuel price subsidies to start a public debate raising awareness that these subsidies impede reaching targets to reduce greenhouse gas emissions.

The aim of learning is to create a ground for joint action

Capacity WORKS identifies learning and innovation as one of the five success factors for managing programs in complex environments successfully. Learning is thus an integral element of GIZ program design. It is generally approached by offering learning opportunities at the individual, organizational, and societal levels. The formal learning instruments most often mentioned in the case studies were workshops, formal or informal monitoring and evaluation exercises, field visits, study tours, and action learning events. However, more informal reflection and feedback sessions and learning events – internally and with partners – were also mentioned several times. Implementers refer to the basic logic of program cycle management, in which a cycle of short planning, action, and review phases is established. This "learning by doing" approach provides scope to alter activities and the course of implementation based on what is learned. The main purpose of learning was described as creating a ground for innovation and joint action (Valters, Cummings, & Nixon, 2016; Valters, 2016; Green, 2016a; Wild, Booth, & Valters, 2017, p. 20).

The iteration between identifying an option and planning, trying, and reviewing it, which leads to a change of course and the identification of alternative ideas, is most prominently described in the **Peru** case study. Here, the team tried several avenues to get the attention of businesses to act on violence against women.

The **Costa Rica** team sees their contribution for creating collective spaces for learning as one of their greatest successes:

"[T]he project was able to attract and include an increasingly large number of diverse voices over time and build a platform for collective learning and impact. This did not happen by chance.... The project identified and approached cooperation partners deliberately and opened options for their participation and involvement. ... Spaces and processes for reflection, learning, and cooperation were created." (See the Costa Rica case study from Sabrina Storm in this publication)

The program in **Tunisia** adopted an action-learning approach for the International Academy for Good Governance, because this approach makes real change more likely compared to theoretical learning, in which problems with the transfer of knowledge to local contexts may occur.

A mutual focus on results and process provides sound orientation for implementers

The third question asked how program teams integrate the two differing logics of result and process in program implementation.

The results logic defines measurable objectives and outcomes to be achieved by implementing the program. Results are defined during the program design phase and evaluated when the program has come to a close. A program's success or failure is assessed by comparing the planned results against what has been achieved. The process logic emphasizes how these results have come about: "Results are not simply delivered to the partner but co-produced in a flexible process of search, negotiation, and implementation" (Deutsche Gesellschaft für Technische Zusammenarbeit, 2008, pp. 3, 9; author's translation). A process orientation emphasizes staying tuned with the course of a transformation and adopting strategies and activities when the process requires it. Success is measured here in the degree of ownership, the acceptance, and the legitimacy of the proposed changes and solutions offered for problems.

As can be seen in the case studies, "planning for results" and "implementation as a process" are not mutually exclusive concepts in these programs. They are different perspectives on the same program,[1] co-existing in GIZ programs. One of the essential ingredients in the craft of implementation is how to achieve results, not as stand-alone elements but as integral parts of an ongoing process.

Both perspectives serve as milestones along the way and mark the corridor in which implementation takes place in a non-linear change process. As the case studies deal with specific challenges, with critical junctures and tipping points, discussions revolve around staying tuned to the local processes and finding ways to bring the program back on track or find alternative avenues. In this regard, results and process orientation are complementary concepts. However, the established form to present success and progress to commissioners is in the logic of results. Narratives that show legitimacy and acceptance are less well-known but helpful for assessing progress in multi-stakeholder constellations. Flexibility to adjust the elements of the results matrix or log frame in due course, if the process requires it, is pivotal for integrating the two logics in program management. Otherwise, there is a risk that external rather than local demands will determine the implementation path, which can lead to unsustainable results and isomorphic mimicry (see Andrews, Pritchett, & Woolcock, 2012, pp. 1, 3, 5; Andrews, 2009; Pritchett & Woolcock, 2002). Considering that a conflict of interest between these two dimensions surfaced only in the one case study points to sufficient flexibility in the institutional arrangement between commissioner and implementer in German development cooperation to operate with both perspectives.

> The program in **Azerbaijan** offered capacity development for government staff to prepare for an EU rapprochement process. At the beginning of the program's implementation, the government of Azerbaijan suspended this intention and thus altered an important precondition for achieving the program objective. The program adjusted the initial plan by altering the time frame, quality, and format of the program, but it kept the originally agreed upon objectives. However, this was not the team's preferred option, and concerns regarding the sustainability of results were raised.
>
> In the case of **Indonesia**, two programs received a request from the

---

1 The *World Development Report 2017: Governance and the Law* refers to this duality by introducing two domains that have to be considered: the rules game and the outcome game. The World Bank proposes to start paying more attention to the rules game again, which, in our case, is referred to as process orientation that works with and shapes the rules of the game (World Bank, 2017, p. 18).

Ministry of Finance for support in a line of work that was not captured in their design during the planning stage. The program had sufficient flexibility to accommodate the partner's demand mid-course, informed the commissioner accordingly, and incorporated the new line of engagement in the designs during the following phase.

The team from the **Philippines** explains how the results logic facilitated communication and agreement among parties. The team decided to develop indicators jointly with the stakeholders. Deciding on a measurement for success together was an important trust-building element among conflicting parties. Here, the results framework was used to enhance accountability and transparency in decision-making and to forge common agreement among conflicting parties. Interestingly, it is also this team that states explicitly: "The fact that today both the City and the local population of the project area are benefiting from inclusive socio-economic development is first and foremost a result of the process that was applied" (see the Philippines case study from Yvonne Müller and Stephanie Schell-Faucon in this publication).

The governance program in **Tunisia** was a response to a political demand in the aftermath of the Arab Spring. The political environment had changed considerably since the program started and is still in flux. Thus, the program gave preference to a process orientation focusing on staying tuned to the partner's demands and adapted the program outputs several time during implementation.

Supportive and impeding conditions for implementation

Supportive and impeding frame conditions for implementation in complex environments was the topic of the fourth question posed to case study writers.

The case study authors mention several aspects that influence the success of program implementation: Long-term engagement in a transformation process, strong ownership for reform and change in partner institutions, and flexibility to respond to local demands were mentioned as conducive frame conditions. Political changes that led to ruptures, imposed interests, policies that have no grounding in local issues, and lack of ownership on the partner's side were mentioned as impeding factors to successful implementation.

Long-term engagement shapes implementation

Supporting transformation in partner countries requires engagement in a sector for a longer period of time – even spanning more than two or three decades.[2] GIZ often has the opportunity to provide long-term support to partner countries by offering a sequence of consecutive programs. The content, partners, institutions, and program designs change over time as the transformation progresses, but there is continuous engagement and support offered for the theme of the transformation and its stakeholders. A great advantage of this approach is the knowledge and understanding of the context, as well as the relationships and levels of trust that are built over time, all of which provide an indispensable source of information for implementers. Thus, short- or long-term engagement shapes the opportunities for implementation and the quality of results a program can achieve.

Four of the nine cases (South Africa, Philippines, South Caucasus, and Indonesia) describe their contribution as a step or phase of a longer engagement and explain their challenges in relation to the transition the program tries to support. In three cases, the long-lasting support was not confined to a country but benefited the development of a region.

The program in **South Africa** has been supporting the government in transforming the public administration into a transparent and development-oriented service provider since 1994. The authors state that the way they implemented the program would not have been doable without the mutual understanding and trust among parties, which had been established in the sector via a succession of different governance programs over a 20-year period. The way the program phase was designed and implemented was partially determined by the history and long-term perspective of the program as a whole.

In the case of **Indonesia**, the government's request for assistance in developing financing mechanisms for climate mitigation would have hardly occurred without the close and long working relationship between the Ministry of Finance and the two GIZ programs.

The case studies from **Liberia, South Caucasus, and Peru** outline how a regional program design assisted in fostering change in countries where the issue still had low priority. An exchange of experiences as well as competition among neighboring

---

2 As an example, see the evaluation on "German Development Support to Rwanda's Health Sector" over a span of 30 years before it was finalized in 2014 (Schwedersky, Noltze, & Gaisbauer, 2014).

countries was deliberately used to inject incentives for change or to overcome national blockages. The **Liberia** team used the positive experience in Sierra Leone to demonstrate that a single and independent approval system for mine licensing was key for keeping the vested interests of actors at bay. The **South Caucasus** team used the successful implementation of the new adminis-

trative law in Georgia to challenge Azerbaijan and Armenia not to stay behind.
On the contrary, the short implementation period of 28 months in **Azerbaijan** was perceived as a hindrance to achieving sustainable results. Only through the integration of this component into a broader governance program was it possible to make results last.

Ownership defines, and at times constrains, what is implemented and how implementation occurs

As explained in the introductory chapter, GIZ adopts the principle of joint responsibility for implementation between the partner institution and the advisory team. In this logic, ownership is a prerequisite for achieving sustainable results. Yet, ownership is not static but alters with changing actor constellations and their priorities in a transformation over time (e.g., after a change of government and different parties heading partner institutions). Such situations lead to pain or inflection points during implementation, requiring the program to change course and adapt. Frequent changes in political or leadership constellations and fluctuating ownership can cause severe disruptions or delays for program implementation. In this setup, ownership influences the pace, scope, and direction of the implementation process and determines what is done when and how. A lack of ownership restricts the options for implementation and can cause unsustainable results if ignored. Smart implementation is based on partner ownership; it probes and ensures ownership of each aspect of the program throughout implementation and adjusts respective parameters if a lack of ownership becomes apparent.

In the beginning, the **South Caucasus** team invited a selected group of leaders and legal experts for study trips to Europe as an instrument to assist in creating ownership across states and systems for a common reform process. This ownership was

later tested when the legal text of the administrative law was submitted to parliament for debate, which meant political exposure and defending the draft against opposing interests.
The program in **Costa Rica** noticed that partner ownership began to

decline after a new procedure was introduced, and the reasons were subsequently investigated. The program initiated a contest in which ministries could win resources to conduct results-oriented evaluations. This process generated competition and resentment between ministries and led to a disengagement of actors. Once the mismatch became apparent during a workshop, the program proposed a different selection procedure with a focus on enhancing cooperation.

The advocacy program in **Peru** faced very different conditions. Here, obtaining ownership from the private sector to address violence against women was an objective and not a precondition. It took a considerable amount of time and effort before Peruvian companies introduced measures to protect women against violence.

Program implementation is a local affair, which requires discretion for local decision-making

Development programs are support structures for complex change processes in partner countries. In this understanding, implementation is predominantly a local affair that requires frequent and quick decisions at the local level. From a managerial point of view, this implies that program staff require discretion to take decisions jointly with their partners. These decisions need to strike a balance between local interests, national policies, the program's mandate, and the commissioner's guidelines. The institutional arrangement in German development cooperation supports adaptive management in program implementation and requires program personnel to use their discretion in managing the program in keeping with local needs and conditions. The intention here is to enable the implementing agency to react to constraints and opportunities as they arise, in a timely manner. There are, of course, instances where objectives, outcomes, and indicators need to be renegotiated and accordingly adjusted during a program phase. The commissioning framework between the German Federal Ministry for Economic Cooperation and Development (BMZ) and GIZ allows for such cases, in which GIZ submits an adjusted program document to the commissioner for approval.

This managerial space is perceived as an essential instrument to be able to work in a problem-focused, locally-led, and incremental way. How this discretion is applied in practice is illustrated in the following case study examples.

The situation in the aftermath of the Arab Spring meant that political decision-makers needed time to decide how they wanted to use and govern decentralization in their country. The program in **Tunisia** started several initiatives in parallel, experimenting in order to discover the best fit for the Tunisian partners in this situation. For example, the team responded to specific training needs and expanded the scope of its support. Flexible funding and decentralized decision-making structures made these adaptations possible. The team further stressed that building trust among actors and confidence in their own capacities to master the challenges were preconditions before partners really committed to an action plan and felt that they possessed ownership for a common program.

In **Peru**, the implementation process was shaped by various experiments. The decisions – to hold business breakfasts to create a space where actors from the private sector could exchange their experiences regarding the impacts of violence against women, to collaborate with research in order to build a solid argument to act on violence against women, and the collaboration with the GIZ water program to reach utilities for PR campaigns – were all taken by the program team and enabled them to conduct experiments on a small scale and to quickly respond to emerging opportunities.

Implementation is a craft with some transferrable skills

The final question asked what aspects of implementation were transferrable between contexts and countries, and what was context-specific and needed to be newly designed.

Practitioners mention transferring their knowledge and experiences from previous posts to different contexts. Such knowledge can include acquired theories, techniques, conceptual bits and pieces, rules of thumb, or elements of best practices that can be tried out in different contexts and which serve as entry points for implementation. These elements are comparable to crafting tools that one learns to use skillfully over time. However, it still requires talent and experience to customize each element so that it fits the context and the parts can be assembled into a functional product. In this picture, implementation is a craft rather than a science. In more complicated or even complex settings, the experiences of one person are not sufficient, but the experiences of several people with different areas of expertise are required to reach the objective. A program advisor team resembles this picture: The expertise of people with different professional backgrounds is combined in interdisciplinary teams working hand in hand to provide assistance to a complex change process. This team works in close collaboration with a broad range of organizations (NGOs, think tanks, universities, agencies, the private sector), and thus expands the network for support.

Facilitating implementation in transformative settings requires inside and outside; practical; technical and theoretical; as well as national and international expertise and skills. The composition of a GIZ advisory team in country ideally tries to capture these dimensions: GIZ advisors work permanently in the field, often for several years in one country and in one sector. There is one set of advisors who provide services to partner organizations, operating at arm's length with the partner institution (Booth, 2013). They support domestic actors in their capacity to lead and drive the change process forward. A second set of advisors are fully embedded in partner organizations and work as either development workers or integrated experts and report to the partner organization. The vast majority of staff (presently two-thirds) are national advisors, and thus non-expatriate staff. They provide indispensable insights into the dynamics and politics of the transformation and ensure close proximity to the demands and interests of stakeholders. Different advisory teams who work in different sectors in a country form a network or platform that combines different capabilities, yet all of them actively implement a (joint) reform program. In these networks, professional and political knowledge and savvy are combined to assist in driving national reforms.

The composition and roles of advisory teams change throughout implementation

Advisors take up different roles throughout the process that are, to a certain extent, transferrable between contexts. The advisor's role and that of the team change throughout the implementation process. Likewise, several roles can be needed at the same time. The roles include that of a broker, facilitator, and convener; an organizational development advisor; an analyst and experimenter; or that of a technical or political expert with international know-how and expertise. Facilitating, accompanying, and assisting roles are valued most by partners, for example as conveners of hitherto opposing groups or institutions, and as brokers of ideas or standpoints to generate new options (Ernsthofer & Stockmayer, 2009; Frenken & Müller, 2010; Richter, 2017). The partner's request for support alters according to the shifts and turns of the change process, and the team's composition adapts to it accordingly from program phase to phase.

These two functions of advisory teams – the advisory networks and the multiple roles they offer – are resources to support driving the change process. Offering and utilizing these skills purposefully and strategically during program implementation is the art in the craft of smart implementation.

The role of broker and convener is emphasized in the **South Africa** case study in particular, where the program supported interdepartmental coordination. It did so by moderating and facilitating a series of meetings and workshops, which led to joint decision-making and monitoring of activities across departments.

Actors in **Liberia** perceived GIZ staff as independent facilitators, honest brokers, and well-trusted partners. The fact that Germany does not have a large mining industry, and thus very few national interests in the sector, was noticed by partners and helped the team to fulfill these roles.

In **Tunisia** the team had an important role in facilitating a common understanding among government entities on the purpose and type of decentralization the country wants to pursue.

An example for utilizing an advisory network or platform is best illustrated in the case of the **Philippines**, where a local NGO partnered with the advisory team. The NGO started to work with communities in the conflict area, which was inaccessible to all other stakeholders. The NGO managed to become a trusted party for these communities and was eventually able to establish communication between them and the city authorities. In this case, expanding the advisory network led to new options for peace-building. Working with inside and outside expertise is illustrated in the **South Caucasus** case. The technical expertise of a deployed German professor helped push the agenda forward in one instance.

Linking smart implementation to doing development differently

In this final section, we relate the findings of the case study analysis back to the discussion on DDD and explore whether the praxis of an implementing agency operating between donors, national policies, and partners can follow these principles, and to which extent. We do so by reviewing our institutional and conceptual frameworks and by presenting the implementation experiences of our governance programs – and not by presenting examples in which programs deliberately tried to do something differently or tried to put the DDD principles into operation. In this regard, we present the experiences and learnings from our present position, relate them to what DDD envisaged, and thus give a siting of an international development organization.

The DDD initiative aims at enhancing the impact of development assistance. A manifesto issued in 2014 outlines that many development initiatives fail because they do not address the complexities of the development process adequately. The initiators identified six principles for DDD in development cooperation (DDD Manifesto Community, 2014; Wild & Booth 2016; Wild, Andrews, Pett, & Dempster, 2016).

Box 1: The Doing Development Differently Manifesto

Six Principles for more effective development cooperation in complex setting:

- Focus on solving local problems that are debated, defined and refined by local people in an ongoing process
- Legitimise reform at all levels (political, managerial, social), building ownership and momentum throughout the process
- Work through local convenors who mobilise all those with a stake in progress
- Blend design and implementation through rapid cycles of planning, action, reflection and revision
- Manage risks by making "small bets," pursuing activities with promise and dropping others
- Foster real results – real solutions to real problems that have real impact

Source: DDD Manifesto Community (2014)

Subsequently, we discuss factors that support or hinder GIZ in following the envisaged principles and how doing so might affect our work in the future.

To briefly recap, we explained in the introductory chapter how GIZ perceives complex social change and what our role as advisors can be within it. Adapting a systems approach and the concept of transformation to program management are responses to the outlined challenges and influence how we plan, implement, and evaluate programs. A systemic view on social change is more and more shared by other development organizations (Green, 2016a, 2016b). Guidance on how to translate this thinking into program management is, in GIZ, provided by the management model Capacity WORKS.

The case studies reveal how the conceptual understanding of complexity and transformation not only informs but shapes the implementation of GIZ governance programs.[3] The following list summarizes a few prominent points, which also constitute core elements of what GIZ terms "smart implementation."[4]

- Implementation is perceived as a predominantly local and time-intensive affair that requires active engagement and patience. Thus, advisory teams work on site and have a high level of discretion to take decisions locally and jointly with their partners. This is in response to the understanding that certain aspects in implementation are not predictable; they cannot be foreseen or planned. Teams focus on solving problems that local partners identify. They operate in messy situations that require flexibility and autonomy to develop a process that can generate solutions and achieve sustainable results.
- The principle of joint responsibility for implementation between GIZ teams and partner organizations supports a focus on solving local problems. Joint responsibility also requires ownership by partner organizations. Ownership shapes how implementation occurs. A lack of – or fluctuating – ownership by partners impedes the scope and pace that implementation can take. Most program teams invested a lot of effort in forging ownership with partner institutions and adapted approaches if it was weakening.
- Long-term engagement is pivotal for achieving sustainable results in a transformation that aims at changing behaviors and attitudes. Behavioral change is difficult to accomplish and easy to reverse until it is rooted in social norms, which takes time. Lasting support that helps to ingrain these behavioral changes increases the chances for sustainable change (Wild, Booth, & Valters, 2017). The case studies covered the period of one or two program phases, but most programs placed this contribution in perspective of the long-term engagement in the sector, which in some instances had a history of 20 years.

---

3 For a more elaborate discussion see Whaites, Gonzalez, Fyson, and Teskey (2015).
4 Graham Teskey discusses in a blog contribution that a lot of work which is labeled DDD is actually only DDP – doing development properly. He describes this work as "based on data, designed and managed with extensive citizen participation, real-time monitoring" (Tesky, 2017, p. 3). Some of the smart implementation points relate to this. According to Teskey, the risk to this practice is that it possibly dilutes the core features of DDD.

- Most programs adopted a multi-level program design, acknowledging that change occurs on different levels simultaneously. This enabled teams to respond to dynamics wherever and whenever they occurred in the system. Teams could stay engaged overall, even when specific areas stagnated temporarily. A multi-level program design helps in aligning the pace of implementation to the partner's demands. Joint responsibility requires the advisory program to adjust to the pace of reform in the partner country and to accept when decision-making takes more time than the proposed program design. A multi-level approach provides flexibility to divert resources to a different layer, if the process takes more time at one level.

- The case studies confirm that most implementation is political by nature. Program teams addressed this by working in a politically informed and astute manner. Some answers that program teams found to overcome challenges during implementation were, for example, attending to conflicting interests, investing in negotiating compromises, and forging coalitions for change and collaboration among parties. In one instance, it was even the conscious decision to stay out of local politics when legal borders started to be stretched. "Crawling" the program space to address political issues required longer and more deliberate strategic approaches in some cases than in others (Pritchett, Samji, & Hammer, 2012).

- All teams adopted an experimental, iterative, and incremental approach to implementation in complex environments because it allows for gradual and flexible adaptations rather than abrupt shifts. This incremental and adaptive management style operates with short intervals between planning and implementation with short but frequent reflections. These feedback loops provide the information needed to assess the situation and the position of the program in relation to it, based on which frequent, small course corrections are made. Experiments and adaptations are done in the understanding that the knowledge for solving even severe problems exists predominantly locally, where the system's intelligence resides.

- The advisory teams' knowledge, experience, and skills provide the starting point for engagement. However, each element of the implementation strategy is then tested and tailored to fit the specificity of the local context. In this regard, smart implementation is staff- and skill-intensive. Knowledge and learning is the single most important input for implementation, helping to develop skills that can contribute to overcoming new and unknown challenges. In this understanding, implementation is a craft rather than a science, in which practitioners adopt several roles throughout the process. The predominant role is that of facilitators and conveners of new cooperation, where support is mainly provided in kind.

• Last but not least, cooperation is a central principle to facilitate progress in complex environments. This is why GIZ's management model Capacity WORKS adopts cooperation management as the leading concept for design and implementation.[5] It promotes in-depth analysis of the context in which programs operate as well as the development of a strategy for implementation. Thus, it does this only along selected parameters, reiterating the need for constant, short, and ad-hoc analysis to assess the context dynamics as well as flexibility to continuously adapt to a moving process.

These findings – derived from the analysis of nine case studies of GIZ governance programs – offer insights into how, and to which extent, the six identified DDD principles are used in daily management. Furthermore, the institutional setup of development organizations has tremendous implications for how they implement programs (Andrews, Pritchett, & Woolcock, 2017). The terms of engagement between GIZ and its main commissioning party (BMZ) have been explained in the introductory chapter. A few points in the authority structure of German development cooperation seem formative for the way we work and encourage further discussion.

The conditions of engagement between GIZ and its main commissioner (BMZ) provide space and flexibility for the implementing agency to respond to local problems and to move with the local process. Two arrangements facilitate this orientation: The first is the freedom to adapt elements of the original program design, the implementation strategy, and the results framework at any point if the dynamics of the local context require it. This includes changes to budget allocations and time frame. Changes at the outcome level during a program phase require agreement by the commissioners but are generally supported in practice. Commissioner and implementer come to a decision for adaptation through a common understanding of the change process and transparent communication.

---

5 The *World Development Report 2017: Governance and the Law* stresses this point as well when identifying commitment, coordination, and cooperation as drivers of effectiveness in development cooperation (World Bank, 2017, p. 5).

A second mechanism supporting problem-driven and locally-led implementation is the margin of discretion for decision-making at the program level, with periodic involvement, supervision, and control from headquarters to ensure transparency and accountability. This space permits new solutions that were not considered at the outset to emerge as the action unfolds. These solutions can respond to local specificities – a condition for more effective and sustainable results.

Trust is needed on multiple levels in this authority structure to institutionalize these mechanisms. It requires constant, open communication and deliberation between the BMZ and GIZ to generate a common understanding of the situation and responsible and transparent management on the implementer's side to earn this trust. All of this creates additional complexity in the setup, but these mechanisms strongly determine the way GIZ implements its programs and the kinds of results they achieve. A recent study shows that development organizations that gave staff autonomy in decision-making and space for judgment performed better in fragile states than those that focused on upward reporting, control, and narrow measurements (Honig, 2015, in Wild, Booth, & Valters, 2017). The commissioning framework between GIZ and its main commissioner, BMZ, is not merely a "conducive environment" but a fundamental and formative condition for technical assistance to play the role it has in development cooperation as a qualifier of people, a supporter of the long-term establishment of organizations, and a facilitator of societal processes.[6]

A last point regarding the authority structure relates to the development discourse on results. In GIZ's experience (and supported by the DDD principles), a results orientation has to be combined with a process orientation to ensure locally-led and problem-driven development. The case studies show that they are guided by objectives and indicators that are clearly spelled out and do not lose their validity in the face of complexity. However, the case descriptions also show that the assumed implementation path is changing all the time and that a focus on process is equally important. Hence, the art is to find the right balance between the two perspec-

---

6 Cornelia Richter, Managing Director of GIZ, stated in a blog contribution on the future of technical assistance in development cooperation: "To ensure that German technical assistance is able to continue to fulfill its role, it is dependent on flexibility, scope for design within the commissioning framework, including budget allocation, innovative modalities, and alliances as well as excellent cooperation with local partners" (Richter, 2017; author's translation).

tives. The case studies demonstrate that combining adaptive management with a results logic is doable. However, it is a shaky balance that requires attention by commissioning parties and implementers alike.[7] The established form to demonstrate evidence is results. Narratives that show legitimacy and acceptance, as evidence for a successful process, are less well-known but of importance in constellations with multiple actors, contributors, and owners of a program. Ideally, success should be portrayed as a combination of impacts *and* legitimacy. Program teams air their concerns over this existing duality by saying that they find it difficult to measure and present results they think the program has achieved. They complain about an inadequate fit between actually achieved and predefined results. A second, yet related observation is that it has proven difficult to apply rigorous evaluation designs to GIZ programs. The reason for this might be the team's focus on process, which leads to frequent small adaptations. Rigorous evaluation techniques, such as randomized controlled trials, establish a causal relation between a set of activities and the result (here understood as outcomes or impacts). Adaptations cause interruptions to this cause–effect relationship, making it harder to portray which effects can be attributed to the program's intervention and which cannot – whereas results that occur as the process unfolds and which were not considered at the outset can be overlooked. Measuring and portraying results produced by a non-linear and adaptive implementation approach requires measurements and evaluation designs that also detect and assess process results. This is worth considering because the case studies show that sustainability is also influenced by the way people and institutions interact, the values they bring to the table, and how they negotiate outcomes. Sustainability is hence not only determined by impacts but also by process characteristics.

Neil Hatton summarizes this disaccord nicely in his contribution in this book when saying that, at present, implementing organizations such as GIZ are already letting practitioners out in the field improvise and develop jazz music (with a high degree of improvisation and context-specificity) together with their partners, "but when they come back to their organizational bases, they often struggle to capture what they have done in classical notation." He advocates for taking the skills and knowledge acquired

---

7 For a more elaborate discussion on results orientation and DDD, see Valters (2014a, 2014b, 2015a, 2015b).

in the field out of the realm of personal gut feeling and individual intuition and giving these skills a hearing in the decision-making of development organizations and networks. The challenge he sees is to change the authority structure of development organizations in such a manner that an implicit individual intuitive skill can be turned into an explicit organizational core competence. In his assessment, GIZ managed to do this, in part, with the introduction of Capacity WORKS (see Neil Hatton's contribution in this publication).

Wild, Booth, and Valters also refer to this tension in their review on DDD at DFID. There, the emphasis on results "conveys a strong bias against the notion that a process ... could be considered a legitimate output" (Wild, Booth, & Valters, 2017, p. 24). The DDD community calls for a shift from a "log-frame" to a "search-frame" logic to better balance results and process logic. This can be done by introducing scheduled short context assessments that lead to subsequent, formally noted adaptations in the implementation strategy and program design (Andrews, Pritchett, & Woolcock, 2017). Other development organizations are experimenting with making their planning frameworks more flexible to support program learning and adaptation. DFID, for example, is testing an adaptive logframe. "It sets out a set of clear objectives at the outcome level, and focuses monitoring of outputs on the quality of the agreed rapid-cycle learning process" (Wild, Booth, & Valters, 2017, p. 24; also Bain, Booth, & Wild, 2016, for DDD at the World Bank). Accompanying this kind of experimentation at the institutional level and acquiring lessons from it in a wider community is a great opportunity that needs to be set in value.

Next to the abovementioned favorable aspects of GIZ's institutional setup, there are also some challenges that need further observation and deliberation.

- The budgets of GIZ programs have increased consistently over the years. There is also greater diversification in commissioning partners that jointly fund GIZ programs (i.e., co-financing of programs), each of whom introduces a new set of rules and regulations. This trend has been recognized in other development organizations as well and is likely to persist. Both developments increase the levels of complexity in managing programs and might not be favorable for an approach that emphasizes staff-intensive cooperation and deep skills.[8]

- Scaling-up incremental results is a challenge for GIZ's mode of operation but important for achieving effectiveness. Bringing results to scale occurs mostly when concepts for scaling-up are included in the design of the program and planned for with specific activities. The case studies hardly mentioned strategies or instruments to achieve scale or to bring incrementally achieved changes to scale.[9]

- A related issue is the kind of innovation generated by a focus on local problems. Can a focus on local problems and finding local solutions tackle regional or global development challenges? The example from the two regional programs presented in this book (South Caucasus, Latin America) shows that peer learning and pressure can be an instrument to advance the process. However, more observation and learning is required to better understand if and how local solutions can influence addressing regional and global challenges.

- Like most development organizations, GIZ's program portfolio is also increasing in fragile states. Conditions for implementation differ in fragile and conflict situations. A recent analysis on the evaluative work of German development cooperation in Afghanistan highlights the political economy in donor countries, which emphasizes a short-term perspective on aid in such contexts and a focus on tangible outputs rather than long-term impacts (Kirsch, 2014). Such a perspective can impede the addressing of local problems and the facilitation of local or regional reform processes.

- David Booth calls for bringing political economy work out of the governance ghetto and engaging more strongly with sector specialists (Booth, 2015, p. 21) – a challenge that GIZ has to tackle as well. The notion that transformation is political by nature is most advanced in GIZ's governance and conflict division. Other sector divisions acknowledge the fact but remain more implicit in addressing it. Booth calls for treating governance as a skill-set rather than as sector work,

---

8 Green acknowledges this constraint by saying "DDD requires skills like facilitation to identify problems and convene lots of different players to solve them, and lots of time, but big money is often neither necessary nor particularly helpful" (Green, 2016c).

9 DDD and PDIA do not address scaling-up but propose replication and diffusion (Andrews, Pritchett, & Woolcock, 2017).

and for deploying governance advisory resources into multidisciplinary teams to solve specific problems (Booth, 2015). This is a suggestion that could work for GIZ as a long-term goal. For the time being, a combination of governance as sector work and skill-set still seems inevitable (GIZ, 2012).

- Digitalization makes knowledge universally available, particularly technical knowledge, and provides tremendous opportunities for innovation and new solutions to development issues. It adds a layer of complexity, as it injects new information into the system without direct intention or orientation toward results. In this regard, digitalization has characteristics of transformation, but it does not offer a process for how to use the available information. Furthermore, the effects of digitalization are only partly predictable and manageable. Digitalization will change the role of advisors, diminish the relevance of technical expertise and expand the role of knowledge brokers.

Finally, we see three challenges that address the DDD agenda itself.

- The initiative has been very quiet about discussing the implications of DDD on partners and local actors. It is stated that "donors don't actually 'do' development" but rather governments and people in partner countries do (Wild, Andrews, Pett, & Dempster, 2016, p. 3). Yet, DDD primarily discusses the role of outsiders. There are important aspects to the interface of this relationship (e.g., whose knowledge is it that is used to find local solutions?) as well as issues affecting the relationship between outsiders (donors, implementers, advocators) and insiders (partner governments and local actors) that should be debated. Including the partner's perspective more rigorously in what is done differently as well as discussing potential consequences for the relationships is a pivotal aspect of success that should be brought center stage.
- Furthermore, the relevance and influence of official development assistance in partner countries is diminishing; consequently, the form and function of development cooperation is changing rapidly. New financing mechanisms, partnerships, and coalitions are springing up with their own rules and experiences. The 2030 Agenda for Sustainable Development stresses the importance of new global partnerships and programs that represent joint responsibility for the global goods and a different notion of partnership – one that overcomes a donor and recipient relationship. These new partnerships are realized with the help of multi-actor approaches, in which new alliances for learning,

knowledge-exchange, standard-setting, and political agenda-setting are forged. In this context, the DDD agenda seems too focused on the traditional role of donors in partner countries and does not yet capture the options that the approaching changes can offer for doing developing differently. It would be worthwhile exploring how the DDD learnings can be actively used to shape new alliances and international cooperation in the spirit of the new global partnerships.

- A final concern relates to showing that working in the spirit of doing development differently makes a difference and actually leads to more effective and sustainable development. Evidence that this assumption is reliable needs to be developed.[10] Reporting, monitoring, and evaluation designs need to be adjusted, and methods need to be expanded beyond case studies that pay attention to progress on DDD dimensions.

Finding new ways to support locally-led problem-solving by taking a more strategic approach to delivery and results and to better integrate flexibility for adaptation into the design stage are recommendations that point to the way forward (Wild, Booth, & Valters, 2017, pp. 31–32). Creating multi-actor partnerships, as promoted by the 2030 Agenda for Sustainable Development, is likely to address identified constraints in the relationship between reformers and outside supporters that should be tried out and learned from bravely.

References

Andrews, M. (2009, May). *Isomorphism and the limits of African public financial management reform* (HKSG, RWP 09-012). Cambridge, MA: Harvard University.

Andrews, M. (2015). Protecting development projects from the habit of repetitive codified solutions. *The Limits of Institutional Reform in Development*. Retrieved from http://matthewandrews.typepad.com/the_limits_of_institution/2015/03/protecting-d evelopment-projects-from-the-habit-of-repetitive-codified-solutions.html

Andrews, M., Pritchett, L., & Woolcock, M. (2012). *Escaping capability traps through Problem-Driven Iterative Adaptation (PDIA)* (CGD Working Paper 299). Washington, DC: Center for Global Development. Retrieved from http://www.cgdev.org/con tent/publications/detail/1426292

Andrews, M., Pritchett, L., & Woolcock, M. (2017). *Building state capability. Evidence, analysis, action*. Oxford: Oxford University Press.

---

10 For a discussion about German development cooperation on this issue, see Faust, Leiderer, Masaki, and Parks (2016).

Bain, K., Booth, D., & Wild, L. (2016). *Doing Development Differently at the World Bank. Updating the plumbing to fit the architecture.* London: Overseas Development Institute.

Booth, D. (2013). *Facilitating development. An arm's length approach to aid* (ODI Politics and Governance Programme Discussion Paper). London: Overseas Development Institute. Retrieved from https://www.odi.org/sites/odi.org.uk/files/odi-asset s/publications-opinion-files/8330.pdf

Booth, D. (2015). *Five steps for reorienting governance work in development.* London: Overseas Development Institute. Retrieved from https://www.odi.org/comment/946 8-five-steps-reorienting-governance-work-development

Booth, D., Harris, D., & Wild, L. (2016). *From political economy analysis to Doing Development Differently: A learning experience.* London: Overseas Development Institute. Retrieved from https://www.odi.org/sites/odi.org.uk/files/odi-assets/public ations-opinion-files/10205.pdf

DDD Manifesto Community. (2014). *Doing Development Differently manifesto.* Retrieved from http://doingdevelopmentdifferently.com/the-ddd-manifesto/

Deutsche Gesellschaft für Technische Zusammenarbeit. (2008, December). *Orientierung zur Technischen Zusammenarbeit.* Eschborn: Author.

Ernsthofer, A., & Stockmayer, A. (Eds.). (2009). *Capacity development for good governance.* Baden-Baden: Nomos.

Faust, J., Leiderer, L., Masaki, T., & Parks, B. (2016). *German aid from a partner perspective. Experience-based perceptions from AidData's 2014 reform efforts survey.* Bonn: German Institute for Development Evaluation (DEval).

Frenken, S., & Müller, U. (Eds.). (2010). *Ownership and political steering in developing countries.* Baden-Baden: Nomos.

Fritz, V., Levy, B., & Ort, R. (2014). *Problem-driven political economy analysis: The World Bank's experience.* Washington, DC: World Bank.

GIZ (Deutsche Gesellschaft für Internationale Zusammenarbeit). (2012). *Das Zusammenspiel zwischen Sektoren und Governance aus Sicht der Abteilung 42.* GIZ Abteilung 42 Good Governance und Menschenrechte. Taskforce Governance in Sektoren. Eschborn: Author.

GIZ. (2015). *Cooperation management for practitioners: Managing social change with Capacity WORKS.* Wiesbaden: Springer Gabler.

Green, D. (2016a). *How change happens.* Oxford: Oxford University Press.

Green, D. (2016b, December 8). Adaptive Management looks like it's here to stay. Here's why that matters. *From Poverty to Power.* Retrieved from http://oxfamblogs. org/fp2p/adaptive-management-looks-like-its-hear-to-stay-heres-why-that-matters/

Green, D. (2016c, November 22). Where has the Doing Development Differently movement got to, two years on? *From Poverty to Power.* Retrieved from http://oxfa mblogs.org/fp2p/where-has-the-doing-development-differently-movement-got-to-t wo-years-on/

Honig, D. (2015). *Navigating by judgement: Organizational structure, autonomy and country context in delivering foreign aid.* Doctoral dissertation. Cambridge, MA: Harvard University, Graduate School of Arts & Sciences.

Hudson, D., Marquette, H., & Waldock, S. (2016). *Everyday political analysis*. Birmingham: Developmental Leadership Program.

Kirsch, R. (2014). *Ein Review der Evaluierungsarbeit zur deutschen Entwicklungszusammenarbeit in Afghanistan*. Report. Bonn: German Institute for Development Evaluation (DEval).

Levy, B. (2014). *Working with the grain. Integrating governance and growth in development strategies*. Oxford: Oxford University Press.

Melia, E. (2016). *The political economy of extractive resources* (GIZ Discussion Paper). Eschborn: Deutsche Gesellschaft für Internationale Zusammenarbeit.

Organisation for Economic Co-operation and Development. (2015). *The case for thinking and working politically: The implications of "doing development differently."* Retrieved from http://publications.dlprog.org/TWP.pdf

Pritchett, L., Samji, S., & Hammer, J. (2012). *It's all about meE: Using structured experiential learning ('e') to crawl the design space*. Retrieved from https://www.princeton.edu/rpds/papers/Hammer_Its_All_About_Me.pdf

Pritchett, L., & Woolcock, M. (2002, September). *Solutions when the solution is the problem: Arraying the disarray in development* (CGD Working Paper No. 10). Washington, DC: Center for Global Development.

Richter, C. (2017, March 21). *Welche Rolle soll künftig die technische Zusammenarbeit in der deutschen Entwicklungszusammenarbeit spielen?* Retrieved from http://blogs.die-gdi.de/2017/03/21/welche-rolle-soll-kuenftig-die-technische-zusammenarbeit-in-der-deutschen-entwicklungszusammenarbeit-spielen/

Schwedersky, T., Noltze, M., & Gaisbauer, F. (2014). *Evaluierungsbericht. 30 Jahre ruandisch-deutsche Entwicklungszusammenarbeit im Gesundheitswesen*. Bonn: German Institute for Development Evaluation (DEval).

Tesky, G. (2017, March 30). *So is "Doing Development Differently" a movement now? And if so, where's it going?* Retrieved from http://oxfamblogs.org/fp2p/so-is-doing-development-differently-a-movement-now-and-if-so-wheres-it-going/

Valters, C. (2014a). *Can theories of change help us "Do Development Differently?"* Retrieved from http://asiafoundation.org/2014/12/10/can-theories-of-change-help-us-do-development-differently/

Valters, C. (2014b). *Six key findings on the use of theories of change in international development*. Retrieved from http://blogs.lse.ac.uk/jsrp/2014/08/18/six-key-findings-on-the-use-of-theories-of-change-in-international-development/

Valters, C. (2015a). *3 big problems with how we think about results and development*. Retrieved from http://blogs.worldbank.org/publicsphere/3-big-problems-how-we-think-about-results-and-development

Valters, C. (2015b). *Four principles for Theories of Change in global development*. Retrieved from https://www.odi.org/comment/9882-four-principles-theories-change-global-development

Valters, C. (2016). *Learning and adaptation: 6 pitfalls to avoid*. Retrieved from https://www.devex.com/news/learning-and-adaptation-6-pitfalls-to-avoid-88032

Valters, C., Cummings, C., & Nixon, H. (2016). *Putting learning at the centre: Adaptive development programming in practice* (ODI report). London: Overseas Development Institute. Retrieved from https://www.odi.org/sites/odi.org.uk/files/resource-documents/10401.pdf

Whaites, A., Gonzalez, E., Fyson, S., & Teskey, G. (2015). *A governance practitioner's notebook: Alternative ideas and approaches.* The DAC Network on Governance (GOVNET). Retrieved from https://www.oecd.org/dac/governance-peace/governance/docs/Governance%20Notebook.pdf

Wild, L., Andrews, M., Pett, J., & Dempster, H. (2016, December). *Doing development differently: Who we are, what we're doing and what we're learning.* Bibliography and literature reviews. London: Overseas Development Institute. Retrieved from https://www.odi.org/publications/10662-doing-development-differently-who-we-are-what-were-doing-and-what-were-learning

Wild, L., & Booth, D. (2016, November). *Doing Development Differently: Two years on, what have we done?* Bibliography and literature reviews. London: Overseas Development Institute. Retrieved from https://www.odi.org/publications/10631-doing-development-differently-two-years-what-have-we-done

Wild, L., Booth, D., & Valters, C. (2017). *Putting theory into practice. How DFID is doing development differently* (ODI report). London: Overseas Development Institute. Retrieved from https://www.odi.org/sites/odi.org.uk/files/resource-documents/11332.pdf

World Bank. (2017). *World Development Report 2017: Governance and the law.* Washington, DC: Author. Retrieved from http://www.worldbank.org/en/publication/wdr2017

About the authors

Tim Auracher has worked for the past 15 years as Project Manager and Technical Advisor for German development cooperation in several African and South-East Asian countries, especially Senegal, Ghana, Benin, Cambodia, and Indonesia. In Indonesia, he was responsible for a component on fiscal decentralization within a GIZ-supported program between 2010 and 2013, advising the Indonesian Ministry of Finance. After three years as Senior Advisor on Good Governance in GIZ  headquarters, he became head of a decentralization support program in Benin in 2017. His mains subject areas are (fiscal) decentralization, administration reform, and civil society participation.

Godje Bialluch (MSc) is the Program Manager for the Governance Support Programme. Prior to this assignment, she worked for GIZ and other development agencies on governance reform processes in Zambia, Kenya, and Tanzania. All in all, she has nearly 20 years of long-term work experience in southern and East Africa. She received her master's degree in Political Science from the Freie Universität Berlin.

Franziska Böhm is a lawyer and currently working in the Saxon State Ministry of Justice in Dresden. As Head of Division, she is responsible for the education and advanced training, foreign contacts, and legal education at schools. During her professional career, Böhm has worked as a judge in different legal fields as well as a public prosecutor, and as desk officer in the Saxon State Ministry  of Justice. From 2007 until 2011 she acted as team leader for GIZ projects in Georgia and Cambodia. After returning to her post in Germany, Böhm continued to work for GIZ as a freelancer. She holds the Open University Postgraduate Certificate Conflict and Development (2011).

Christine Brendel, a German pedagogue and sociologist, is the Manager of the regional program ComVoMujer (Combating Violence Against Women in Latin America) of the German development cooperation, implemented by GIZ. The program is based in Peru but also operates in Bolivia, Ecuador, and Paraguay. She has more than 20 years of work experience in development cooperation, mainly  in Latin America and Africa, but also in Germany and the United States. She focuses on gender equality, democracy promotion, organizational change, development processes, results-based program management, as well as capacity development in economic and employment fields. Brendel is also the author/co-author of numerous publications and education materials.

Thomas Fiegle (PhD) studied administrational science at the University of Constance (Germany) and received his doctoral degree in Political Science from the Ecole des Hautes Etudes en Sciences Sociales in Paris and the University of Potsdam. Following his academic career as an Assistant Professor at the University of Potsdam from 2005 to 2013, he has been working for GIZ since 2015. He is currently the Project Director of the German-Tunisian Academy for Good Governance in Tunis  as well as of an anti-corruption project in Tunisia. He has published extensively on matters of political theory and administrational science.

Verena Fritz (PhD) is a Senior Public Sector Specialist with the World Bank Group's Governance Global Practice. Her areas of expertise include state-building processes, political economy analysis, and public-sector and public financial management reforms. She has undertaken analytic, advisory, and operational work, mainly in East Asia, Europe, Central Asia, as well as in Africa, where she currently task manages three projects aimed at institutional strengthening, as well as  related analytic work. Fritz received her doctoral degree in Political Science from the European University Institute in Florence and has published a number of articles, working papers, and books in her areas of interest, including *Strengthening Public Financial Management: Exploring Drivers and Effects* (with Stephanie Sweet and Marijn Verhoeven, 2014); *Problem-Driven Political Economy Analysis: The World Bank's Experience* (with Brian Levy and Rachel Ort, World Bank Group, 2014); *Public Financial Management Reforms in Post-Conflict Countries* (with Ana Paula Fialho Lopes, Ed Hedger, and Heidi Tavakoli); *Making Public Sector Reforms Work – Political and Economic Contexts, Incentives, and Strategies* (with Simone Bunse, World Bank Policy Research Working Paper no. 6174, 2012); *Problem-Driven Political Economy Analysis: A Good Practice Framework* (with Brian Levy and Kai Kaiser, World Bank, 2009); *Understanding State-Building from a Political Economy Perspective* (with Alina Rocha Menocal, ODI, 2007); and *Developmental States in the New Millennium* (with Alina Rocha Menocal, 2007).

Franziska Gutzeit, a German political scientist and Technical Advisor for the regional program ComVo-Mujer (Combating Violence Against Women in Latin America) of the German development cooperation, implemented by GIZ, has a deep interest in democracy and good governance, human rights, and equality as well as an affinity for Latin America. She has been working in Latin America, the United States, and Germany and was also able to study and learn in Portugal, Malaysia, and Canada. Her main working fields  are gender equality, development cooperation, South-South Cooperation, political participation and migration, and refugee protection.

Neil Hatton (MBA, MSc Econ.) is currently a Partner and Managing Director of the frankfurt corporate development group. Prior to that, he worked for many years as a freelance consultant for international management and organizational development. He was a Senior Consultant for GIZ and responsible, among other things, for the development of Capacity WORKS. He has lived and worked in Europe, Southeast Asia, and Latin America and has been active as a consultant in  Africa and the Middle East. He has qualifications in systemic organizational development, project management, agile management and leadership (accredited Scrum Master®), as well as leadership, coaching, and counseling. His consultancy focus includes strategy development and implementation in commercial and international contexts; the design and moderation of workshops, conferences, and large group formats for project and international groups; executive development; as well as coaching, training, and consultancy in the development of leadership and talent. He is involved in project evaluations as well as capacity assessments worldwide.

Pauline Heusterberg (MPhil) has been interning with GIZ's Governance and Conflict department. She is an MA candidate in Human Geography at the Goethe University of Frankfurt and holds an MPhil in Development Studies from the University of Cambridge and a BA in Anthropology and Law from the Ludwig Maximilans University of Munich. Her previous experience includes working as a legal advisor for refugees, interning with an NGO focussing on women's rights in northern Tan-  zania, and co-founding the Munich branch of 180 Degrees Consulting, a student consultancy for NGOs and social entrepreneurs.

Lisa Hiemer (MSc) worked as an Advisor for media, communication, and citizen engagement under the GIZ Strengthening Local Governance Programme and the GIZ Governance Support Programme. She mostly worked on the provincial and local levels in the Eastern Cape of South Africa and thus gathered valuable insights on challenges and opportunities for effective, cooperative implementation in this context. She received her master's degree in Politics and Communication from the London School of Economics and Political Science.

Anne Hitzegrad holds degrees in Law and in Administrative Studies. Since 2016, she has been a Senior Policy Advisor for Migration Issues at the German Federal Foreign Office. From 2012 to 2016, she worked as a Governance Advisor with GIZ in Tunisia, with a focus on municipalities and local democracy. As a consultant, she has worked on topics such as rule of law, human rights, youth policy, and intercultural communication.

Astrid Karamira has been working in the field of extractive industries governance for many years. After spending five years as an expert in the field based at GIZ headquarters, she recently moved to Kigali, Rwanda, where she is working as Head of the GIZ program supporting the International Conference on the Great Lakes Region. A political scientist, Karamira has more than eight years of work and life experience in Africa.

Renate Kirsch (MA) has been Lead Governance Specialist at GIZ since 2015. Prior to this position, she was Head of Department at the newly founded German Institute for Development Evaluation (DEVAL). Between 2009 and 2012, she worked in the Good Governance and Human Rights division of GIZ, where she headed the "Democracy and Rule of Law Unit." Between 2003 and 2009, Kirsch worked at the World Bank as a Senior Social Scientist in the Social Policy and Social Analysis Unit. In 2010 she was seconded to the EU Delegation to Pakistan, where she represented the EU in a Peace and Conflict Needs Assessment for the province Khyber Pakhtunkhwa. Her operational and country experience is based on long-term assignments as a Government Advisor for GTZ. Kirsch received her master's degree in Sociology from the University of Bielefeld in Germany and graduated from the Centre for Advanced Training on Agricultural Development (Seminar für Ländliche Entwicklung) in Berlin.

Ruan Kitshoff is a team member of the Governance Support Programme, focusing on accountability, integrity, administrative justice, and citizen engagement. Previously, he worked in the Public Service Reform Programme of GIZ in South Africa. He has worked extensively in the fields of governance and public-sector reform in South Africa and the rest of Africa. Kitshoff has studied political science and holds executive qualifications from the business schools at Harvard and Wits.

Heiner von Lüpke (MA) received his master's degree in Tropical Forestry and Management from the Technical University of Dresden and has worked on climate policy issues ever since he graduated in 2003. Between 2004 and 2007, he worked as Officer Responsible for Climate Change and Forestry for the UN-FAO in Rome, subsequently moving to Jakarta, Indonesia, where he advised the Indonesian government on climate policy issues from 2007 until 2015 within various project assignments of GIZ. Gradually moving from a forestry background toward climate change policy issues on a cross-cutting level, he is currently advising the German Federal Ministry for Economic Cooperation and Development (BMZ) for GIZ.

Mark Mattner (PhD) heads the GIZ program Regional Resource Governance in West Africa, based in Freetown, Sierra Leone. In this capacity, he oversees activities to help enhance the development impact of mining in Guinea, Liberia, Sierra Leone, and Côte d'Ivoire. Prior to joining GIZ, Mattner was a Conflict Specialist with the World Bank's Conflict Prevention and Reconstruction Team and a Visiting Researcher in the Center for the Study of Human Rights at Columbia University. His doctoral research at McGill University was on local governance and oil production in the Niger Delta region of Nigeria, where he conducted qualitative fieldwork in oil-bearing communities.

Yvonne Müller has a professional background in land administration and land governance. She has been working for GIZ since 2006 in the field of governance, with a strong focus in recent years on contexts of conflict and fragility. Between 2011 and 2014, she was Chief Advisor of the COSERAM Program in the Philippines. Since mid-2014 she has worked as Senior Advisor in the Competence Center "Democracy, Political Dialogue, Urban Development" at GIZ headquarters.

Jazmín Ponce is a Peruvian academic researcher and a professional of International Business Administration. She is a Technical Advisor for the regional program ComVoMujer (Combating Violence Against Women in Latin America) of the German development cooperation, implemented by GIZ, and works in Peru but also closely with Ecuador, Bolivia, and Paraguay. She focuses on violence against women (VAW) and its relation with the business sector, gender equality, women  entrepreneurs, and development cooperation. She has experience in advisory services for companies; studies the economic impact of violence against women in big, medium, and small enterprises as well as on women entrepreneurs; and also has experience in the development of instruments for specialized surveys on VAW.

Stephanie Schell-Faucon (PhD) is a teacher and also worked as a lecturer in adult education. She has conducted research on peace education, conflict transformation, and transitional justice in divided societies. For many years, she has been involved in dealing with the past in Germany as well as with intercultural exchanges, being a co-founder of the South African German Exchange Network. Since 2003 she has worked for GIZ in long- and  short-term assignments in contexts of conflict and fragility. From 2011 to 2015 she was Team Leader of the COSERAM Program in the Philippines. Since 2016 she has worked as Senior Advisor in the Competence Center "Relief, Reconstruction and Peace" at GIZ headquarters.

Elke Siehl (PhD) has been Director General of the Corporate Development Unit of GIZ since April 2015. She is in charge of corporate strategy and policy, organizational development, support of the governance board, quality, and corporate sustainability. Prior to this, she was Director of the sector division Good Governance, Democracy and Human Rights and has worked in different positions for GIZ (formerly GTZ) in Germany and abroad since  joining in 1999. Since November 2015 she has also been the Corporate Sustainability Manager at GIZ. She received her doctoral degree in Economics from Johann Wolfgang Goethe-University, Frankfurt (Germany), specializing in New Institutional Economics, Economies in Transition, and Privatization. She has also lectured at the University Witten-Herdecke on the design and management of complex reform projects (Capacity WORKS, smart implementation, iterative project management).

Markus Steinich (PhD) is a Senior Governance Specialist who has been working at GIZ headquarters as well as for GIZ projects in Latin America and Africa. He is currently coordinator of the governance cluster in Tunisia.

Albrecht Stockmayer (PhD) was trained as a lawyer and a business administrator in Germany and the United States. He worked for the World Bank and the UN (UNIDO, UNCTAD, UN/DTCD) as an Advisor for institutional and legal development in mining and energy in Africa and Latin America. He joined a newly created unit in GTZ as an Advisor on public-sector institutions, later as Principal Advisor on state reform, with focal points in public  finance administration, decentralization, and civil society participation. He left GTZ for OECD/PUMA (now GOV) to head its Governance Outreach

Division and the OECD-wide Governance Outreach Initiative. At the end of 2002, he joined GTZ again, first as Head of the Governance and Gender team, Planning and Development Department. In 2008, he began heading the Governance Cluster, a unit that looks into issues of sector governance, promotes governance as a key issue, and seeks innovative ways for governance in development cooperation. In 2011 he was made Lead Governance Specialist of GIZ. After his retirement in 2014, he has been pursuing some academic work and has a consultancy for public governance and the rule of law.

Sabrina Storm (MA) is an Advisor to the sectoral department at GIZ in Eschborn. From 2011 to 2014 she was Director of GIZ's FOCEVAL program, which supported the Costa Rican government in strengthening evaluation capacities. She is a psychologist with an extensive background in organizational development and change management and has a master's degree in Public Administration from New York University. Her professional and research interests are focused on innovation and organizational learning within the public sector.

Tobias Tschappe works as an Advisor in the Governance Support Programme in South Africa on issues of integrity, anti-corruption, as well as organizational and strategy development. He works with national institutions and civil society and has prior international work experience in Kosovo and Japan. He holds a diploma in Political Science, Economics, and Public Law from the University of Göttingen.

Christopher Weigand is a fully qualified lawyer and a research fellow at the Institute for International Affairs at Hamburg University. He received his legal education in Leipzig, Madrid, Berlin, Mexico City, and Buenos Aires. His current research interests include international development policy, institution-building, and legal trans-plants. In his doctoral thesis, he focuses on the possibilities and limits of external Rule of Law promotion.

Agnes Wiedemann is a governance expert with a special interest in local governance and citizen participation. Currently, she is leading the GIZ project "Capacity Development for Municipalities in Tunisia and Libya." Focusing on the Mediterranean and Maghreb region, she worked from 2011 to 2015 at the Center for Mediterranean Integration in Marseille as Regional Coordinator for the GIZ program CoMun, "Strengthening municipalities of Morocco, Algeria and Tunisia." From 2008 to 2010 she worked as Component Leader for decentralization of the health sector at GTZ Malawi.

Melanie Wiskow (MA) is currently working as Specialist in the Academy for International Cooperation of GIZ in Bonn. In her previous assignment, she led the projects "Support to civil service training capacities with a focus on EU affairs" (co-funded by the European Union) and "Reform of civil service" in Azerbaijan. Before Azerbaijan, Wiskow was based in Germany and Ukraine working on topics such as public administration reform, good governance, corruption prevention, and poverty reduction. She holds a master's degree from the University of Tübingen in Political Science and International Relations.